Thank you for picking up *Haikyu!!* volume 3. We started working on this volume just as the 2012 Summer Olympics in London were wrapping up. In other words, it was right after the Japanese women's Olympic volleyball team, for the first time in 28 years, won an Olympic medal (bronze). So basically, what I'm trying to say is that we were all really excited. Woo!

HARUICHI FURUDATE began his manga career when he was 25 years old with the one-shot *Ousama Kid* (King Kid), which won an honorable mention for the 14th Jump Treasure Newcomer Manga Prize. His first series, *Kiben Gakuha, Yotsuya Sensei no Kaidan* (Philosophy School, Yotsuya Sensei's Ghost Stories), was serialized in Weekly Shonen Jump in 2010. In 2012, he began serializing *Haikyu!!* in Weekly Shonen Jump, where it became his most popular work to date.

HAIKYU!!
VOLUME 3
SHONEN JUMP Manga Edition

Story and Art by
HARUICHI FURUDATE

Translation ❶ **ADRIENNE BECK**
Touch-Up Art & Lettering ❷ **ERIKA TERRIQUEZ**
Design ❸ **FAWN LAU**
Editor ❹ **MARLENE FIRST**

Printed in the U.S.A.

Published by VIZ Media, LLC
P.O. Box 77010
San Francisco, CA 94107

10 9 8 7 6 5 4 3 2
First printing, September 2016
Second printing, March 2017

www.shonenjump.com

www.viz.com

SHONENJUMP MANGA

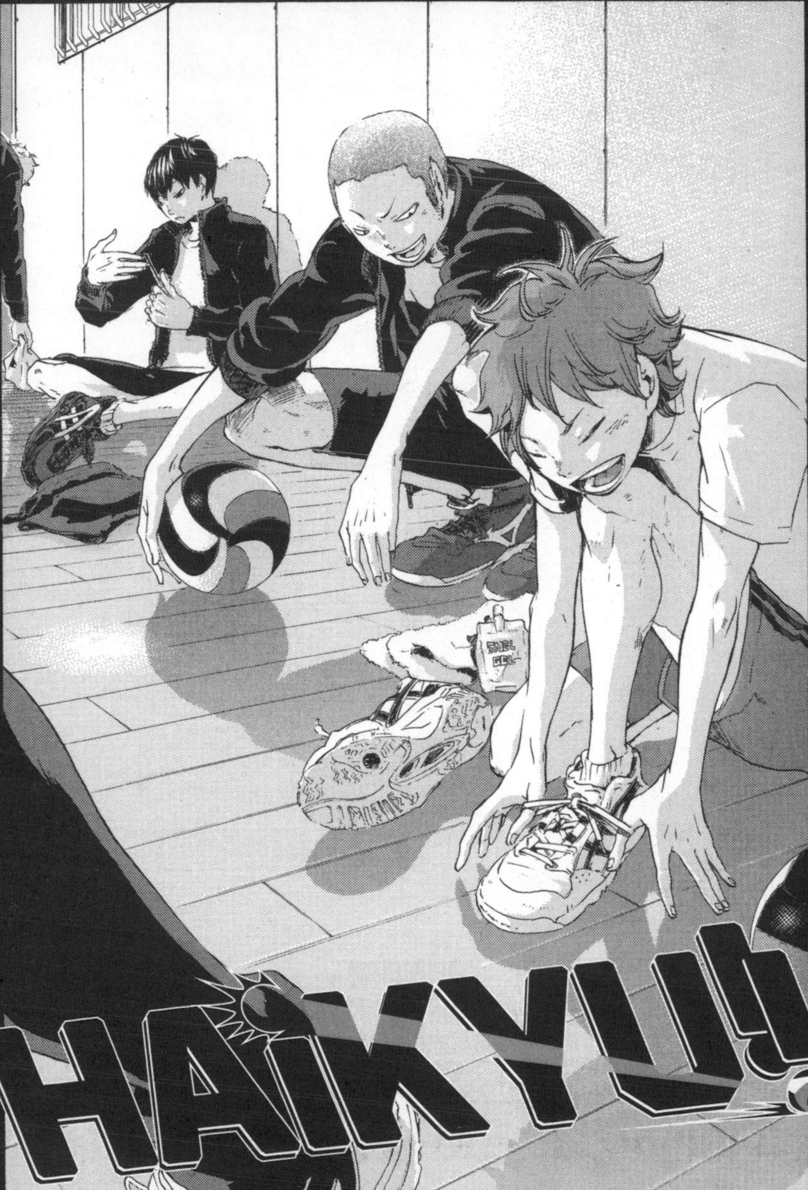
HAIKYU!!

HARUICHI
FURUDATE

3

GO, TEAM KARASUNO!

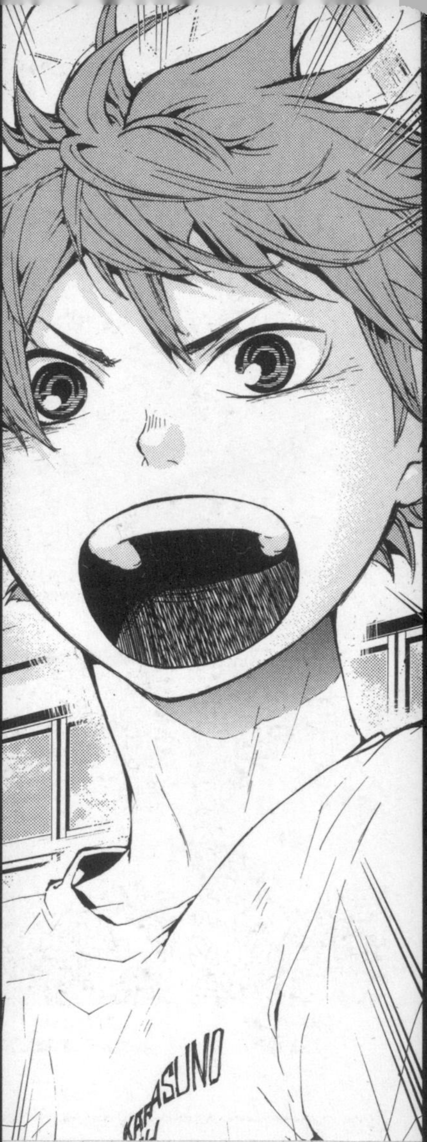

SHOYO HINATA

1ST YEAR / WING SPIKER

Even though he doesn't have the best body type for volleyball, he is super athletic. Gets nervous easily.

TOBIO KAGEYAMA

1ST YEAR / SETTER

His instincts and athletic talent are so good that he's like a "king" who rules the court. Demanding and egocentric.

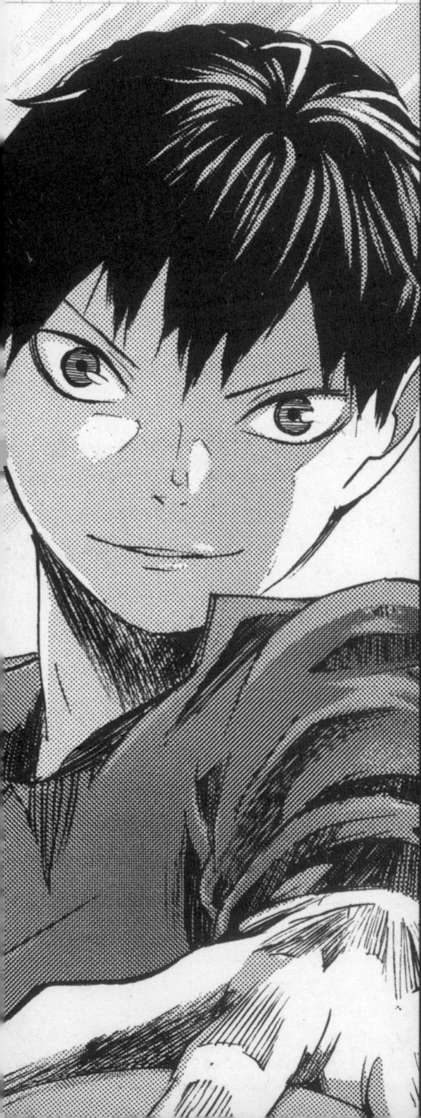

CHARACTERS

Karasuno High School Volleyball Club

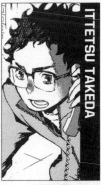

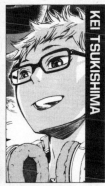

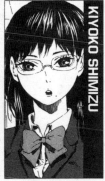

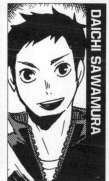

DAICHI SAWAMURA

3RD YEAR (CAPTAIN)
WING SPIKER

KIYOKO SHIMIZU

3RD YEAR
MANAGER

KEI TSUKISHIMA

1ST YEAR
MIDDLE BLOCKER

ITTETSU TAKEDA

ADVISER

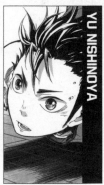

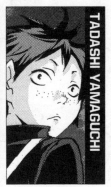

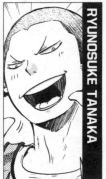

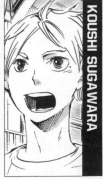

KOUSHI SUGAWARA

3RD YEAR (VICE CAPTAIN)
SETTER

RYUNOSUKE TANAKA

2ND YEAR
WING SPIKER

TADASHI YAMAGUCHI

1ST YEAR
MIDDLE BLOCKER

YU NISHINOYA

2ND YEAR
LIBERO

Ever since he saw the legendary player known as "the Little Giant" compete at the national volleyball finals, Shoyo Hinata has been aiming to be the best volleyball player ever! He decides to join the volleyball club at his middle school and gets to play in an official tournament during his third year. His team is crushed by a team led by volleyball prodigy Tobio Kageyama, also known as "the King of the Court." Swearing revenge on Kageyama, Hinata graduates middle school and enters Karasuno High School, the school where the Little Giant played. However, upon joining the club, he finds out that Kageyama is there too! The two of them bicker constantly, but they bring out the best in each other's talents and become a powerful combo! Karasuno then takes on one of the top four volleyball teams in the prefecture and wins! Now the team is looking to get an old member back...a second-year libero named Yu Nishinoya.

HAIKYU!!

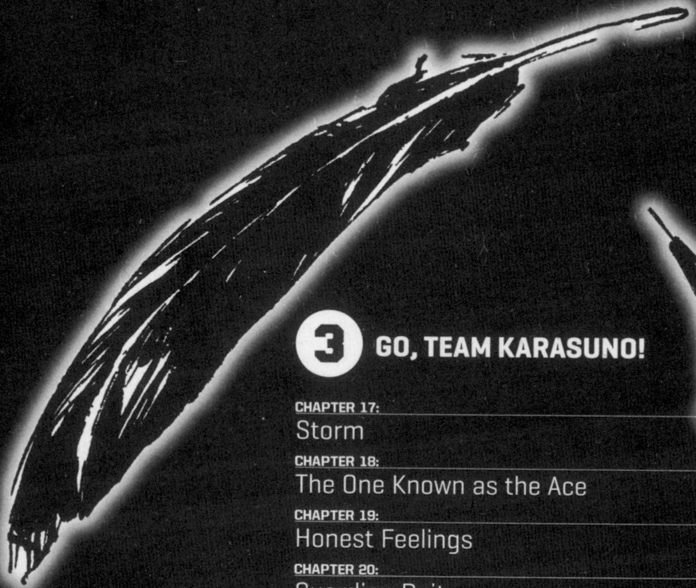

3 GO, TEAM KARASUNO!

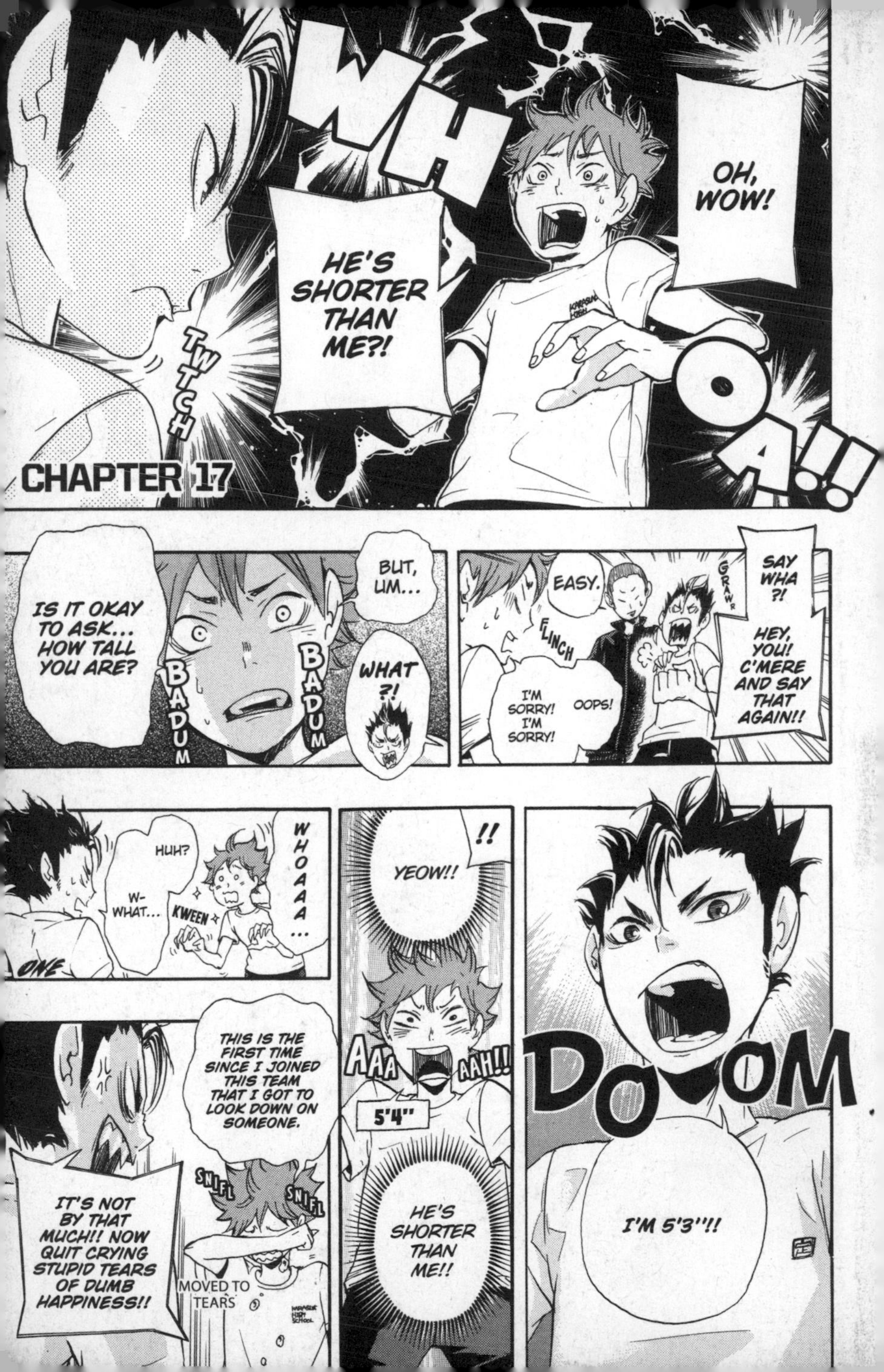
WHOA!!
OH, WOW!
HE'S SHORTER THAN ME?!
TWITCH
CHAPTER 17
SAY WHA?!
GRAWR
HEY, YOU! C'MERE AND SAY THAT AGAIN!!
EASY.
FLINCH
OOPS!
I'M SORRY! I'M SORRY!
BUT, UM...
BADUM
WHAT?!
IS IT OKAY TO ASK... HOW TALL YOU ARE?
BADUM
DOOM
I'M 5'3''!!
!!
YEOW!!
AAAAAH!!
5'4''
HE'S SHORTER THAN ME!!
WHOAAA...
HUH?
W- WHAT...
KWEEN
ONE
THIS IS THE FIRST TIME SINCE I JOINED THIS TEAM THAT I GOT TO LOOK DOWN ON SOMEONE.
SNIFL
SNIFL
IT'S NOT BY THAT MUCH!! NOW QUIT CRYING STUPID TEARS OF DUMB HAPPINESS!!
MOVED TO TEARS

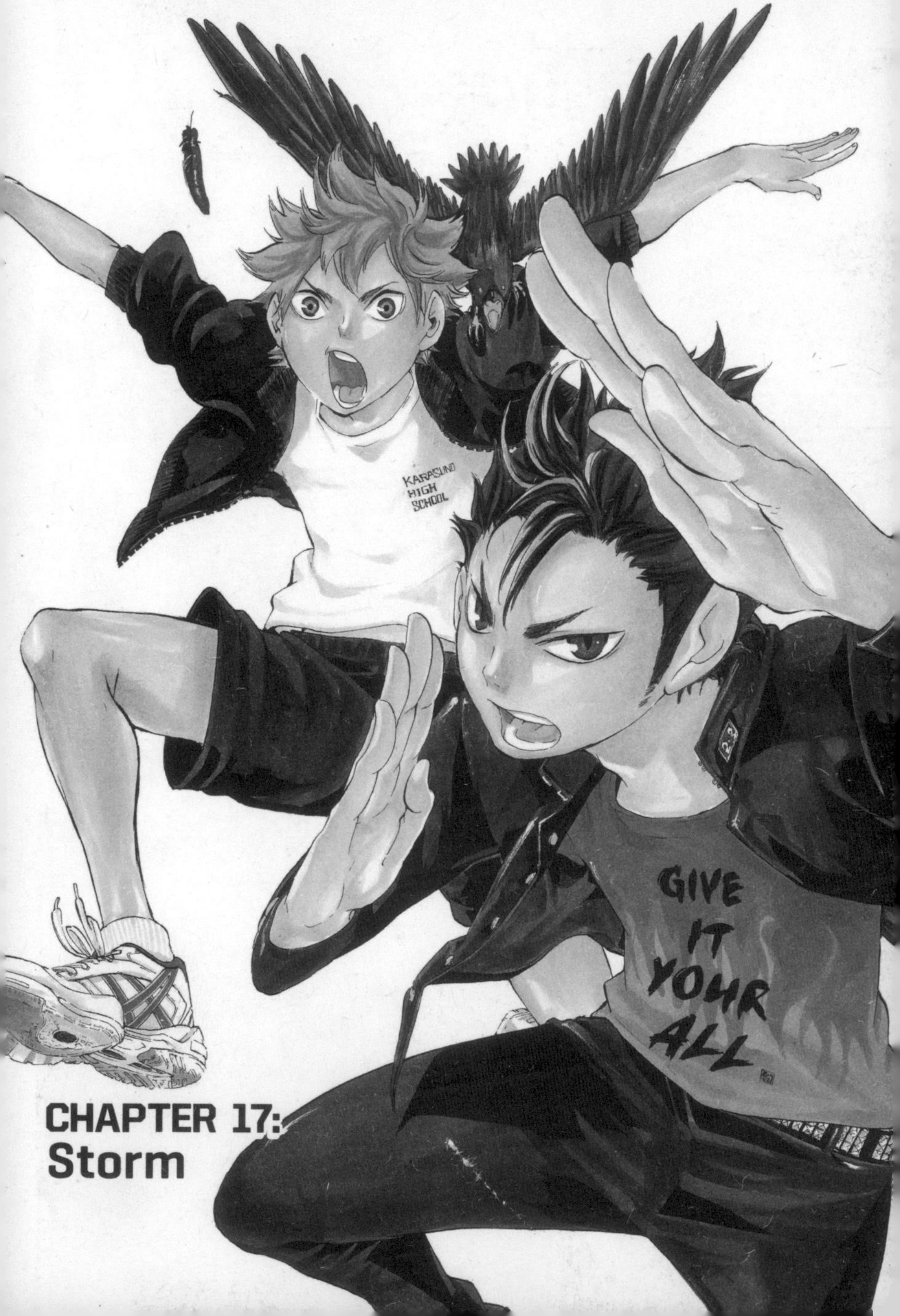
KARASUNO HIGH SCHOOL
GIVE IT YOUR ALL

CHAPTER 17: Storm

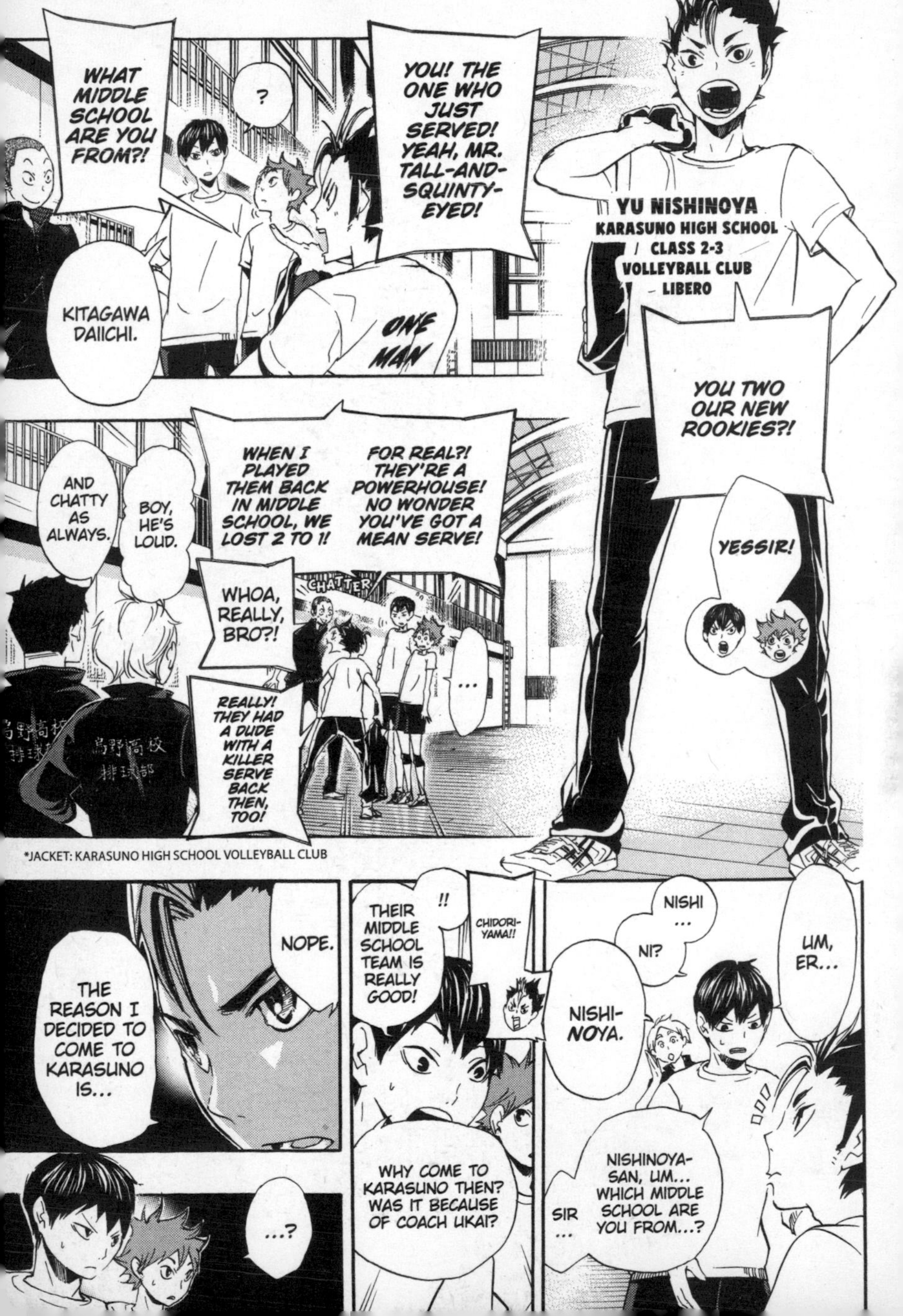
YU NISHINOYA
KARASUNO HIGH SCHOOL
CLASS 2-3
VOLLEYBALL CLUB
LIBERO
YOU TWO OUR NEW ROOKIES?!
YESSIR!
YOU! THE ONE WHO JUST SERVED! YEAH, MR. TALL-AND-SQUINTY-EYED!
?
WHAT MIDDLE SCHOOL ARE YOU FROM?!
ONE MAN
KITAGAWA DAIICHI.
FOR REAL?! THEY'RE A POWERHOUSE! NO WONDER YOU'VE GOT A MEAN SERVE!
WHEN I PLAYED THEM BACK IN MIDDLE SCHOOL, WE LOST 2 TO 1!
...
CHATTER
WHOA, REALLY, BRO?!
REALLY! THEY HAD A DUDE WITH A KILLER SERVE BACK THEN, TOO!
BOY, HE'S LOUD.
AND CHATTY AS ALWAYS.
烏野高校 排球部
UM, ER...
NISHI ...
NI?
NISHI-NOYA.
NISHINOYA-SAN, UM... WHICH MIDDLE SCHOOL ARE YOU FROM...?
SIR ...
!!
CHIDORI-YAMA!!
THEIR MIDDLE SCHOOL TEAM IS REALLY GOOD!
WHY COME TO KARASUNO THEN? WAS IT BECAUSE OF COACH UKAI?
NOPE.
THE REASON I DECIDED TO COME TO KARASUNO IS...
...?
*JACKET: KARASUNO HIGH SCHOOL VOLLEYBALL CLUB

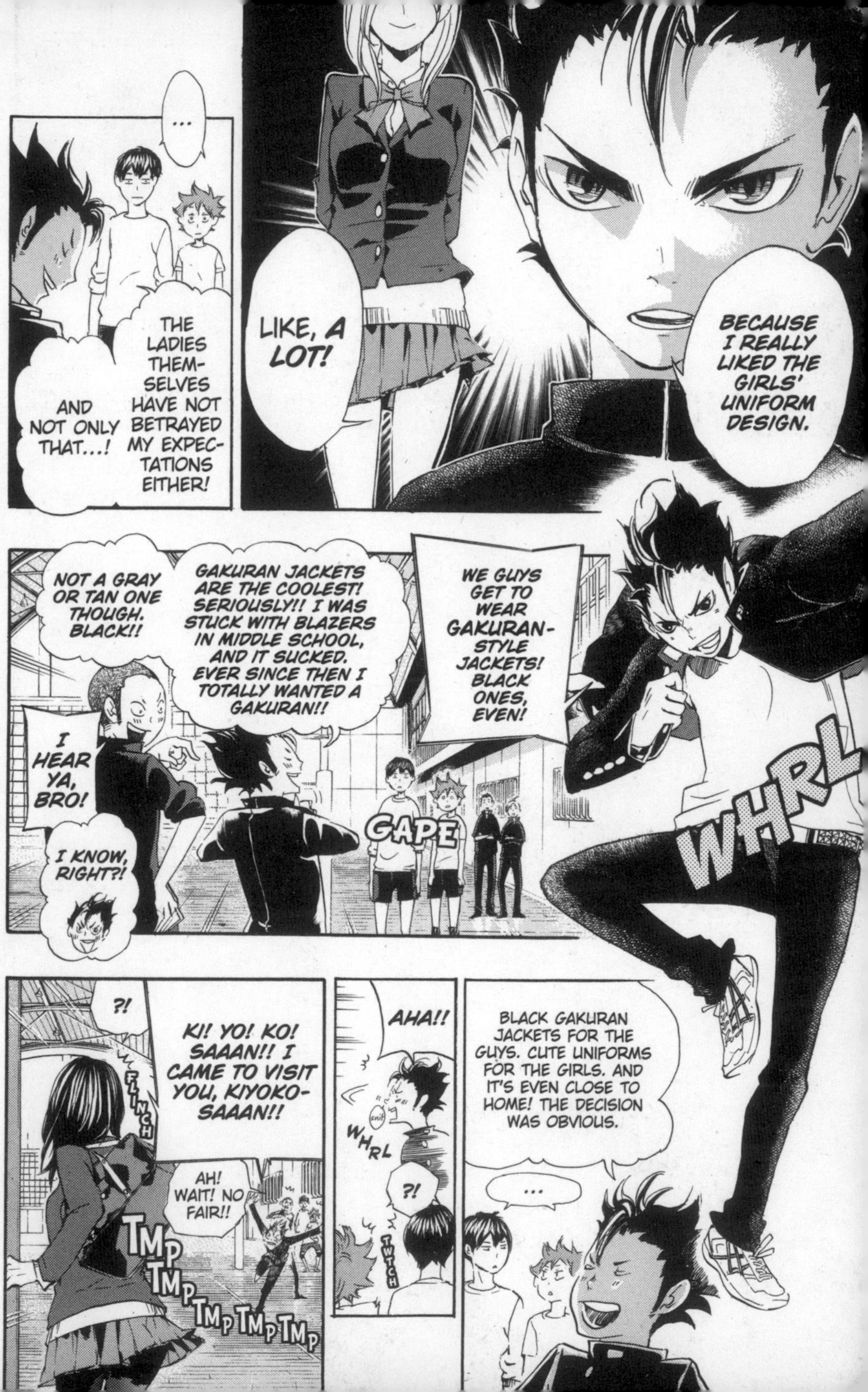
BECAUSE I REALLY LIKED THE GIRLS' UNIFORM DESIGN.
LIKE, A LOT!
...
THE LADIES THEMSELVES HAVE NOT BETRAYED MY EXPECTATIONS EITHER!
AND NOT ONLY THAT...!
WE GUYS GET TO WEAR GAKURAN-STYLE JACKETS! BLACK ONES, EVEN!
WHRL
GAKURAN JACKETS ARE THE COOLEST! SERIOUSLY!! I WAS STUCK WITH BLAZERS IN MIDDLE SCHOOL, AND IT SUCKED. EVER SINCE THEN I TOTALLY WANTED A GAKURAN!!
NOT A GRAY OR TAN ONE THOUGH. BLACK!!
GAPE
I HEAR YA, BRO!
I KNOW, RIGHT?!
BLACK GAKURAN JACKETS FOR THE GUYS. CUTE UNIFORMS FOR THE GIRLS. AND IT'S EVEN CLOSE TO HOME! THE DECISION WAS OBVIOUS.
...
AHA!!
sniff
WHRL
?!
TWTCH
?!
KI! YO! KO! SAAAN!! I CAME TO VISIT YOU, KIYOKO-SAAAN!!
FLINCH
AH! WAIT! NO FAIR!!
TMP TMP TMP TMP TMP TMP

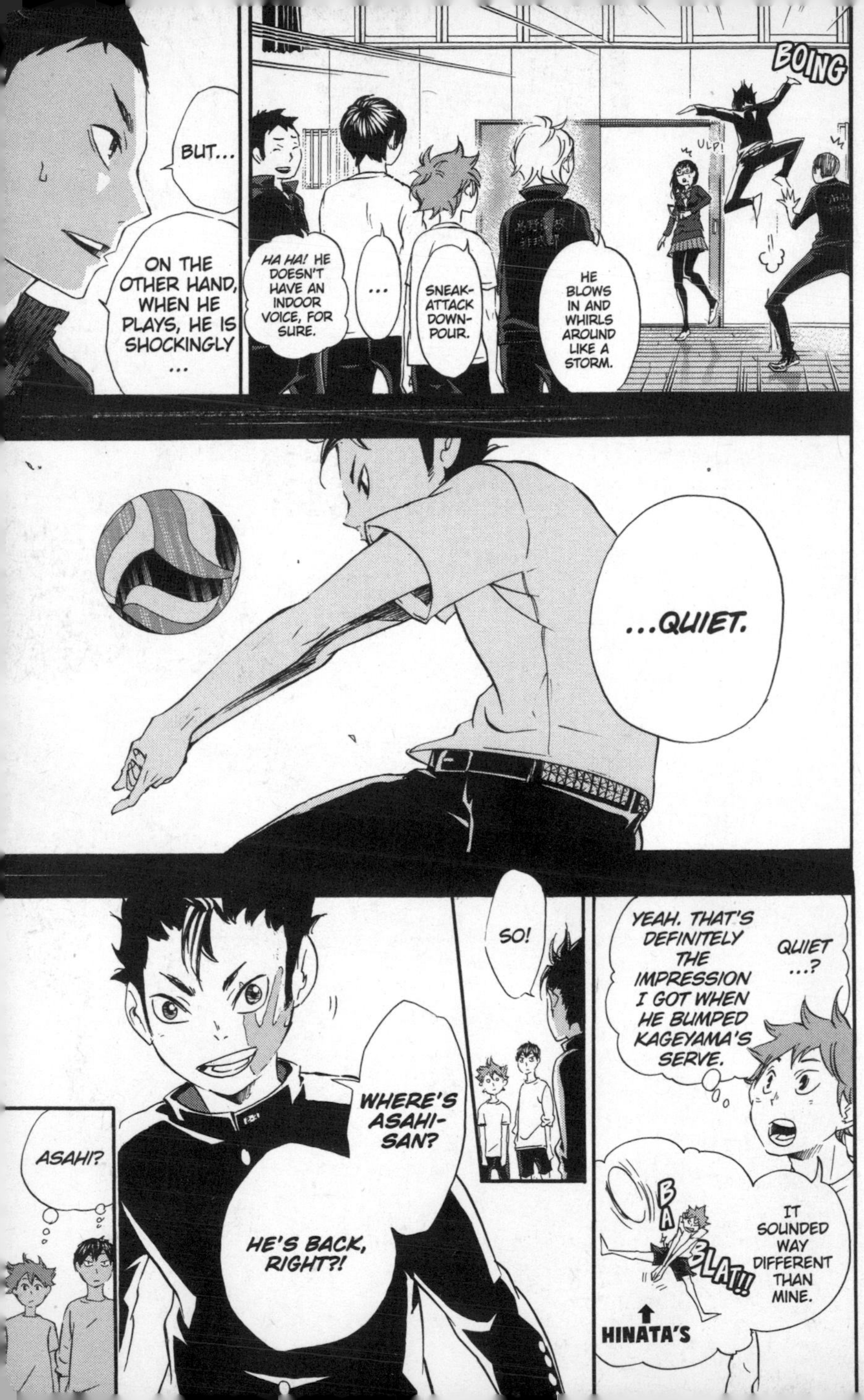
BOING
ULP!
HE BLOWS IN AND WHIRLS AROUND LIKE A STORM.
SNEAK-ATTACK DOWNPOUR.
...
HA HA! HE DOESN'T HAVE AN INDOOR VOICE, FOR SURE.
BUT...
ON THE OTHER HAND, WHEN HE PLAYS, HE IS SHOCKINGLY ...
...QUIET.
QUIET ...?
YEAH. THAT'S DEFINITELY THE IMPRESSION I GOT WHEN HE BUMPED KAGEYAMA'S SERVE.
IT SOUNDED WAY DIFFERENT THAN MINE.
BA BLAT!!
HINATA'S
SO!
WHERE'S ASAHI-SAN?
HE'S BACK, RIGHT?!
ASAHI?

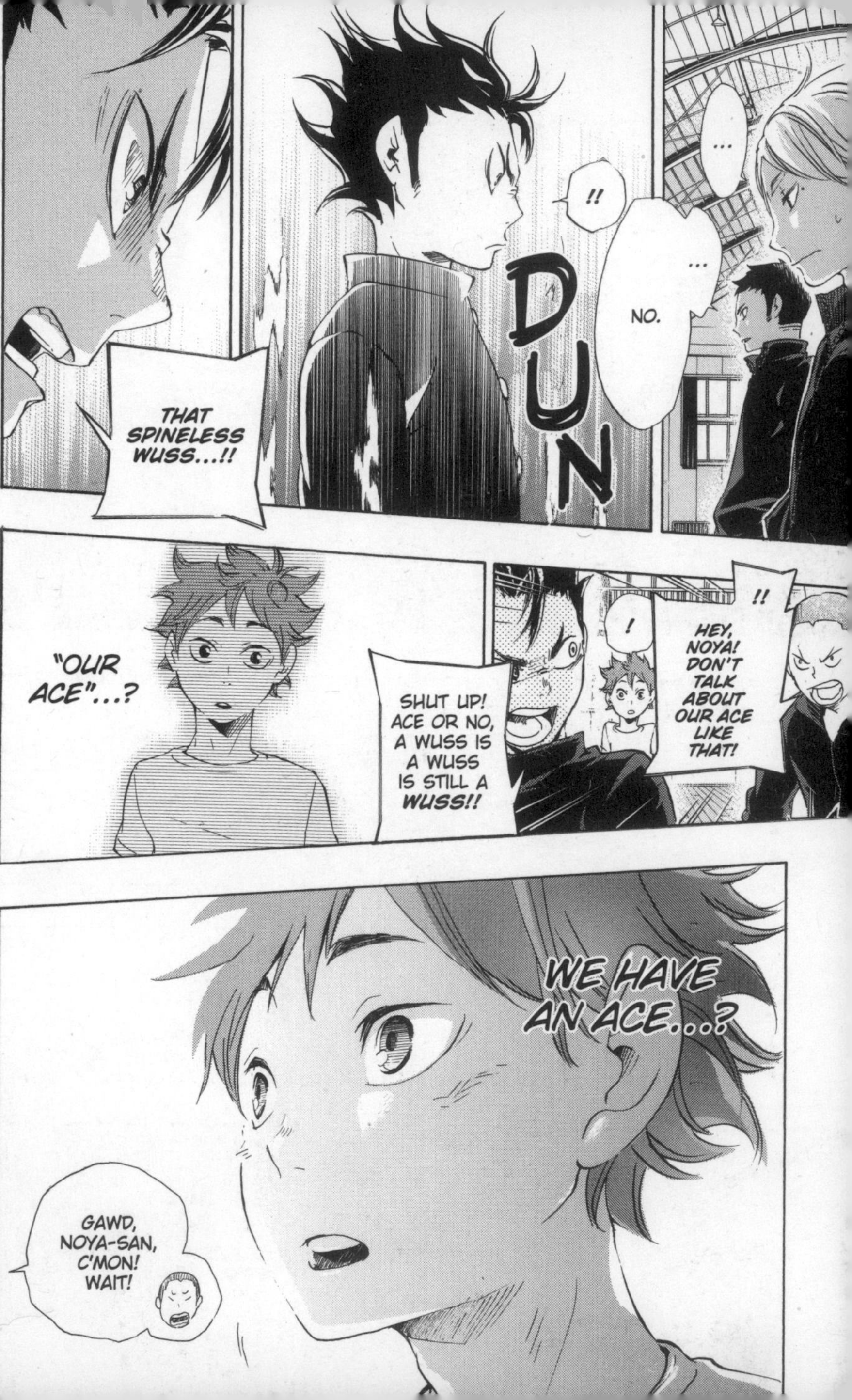
...
...
NO.
!!
DUN
THAT SPINELESS WUSS...!!
!!
HEY, NOYA! DON'T TALK ABOUT OUR ACE LIKE THAT!
!
SHUT UP! ACE OR NO, A WUSS IS A WUSS IS STILL A WUSS!!
"OUR ACE"...?
WE HAVE AN ACE...?
GAWD, NOYA-SAN, C'MON! WAIT!

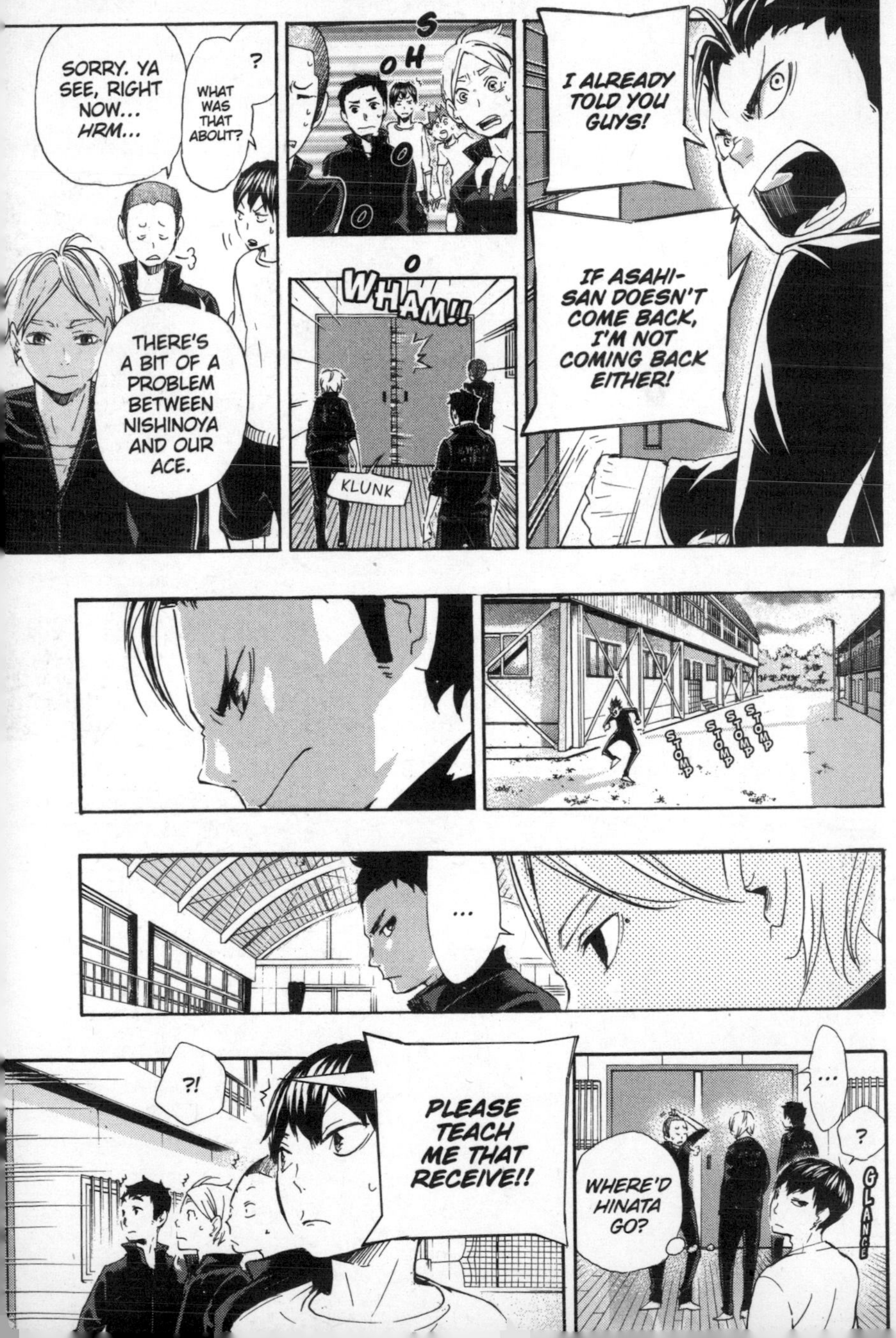
I ALREADY TOLD YOU GUYS!
IF ASAHI-SAN DOESN'T COME BACK, I'M NOT COMING BACK EITHER!
SHOOOO
WHAM!!
KLUNK
?
WHAT WAS THAT ABOUT?
SORRY. YA SEE, RIGHT NOW... HRM...
THERE'S A BIT OF A PROBLEM BETWEEN NISHINOYA AND OUR ACE.
STOMP STOMP STOMP STOMP
...
...
?
GLANCE
WHERE'D HINATA GO?
?!
PLEASE TEACH ME THAT RECEIVE!!

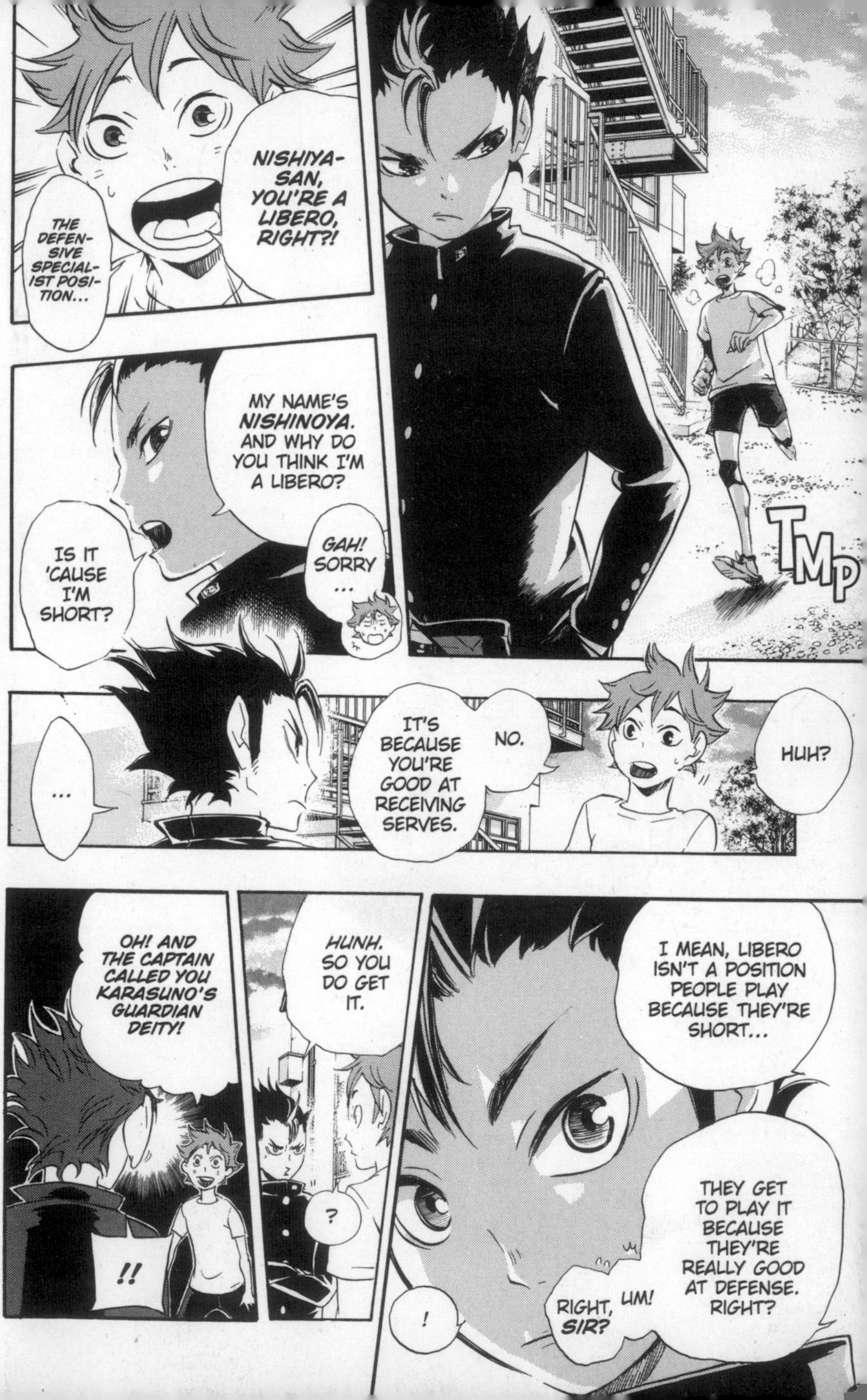
TMP
NISHIYA-SAN, YOU'RE A LIBERO, RIGHT?!
THE DEFENSIVE SPECIALIST POSITION...
MY NAME'S NISHINOYA. AND WHY DO YOU THINK I'M A LIBERO?
GAH! SORRY...
IS IT 'CAUSE I'M SHORT?
HUH?
NO.
IT'S BECAUSE YOU'RE GOOD AT RECEIVING SERVES.
...
I MEAN, LIBERO ISN'T A POSITION PEOPLE PLAY BECAUSE THEY'RE SHORT...
THEY GET TO PLAY IT BECAUSE THEY'RE REALLY GOOD AT DEFENSE. RIGHT?
UM!
RIGHT, SIR?
!
HUNH. SO YOU DO GET IT.
?
OH! AND THE CAPTAIN CALLED YOU KARASUNO'S GUARDIAN DEITY!
!!

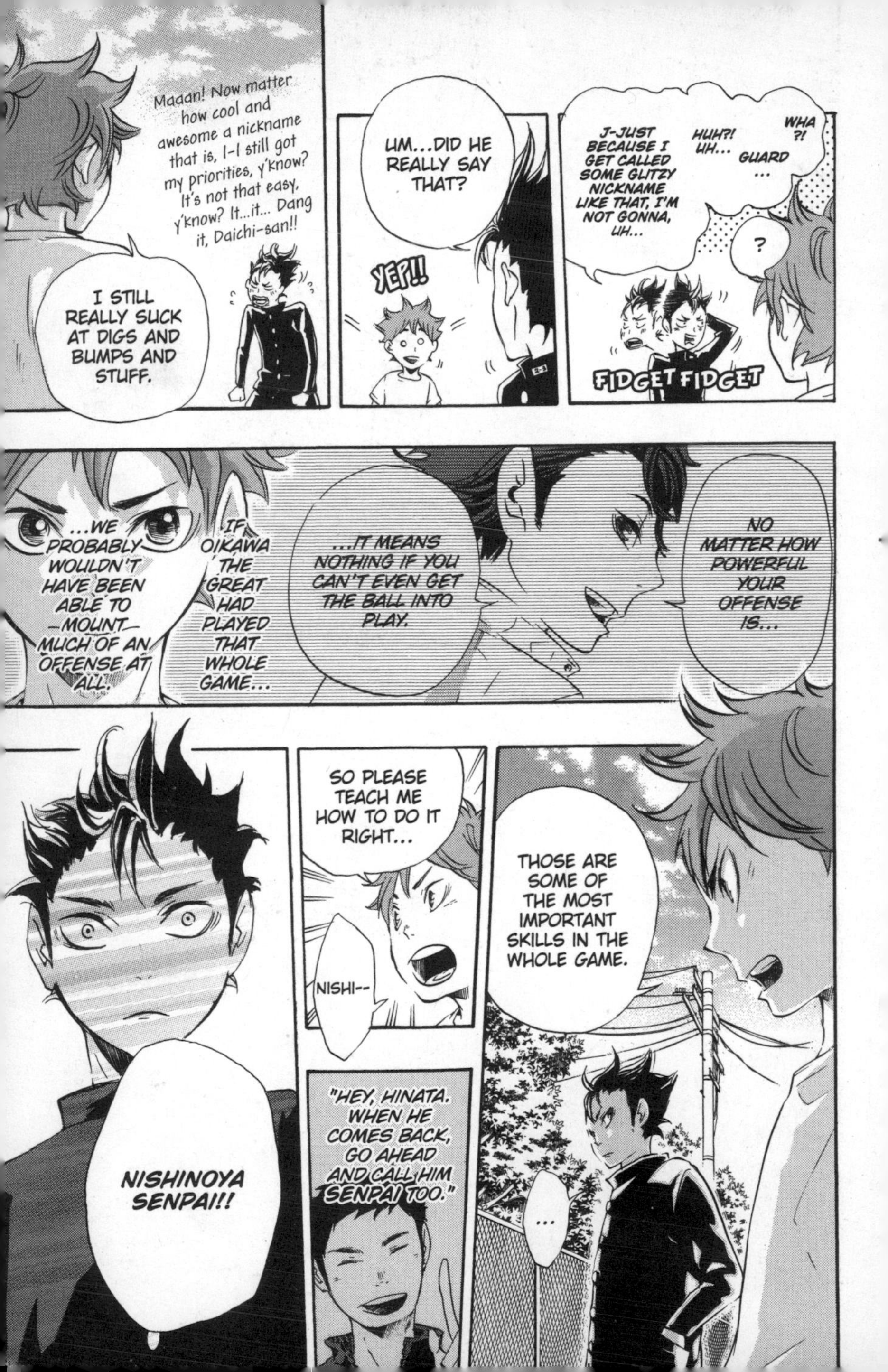
WHA ?!
GUARD ...
HUH?! UH...
J-JUST BECAUSE I GET CALLED SOME GLITZY NICKNAME LIKE THAT, I'M NOT GONNA, UH...
?
FIDGET FIDGET
UM...DID HE REALLY SAY THAT?
YEP!!
Maaan! Now matter how cool and awesome a nickname that is, I-I still got my priorities, y'know? It's not that easy, y'know? It...it... Dang it, Daichi-san!!
I STILL REALLY SUCK AT DIGS AND BUMPS AND STUFF.
NO MATTER HOW POWERFUL YOUR OFFENSE IS...
...IT MEANS NOTHING IF YOU CAN'T EVEN GET THE BALL INTO PLAY.
IF OIKAWA THE GREAT HAD PLAYED THAT WHOLE GAME...
...WE PROBABLY WOULDN'T HAVE BEEN ABLE TO MOUNT MUCH OF AN OFFENSE AT ALL.
THOSE ARE SOME OF THE MOST IMPORTANT SKILLS IN THE WHOLE GAME.
...
SO PLEASE TEACH ME HOW TO DO IT RIGHT...
NISHI--
"HEY, HINATA. WHEN HE COMES BACK, GO AHEAD AND CALL HIM SENPAI TOO."
NISHINOYA SENPAI!!

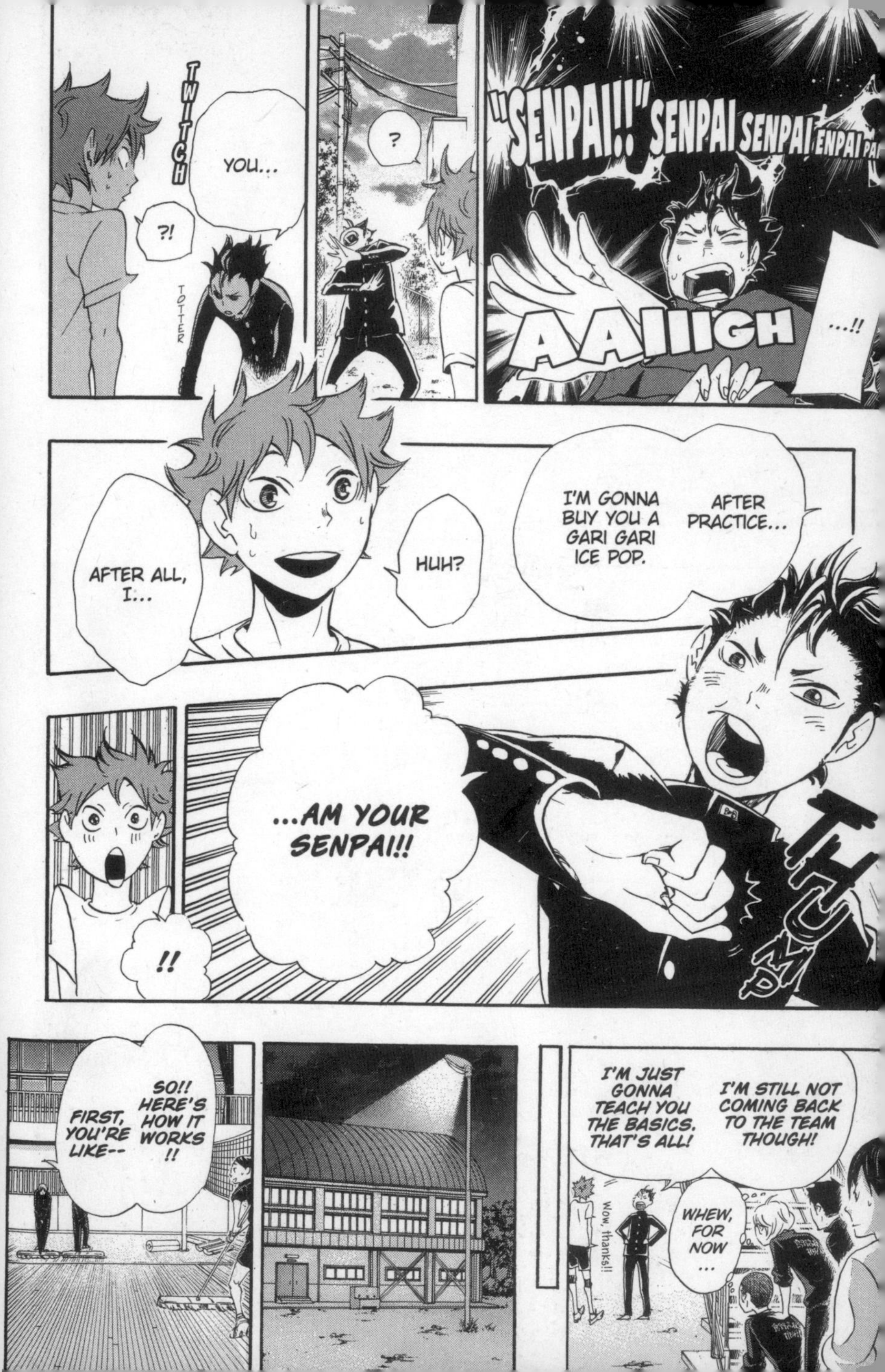
"SENPAI!!" SENPAI SENPAI ENPAI PAI
AAIIIGH
...!!
?
TWITCH
YOU...
?!
TOTTER
AFTER PRACTICE...
I'M GONNA BUY YOU A GARI GARI ICE POP.
HUH?
AFTER ALL, I...
THUMP
...AM YOUR SENPAI!!
!!
I'M STILL NOT COMING BACK TO THE TEAM THOUGH!
I'M JUST GONNA TEACH YOU THE BASICS. THAT'S ALL!
WHEW, FOR NOW...
Wow, thanks!!
SO!! HERE'S HOW IT WORKS!!
FIRST, YOU'RE LIKE--

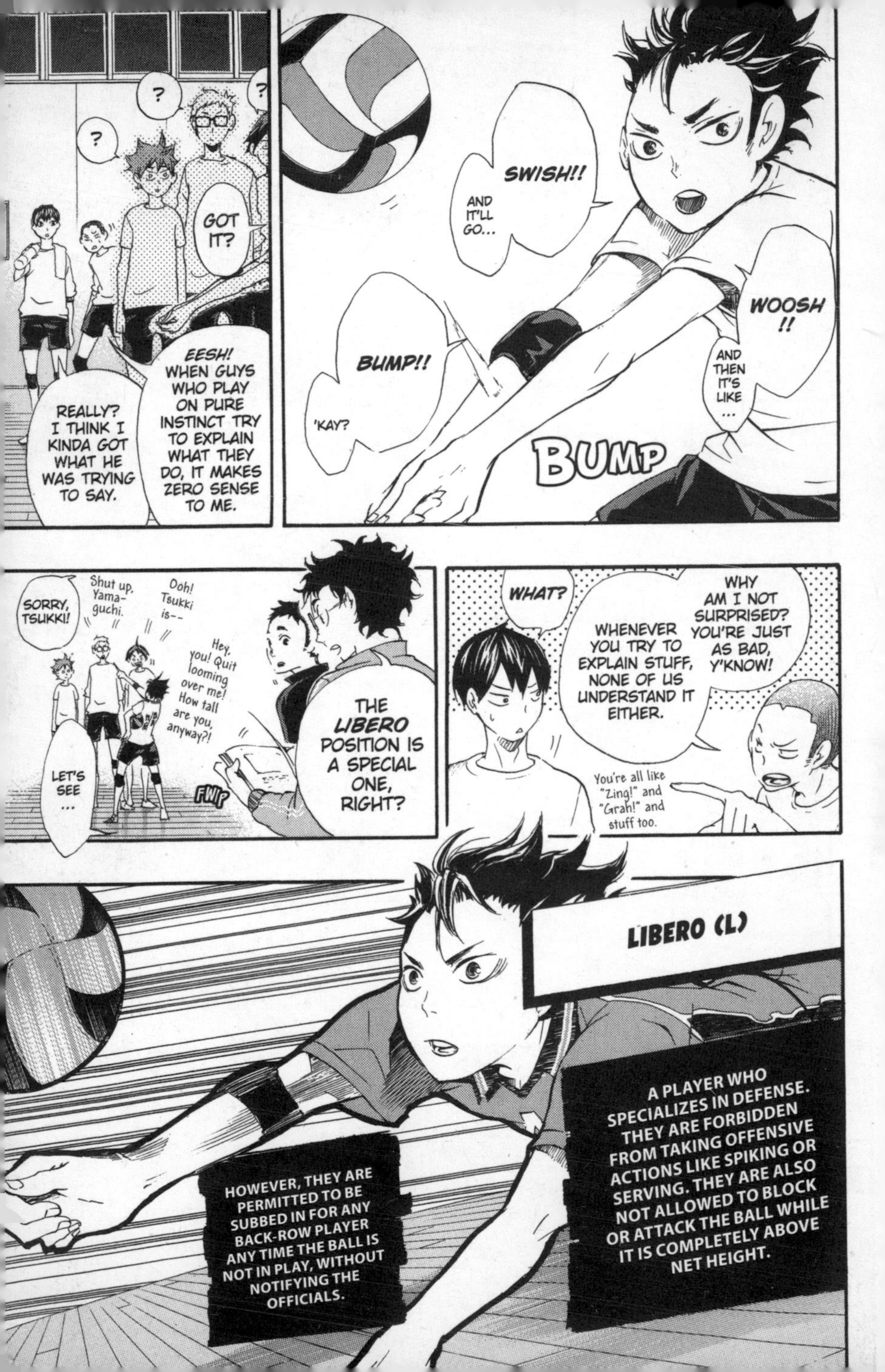
AND IT'LL GO...
SWISH!!
AND THEN IT'S LIKE...
WOOSH!!
BUMP!!
'KAY?
BUMP
?
?
?
GOT IT?
EESH! WHEN GUYS WHO PLAY ON PURE INSTINCT TRY TO EXPLAIN WHAT THEY DO, IT MAKES ZERO SENSE TO ME.
REALLY? I THINK I KINDA GOT WHAT HE WAS TRYING TO SAY.
WHY AM I NOT SURPRISED? YOU'RE JUST AS BAD, Y'KNOW!
WHAT?
WHENEVER YOU TRY TO EXPLAIN STUFF, NONE OF US UNDERSTAND IT EITHER.
You're all like "Zing!" and "Grah!" and stuff too.
THE LIBERO POSITION IS A SPECIAL ONE, RIGHT?
FWIP
Hey, you! Quit looming over me! How tall are you, anyway?!
Ooh! Tsukki is--
Shut up, Yamaguchi.
SORRY, TSUKKI!
LET'S SEE...
LIBERO (L)
A PLAYER WHO SPECIALIZES IN DEFENSE. THEY ARE FORBIDDEN FROM TAKING OFFENSIVE ACTIONS LIKE SPIKING OR SERVING. THEY ARE ALSO NOT ALLOWED TO BLOCK OR ATTACK THE BALL WHILE IT IS COMPLETELY ABOVE NET HEIGHT.
HOWEVER, THEY ARE PERMITTED TO BE SUBBED IN FOR ANY BACK-ROW PLAYER ANY TIME THE BALL IS NOT IN PLAY, WITHOUT NOTIFYING THE OFFICIALS.

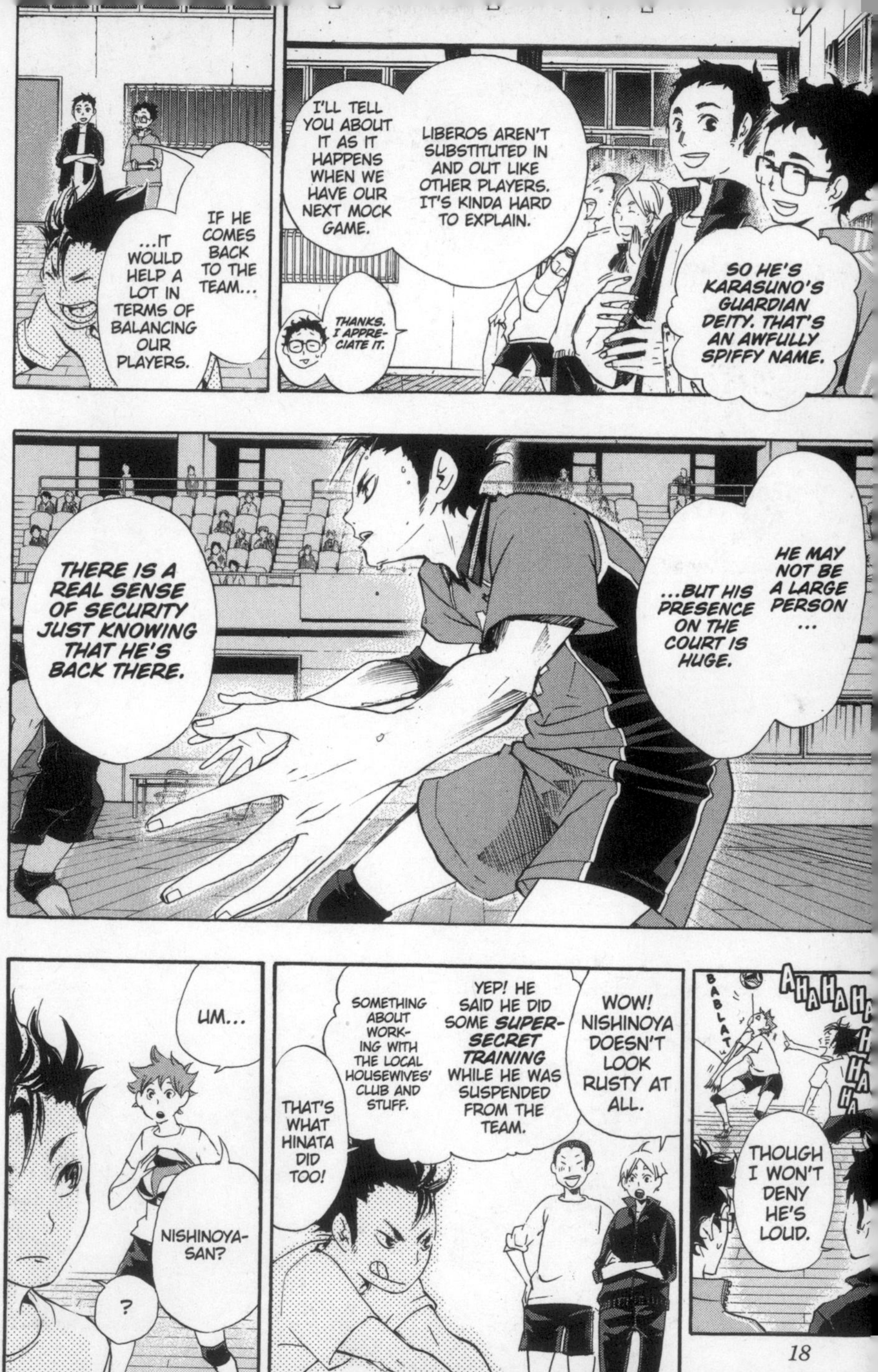
SO HE'S KARASUNO'S GUARDIAN DEITY. THAT'S AN AWFULLY SPIFFY NAME.
LIBEROS AREN'T SUBSTITUTED IN AND OUT LIKE OTHER PLAYERS. IT'S KINDA HARD TO EXPLAIN.
I'LL TELL YOU ABOUT IT AS IT HAPPENS WHEN WE HAVE OUR NEXT MOCK GAME.
THANKS. I APPRECIATE IT.
IF HE COMES BACK TO THE TEAM...
...IT WOULD HELP A LOT IN TERMS OF BALANCING OUR PLAYERS.
HE MAY NOT BE A LARGE PERSON ...
...BUT HIS PRESENCE ON THE COURT IS HUGE.
THERE IS A REAL SENSE OF SECURITY JUST KNOWING THAT HE'S BACK THERE.
AHAHAHAHAHA
BABLAT
THOUGH I WON'T DENY HE'S LOUD.
WOW! NISHINOYA DOESN'T LOOK RUSTY AT ALL.
YEP! HE SAID HE DID SOME SUPER-SECRET TRAINING WHILE HE WAS SUSPENDED FROM THE TEAM.
SOMETHING ABOUT WORKING WITH THE LOCAL HOUSEWIVES' CLUB AND STUFF.
THAT'S WHAT HINATA DID TOO!
UM...
NISHINOYA-SAN?
?

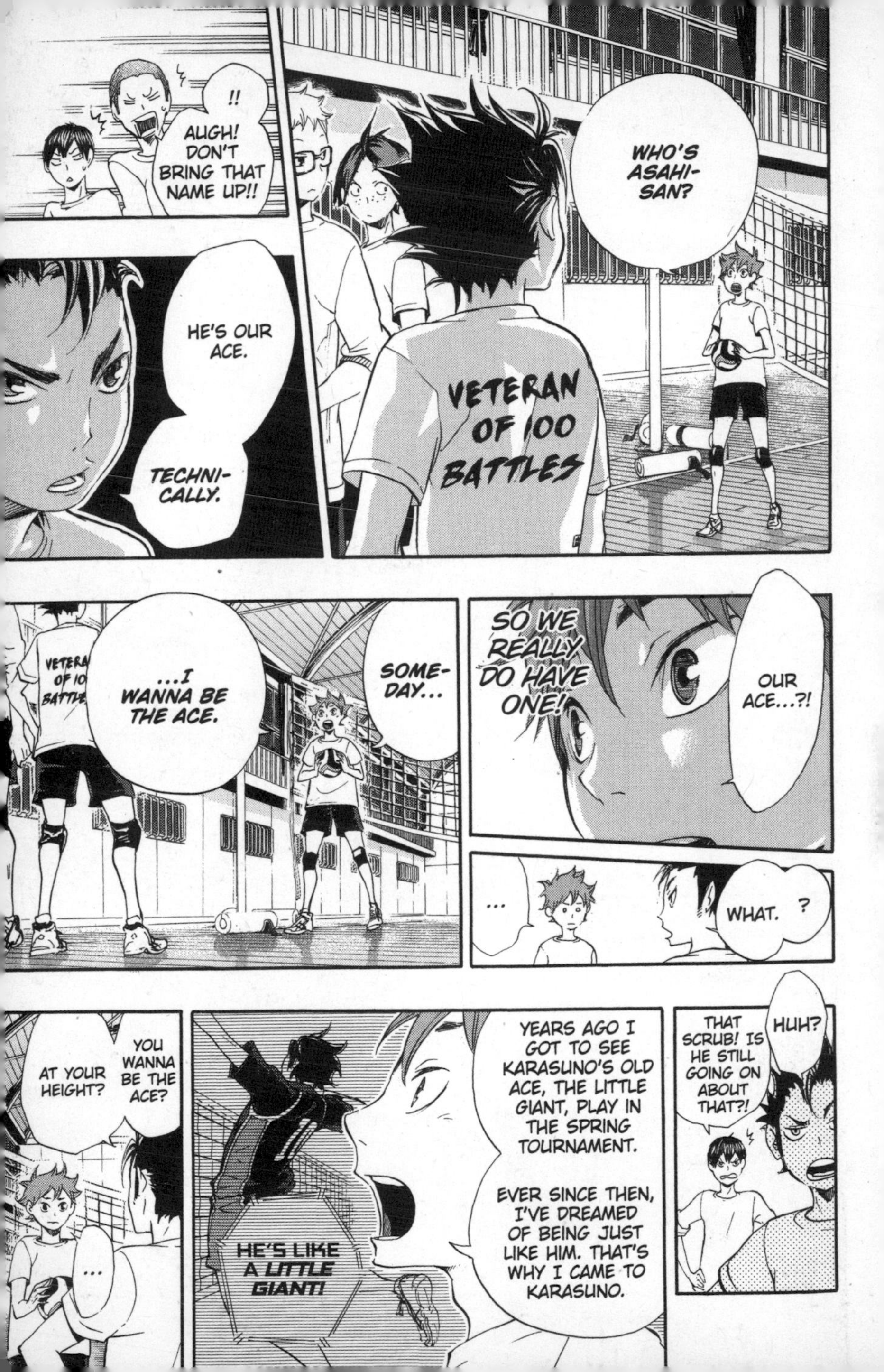
WHO'S ASAHI-SAN?
VETERAN OF 100 BATTLES
!!
AUGH! DON'T BRING THAT NAME UP!!
HE'S OUR ACE.
TECHNI-CALLY.
OUR ACE...?!
SO WE REALLY DO HAVE ONE!
WHAT. ?
...
SOME-DAY...
...I WANNA BE THE ACE.
HUH?
THAT SCRUB! IS HE STILL GOING ON ABOUT THAT?!
YEARS AGO I GOT TO SEE KARASUNO'S OLD ACE, THE LITTLE GIANT, PLAY IN THE SPRING TOURNAMENT.
EVER SINCE THEN, I'VE DREAMED OF BEING JUST LIKE HIM. THAT'S WHY I CAME TO KARASUNO.
HE'S LIKE A LITTLE GIANT!
YOU WANNA BE THE ACE?
AT YOUR HEIGHT?
...

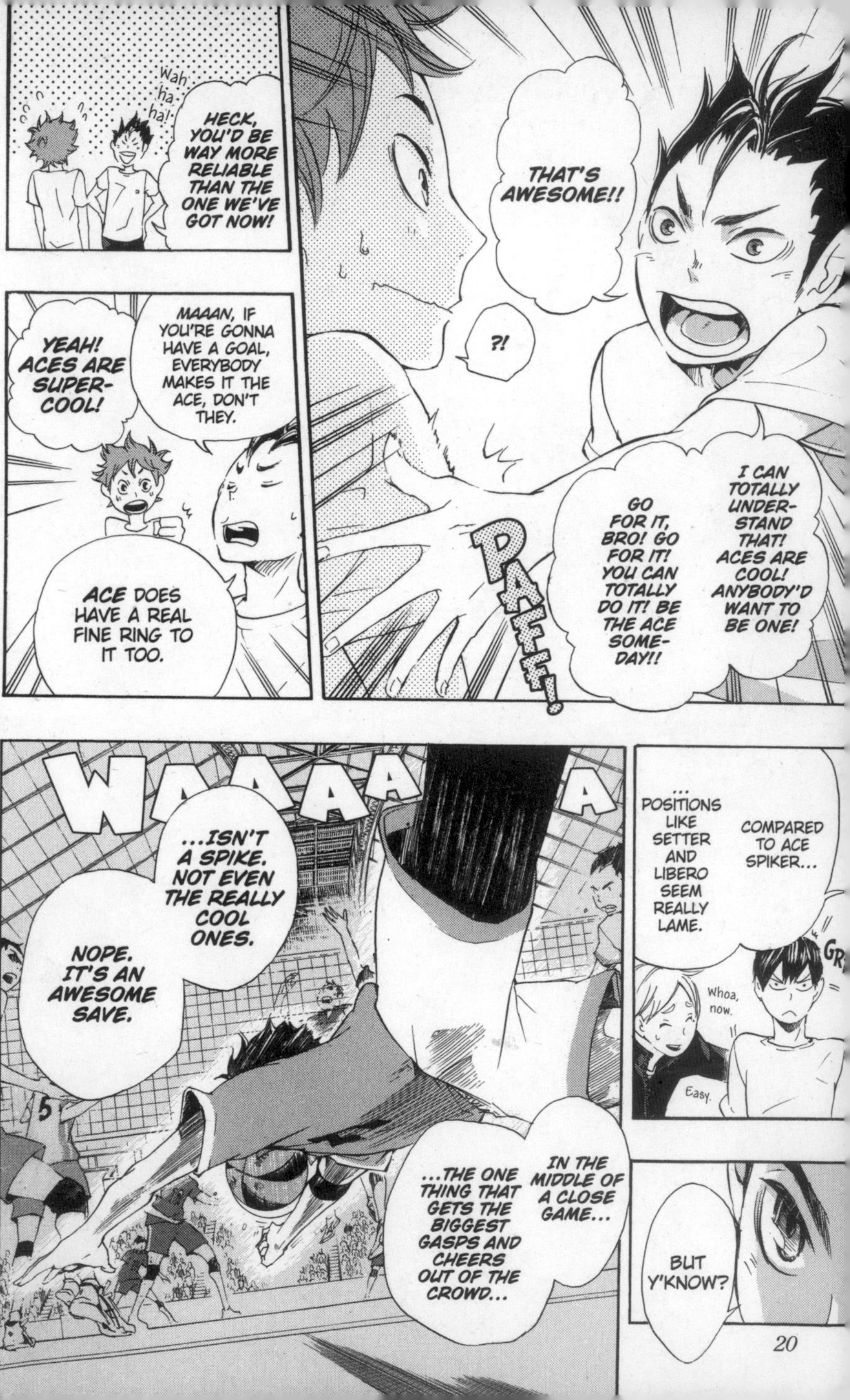

THAT'S AWESOME!!
?!
I CAN TOTALLY UNDERSTAND THAT! ACES ARE COOL! ANYBODY'D WANT TO BE ONE!
GO FOR IT, BRO! GO FOR IT! YOU CAN TOTALLY DO IT! BE THE ACE SOMEDAY!!
PAFF!
Wah ha ha!
HECK, YOU'D BE WAY MORE RELIABLE THAN THE ONE WE'VE GOT NOW!
MAAAN, IF YOU'RE GONNA HAVE A GOAL, EVERYBODY MAKES IT THE ACE, DON'T THEY.
YEAH! ACES ARE SUPER-COOL!
ACE DOES HAVE A REAL FINE RING TO IT TOO.
COMPARED TO ACE SPIKER...
...POSITIONS LIKE SETTER AND LIBERO SEEM REALLY LAME.
GR
Whoa, now.
Easy.
BUT Y'KNOW?
WAAAAA
IN THE MIDDLE OF A CLOSE GAME...
...THE ONE THING THAT GETS THE BIGGEST GASPS AND CHEERS OUT OF THE CROWD...
...ISN'T A SPIKE. NOT EVEN THE REALLY COOL ONES.
NOPE. IT'S AN AWESOME SAVE.

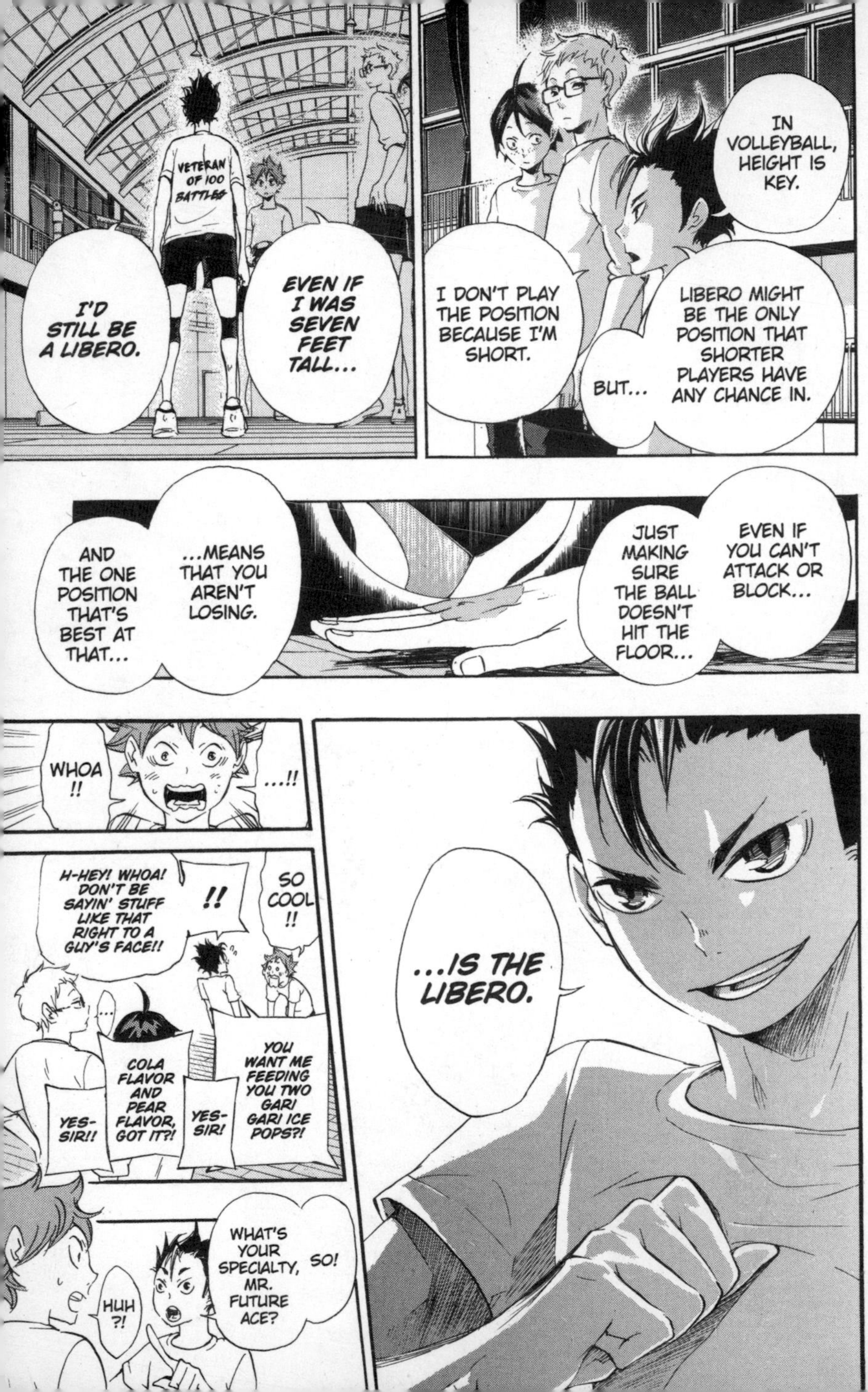
IN VOLLEYBALL, HEIGHT IS KEY.
LIBERO MIGHT BE THE ONLY POSITION THAT SHORTER PLAYERS HAVE ANY CHANCE IN.
BUT...
I DON'T PLAY THE POSITION BECAUSE I'M SHORT.
VETERAN OF 100 BATTLES
EVEN IF I WAS SEVEN FEET TALL...
I'D STILL BE A LIBERO.
EVEN IF YOU CAN'T ATTACK OR BLOCK...
JUST MAKING SURE THE BALL DOESN'T HIT THE FLOOR...
...MEANS THAT YOU AREN'T LOSING.
AND THE ONE POSITION THAT'S BEST AT THAT...
...IS THE LIBERO.
...!!
WHOA !!
SO COOL !!
!!
H-HEY! WHOA! DON'T BE SAYIN' STUFF LIKE THAT RIGHT TO A GUY'S FACE!!
...
YOU WANT ME FEEDING YOU TWO GARI GARI ICE POPS?!
YES-SIR!
COLA FLAVOR AND PEAR FLAVOR, GOT IT?!
YES-SIR!!
SO!
WHAT'S YOUR SPECIALTY, MR. FUTURE ACE?
HUH ?!

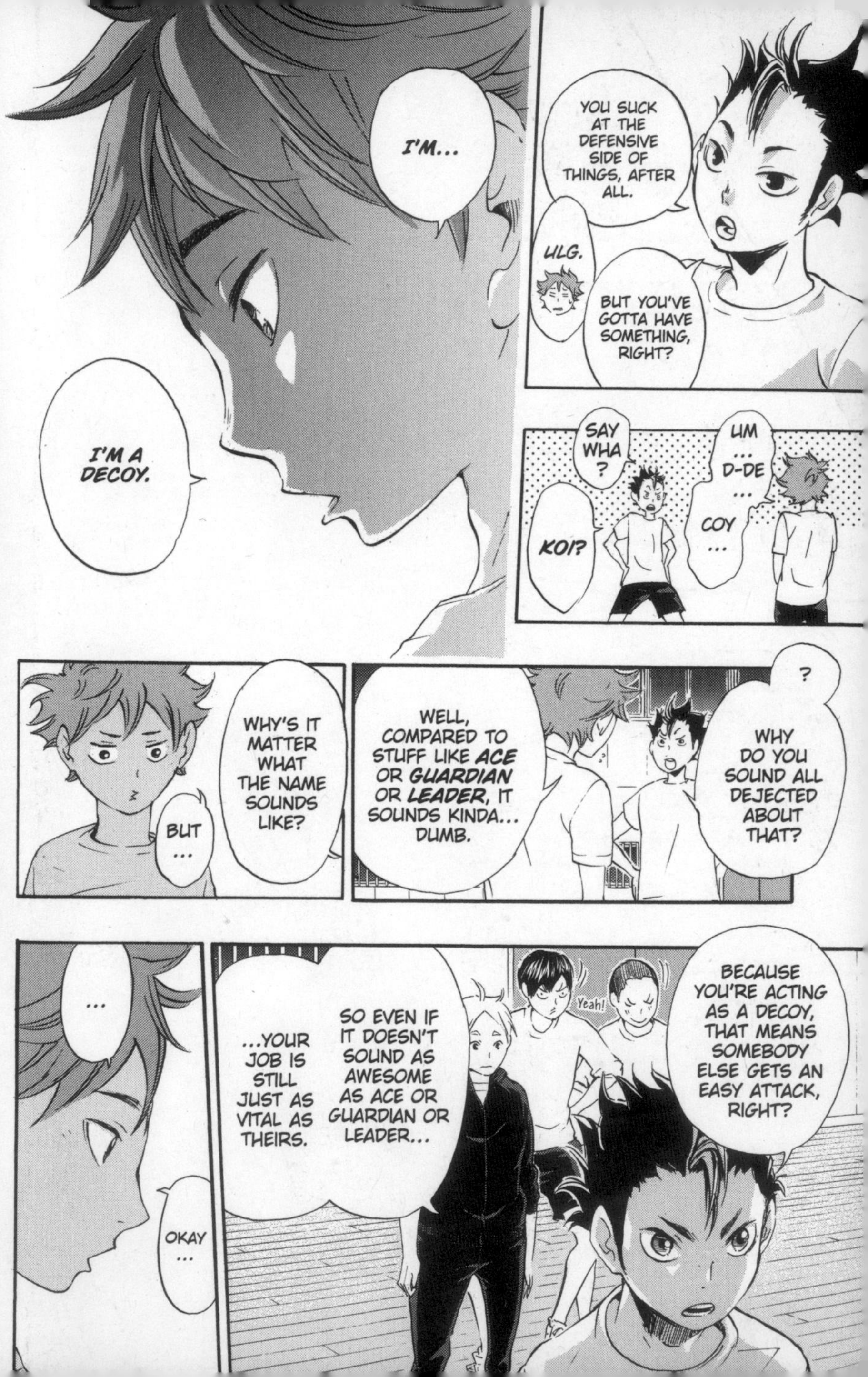
YOU SUCK AT THE DEFENSIVE SIDE OF THINGS, AFTER ALL.
ULG.
BUT YOU'VE GOTTA HAVE SOMETHING, RIGHT?
UM ... D-DE ... COY ...
SAY WHA ?
KOI?
I'M...
I'M A DECOY.
?
WHY DO YOU SOUND ALL DEJECTED ABOUT THAT?
WELL, COMPARED TO STUFF LIKE ACE OR GUARDIAN OR LEADER, IT SOUNDS KINDA... DUMB.
WHY'S IT MATTER WHAT THE NAME SOUNDS LIKE?
BUT ...
BECAUSE YOU'RE ACTING AS A DECOY, THAT MEANS SOMEBODY ELSE GETS AN EASY ATTACK, RIGHT?
Yeah!
SO EVEN IF IT DOESN'T SOUND AS AWESOME AS ACE OR GUARDIAN OR LEADER...
...YOUR JOB IS STILL JUST AS VITAL AS THEIRS.
...
OKAY ...

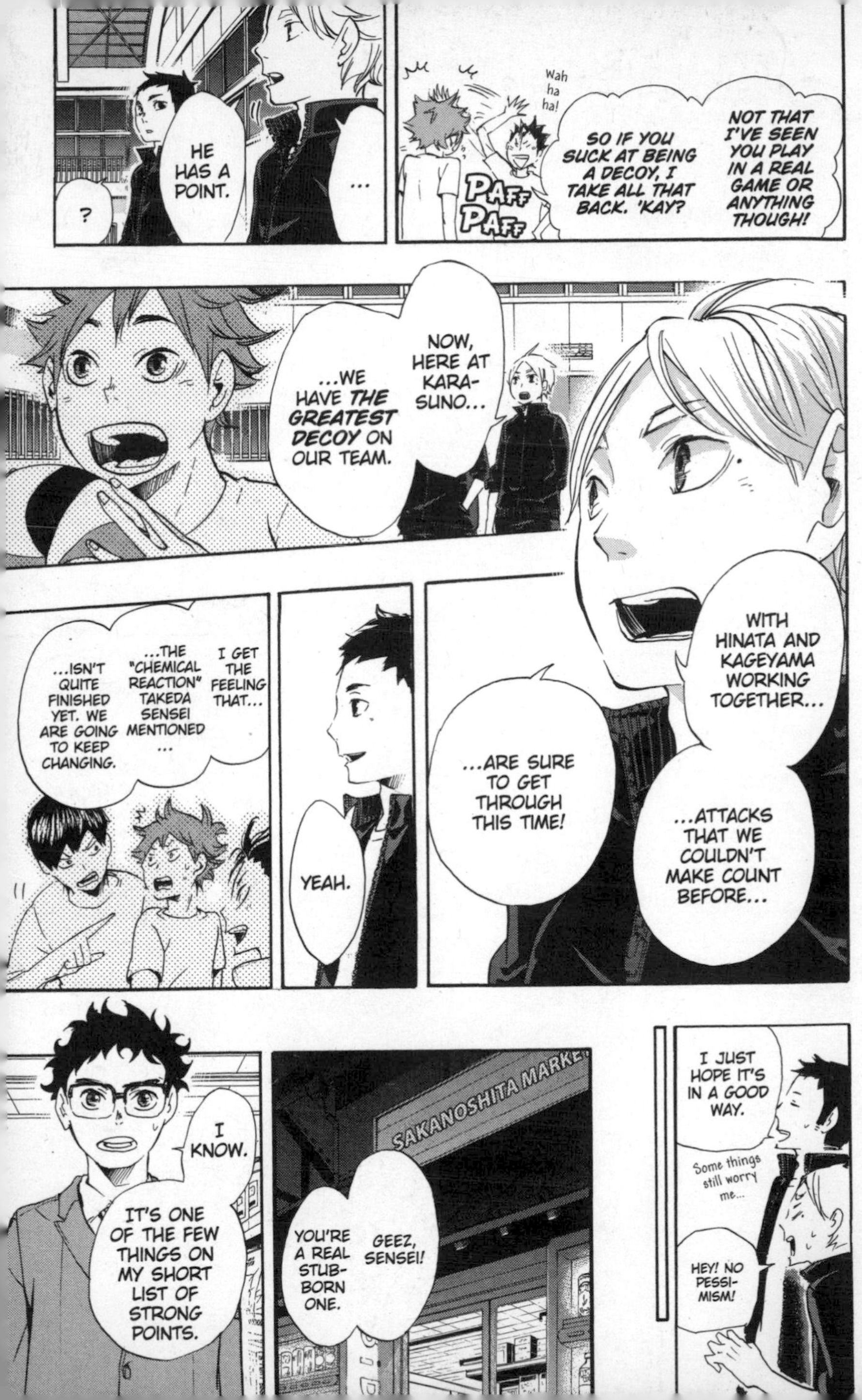
NOT THAT I'VE SEEN YOU PLAY IN A REAL GAME OR ANYTHING THOUGH!
SO IF YOU SUCK AT BEING A DECOY, I TAKE ALL THAT BACK. 'KAY?
Wah ha ha!
PAFF PAFF
...
HE HAS A POINT.
?
NOW, HERE AT KARA-SUNO...
...WE HAVE THE GREATEST DECOY ON OUR TEAM.
WITH HINATA AND KAGEYAMA WORKING TOGETHER...
...ATTACKS THAT WE COULDN'T MAKE COUNT BEFORE...
...ARE SURE TO GET THROUGH THIS TIME!
YEAH.
I GET THE FEELING THAT...
...THE "CHEMICAL REACTION" TAKEDA SENSEI MENTIONED...
...ISN'T QUITE FINISHED YET. WE ARE GOING TO KEEP CHANGING.
I JUST HOPE IT'S IN A GOOD WAY.
Some things still worry me...
HEY! NO PESSI-MISM!
SAKANOSHITA MARKE
GEEZ, SENSEI!
YOU'RE A REAL STUB-BORN ONE.
I KNOW.
IT'S ONE OF THE FEW THINGS ON MY SHORT LIST OF STRONG POINTS.

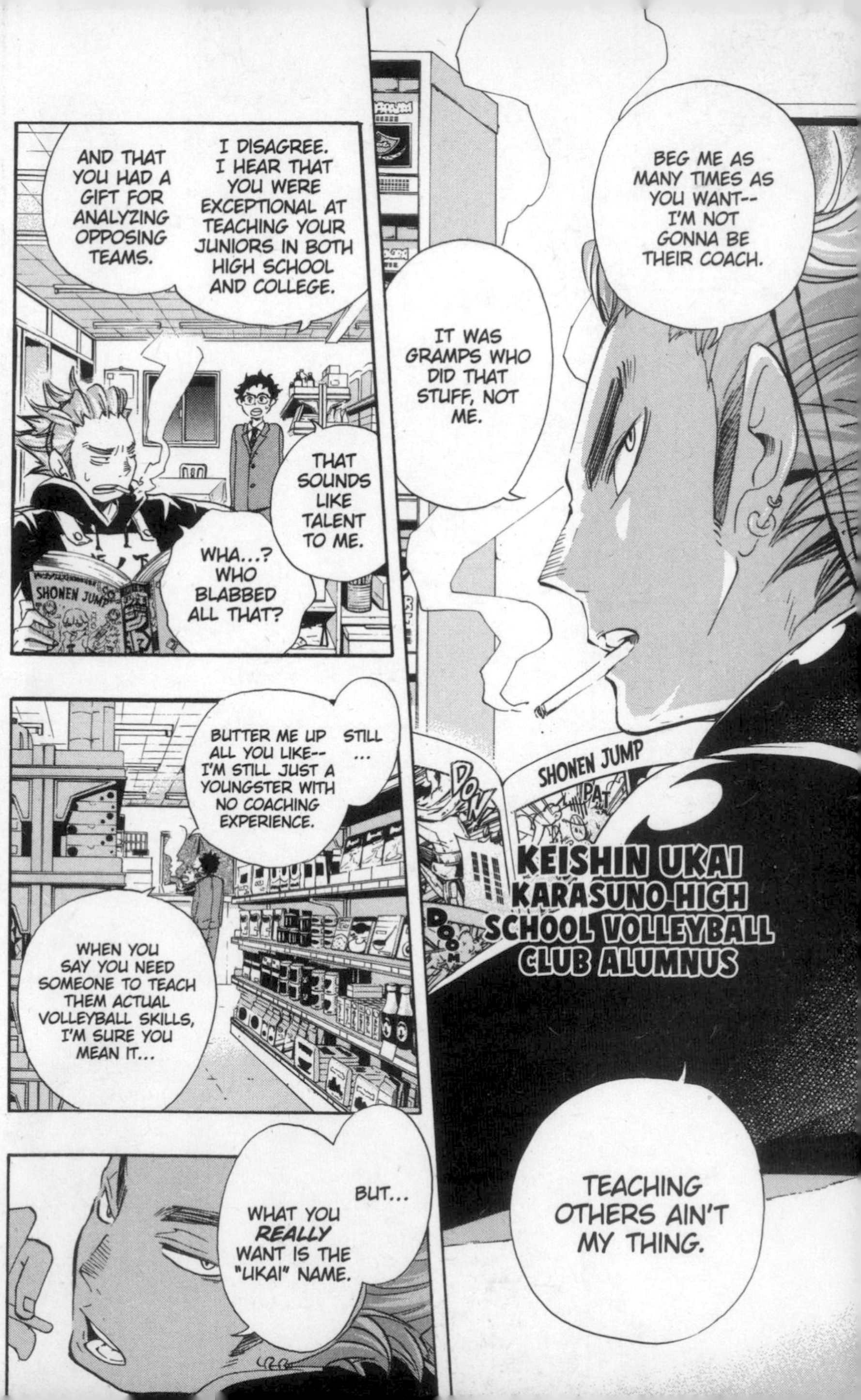
BEG ME AS MANY TIMES AS YOU WANT-- I'M NOT GONNA BE THEIR COACH.
IT WAS GRAMPS WHO DID THAT STUFF, NOT ME.
SHONEN JUMP
DON
PAT
KEISHIN UKAI
KARASUNO HIGH SCHOOL VOLLEYBALL CLUB ALUMNUS
DOOM
TEACHING OTHERS AIN'T MY THING.
I DISAGREE. I HEAR THAT YOU WERE EXCEPTIONAL AT TEACHING YOUR JUNIORS IN BOTH HIGH SCHOOL AND COLLEGE.
AND THAT YOU HAD A GIFT FOR ANALYZING OPPOSING TEAMS.
THAT SOUNDS LIKE TALENT TO ME.
WHA...? WHO BLABBED ALL THAT?
SHONEN JUMP
STILL...
BUTTER ME UP ALL YOU LIKE-- I'M STILL JUST A YOUNGSTER WITH NO COACHING EXPERIENCE.
WHEN YOU SAY YOU NEED SOMEONE TO TEACH THEM ACTUAL VOLLEYBALL SKILLS, I'M SURE YOU MEAN IT...
BUT...
WHAT YOU *REALLY* WANT IS THE "UKAI" NAME.

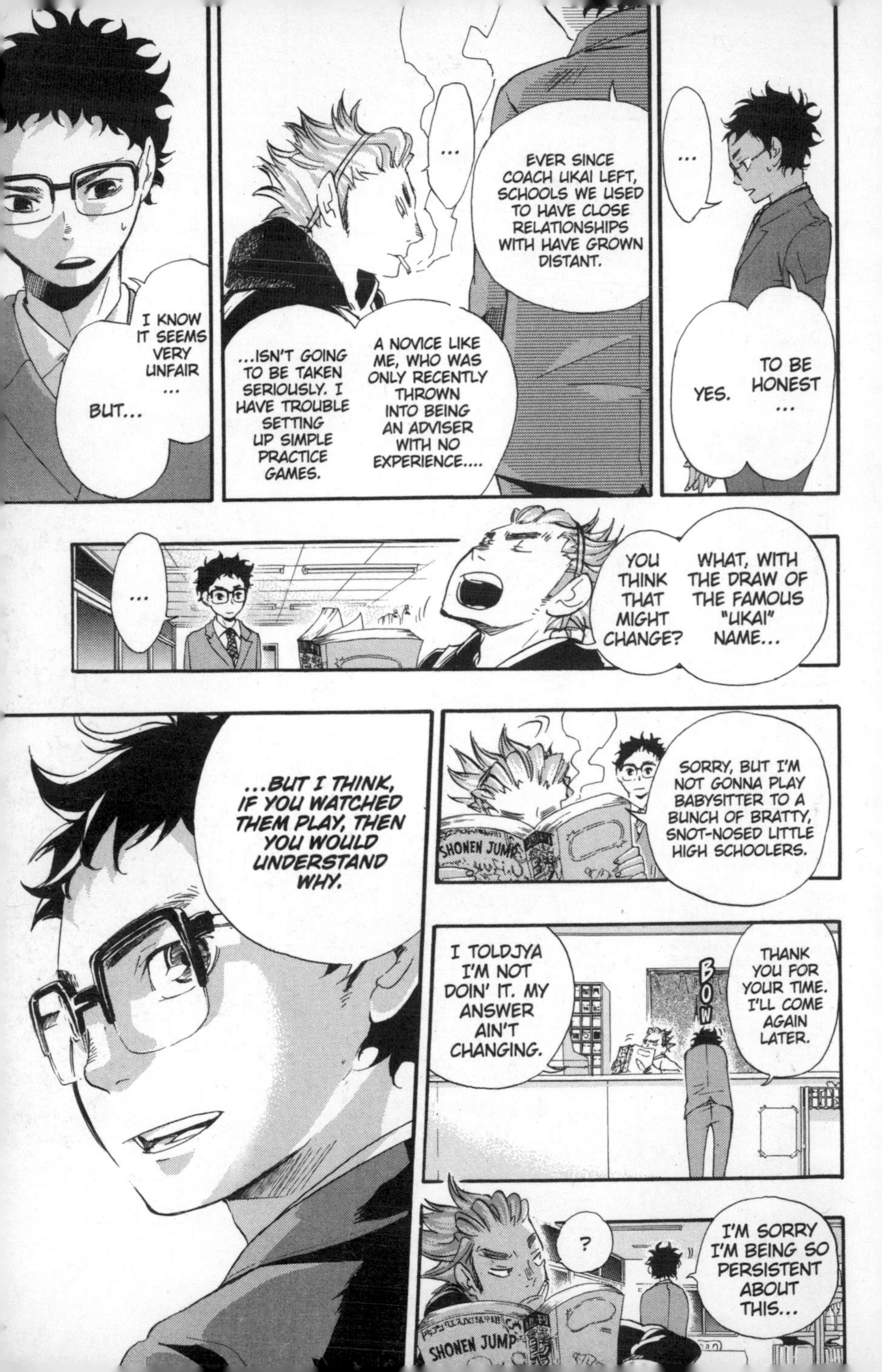
...
TO BE HONEST...
YES.
...
EVER SINCE COACH UKAI LEFT, SCHOOLS WE USED TO HAVE CLOSE RELATIONSHIPS WITH HAVE GROWN DISTANT.
A NOVICE LIKE ME, WHO WAS ONLY RECENTLY THROWN INTO BEING AN ADVISER WITH NO EXPERIENCE....
...ISN'T GOING TO BE TAKEN SERIOUSLY. I HAVE TROUBLE SETTING UP SIMPLE PRACTICE GAMES.
I KNOW IT SEEMS VERY UNFAIR...
BUT...
WHAT, WITH THE DRAW OF THE FAMOUS "UKAI" NAME...
YOU THINK THAT MIGHT CHANGE?
...
SORRY, BUT I'M NOT GONNA PLAY BABYSITTER TO A BUNCH OF BRATTY, SNOT-NOSED LITTLE HIGH SCHOOLERS.
SHONEN JUMP
THANK YOU FOR YOUR TIME. I'LL COME AGAIN LATER.
BOW
I TOLDJYA I'M NOT DOIN' IT. MY ANSWER AIN'T CHANGING.
I'M SORRY I'M BEING SO PERSISTENT ABOUT THIS...
?
SHONEN JUMP
...BUT I THINK, IF YOU WATCHED THEM PLAY, THEN YOU WOULD UNDERSTAND WHY.

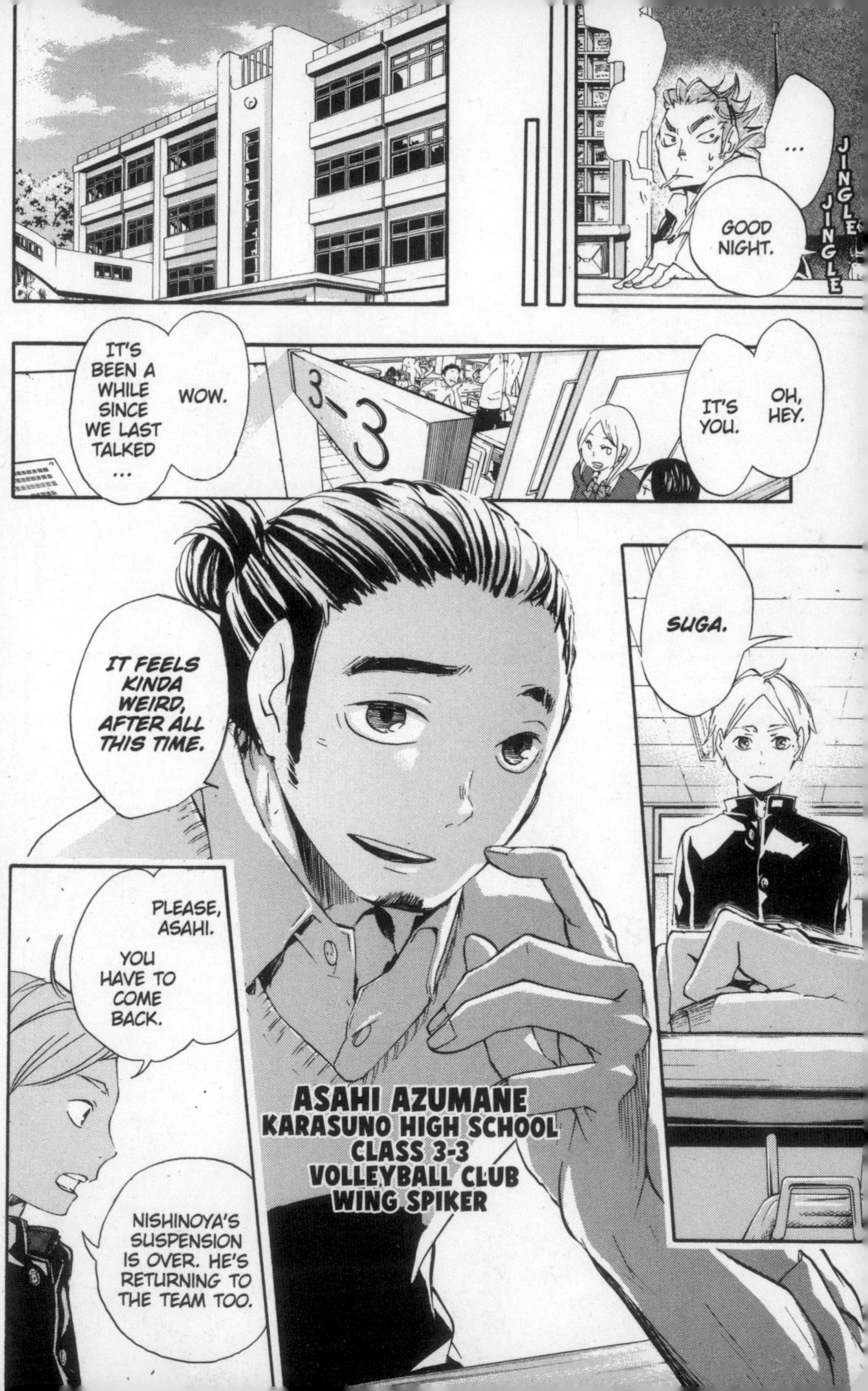
...
GOOD NIGHT.
JINGLE
JINGLE
OH, HEY.
IT'S YOU.
WOW.
IT'S BEEN A WHILE SINCE WE LAST TALKED...
3-3
SUGA.
IT FEELS KINDA WEIRD, AFTER ALL THIS TIME.
ASAHI AZUMANE
KARASUNO HIGH SCHOOL
CLASS 3-3
VOLLEYBALL CLUB
WING SPIKER
PLEASE, ASAHI.
YOU HAVE TO COME BACK.
NISHINOYA'S SUSPENSION IS OVER. HE'S RETURNING TO THE TEAM TOO.

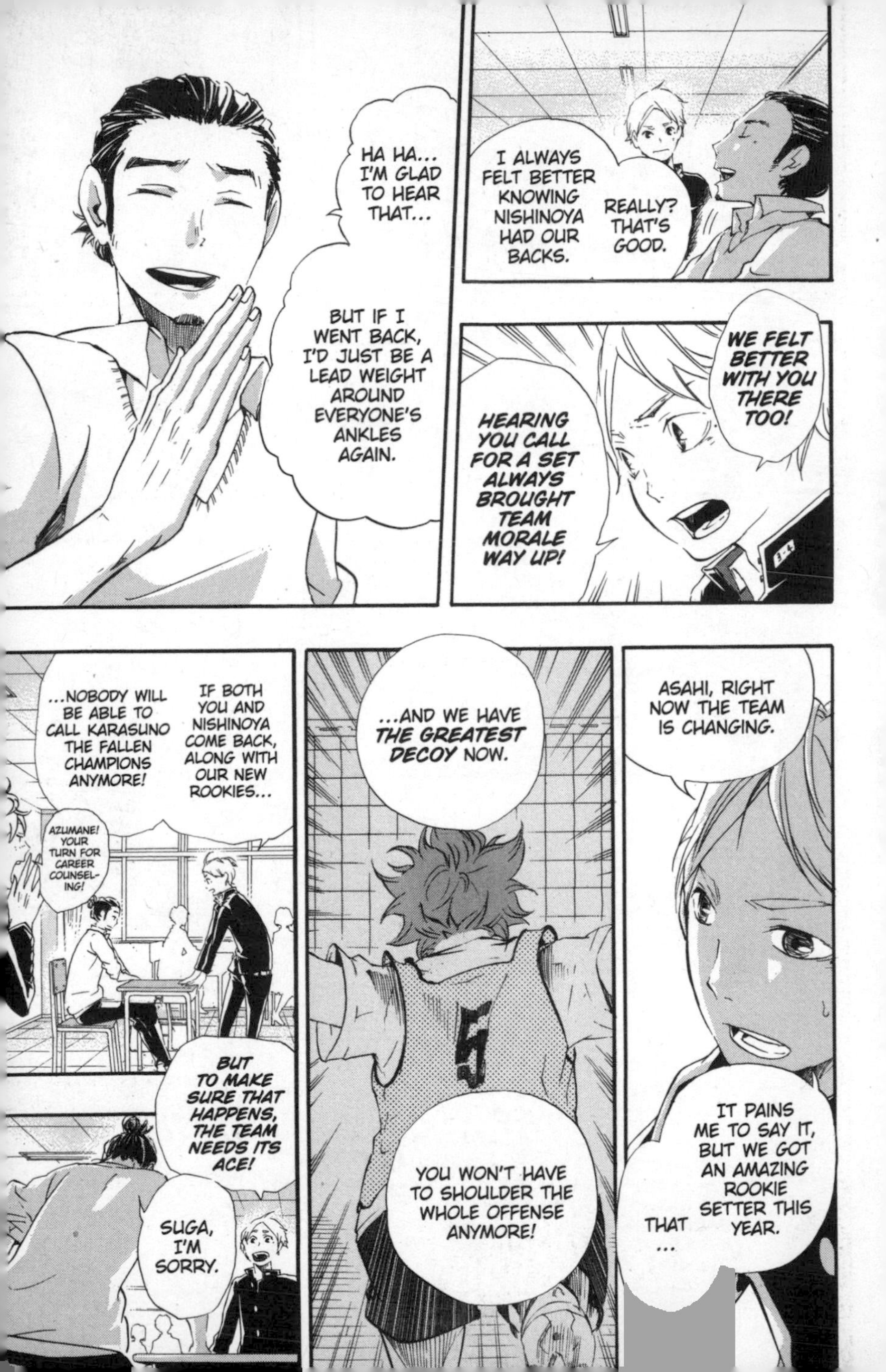
I ALWAYS FELT BETTER KNOWING NISHINOYA HAD OUR BACKS.
REALLY? THAT'S GOOD.
WE FELT BETTER WITH YOU THERE TOO!
HEARING YOU CALL FOR A SET ALWAYS BROUGHT TEAM MORALE WAY UP!
HA HA... I'M GLAD TO HEAR THAT...
BUT IF I WENT BACK, I'D JUST BE A LEAD WEIGHT AROUND EVERYONE'S ANKLES AGAIN.
ASAHI, RIGHT NOW THE TEAM IS CHANGING.
IT PAINS ME TO SAY IT, BUT WE GOT AN AMAZING ROOKIE SETTER THIS YEAR.
THAT...
...AND WE HAVE THE GREATEST DECOY NOW.
YOU WON'T HAVE TO SHOULDER THE WHOLE OFFENSE ANYMORE!
IF BOTH YOU AND NISHINOYA COME BACK, ALONG WITH OUR NEW ROOKIES...
...NOBODY WILL BE ABLE TO CALL KARASUNO THE FALLEN CHAMPIONS ANYMORE!
AZUMANE! YOUR TURN FOR CAREER COUNSEL-ING!
BUT TO MAKE SURE THAT HAPPENS, THE TEAM NEEDS ITS ACE!
SUGA, I'M SORRY.

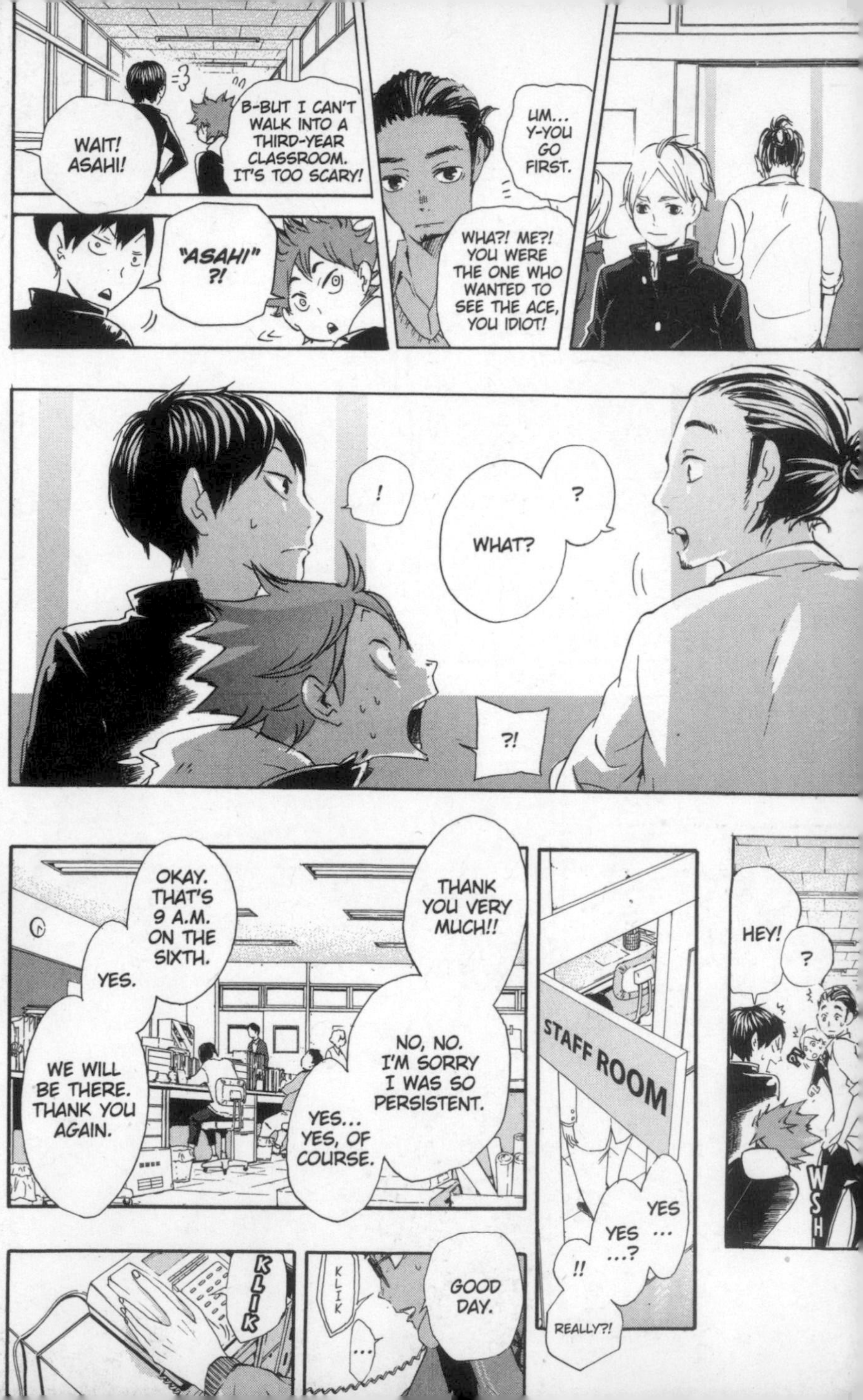
UM... Y-YOU GO FIRST.
WHA?! ME?! YOU WERE THE ONE WHO WANTED TO SEE THE ACE, YOU IDIOT!
B-BUT I CAN'T WALK INTO A THIRD-YEAR CLASSROOM. IT'S TOO SCARY!
WAIT! ASAHI!
"ASAHI" ?!
?
WHAT?
!
?!
HEY!
?
WSH
STAFF ROOM
YES
YES ...?
!!
REALLY?!
THANK YOU VERY MUCH!!
OKAY. THAT'S 9 A.M. ON THE SIXTH.
YES.
NO, NO. I'M SORRY I WAS SO PERSISTENT.
YES... YES, OF COURSE.
WE WILL BE THERE. THANK YOU AGAIN.
GOOD DAY.
KLIK
...
KLIK

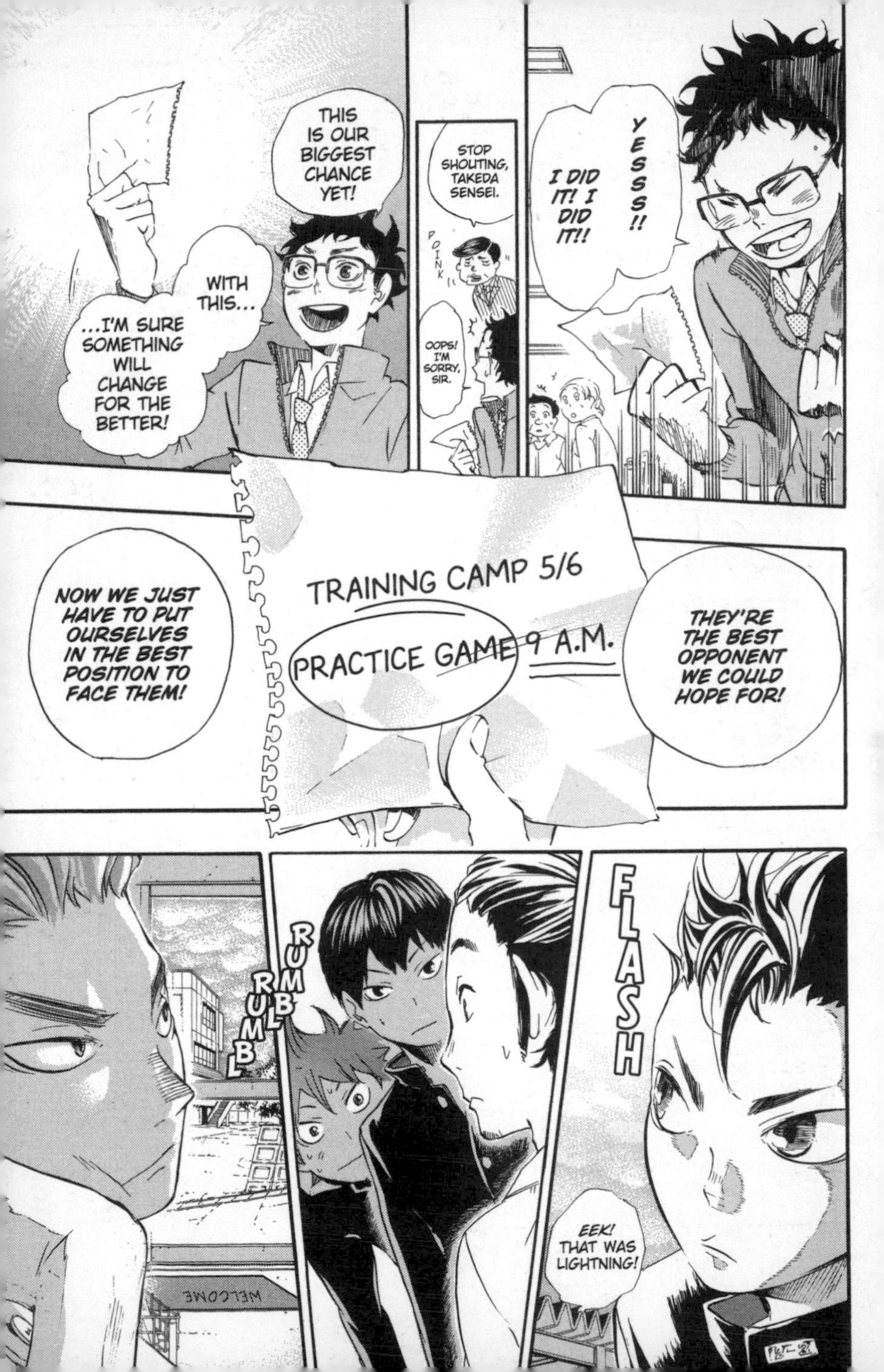
YESSS!!
I DID IT! I DID IT!!
STOP SHOUTING, TAKEDA SENSEI.
POINK
OOPS! I'M SORRY, SIR.
THIS IS OUR BIGGEST CHANCE YET!
WITH THIS...
...I'M SURE SOMETHING WILL CHANGE FOR THE BETTER!
THEY'RE THE BEST OPPONENT WE COULD HOPE FOR!
TRAINING CAMP 5/6
PRACTICE GAME 9 A.M.
NOW WE JUST HAVE TO PUT OURSELVES IN THE BEST POSITION TO FACE THEM!
FLASH
EEK! THAT WAS LIGHTNING!
RUMBL
RUMBL

YU NISHINOYA!!

KARASUNO HIGH SCHOOL
CLASS 2-3!!

POSITION:
LIBERO!!!

HEIGHT: 5'3"!

WEIGHT: 113 LBS.!!
(AS OF APRIL, 2ND YEAR
OF HIGH SCHOOL!)

BIRTHDAY: OCTOBER 10!!

FAVORITE FOOD:
GARI GARI ICE POPS!!
(COLA FLAVOR!)

CURRENT WORRY:
NONE!!

ABILITY PARAMETERS
(5-POINT SCALE)

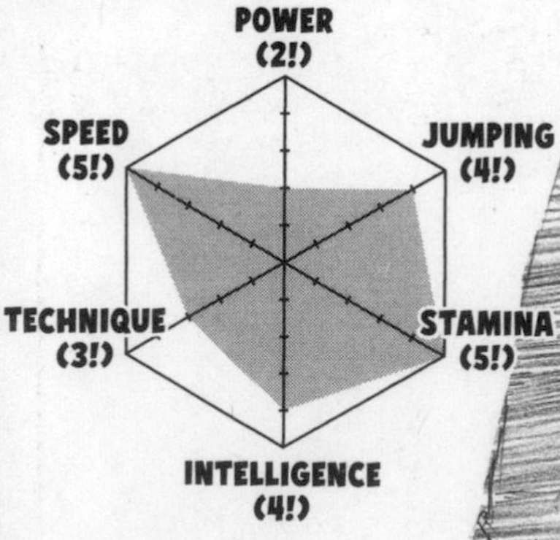
POWER (2!)
JUMPING (4!)
STAMINA (5!)
INTELLIGENCE (4!)
TECHNIQUE (3!)
SPEED (5!)

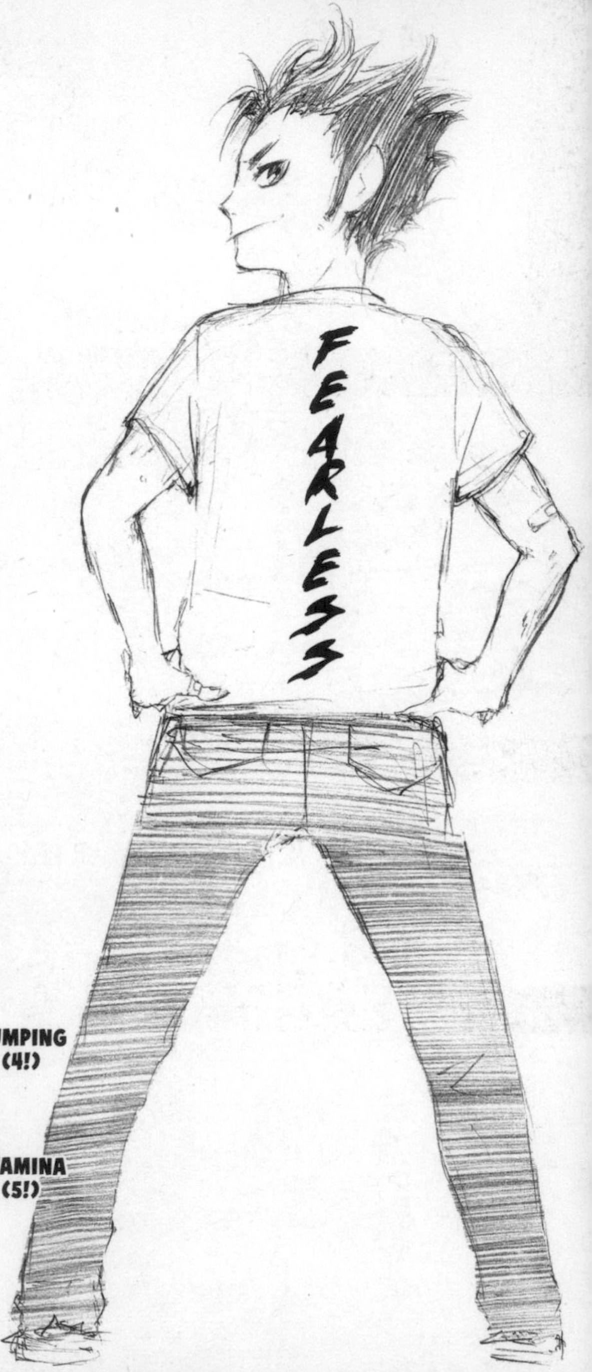
FEARLESS

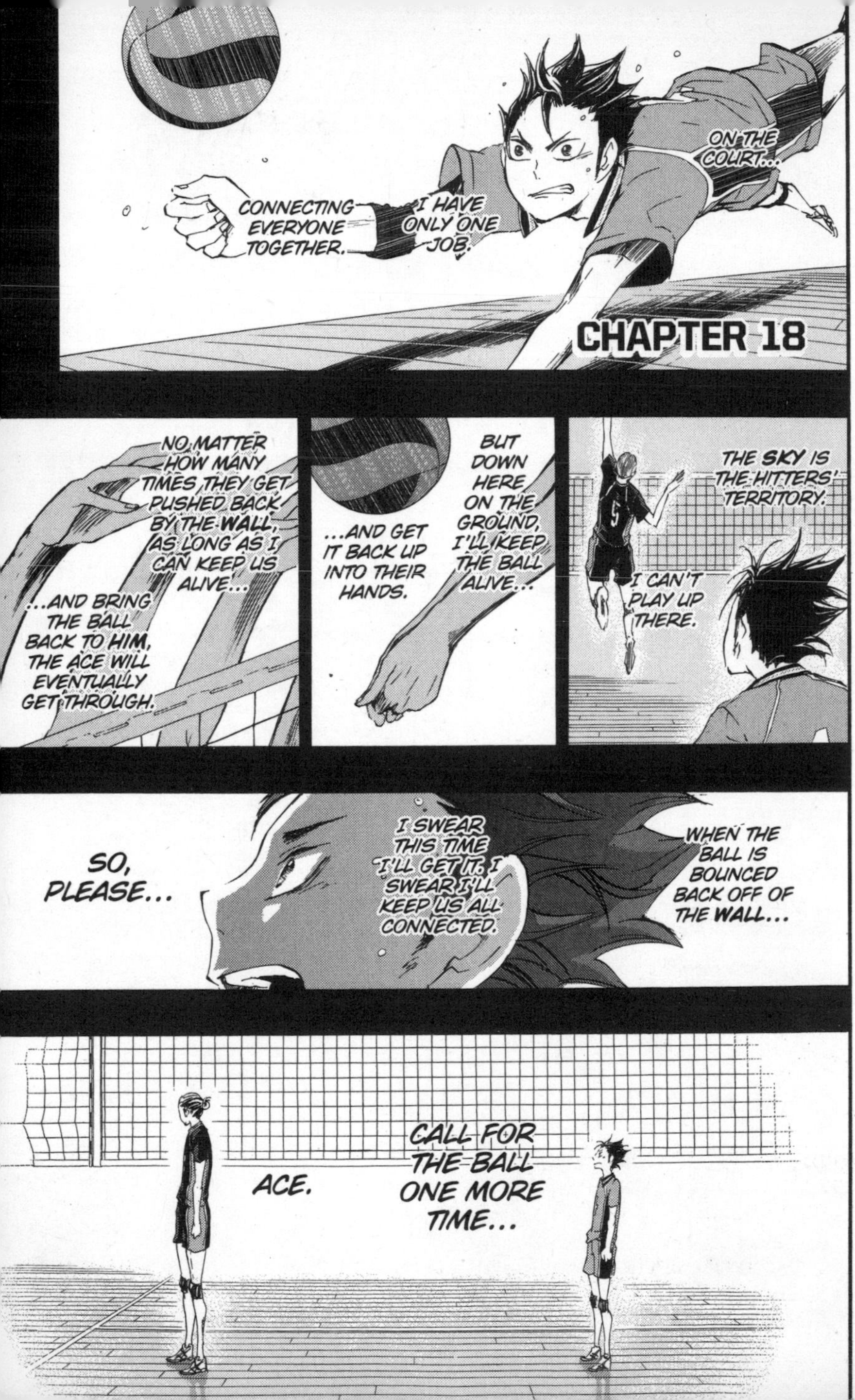
ON THE COURT...
I HAVE ONLY ONE JOB.
CONNECTING EVERYONE TOGETHER.
CHAPTER 18
THE SKY IS THE HITTERS' TERRITORY.
I CAN'T PLAY UP THERE.
BUT DOWN HERE ON THE GROUND, I'LL KEEP THE BALL ALIVE...
...AND GET IT BACK UP INTO THEIR HANDS.
NO MATTER HOW MANY TIMES THEY GET PUSHED BACK BY THE WALL, AS LONG AS I CAN KEEP US ALIVE...
...AND BRING THE BALL BACK TO HIM, THE ACE WILL EVENTUALLY GET THROUGH.
WHEN THE BALL IS BOUNCED BACK OFF OF THE WALL...
I SWEAR THIS TIME I'LL GET IT. I SWEAR I'LL KEEP US ALL CONNECTED.
SO, PLEASE...
CALL FOR THE BALL ONE MORE TIME...
ACE.

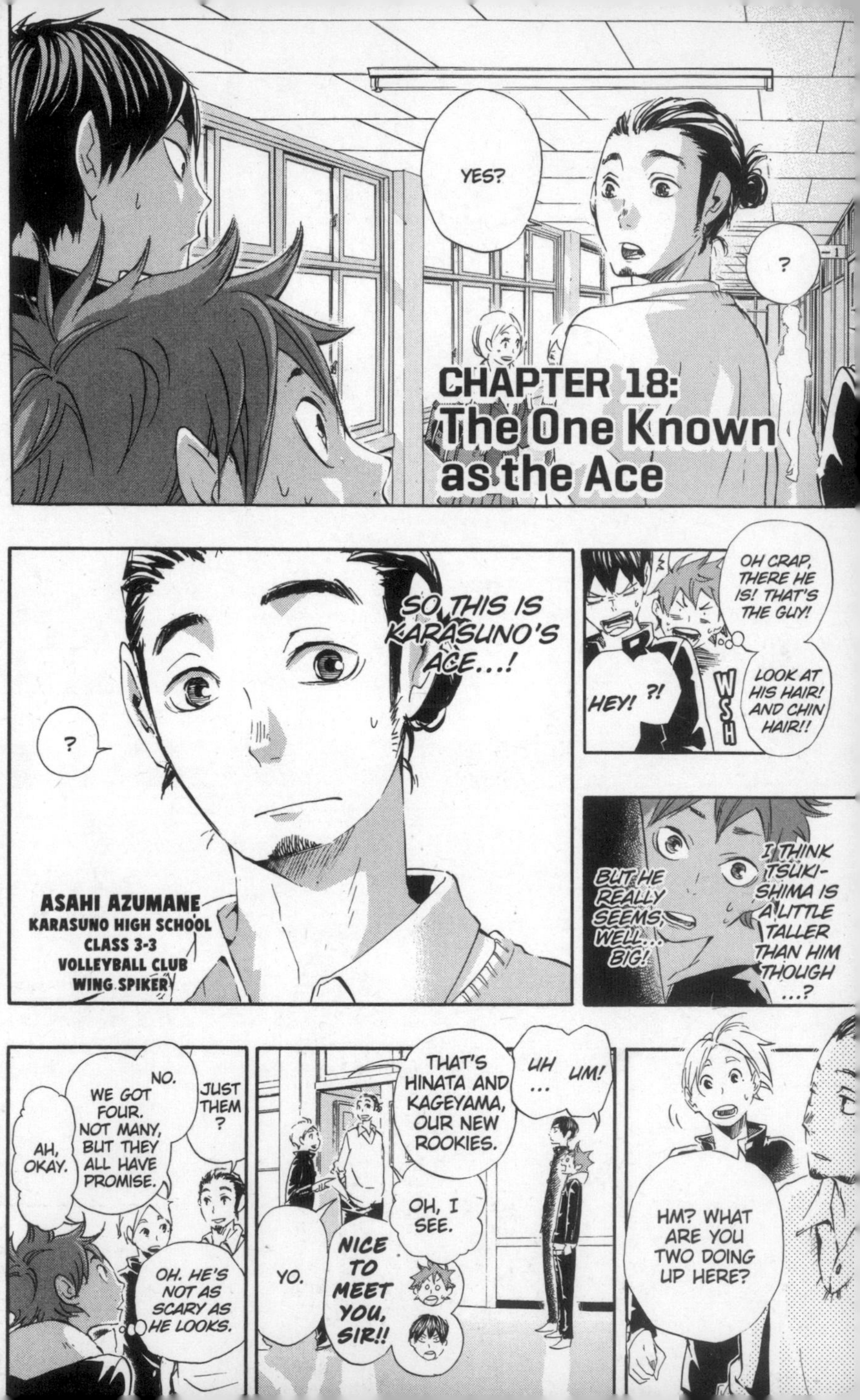
?
YES?
CHAPTER 18:
The One Known as the Ace
OH CRAP, THERE HE IS! THAT'S THE GUY!
LOOK AT HIS HAIR! AND CHIN HAIR!!
WSH
?!
HEY!
I THINK TSUKI-SHIMA IS A LITTLE TALLER THAN HIM THOUGH ...?
BUT HE REALLY SEEMS, WELL... BIG!
SO THIS IS KARASUNO'S ACE...!
?
ASAHI AZUMANE
KARASUNO HIGH SCHOOL
CLASS 3-3
VOLLEYBALL CLUB
WING SPIKER
HM? WHAT ARE YOU TWO DOING UP HERE?
UM!
UH ...
THAT'S HINATA AND KAGEYAMA, OUR NEW ROOKIES.
OH, I SEE.
NICE TO MEET YOU, SIR!!
YO.
JUST THEM?
NO.
WE GOT FOUR. NOT MANY, BUT THEY ALL HAVE PROMISE.
AH, OKAY.
OH. HE'S NOT AS SCARY AS HE LOOKS.

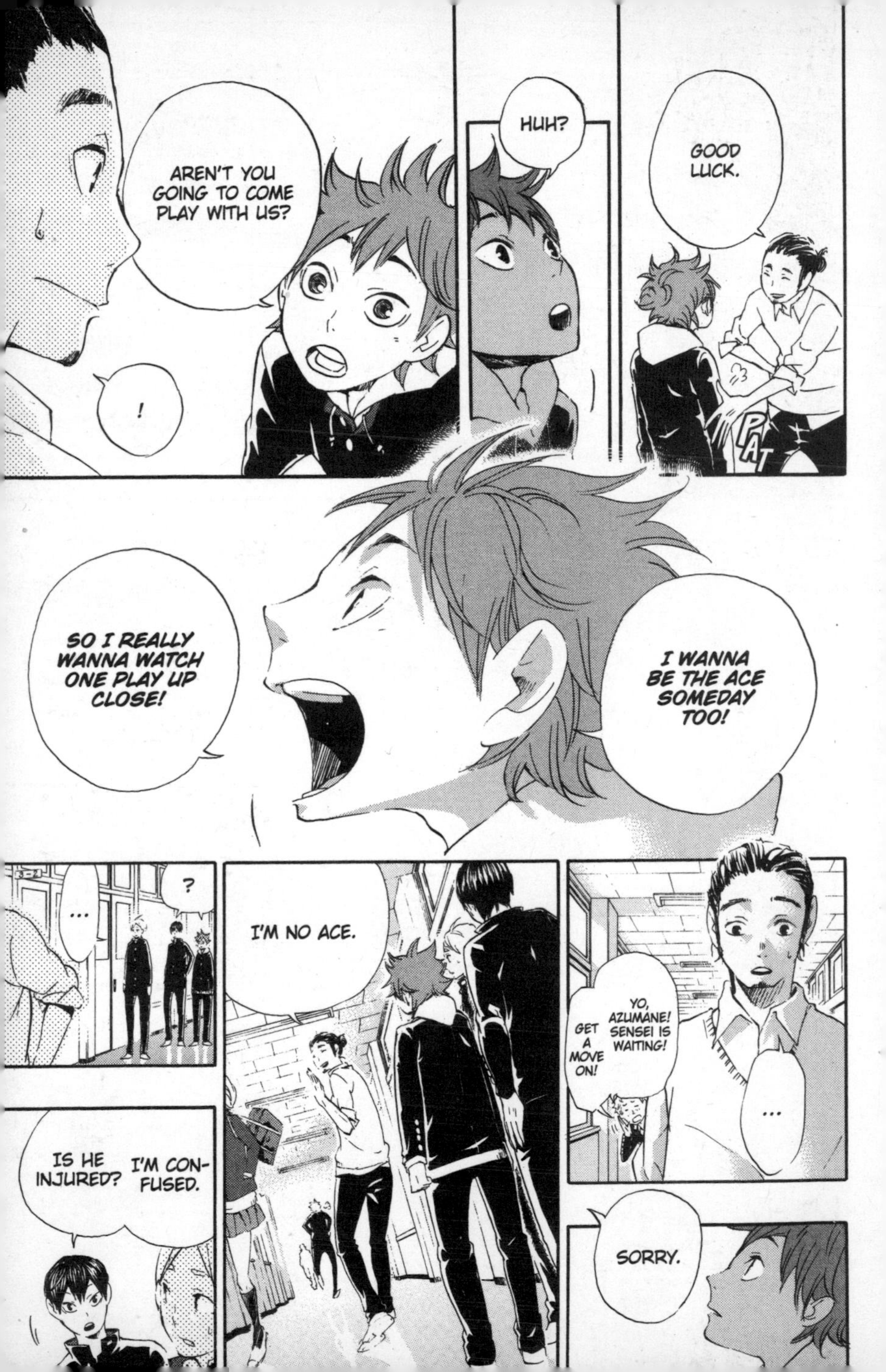
GOOD LUCK.
PAT
HUH?
AREN'T YOU GOING TO COME PLAY WITH US?
!
I WANNA BE THE ACE SOMEDAY TOO!
SO I REALLY WANNA WATCH ONE PLAY UP CLOSE!
YO, AZUMANE! SENSEI IS WAITING!
GET A MOVE ON!
...
SORRY.
I'M NO ACE.
?
...
I'M CON-FUSED.
IS HE INJURED?

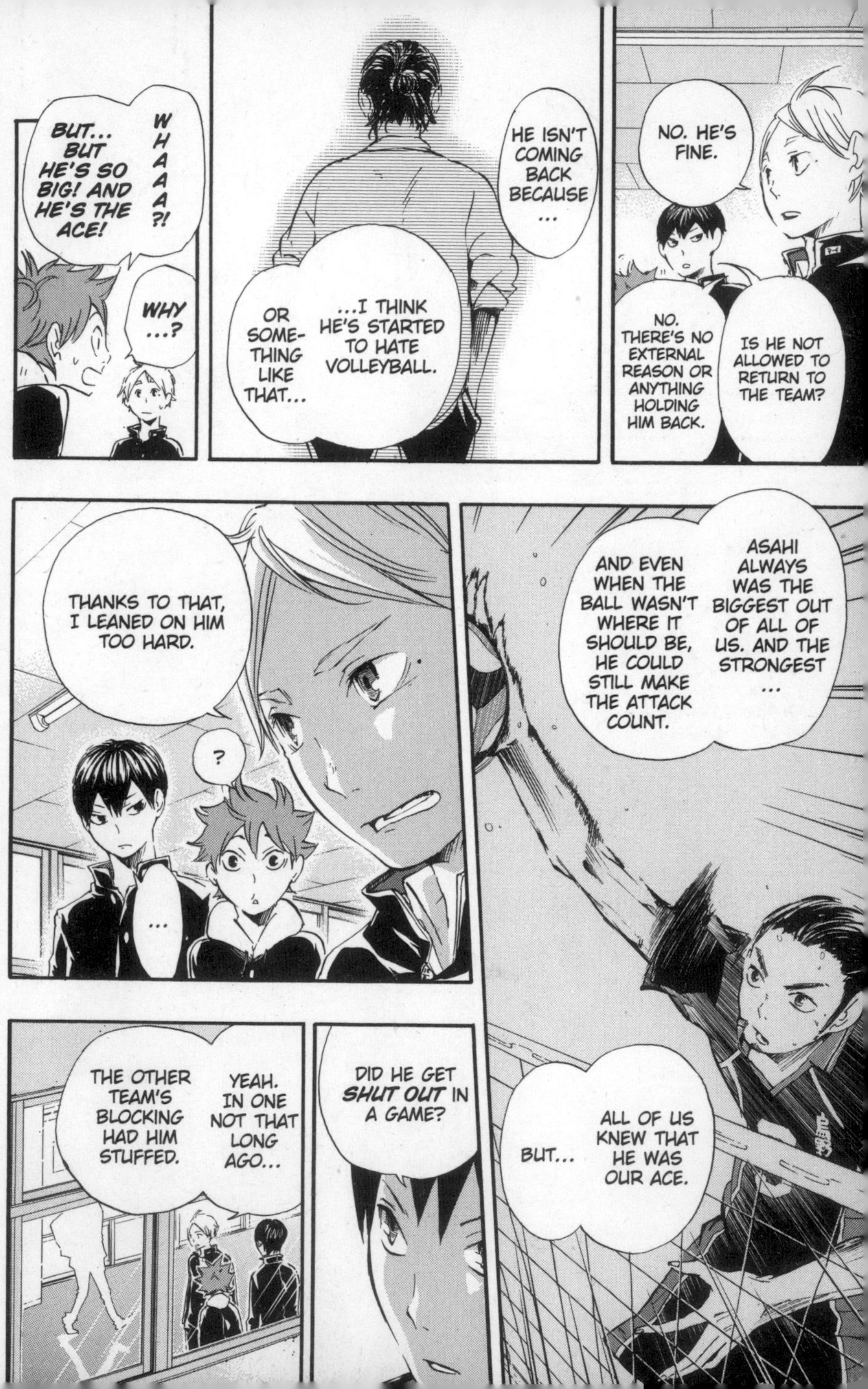
NO. HE'S FINE.
IS HE NOT ALLOWED TO RETURN TO THE TEAM?
NO. THERE'S NO EXTERNAL REASON OR ANYTHING HOLDING HIM BACK.
HE ISN'T COMING BACK BECAUSE...
...I THINK HE'S STARTED TO HATE VOLLEYBALL.
OR SOMETHING LIKE THAT...
WHAAAA?!
BUT... BUT HE'S SO BIG! AND HE'S THE ACE!
WHY...?
ASAHI ALWAYS WAS THE BIGGEST OUT OF ALL OF US. AND THE STRONGEST...
AND EVEN WHEN THE BALL WASN'T WHERE IT SHOULD BE, HE COULD STILL MAKE THE ATTACK COUNT.
ALL OF US KNEW THAT HE WAS OUR ACE.
BUT...
THANKS TO THAT, I LEANED ON HIM TOO HARD.
?
...
DID HE GET SHUT OUT IN A GAME?
YEAH. IN ONE NOT THAT LONG AGO...
THE OTHER TEAM'S BLOCKING HAD HIM STUFFED.

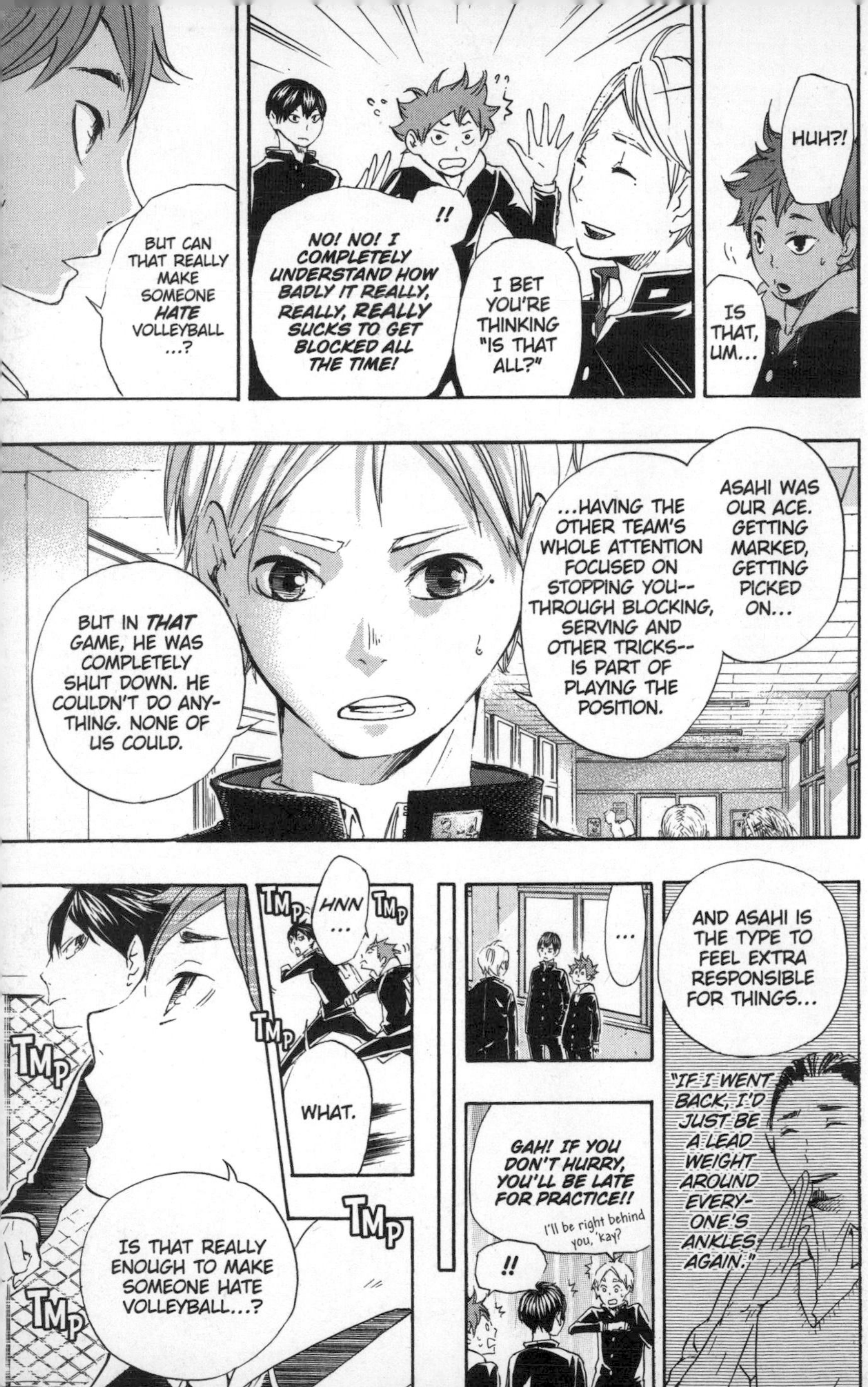
HUH?!
IS THAT, UM...
I BET YOU'RE THINKING "IS THAT ALL?"
!!
NO! NO! I COMPLETELY UNDERSTAND HOW BADLY IT REALLY, REALLY, REALLY SUCKS TO GET BLOCKED ALL THE TIME!
BUT CAN THAT REALLY MAKE SOMEONE HATE VOLLEYBALL ...?
ASAHI WAS OUR ACE. GETTING MARKED, GETTING PICKED ON...
...HAVING THE OTHER TEAM'S WHOLE ATTENTION FOCUSED ON STOPPING YOU-- THROUGH BLOCKING, SERVING AND OTHER TRICKS-- IS PART OF PLAYING THE POSITION.
BUT IN THAT GAME, HE WAS COMPLETELY SHUT DOWN. HE COULDN'T DO ANY-THING. NONE OF US COULD.
AND ASAHI IS THE TYPE TO FEEL EXTRA RESPONSIBLE FOR THINGS...
"IF I WENT BACK, I'D JUST BE A LEAD WEIGHT AROUND EVERY-ONE'S ANKLES AGAIN."
...
GAH! IF YOU DON'T HURRY, YOU'LL BE LATE FOR PRACTICE!!
I'll be right behind you, 'kay?
!!
TMP
HNN ...
TMP
TMP
WHAT.
TMP
TMP
TMP
IS THAT REALLY ENOUGH TO MAKE SOMEONE HATE VOLLEYBALL...?

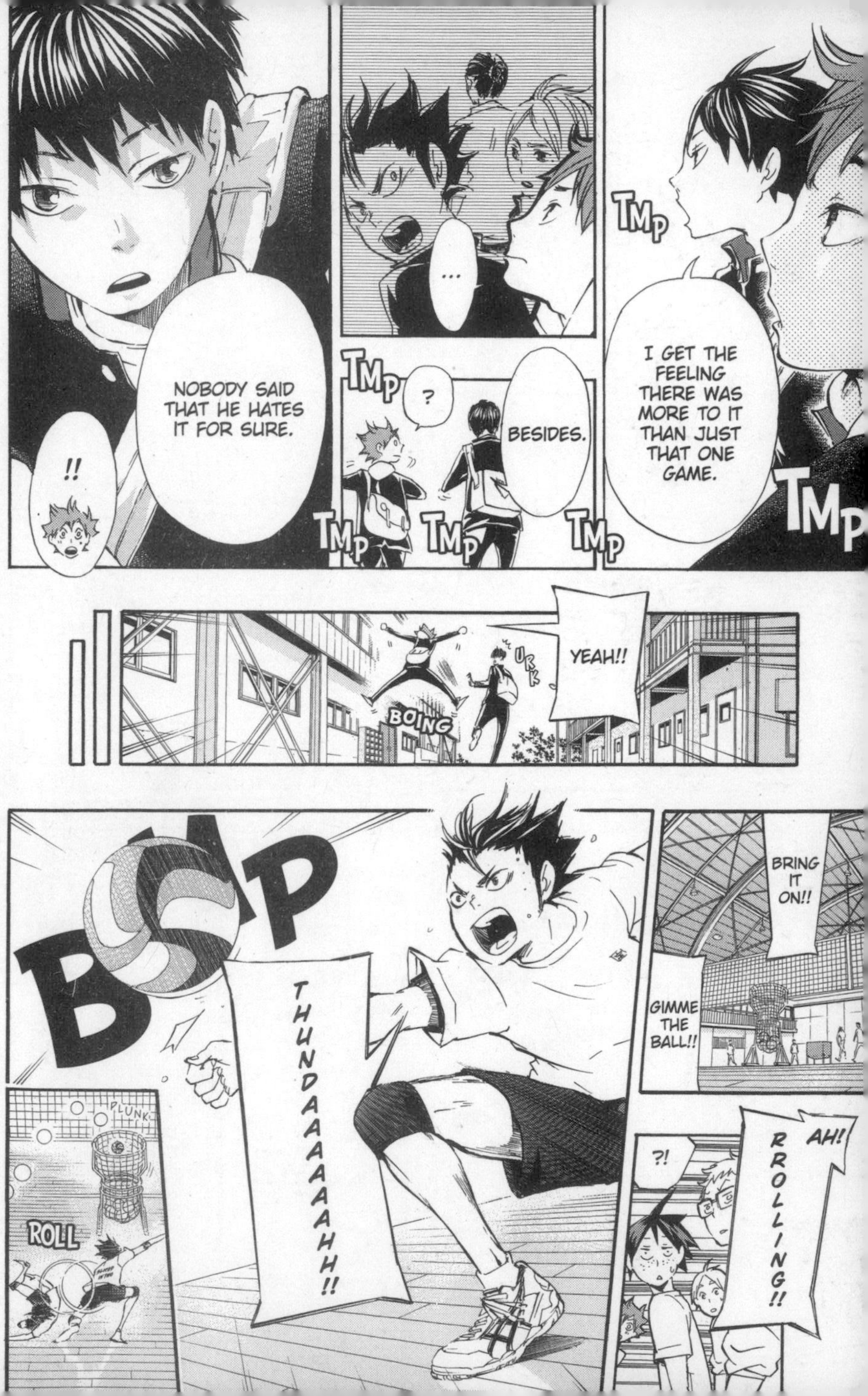
TMP
I GET THE FEELING THERE WAS MORE TO IT THAN JUST THAT ONE GAME.
TMP
...
TMP
?
BESIDES.
TMP
TMP
TMP
NOBODY SAID THAT HE HATES IT FOR SURE.
!!
YEAH!!
URK
BOING
BRING IT ON!!
GIMME THE BALL!!
AH!
RROLLING!!
?!
BAP
THUNDAAAAAAAHH!!
PLUNK
ROLL

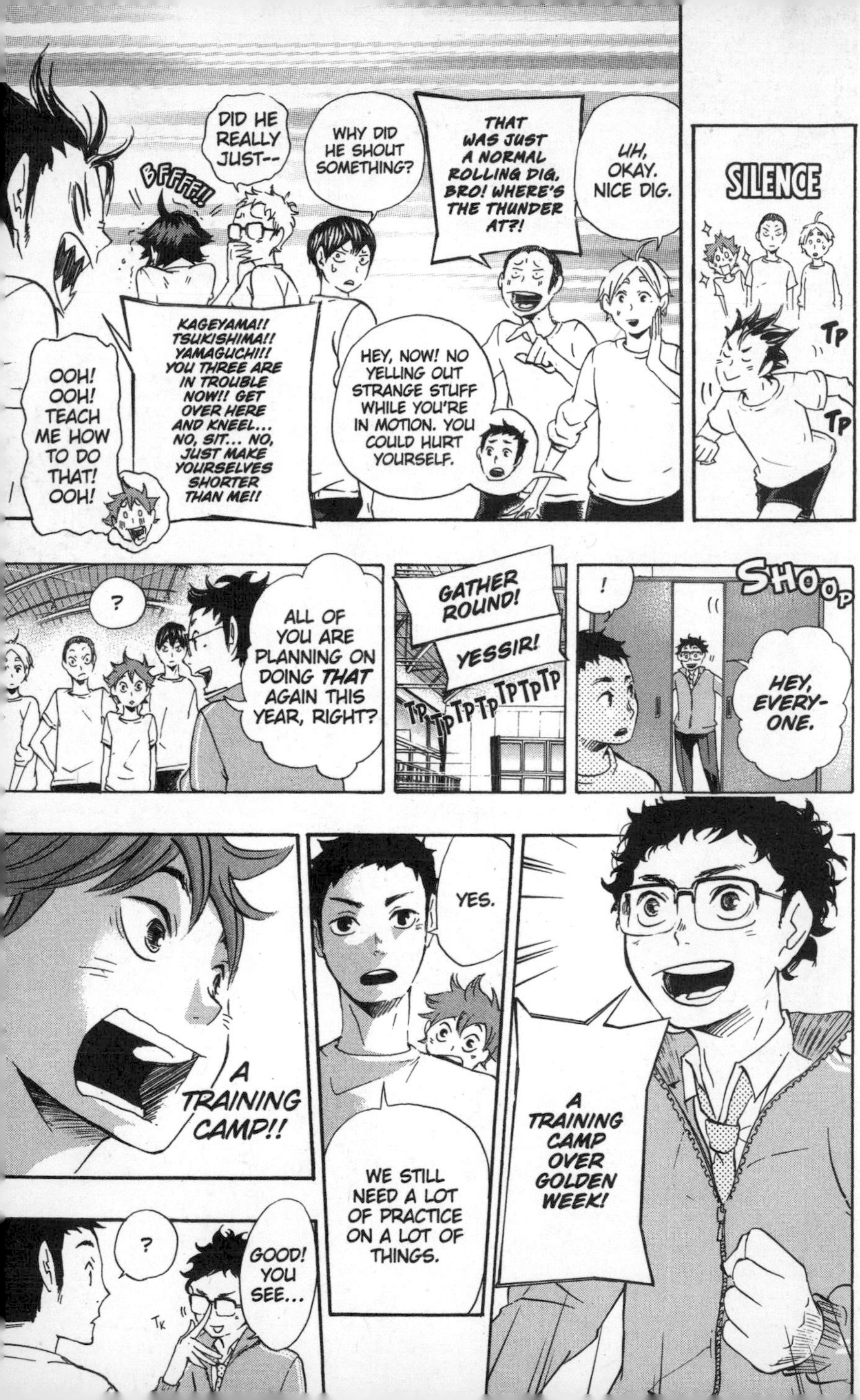
SILENCE
Tp
Tp
UH, OKAY. NICE DIG.
THAT WAS JUST A NORMAL ROLLING DIG, BRO! WHERE'S THE THUNDER AT?!
WHY DID HE SHOUT SOMETHING?
DID HE REALLY JUST--
BFFFF!!
HEY, NOW! NO YELLING OUT STRANGE STUFF WHILE YOU'RE IN MOTION. YOU COULD HURT YOURSELF.
KAGEYAMA!! TSUKISHIMA!! YAMAGUCHI!! YOU THREE ARE IN TROUBLE NOW!! GET OVER HERE AND KNEEL... NO, SIT... NO, JUST MAKE YOURSELVES SHORTER THAN ME!!
OOH! OOH! TEACH ME HOW TO DO THAT! OOH!
SHOOP
!
HEY, EVERYONE.
GATHER ROUND!
YESSIR!
TpTpTpTpTpTpTp
ALL OF YOU ARE PLANNING ON DOING THAT AGAIN THIS YEAR, RIGHT?
?
YES.
WE STILL NEED A LOT OF PRACTICE ON A LOT OF THINGS.
?
GOOD! YOU SEE...
Tk
A TRAINING CAMP OVER GOLDEN WEEK!
A TRAINING CAMP!!

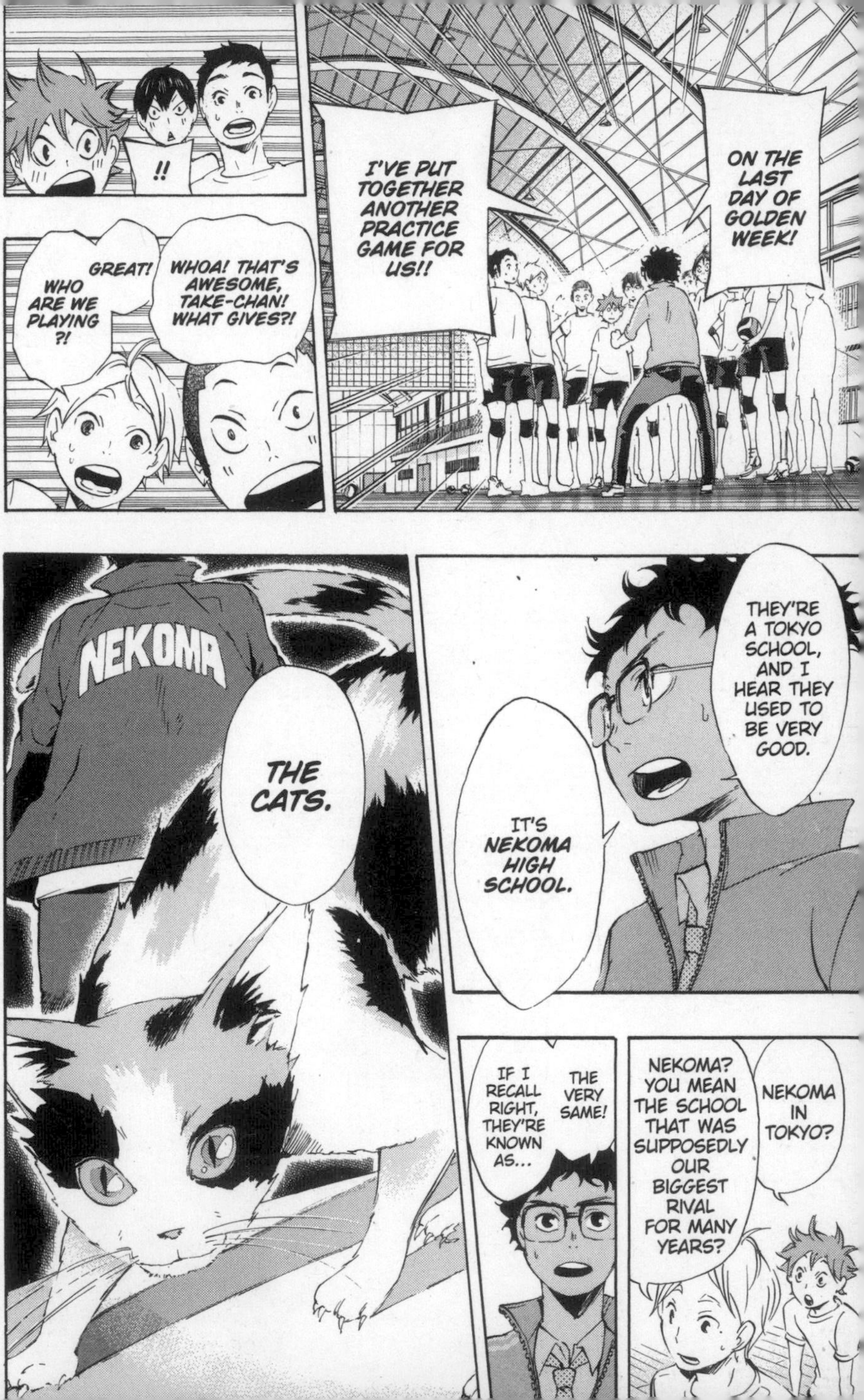
ON THE LAST DAY OF GOLDEN WEEK!
I'VE PUT TOGETHER ANOTHER PRACTICE GAME FOR US!!
!!
WHOA! THAT'S AWESOME, TAKE-CHAN! WHAT GIVES?!
GREAT! WHO ARE WE PLAYING?!
THEY'RE A TOKYO SCHOOL, AND I HEAR THEY USED TO BE VERY GOOD.
IT'S NEKOMA HIGH SCHOOL.
NEKOMA IN TOKYO?
NEKOMA? YOU MEAN THE SCHOOL THAT WAS SUPPOSEDLY OUR BIGGEST RIVAL FOR MANY YEARS?
THE VERY SAME!
IF I RECALL RIGHT, THEY'RE KNOWN AS...
NEKOMA
THE CATS.

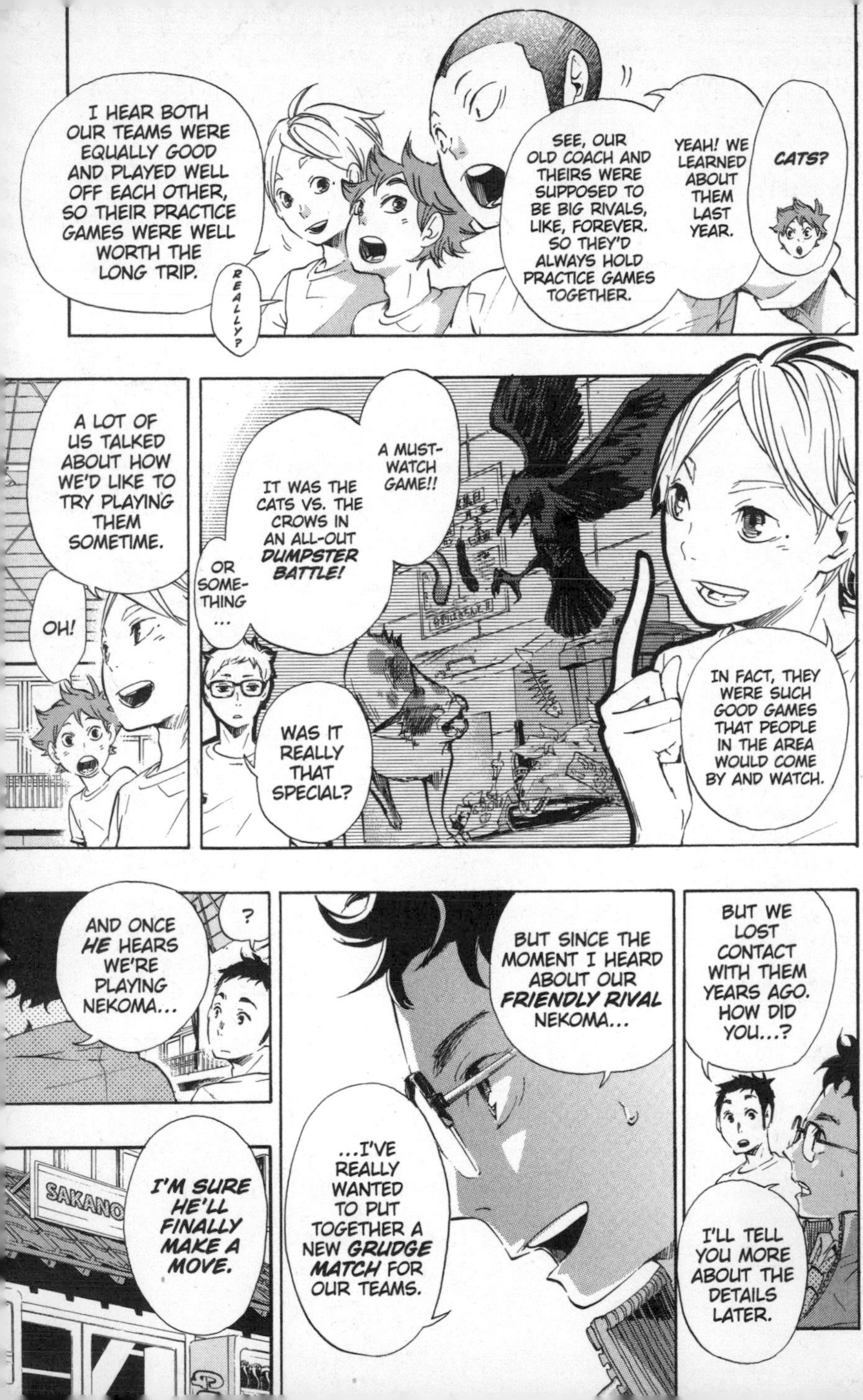

CATS?
YEAH! WE LEARNED ABOUT THEM LAST YEAR.
SEE, OUR OLD COACH AND THEIRS WERE SUPPOSED TO BE BIG RIVALS, LIKE, FOREVER. SO THEY'D ALWAYS HOLD PRACTICE GAMES TOGETHER.
I HEAR BOTH OUR TEAMS WERE EQUALLY GOOD AND PLAYED WELL OFF EACH OTHER, SO THEIR PRACTICE GAMES WERE WELL WORTH THE LONG TRIP.
REALLY?
IN FACT, THEY WERE SUCH GOOD GAMES THAT PEOPLE IN THE AREA WOULD COME BY AND WATCH.
A MUST-WATCH GAME!!
IT WAS THE CATS VS. THE CROWS IN AN ALL-OUT DUMPSTER BATTLE!
OR SOME-THING...
WAS IT REALLY THAT SPECIAL?
A LOT OF US TALKED ABOUT HOW WE'D LIKE TO TRY PLAYING THEM SOMETIME.
OH!
BUT WE LOST CONTACT WITH THEM YEARS AGO. HOW DID YOU...?
I'LL TELL YOU MORE ABOUT THE DETAILS LATER.
BUT SINCE THE MOMENT I HEARD ABOUT OUR FRIENDLY RIVAL NEKOMA...
...I'VE REALLY WANTED TO PUT TOGETHER A NEW GRUDGE MATCH FOR OUR TEAMS.
?
AND ONCE HE HEARS WE'RE PLAYING NEKOMA...
SAKANO
I'M SURE HE'LL FINALLY MAKE A MOVE.

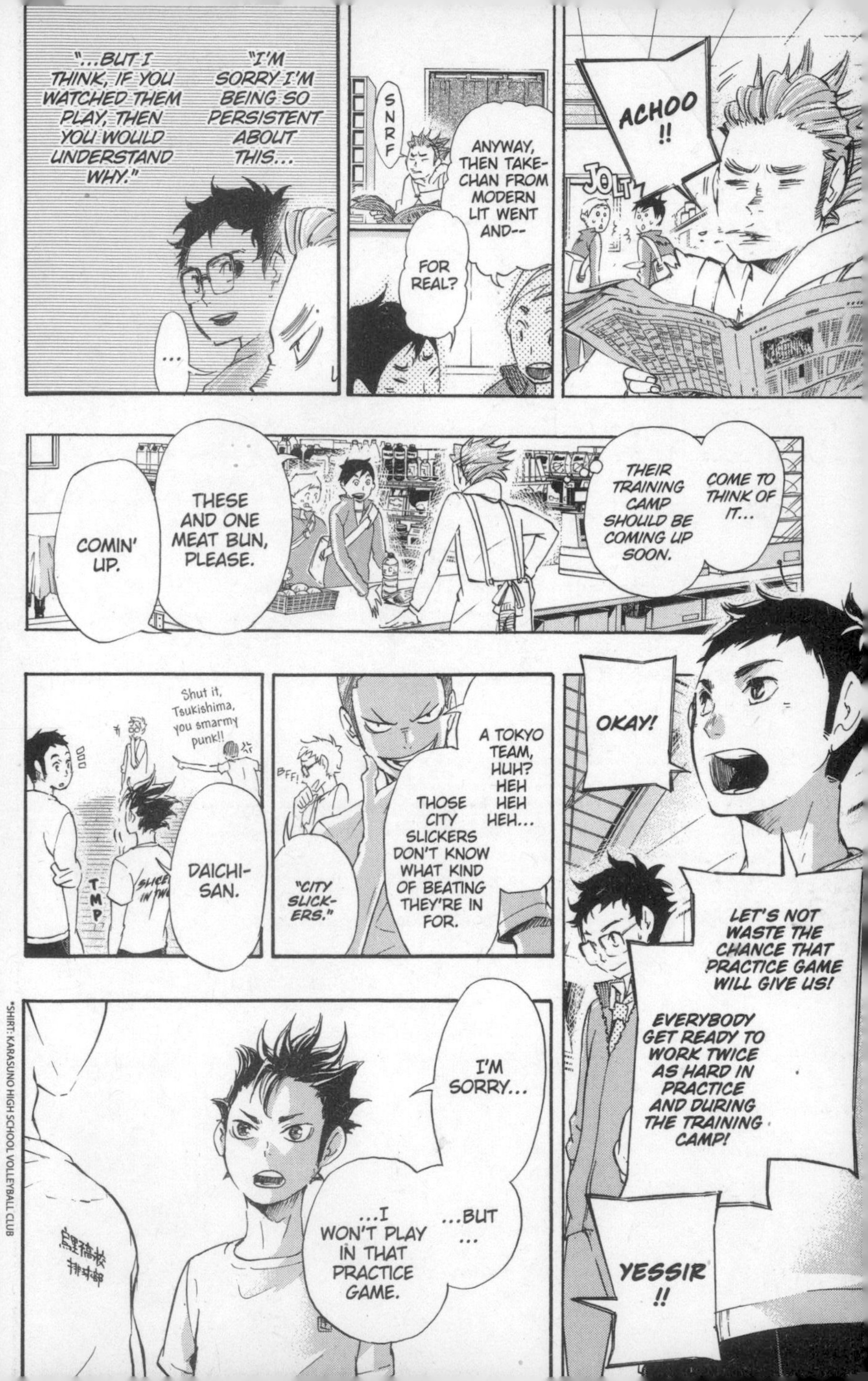
ACHOO !!
JOLT
SNRF
ANYWAY, THEN TAKE-CHAN FROM MODERN LIT WENT AND--
FOR REAL?
"I'M SORRY I'M BEING SO PERSISTENT ABOUT THIS...
"...BUT I THINK, IF YOU WATCHED THEM PLAY, THEN YOU WOULD UNDERSTAND WHY."
...
COME TO THINK OF IT...
THEIR TRAINING CAMP SHOULD BE COMING UP SOON.
THESE AND ONE MEAT BUN, PLEASE.
COMIN' UP.
OKAY!
LET'S NOT WASTE THE CHANCE THAT PRACTICE GAME WILL GIVE US!
EVERYBODY GET READY TO WORK TWICE AS HARD IN PRACTICE AND DURING THE TRAINING CAMP!
YESSIR !!
A TOKYO TEAM, HUH? HEH HEH HEH...
THOSE CITY SLICKERS DON'T KNOW WHAT KIND OF BEATING THEY'RE IN FOR.
BFF!
"CITY SLICK-ERS."
Shut it, Tsukishima, you smarmy punk!!
DAICHI-SAN.
TMP
I'M SORRY...
...BUT...
...I WON'T PLAY IN THAT PRACTICE GAME.
*SHIRT: KARASUNO HIGH SCHOOL VOLLEYBALL CLUB

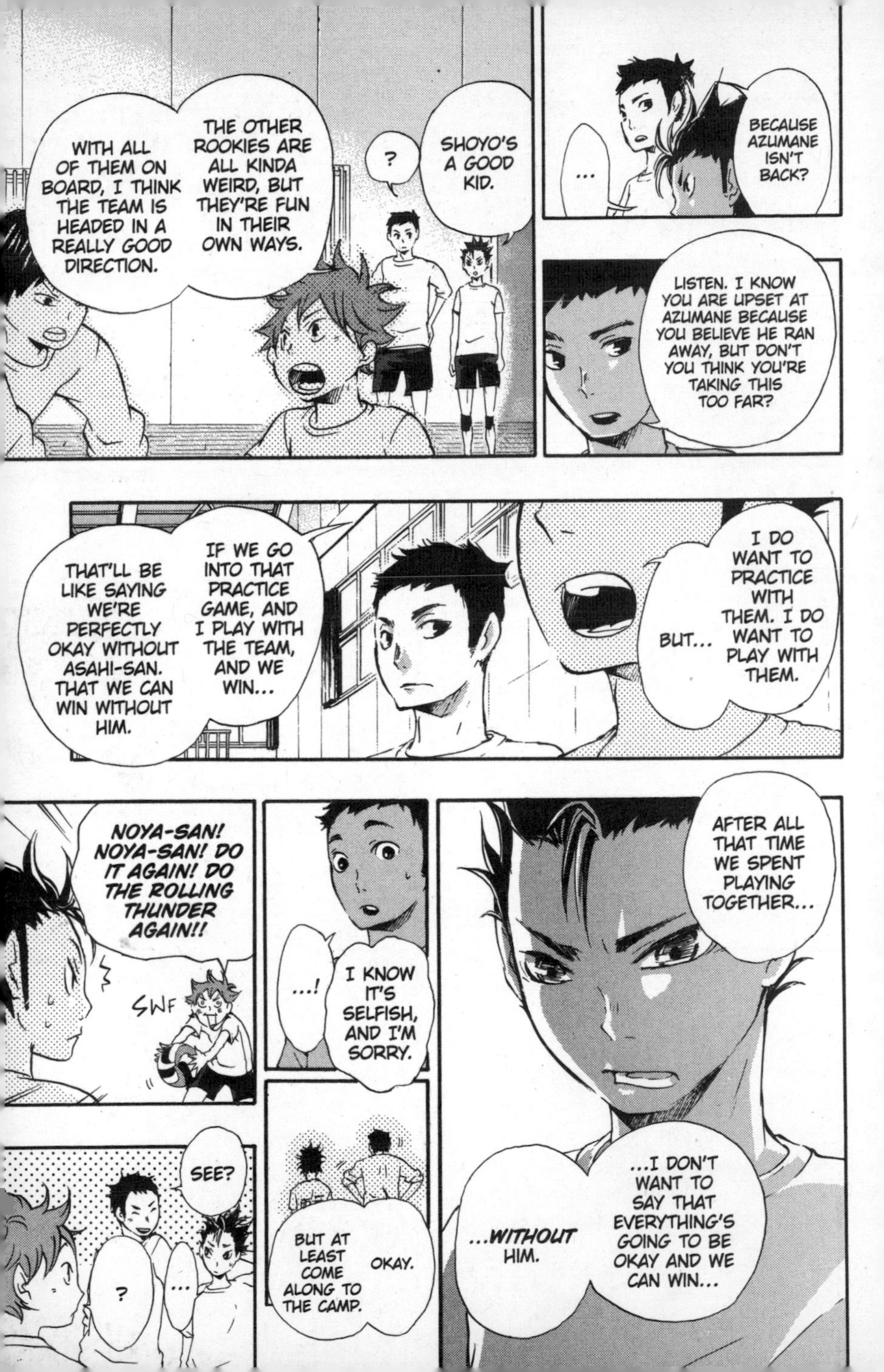
BECAUSE AZUMANE ISN'T BACK?
...
LISTEN. I KNOW YOU ARE UPSET AT AZUMANE BECAUSE YOU BELIEVE HE RAN AWAY, BUT DON'T YOU THINK YOU'RE TAKING THIS TOO FAR?
SHOYO'S A GOOD KID.
?
THE OTHER ROOKIES ARE ALL KINDA WEIRD, BUT THEY'RE FUN IN THEIR OWN WAYS.
WITH ALL OF THEM ON BOARD, I THINK THE TEAM IS HEADED IN A REALLY GOOD DIRECTION.
I DO WANT TO PRACTICE WITH THEM. I DO WANT TO PLAY WITH THEM.
BUT...
IF WE GO INTO THAT PRACTICE GAME, AND I PLAY WITH THE TEAM, AND WE WIN...
THAT'LL BE LIKE SAYING WE'RE PERFECTLY OKAY WITHOUT ASAHI-SAN. THAT WE CAN WIN WITHOUT HIM.
AFTER ALL THAT TIME WE SPENT PLAYING TOGETHER...
...I DON'T WANT TO SAY THAT EVERYTHING'S GOING TO BE OKAY AND WE CAN WIN...
...WITHOUT HIM.
I KNOW IT'S SELFISH, AND I'M SORRY.
...!
OKAY.
BUT AT LEAST COME ALONG TO THE CAMP.
NOYA-SAN! NOYA-SAN! DO IT AGAIN! DO THE ROLLING THUNDER AGAIN!!
SWF
SEE?
...
?

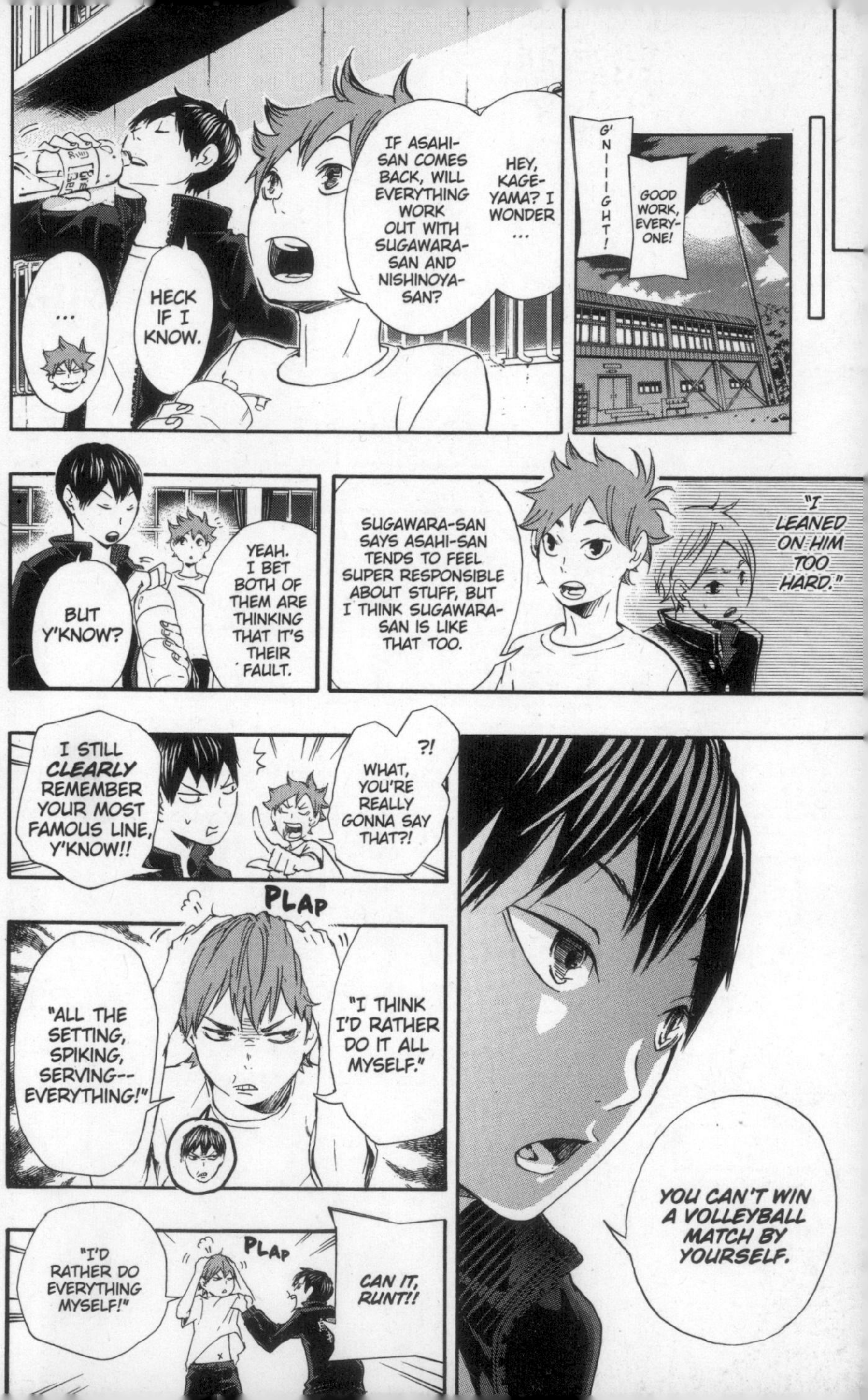
G'NIIIGHT!
GOOD WORK, EVERYONE!
HEY, KAGEYAMA? I WONDER...
IF ASAHI-SAN COMES BACK, WILL EVERYTHING WORK OUT WITH SUGAWARA-SAN AND NISHINOYA-SAN?
HECK IF I KNOW.
...
"I LEANED ON HIM TOO HARD."
SUGAWARA-SAN SAYS ASAHI-SAN TENDS TO FEEL SUPER RESPONSIBLE ABOUT STUFF, BUT I THINK SUGAWARA-SAN IS LIKE THAT TOO.
YEAH. I BET BOTH OF THEM ARE THINKING THAT IT'S THEIR FAULT.
BUT Y'KNOW?
YOU CAN'T WIN A VOLLEYBALL MATCH BY YOURSELF.
?!
WHAT, YOU'RE REALLY GONNA SAY THAT?!
I STILL CLEARLY REMEMBER YOUR MOST FAMOUS LINE, Y'KNOW!!
PLAP
"I THINK I'D RATHER DO IT ALL MYSELF."
"ALL THE SETTING, SPIKING, SERVING--EVERYTHING!"
CAN IT, RUNT!!
PLAP
"I'D RATHER DO EVERYTHING MYSELF!"

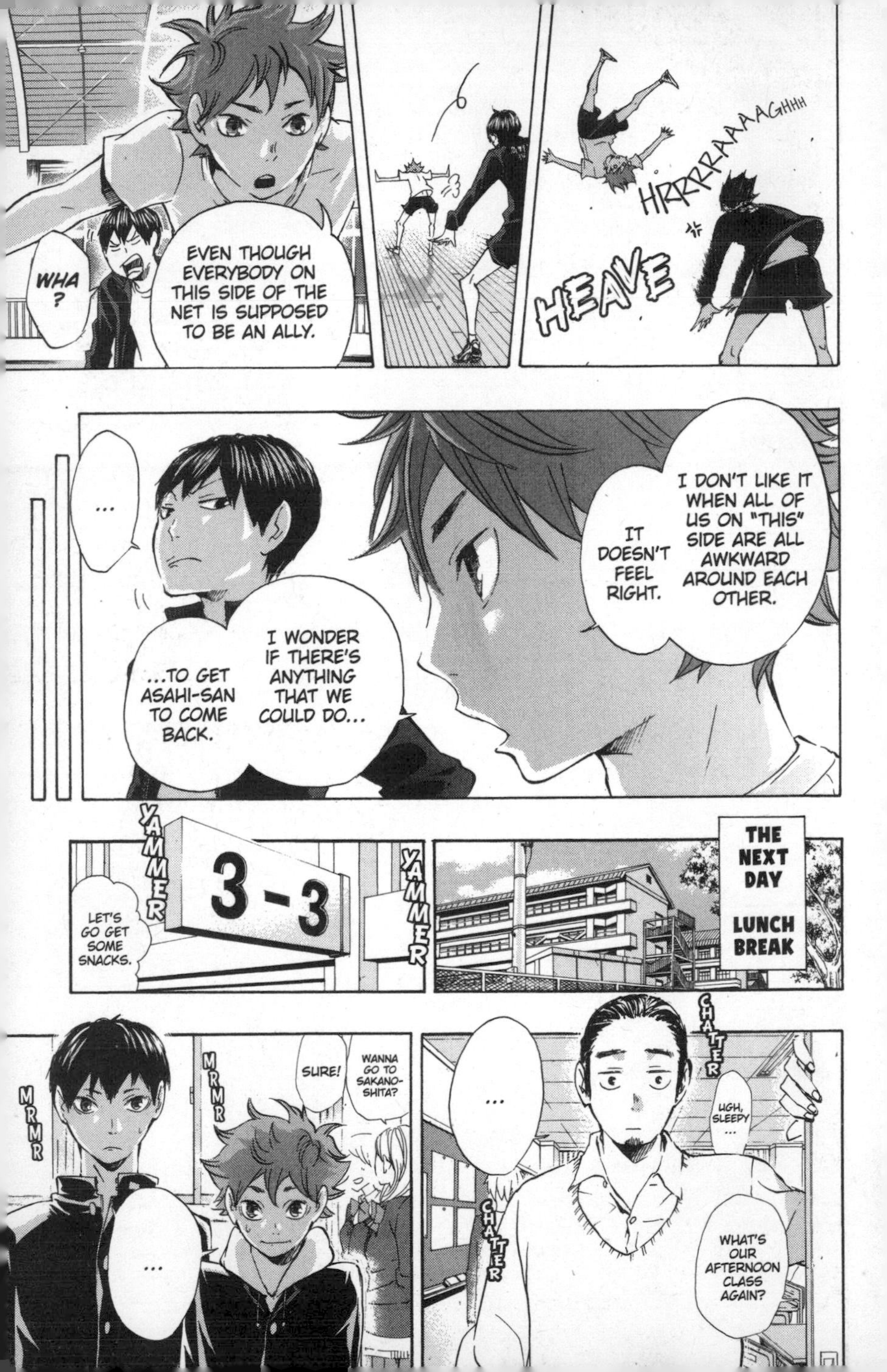
HRRRRAAAAGHHH
HEAVE
EVEN THOUGH EVERYBODY ON THIS SIDE OF THE NET IS SUPPOSED TO BE AN ALLY.
WHA ?
I DON'T LIKE IT WHEN ALL OF US ON "THIS" SIDE ARE ALL AWKWARD AROUND EACH OTHER.
IT DOESN'T FEEL RIGHT.
...
I WONDER IF THERE'S ANYTHING THAT WE COULD DO...
...TO GET ASAHI-SAN TO COME BACK.
THE NEXT DAY
LUNCH BREAK
YAMMER
YAMMER
3-3
LET'S GO GET SOME SNACKS.
CHATTER
...
UGH, SLEEPY ...
CHATTER
WHAT'S OUR AFTERNOON CLASS AGAIN?
WANNA GO TO SAKANOSHITA?
SURE!
MRMR
MRMR
...

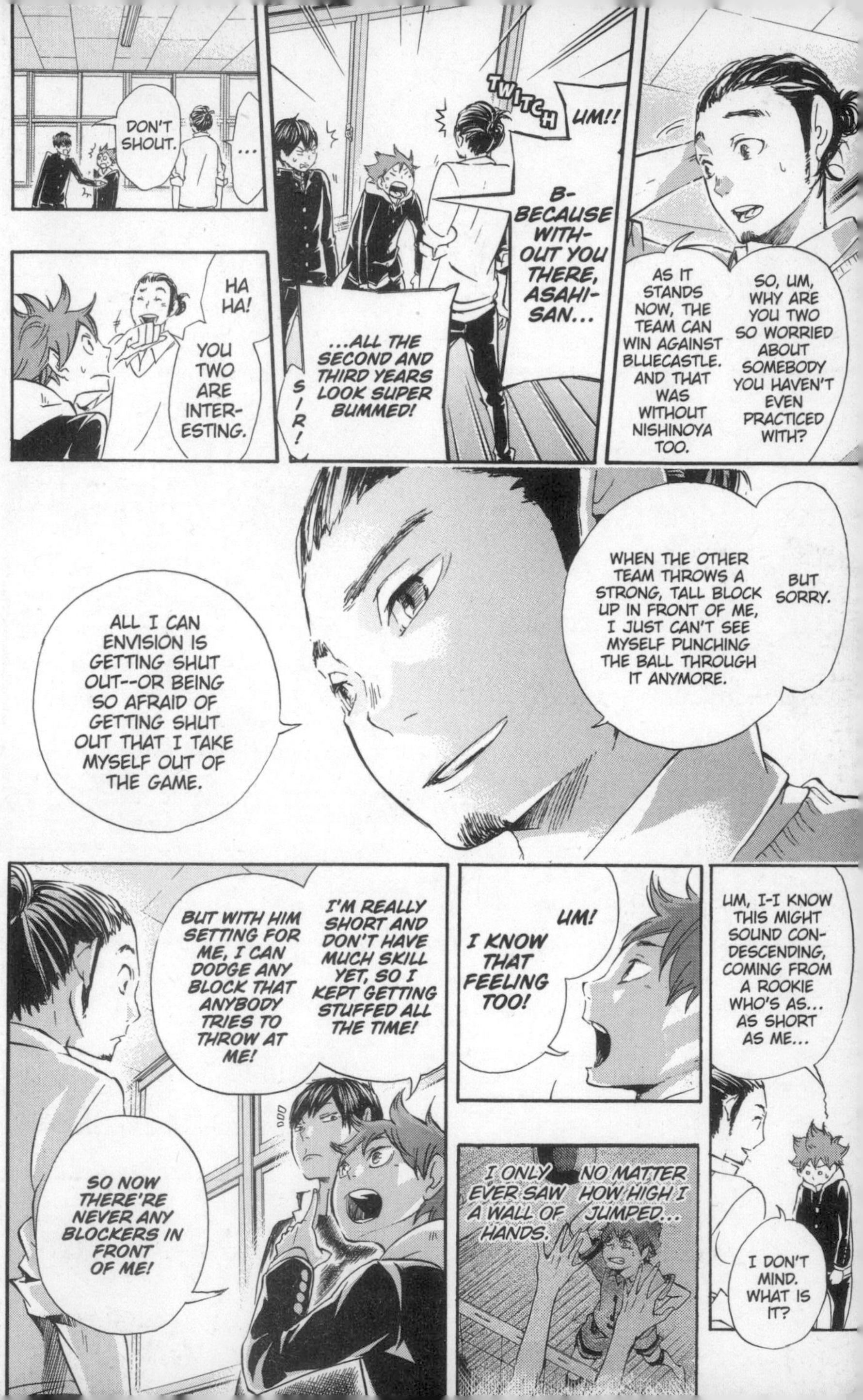
SO, UM, WHY ARE YOU TWO SO WORRIED ABOUT SOMEBODY YOU HAVEN'T EVEN PRACTICED WITH?
AS IT STANDS NOW, THE TEAM CAN WIN AGAINST BLUECASTLE. AND THAT WAS WITHOUT NISHINOYA TOO.
TWITCH
UM!!
B-BECAUSE WITHOUT YOU THERE, ASAHI-SAN...
...ALL THE SECOND AND THIRD YEARS LOOK SUPER BUMMED!
SIR!
DON'T SHOUT.
...
HA HA!
YOU TWO ARE INTERESTING.
BUT SORRY.
WHEN THE OTHER TEAM THROWS A STRONG, TALL BLOCK UP IN FRONT OF ME, I JUST CAN'T SEE MYSELF PUNCHING THE BALL THROUGH IT ANYMORE.
ALL I CAN ENVISION IS GETTING SHUT OUT--OR BEING SO AFRAID OF GETTING SHUT OUT THAT I TAKE MYSELF OUT OF THE GAME.
UM, I-I KNOW THIS MIGHT SOUND CONDESCENDING, COMING FROM A ROOKIE WHO'S AS... AS SHORT AS ME...
I DON'T MIND. WHAT IS IT?
UM!
I KNOW THAT FEELING TOO!
NO MATTER HOW HIGH I JUMPED...
I ONLY EVER SAW A WALL OF HANDS.
I'M REALLY SHORT AND DON'T HAVE MUCH SKILL YET, SO I KEPT GETTING STUFFED ALL THE TIME!
BUT WITH HIM SETTING FOR ME, I CAN DODGE ANY BLOCK THAT ANYBODY TRIES TO THROW AT ME!
SO NOW THERE'RE NEVER ANY BLOCKERS IN FRONT OF ME!

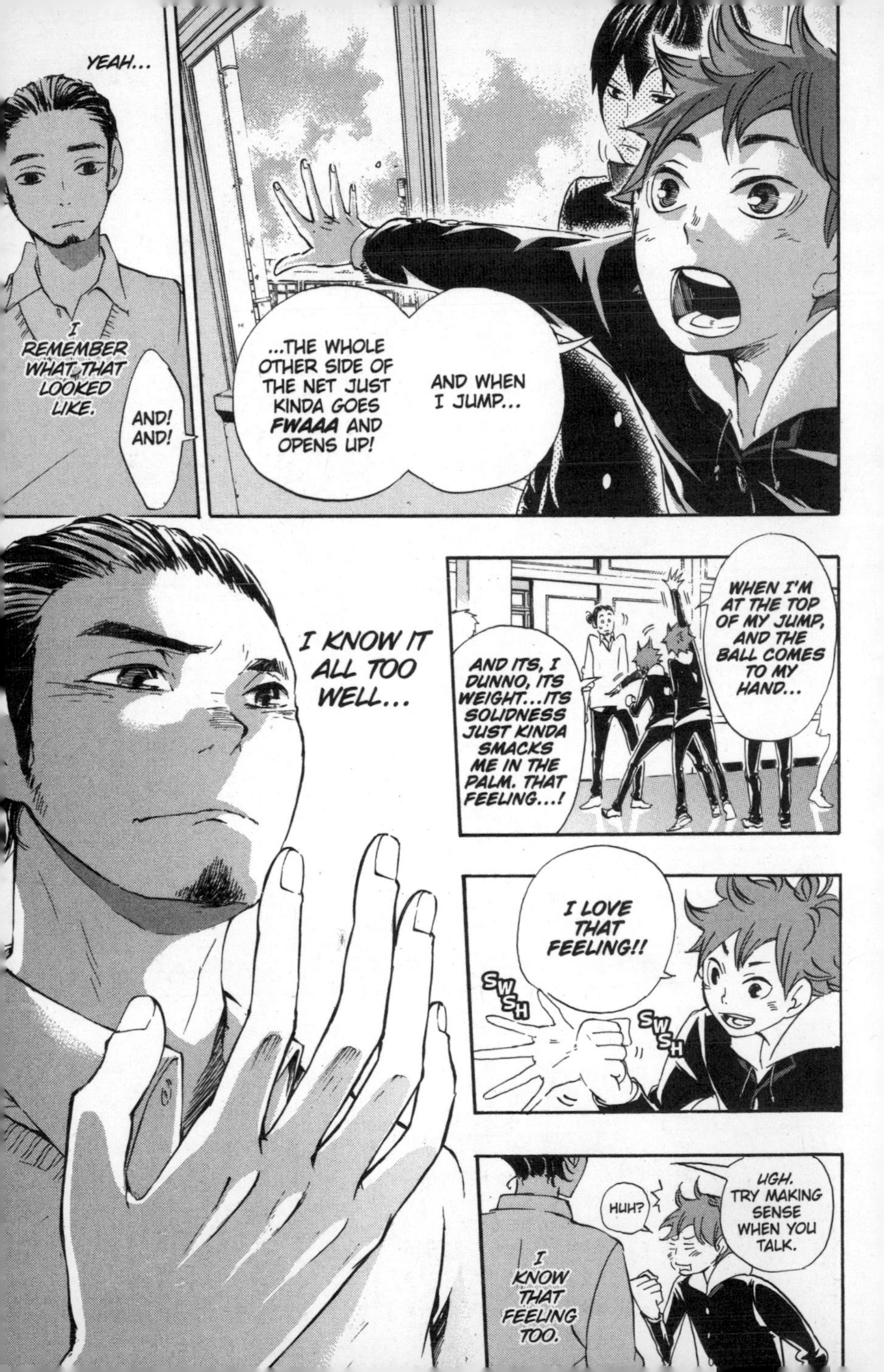
AND WHEN I JUMP...
...THE WHOLE OTHER SIDE OF THE NET JUST KINDA GOES FWAAA AND OPENS UP!
YEAH...
I REMEMBER WHAT THAT LOOKED LIKE.
AND! AND!
WHEN I'M AT THE TOP OF MY JUMP, AND THE BALL COMES TO MY HAND...
AND ITS, I DUNNO, ITS WEIGHT...ITS SOLIDNESS JUST KINDA SMACKS ME IN THE PALM. THAT FEELING...!
I LOVE THAT FEELING!!
SWSH
SWSH
UGH. TRY MAKING SENSE WHEN YOU TALK.
HUH?
I KNOW THAT FEELING TOO.
I KNOW IT ALL TOO WELL...

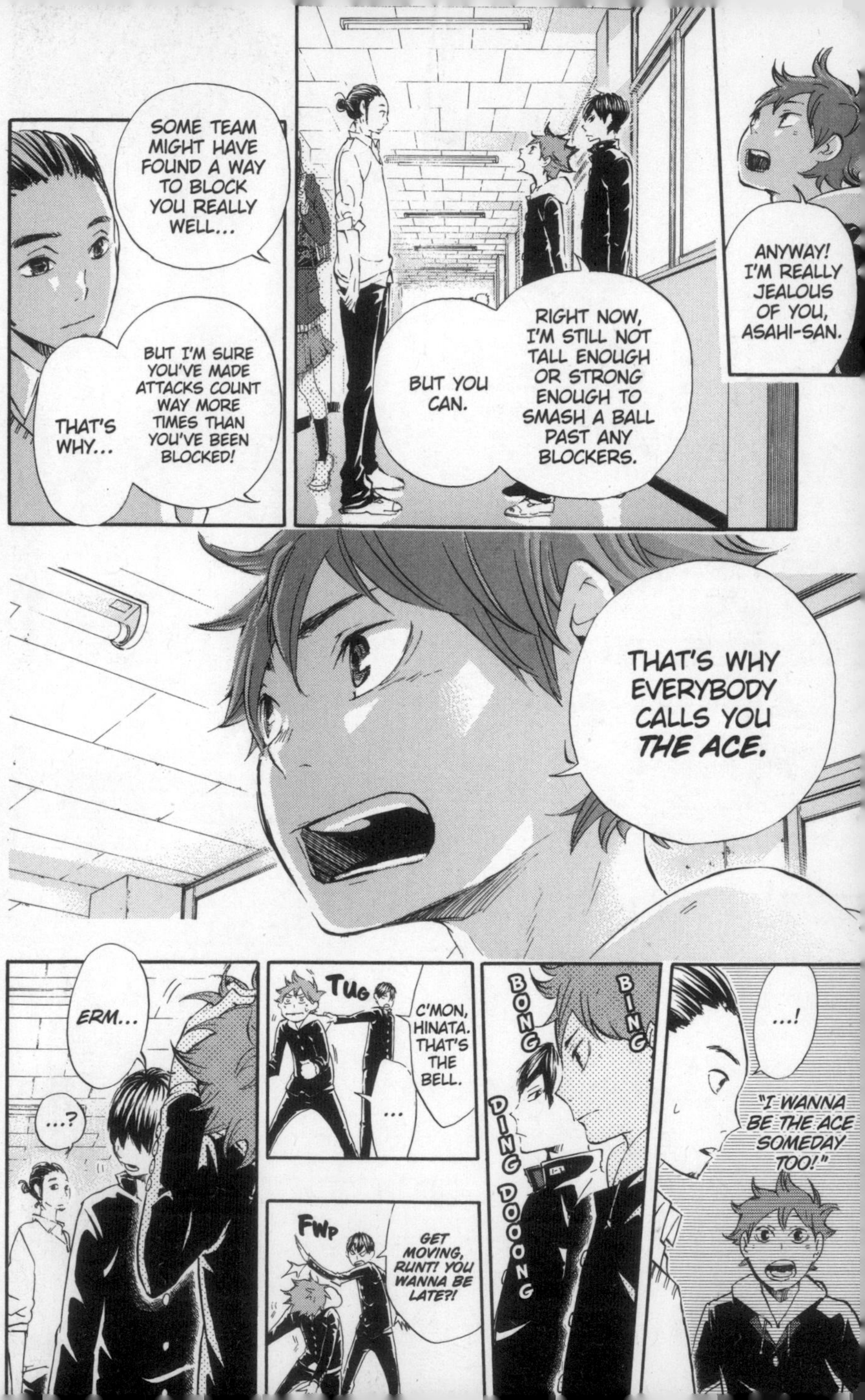
ANYWAY! I'M REALLY JEALOUS OF YOU, ASAHI-SAN.
RIGHT NOW, I'M STILL NOT TALL ENOUGH OR STRONG ENOUGH TO SMASH A BALL PAST ANY BLOCKERS.
BUT YOU CAN.
SOME TEAM MIGHT HAVE FOUND A WAY TO BLOCK YOU REALLY WELL...
BUT I'M SURE YOU'VE MADE ATTACKS COUNT WAY MORE TIMES THAN YOU'VE BEEN BLOCKED!
THAT'S WHY...
THAT'S WHY EVERYBODY CALLS YOU *THE ACE.*
...!
"I WANNA BE THE ACE SOMEDAY TOO!"
BING
BONG
DING
DOOONG
TUG
C'MON, HINATA. THAT'S THE BELL.
...
FWP
GET MOVING, RUNT! YOU WANNA BE LATE?!
ERM...
...?

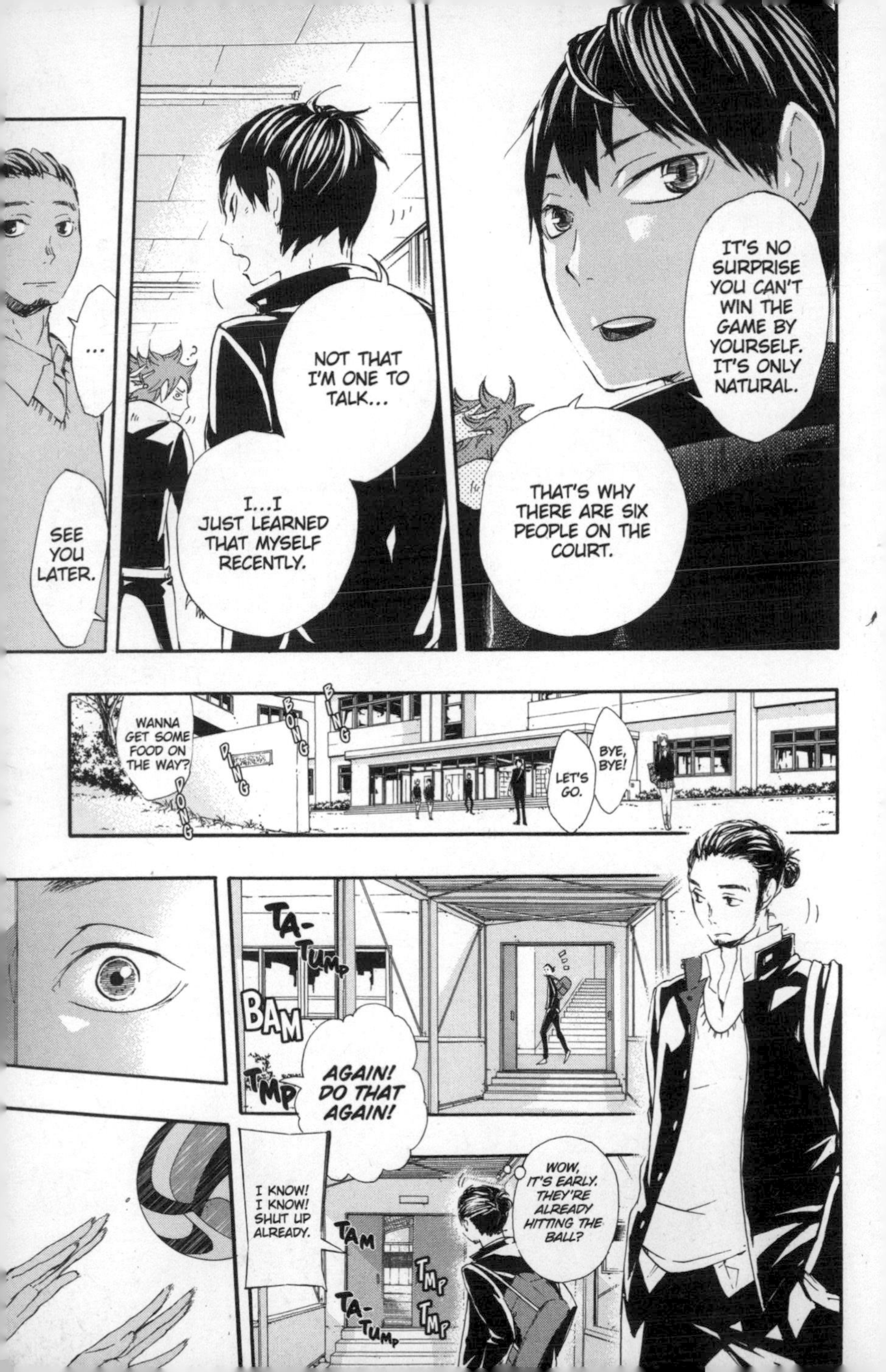
IT'S NO SURPRISE YOU CAN'T WIN THE GAME BY YOURSELF. IT'S ONLY NATURAL.
THAT'S WHY THERE ARE SIX PEOPLE ON THE COURT.
NOT THAT I'M ONE TO TALK...
I...I JUST LEARNED THAT MYSELF RECENTLY.
...
SEE YOU LATER.
BYE, BYE!
LET'S GO.
BING
BONG
DING
DONG
WANNA GET SOME FOOD ON THE WAY?
TA-TUMP
BAM
TMP
AGAIN! DO THAT AGAIN!
WOW, IT'S EARLY. THEY'RE ALREADY HITTING THE BALL?
TAM
TMP
TMP
TA-TUMP
I KNOW! I KNOW! SHUT UP ALREADY.

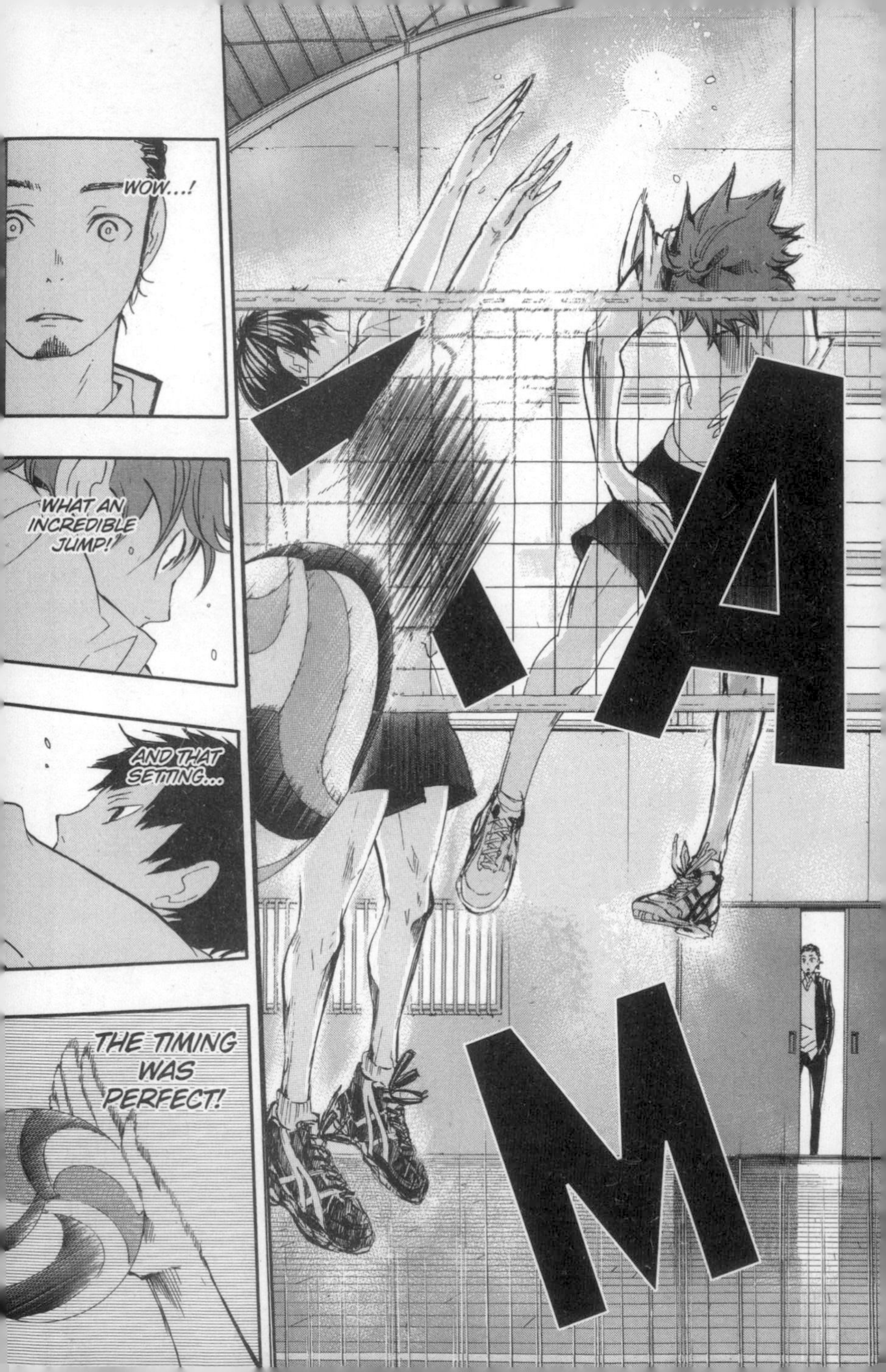
WOW...!
WHAT AN INCREDIBLE JUMP!
AND THAT SETTING...
THE TIMING WAS PERFECT!

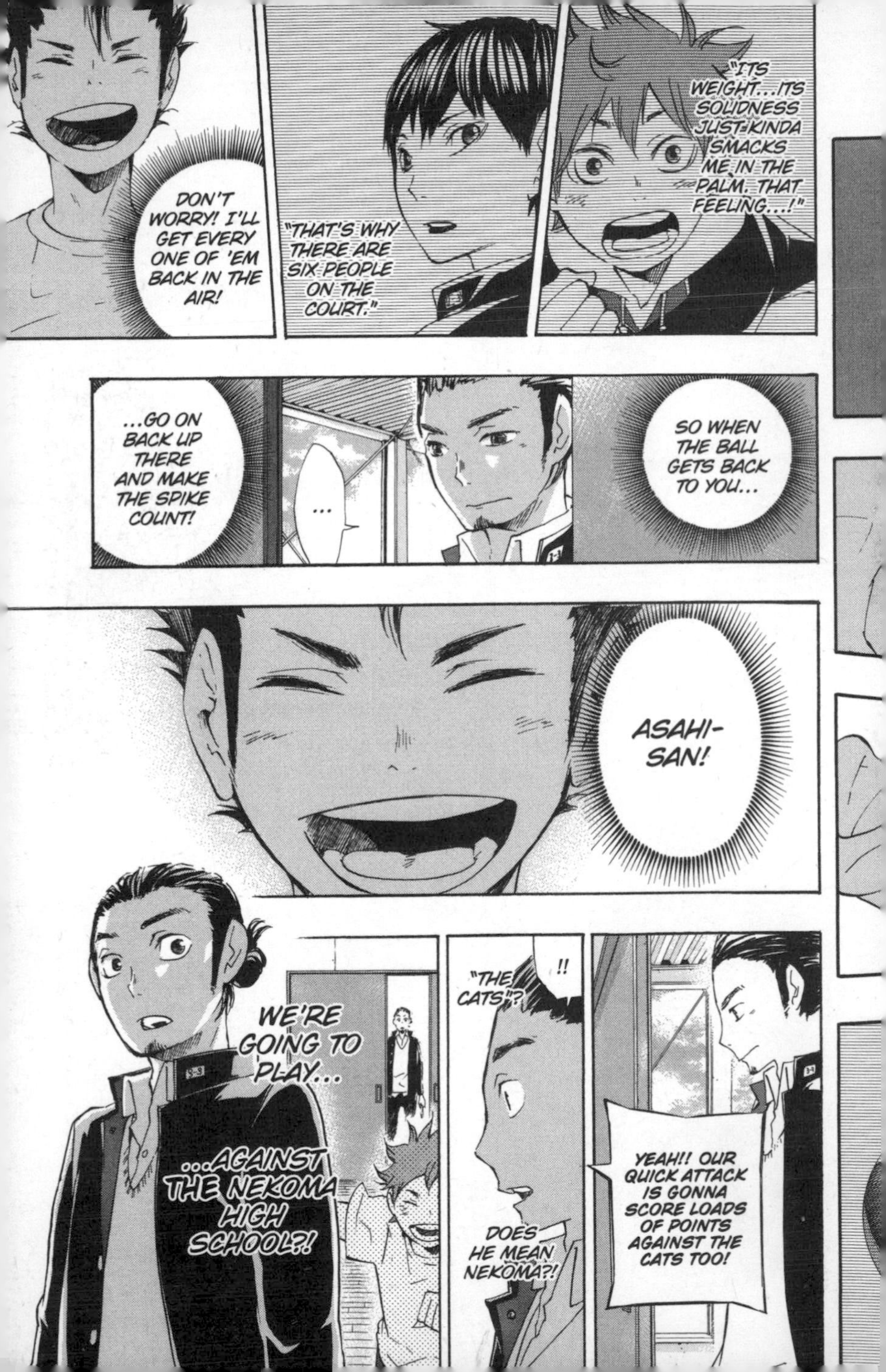
"ITS WEIGHT...ITS SOLIDNESS JUST KINDA SMACKS ME IN THE PALM. THAT FEELING...!"
"THAT'S WHY THERE ARE SIX PEOPLE ON THE COURT."
DON'T WORRY! I'LL GET EVERY ONE OF 'EM BACK IN THE AIR!
SO WHEN THE BALL GETS BACK TO YOU...
...
...GO ON BACK UP THERE AND MAKE THE SPIKE COUNT!
ASAHI-SAN!
YEAH!! OUR QUICK ATTACK IS GONNA SCORE LOADS OF POINTS AGAINST THE CATS TOO!
!!
"THE CATS"?
DOES HE MEAN NEKOMA?!
WE'RE GOING TO PLAY...
...AGAINST THE NEKOMA HIGH SCHOOL?!

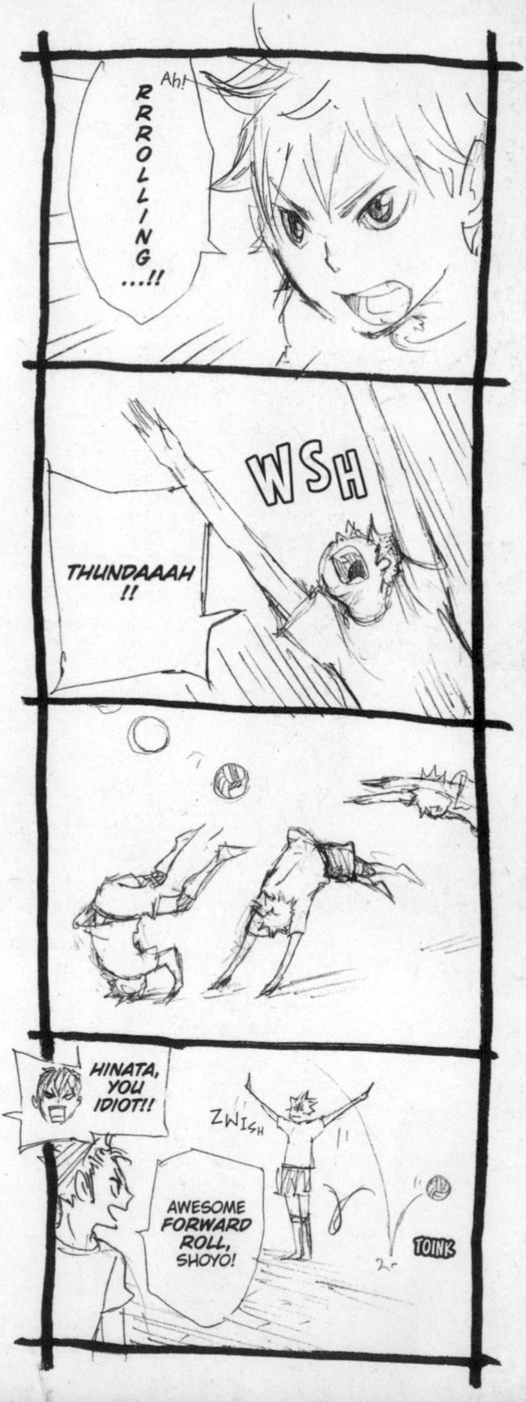
Ah!
RRROLLING...!!
WSH
THUNDAAAH!!
HINATA, YOU IDIOT!!
ZWISH
AWESOME FORWARD ROLL, SHOYO!
TOINK

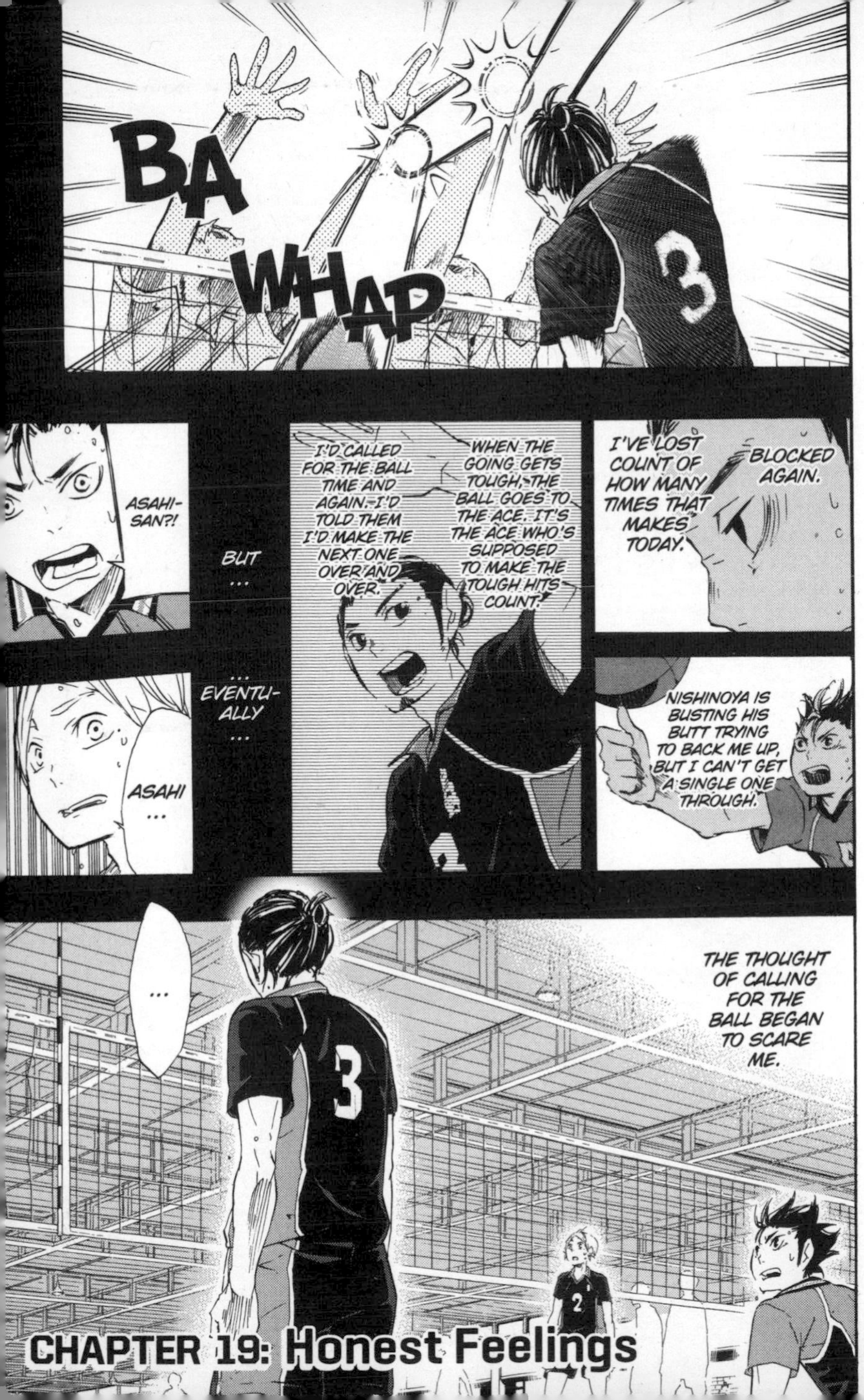
BA WHAP
BLOCKED AGAIN.
I'VE LOST COUNT OF HOW MANY TIMES THAT MAKES TODAY.
NISHINOYA IS BUSTING HIS BUTT TRYING TO BACK ME UP, BUT I CAN'T GET A SINGLE ONE THROUGH.
WHEN THE GOING GETS TOUGH, THE BALL GOES TO THE ACE. IT'S THE ACE WHO'S SUPPOSED TO MAKE THE TOUGH HITS COUNT.
I'D CALLED FOR THE BALL TIME AND AGAIN. I'D TOLD THEM I'D MAKE THE NEXT ONE OVER AND OVER.
BUT ...
... EVENTU-ALLY ...
ASAHI-SAN?!
ASAHI ...
THE THOUGHT OF CALLING FOR THE BALL BEGAN TO SCARE ME.
...
CHAPTER 19: Honest Feelings

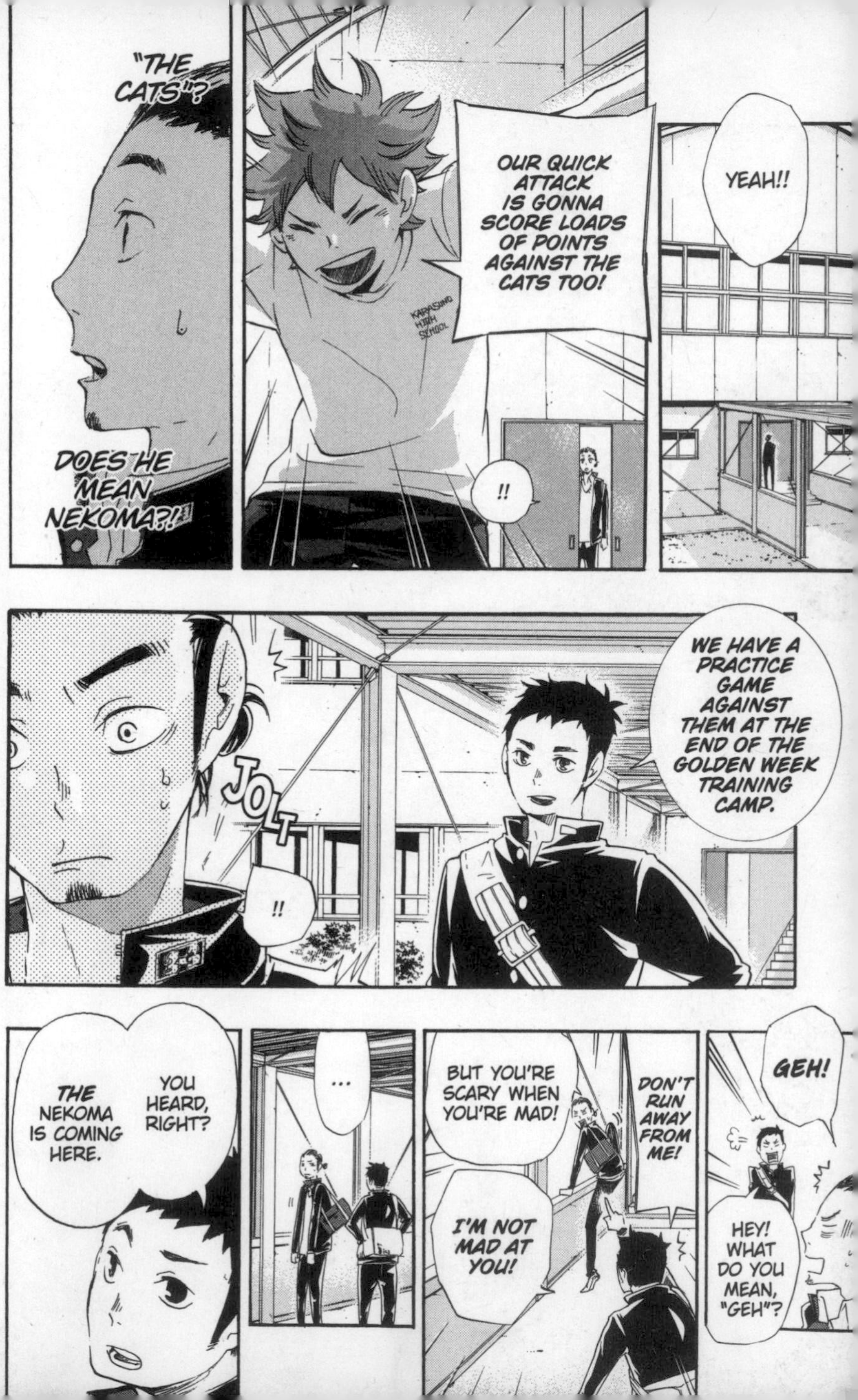
YEAH!!
OUR QUICK ATTACK IS GONNA SCORE LOADS OF POINTS AGAINST THE CATS TOO!
KARASUNO HIGH SCHOOL
!!
"THE CATS"?
DOES HE MEAN NEKOMA?!
WE HAVE A PRACTICE GAME AGAINST THEM AT THE END OF THE GOLDEN WEEK TRAINING CAMP.
JOLT
!!
GEH!
HEY! WHAT DO YOU MEAN, "GEH"?
DON'T RUN AWAY FROM ME!
BUT YOU'RE SCARY WHEN YOU'RE MAD!
I'M NOT MAD AT YOU!
...
YOU HEARD, RIGHT?
THE NEKOMA IS COMING HERE.

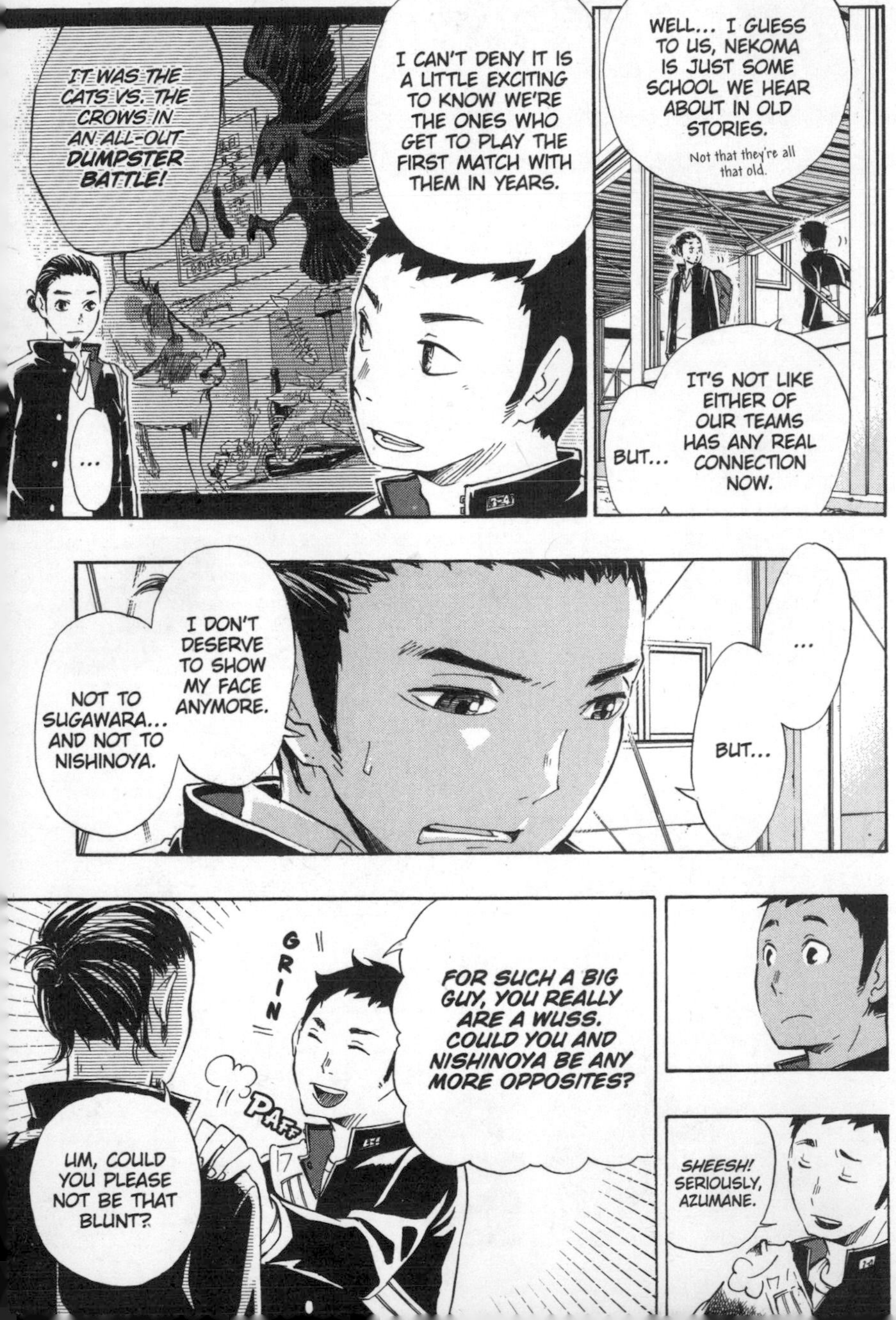
WELL... I GUESS TO US, NEKOMA IS JUST SOME SCHOOL WE HEAR ABOUT IN OLD STORIES.
Not that they're all that old.
IT'S NOT LIKE EITHER OF OUR TEAMS HAS ANY REAL CONNECTION NOW.
BUT...
I CAN'T DENY IT IS A LITTLE EXCITING TO KNOW WE'RE THE ONES WHO GET TO PLAY THE FIRST MATCH WITH THEM IN YEARS.
IT WAS THE CATS VS. THE CROWS IN AN ALL-OUT DUMPSTER BATTLE!
...
...
BUT...
I DON'T DESERVE TO SHOW MY FACE ANYMORE.
NOT TO SUGAWARA... AND NOT TO NISHINOYA.
SHEESH! SERIOUSLY, AZUMANE.
FOR SUCH A BIG GUY, YOU REALLY ARE A WUSS. COULD YOU AND NISHINOYA BE ANY MORE OPPOSITES?
GRIN
PAFF
UM, COULD YOU PLEASE NOT BE THAT BLUNT?

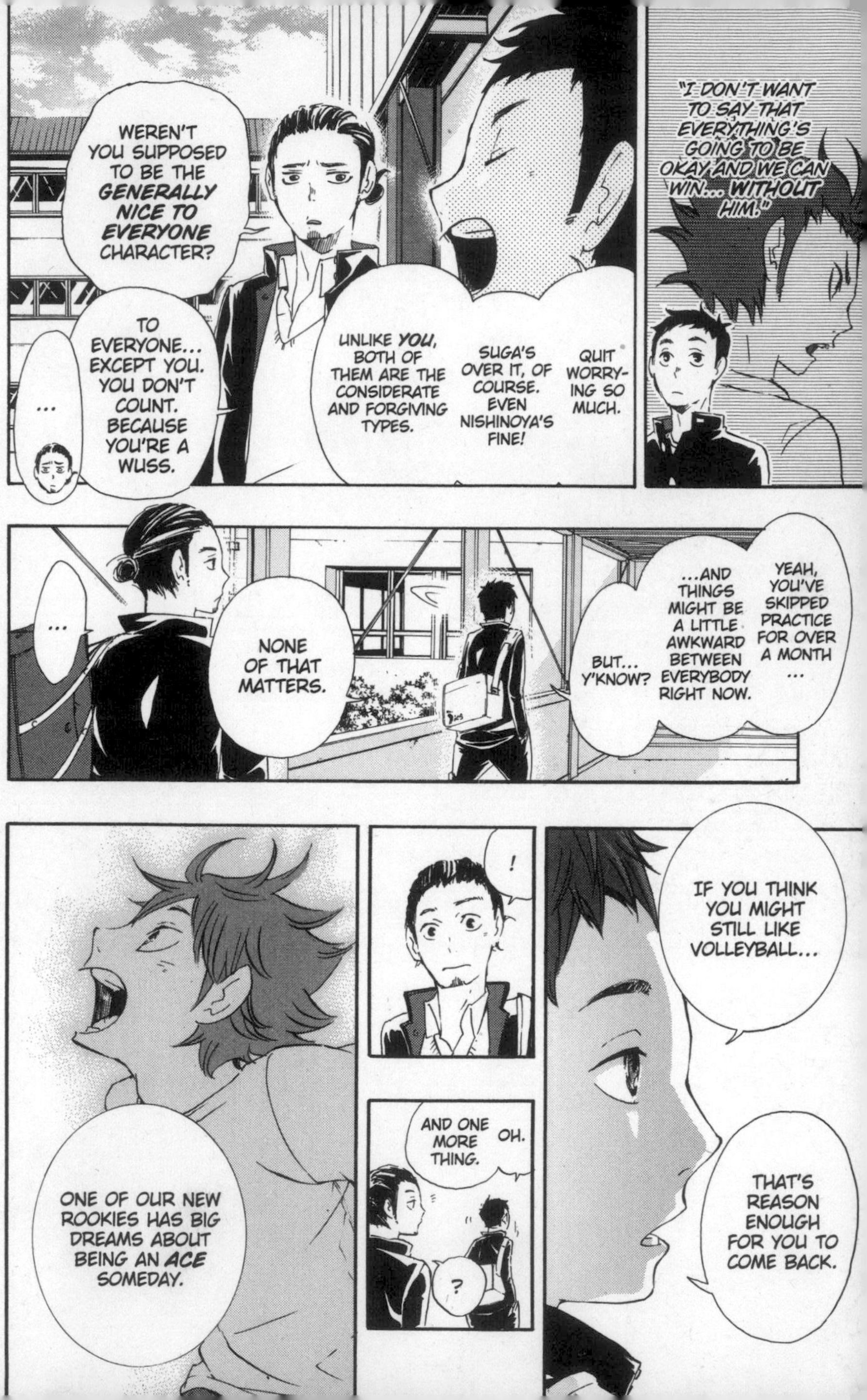
"I DON'T WANT TO SAY THAT EVERYTHING'S GOING TO BE OKAY AND WE CAN WIN... WITHOUT HIM."
QUIT WORRYING SO MUCH.
SUGA'S OVER IT, OF COURSE. EVEN NISHINOYA'S FINE!
UNLIKE YOU, BOTH OF THEM ARE THE CONSIDERATE AND FORGIVING TYPES.
WEREN'T YOU SUPPOSED TO BE THE GENERALLY NICE TO EVERYONE CHARACTER?
TO EVERYONE... EXCEPT YOU. YOU DON'T COUNT. BECAUSE YOU'RE A WUSS.
...
YEAH, YOU'VE SKIPPED PRACTICE FOR OVER A MONTH...
...AND THINGS MIGHT BE A LITTLE AWKWARD BETWEEN EVERYBODY RIGHT NOW.
BUT... Y'KNOW?
NONE OF THAT MATTERS.
...
IF YOU THINK YOU MIGHT STILL LIKE VOLLEYBALL...
THAT'S REASON ENOUGH FOR YOU TO COME BACK.
!
OH.
AND ONE MORE THING.
?
ONE OF OUR NEW ROOKIES HAS BIG DREAMS ABOUT BEING AN ACE SOMEDAY.

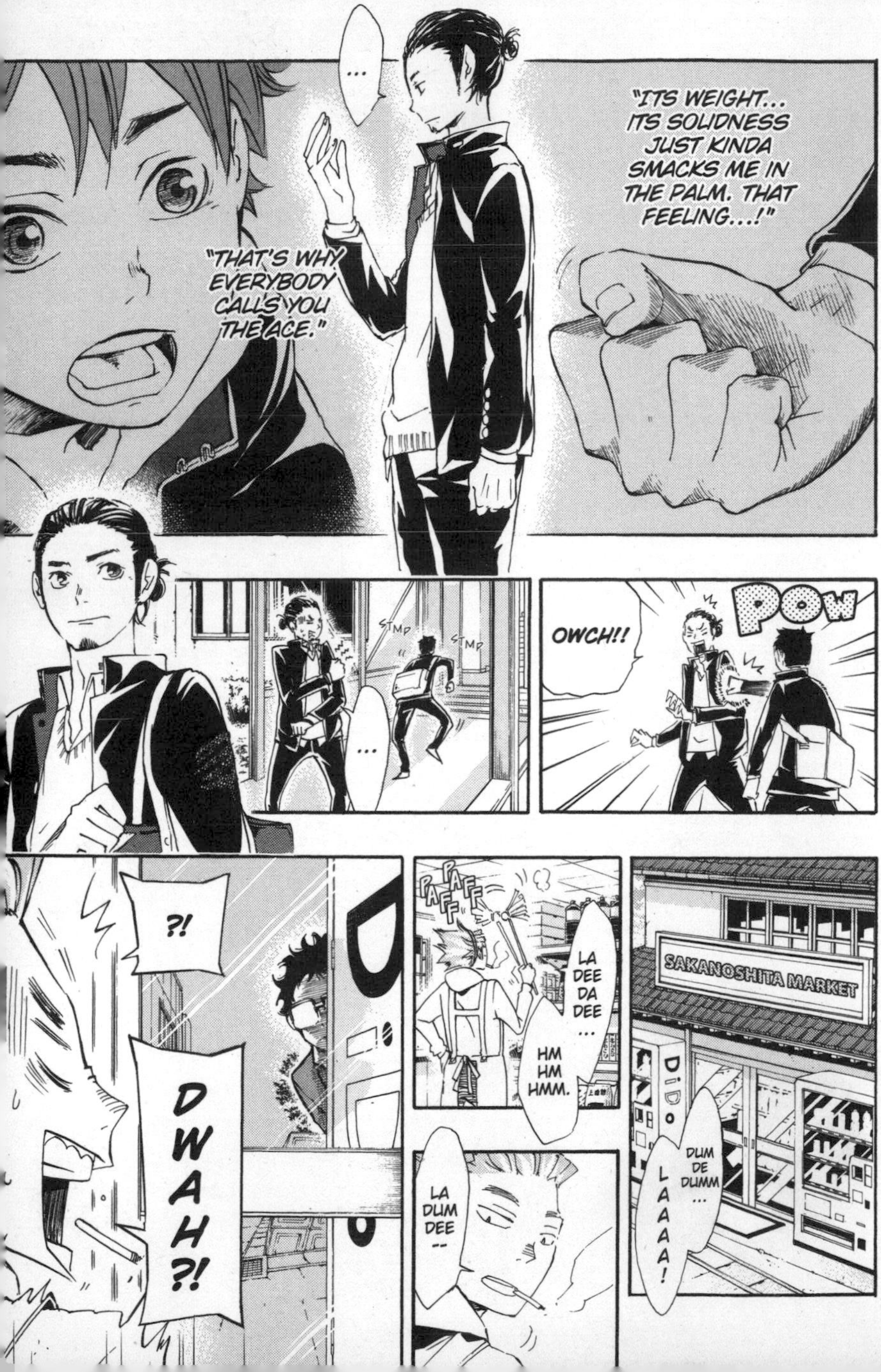
"ITS WEIGHT... ITS SOLIDNESS JUST KINDA SMACKS ME IN THE PALM. THAT FEELING...!"
...
"THAT'S WHY EVERYBODY CALLS YOU THE ACE."
POW
OWCH!!
STMP
STMP
...
SAKANOSHITA MARKET
DiDo
DUM DE DUMM ...
LAAAA!
PAFF PAFF
LA DEE DA DEE ...
HM HM HMM.
LA DUM DEE --
?!
DWAH?!

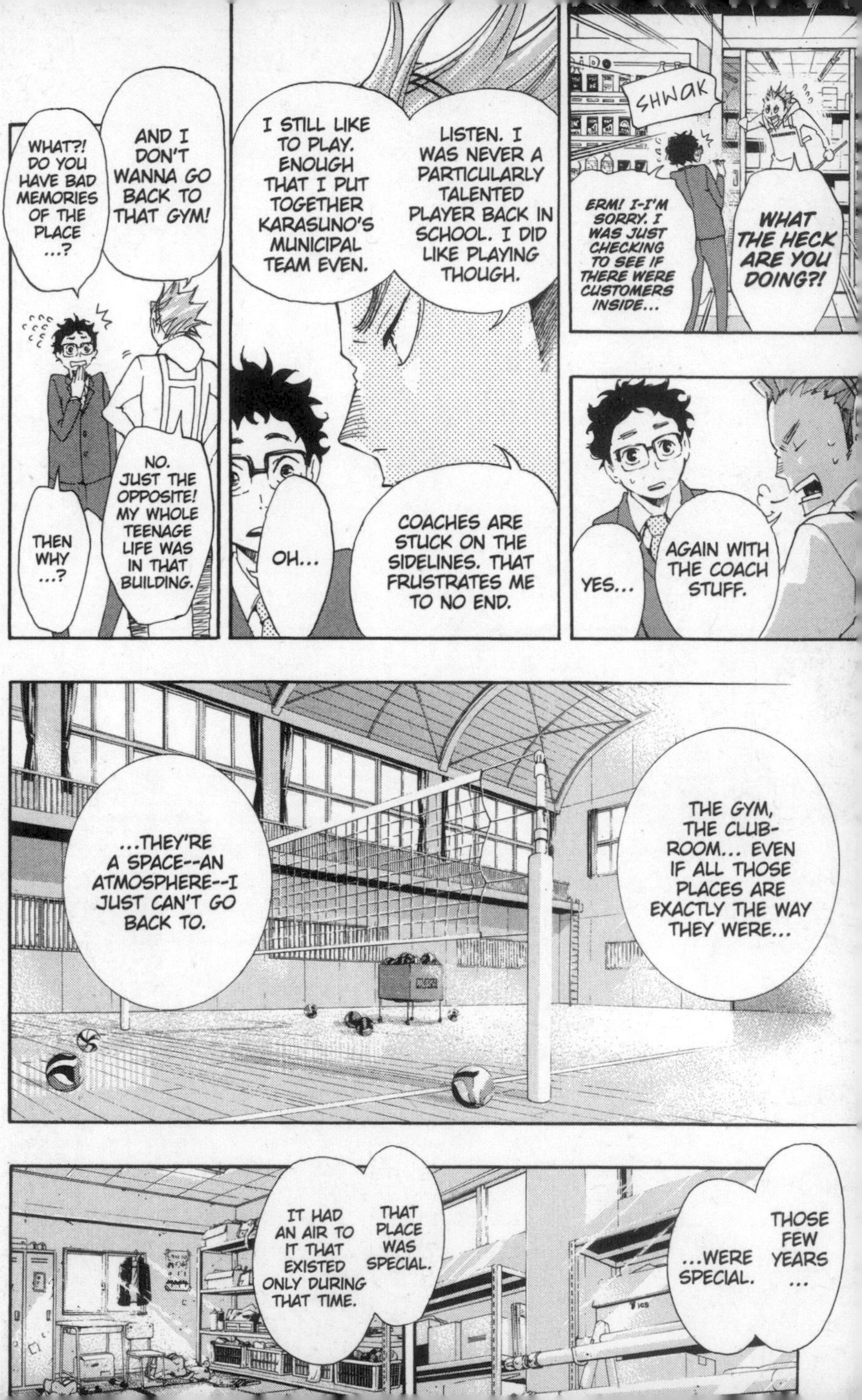
SHWAK
WHAT THE HECK ARE YOU DOING?!
ERM! I-I'M SORRY. I WAS JUST CHECKING TO SEE IF THERE WERE CUSTOMERS INSIDE...
AGAIN WITH THE COACH STUFF.
YES...
LISTEN. I WAS NEVER A PARTICULARLY TALENTED PLAYER BACK IN SCHOOL. I DID LIKE PLAYING THOUGH.
I STILL LIKE TO PLAY. ENOUGH THAT I PUT TOGETHER KARASUNO'S MUNICIPAL TEAM EVEN.
COACHES ARE STUCK ON THE SIDELINES. THAT FRUSTRATES ME TO NO END.
OH...
AND I DON'T WANNA GO BACK TO THAT GYM!
WHAT?! DO YOU HAVE BAD MEMORIES OF THE PLACE ...?
NO. JUST THE OPPOSITE! MY WHOLE TEENAGE LIFE WAS IN THAT BUILDING.
THEN WHY ...?
THE GYM, THE CLUB-ROOM... EVEN IF ALL THOSE PLACES ARE EXACTLY THE WAY THEY WERE...
...THEY'RE A SPACE--AN ATMOSPHERE--I JUST CAN'T GO BACK TO.
THOSE FEW YEARS ...
...WERE SPECIAL.
THAT PLACE WAS SPECIAL.
IT HAD AN AIR TO IT THAT EXISTED ONLY DURING THAT TIME.

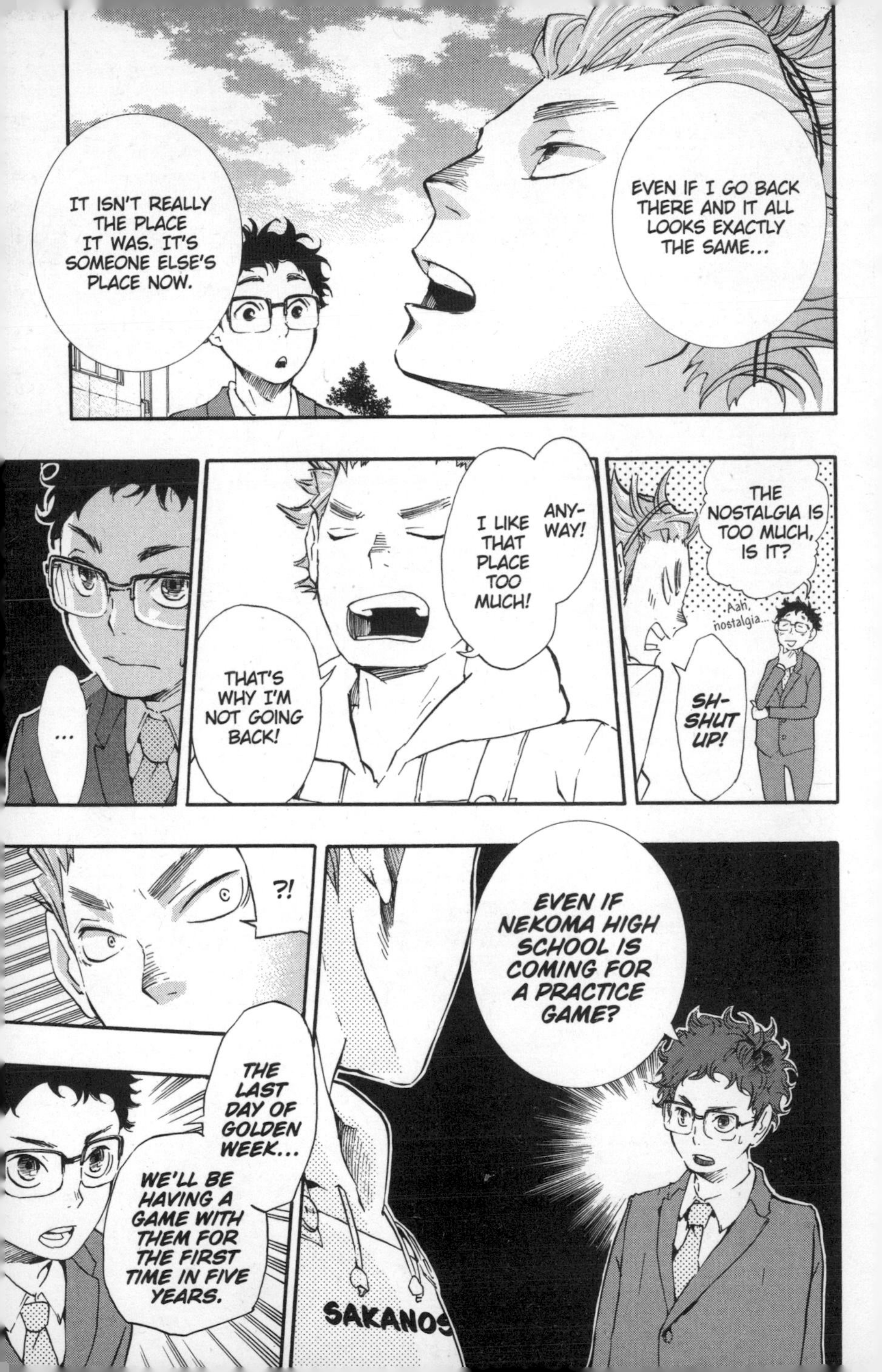
EVEN IF I GO BACK THERE AND IT ALL LOOKS EXACTLY THE SAME...
IT ISN'T REALLY THE PLACE IT WAS. IT'S SOMEONE ELSE'S PLACE NOW.
THE NOSTALGIA IS TOO MUCH, IS IT?
Aah, nostalgia...
SH-SHUT UP!
ANY-WAY!
I LIKE THAT PLACE TOO MUCH!
THAT'S WHY I'M NOT GOING BACK!
...
EVEN IF NEKOMA HIGH SCHOOL IS COMING FOR A PRACTICE GAME?
SAKANOS
?!
THE LAST DAY OF GOLDEN WEEK...
WE'LL BE HAVING A GAME WITH THEM FOR THE FIRST TIME IN FIVE YEARS.

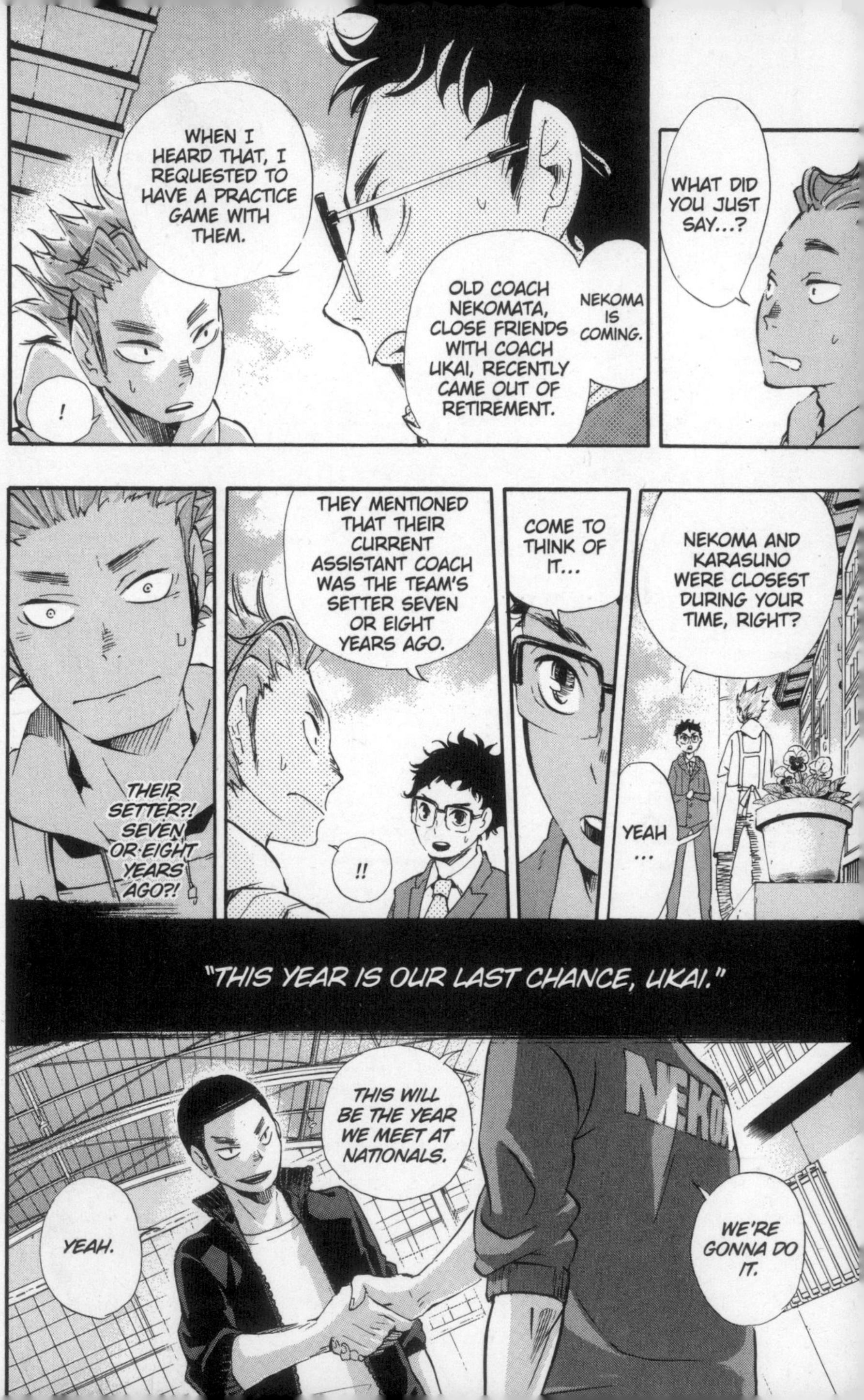
WHAT DID YOU JUST SAY...?
NEKOMA IS COMING.
OLD COACH NEKOMATA, CLOSE FRIENDS WITH COACH UKAI, RECENTLY CAME OUT OF RETIREMENT.
WHEN I HEARD THAT, I REQUESTED TO HAVE A PRACTICE GAME WITH THEM.
!
NEKOMA AND KARASUNO WERE CLOSEST DURING YOUR TIME, RIGHT?
YEAH...
COME TO THINK OF IT...
THEY MENTIONED THAT THEIR CURRENT ASSISTANT COACH WAS THE TEAM'S SETTER SEVEN OR EIGHT YEARS AGO.
!!
THEIR SETTER?! SEVEN OR EIGHT YEARS AGO?!
"THIS YEAR IS OUR LAST CHANCE, UKAI."
THIS WILL BE THE YEAR WE MEET AT NATIONALS.
WE'RE GONNA DO IT.
YEAH.
NEKO

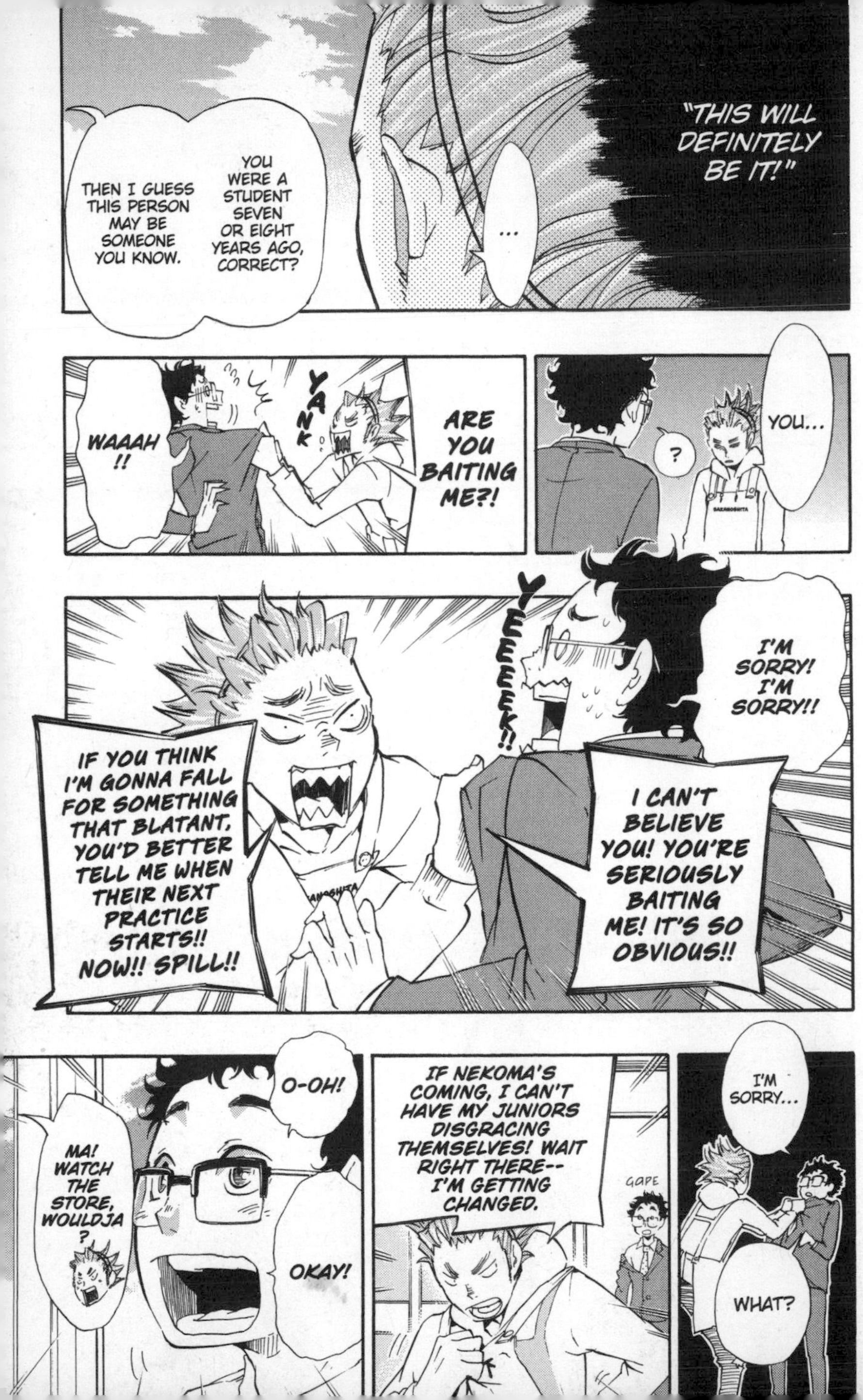
"THIS WILL DEFINITELY BE IT!"
...
YOU WERE A STUDENT SEVEN OR EIGHT YEARS AGO, CORRECT?
THEN I GUESS THIS PERSON MAY BE SOMEONE YOU KNOW.
YOU...
?
ARE YOU BAITING ME?!
YANK
WAAAH!!
I'M SORRY! I'M SORRY!!
YEEEEEK!!
I CAN'T BELIEVE YOU! YOU'RE SERIOUSLY BAITING ME! IT'S SO OBVIOUS!!
IF YOU THINK I'M GONNA FALL FOR SOMETHING THAT BLATANT, YOU'D BETTER TELL ME WHEN THEIR NEXT PRACTICE STARTS!! NOW!! SPILL!!
I'M SORRY...
WHAT?
IF NEKOMA'S COMING, I CAN'T HAVE MY JUNIORS DISGRACING THEMSELVES! WAIT RIGHT THERE-- I'M GETTING CHANGED.
GAPE
O-OH!
MA! WATCH THE STORE, WOULDJA?
OKAY!

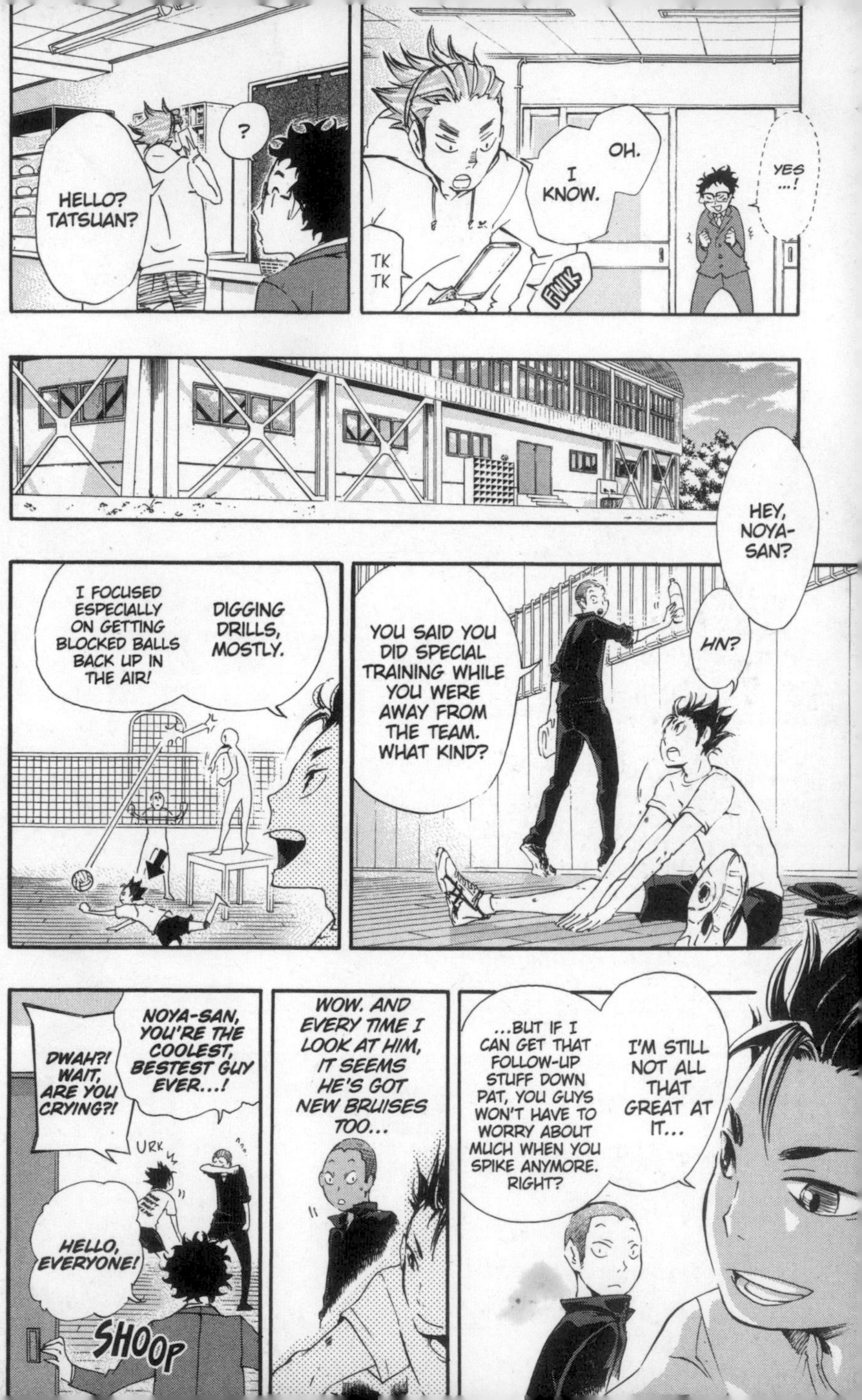
OH.
I KNOW.
TK TK
FWIK
YES ...!
?
HELLO? TATSUAN?
HEY, NOYA-SAN?
HN?
YOU SAID YOU DID SPECIAL TRAINING WHILE YOU WERE AWAY FROM THE TEAM. WHAT KIND?
DIGGING DRILLS, MOSTLY.
I FOCUSED ESPECIALLY ON GETTING BLOCKED BALLS BACK UP IN THE AIR!
I'M STILL NOT ALL THAT GREAT AT IT...
...BUT IF I CAN GET THAT FOLLOW-UP STUFF DOWN PAT, YOU GUYS WON'T HAVE TO WORRY ABOUT MUCH WHEN YOU SPIKE ANYMORE. RIGHT?
WOW. AND EVERY TIME I LOOK AT HIM, IT SEEMS HE'S GOT NEW BRUISES TOO...
NOYA-SAN, YOU'RE THE COOLEST, BESTEST GUY EVER...!
DWAH?! WAIT, ARE YOU CRYING?!
URK
HELLO, EVERYONE!
SHOOP

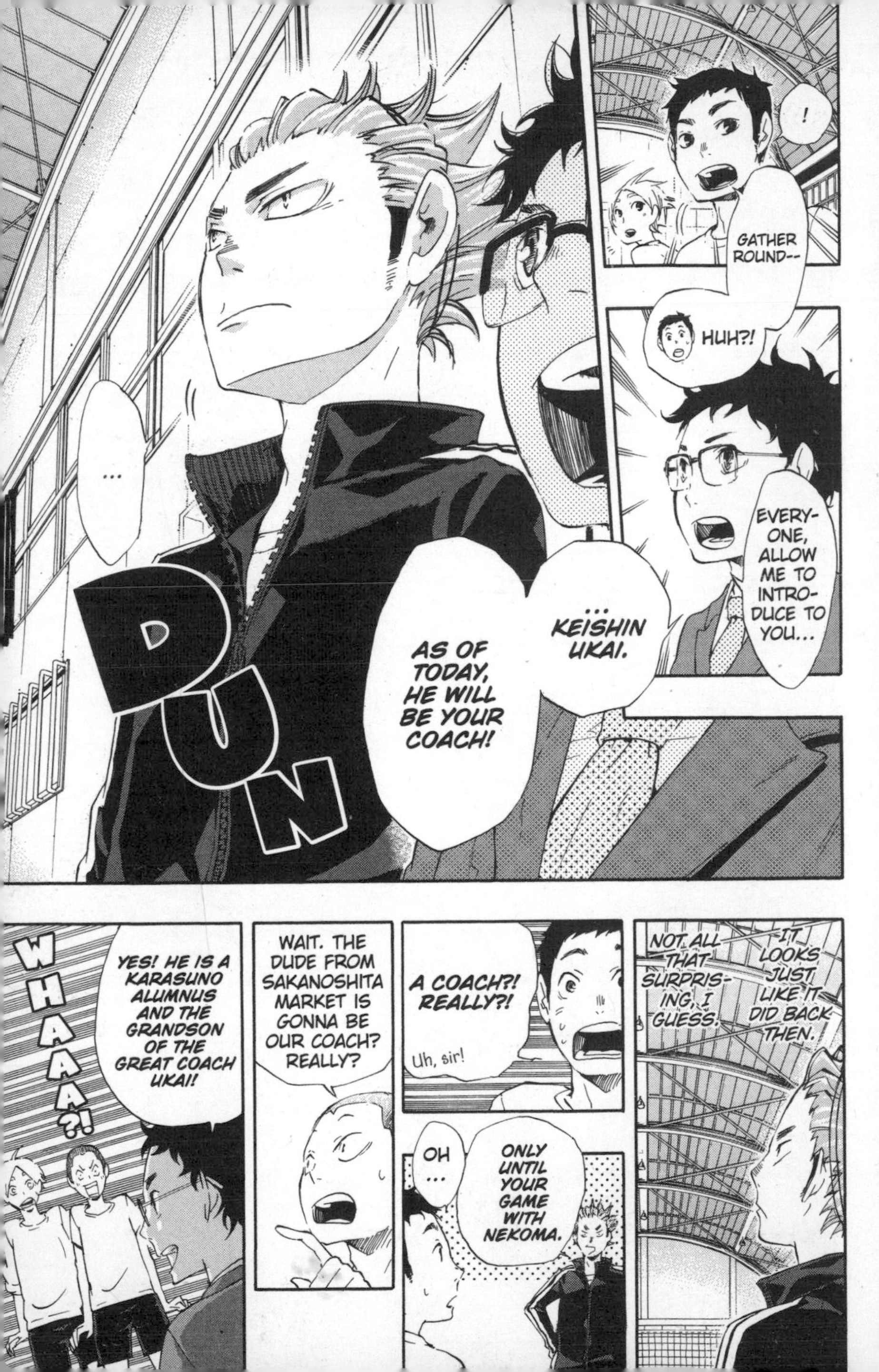
!
GATHER ROUND--
HUH?!
EVERY-ONE, ALLOW ME TO INTRO-DUCE TO YOU...
... KEISHIN UKAI.
AS OF TODAY, HE WILL BE YOUR COACH!
...
DUN
IT LOOKS JUST LIKE IT DID BACK THEN.
NOT ALL THAT SURPRIS-ING, I GUESS.
A COACH?! REALLY?!
Uh, sir!
ONLY UNTIL YOUR GAME WITH NEKOMA.
OH ...
WAIT. THE DUDE FROM SAKANOSHITA MARKET IS GONNA BE OUR COACH? REALLY?
YES! HE IS A KARASUNO ALUMNUS AND THE GRANDSON OF THE GREAT COACH UKAI!
WHAAAA?!

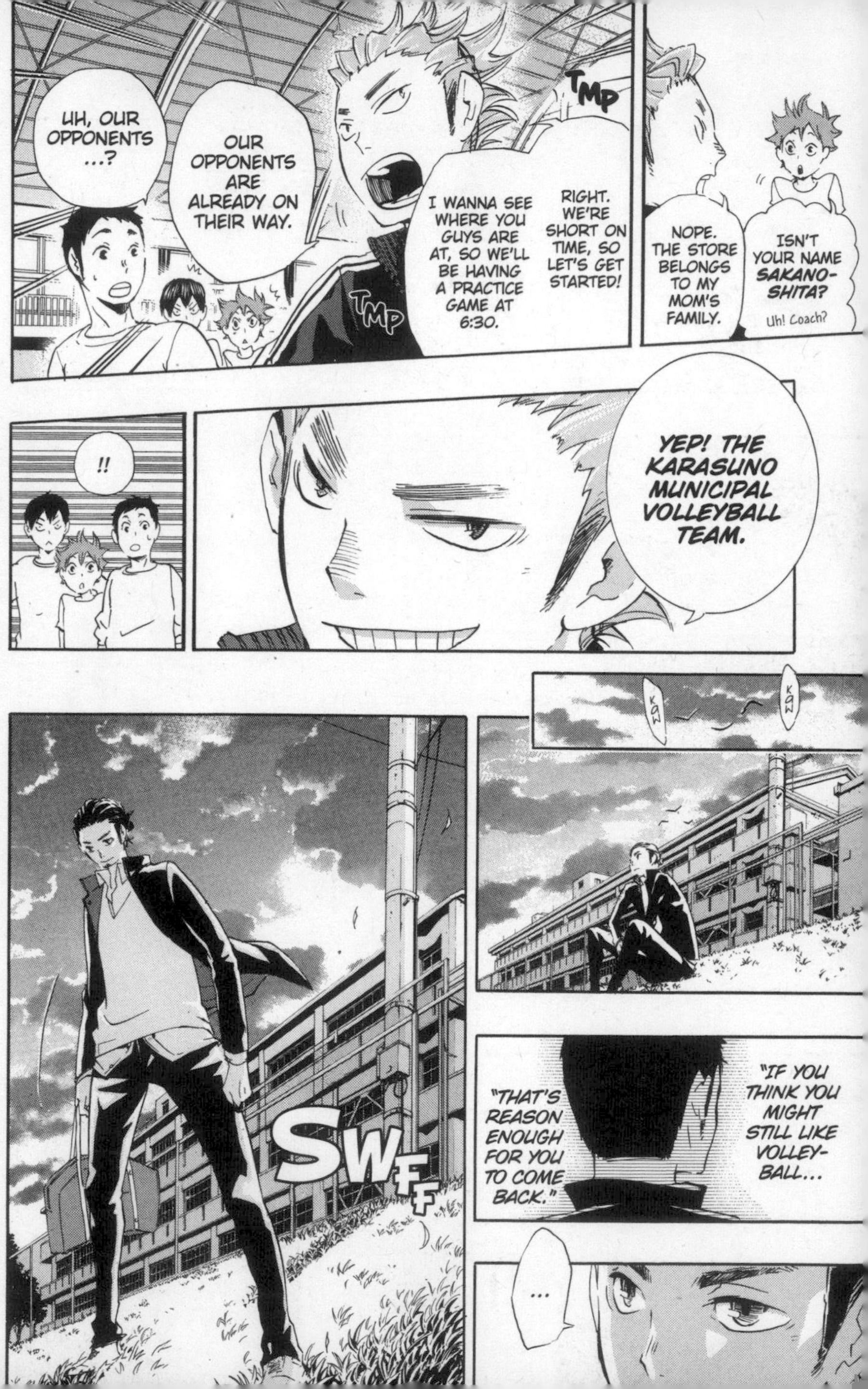
ISN'T YOUR NAME SAKANOSHITA?
Uh! Coach?
NOPE. THE STORE BELONGS TO MY MOM'S FAMILY.
TMP
RIGHT. WE'RE SHORT ON TIME, SO LET'S GET STARTED!
I WANNA SEE WHERE YOU GUYS ARE AT, SO WE'LL BE HAVING A PRACTICE GAME AT 6:30.
TMP
OUR OPPONENTS ARE ALREADY ON THEIR WAY.
UH, OUR OPPONENTS ...?
YEP! THE KARASUNO MUNICIPAL VOLLEYBALL TEAM.
!!
KAW
KAW
"IF YOU THINK YOU MIGHT STILL LIKE VOLLEY-BALL...
"THAT'S REASON ENOUGH FOR YOU TO COME BACK."
...
SWFF

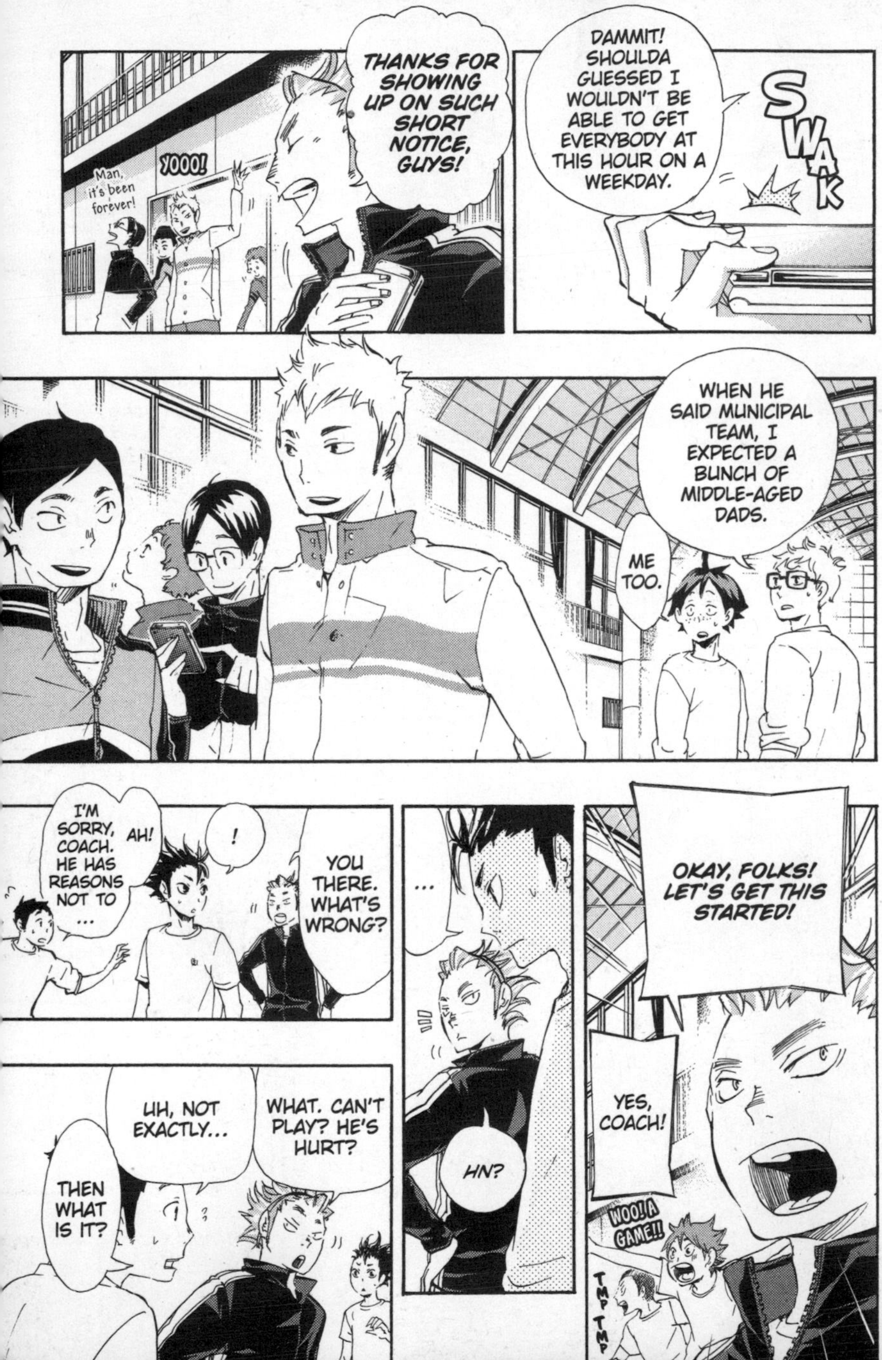
DAMMIT! SHOULDA GUESSED I WOULDN'T BE ABLE TO GET EVERYBODY AT THIS HOUR ON A WEEKDAY.
SWAK
THANKS FOR SHOWING UP ON SUCH SHORT NOTICE, GUYS!
YOOO!
Man, it's been forever!
WHEN HE SAID MUNICIPAL TEAM, I EXPECTED A BUNCH OF MIDDLE-AGED DADS.
ME TOO.
OKAY, FOLKS! LET'S GET THIS STARTED!
YES, COACH!
WOO! A GAME!!
TMP TMP
...
HN?
YOU THERE. WHAT'S WRONG?
!
AH!
I'M SORRY, COACH. HE HAS REASONS NOT TO ...
WHAT. CAN'T PLAY? HE'S HURT?
UH, NOT EXACTLY...
THEN WHAT IS IT?

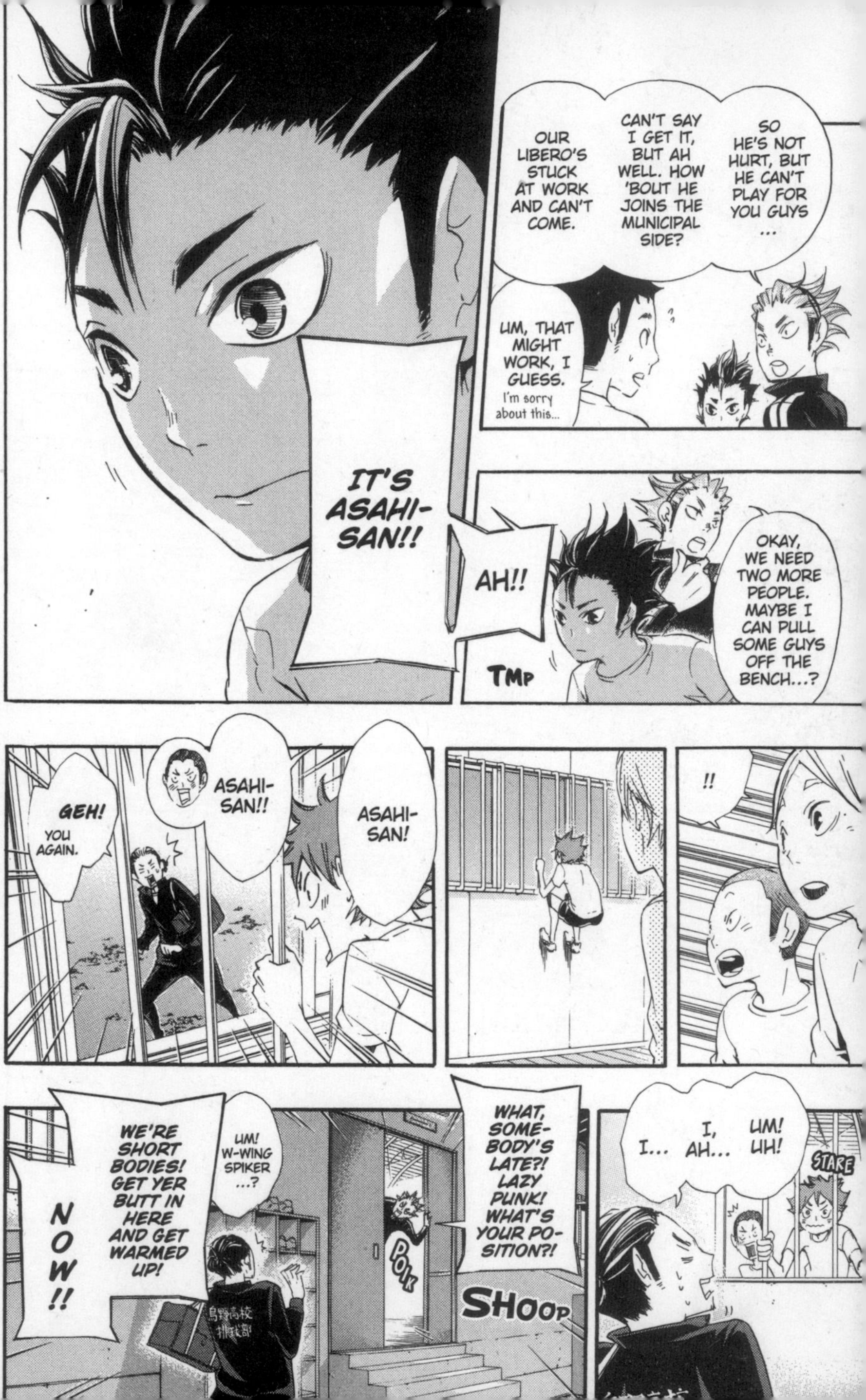
SO HE'S NOT HURT, BUT HE CAN'T PLAY FOR YOU GUYS ...
CAN'T SAY I GET IT, BUT AH WELL. HOW 'BOUT HE JOINS THE MUNICIPAL SIDE?
OUR LIBERO'S STUCK AT WORK AND CAN'T COME.
UM, THAT MIGHT WORK, I GUESS.
I'm sorry about this...
OKAY, WE NEED TWO MORE PEOPLE. MAYBE I CAN PULL SOME GUYS OFF THE BENCH...?
AH!!
TMP
IT'S ASAHI-SAN!!
!!
ASAHI-SAN!
ASAHI-SAN!!
GEH!
YOU AGAIN.
UM! UH!
I, AH...
I...
STARE
WHAT, SOMEBODY'S LATE?! LAZY PUNK! WHAT'S YOUR POSITION?!
POK
SHOOP
UM! W-WING SPIKER ...?
WE'RE SHORT BODIES! GET YER BUTT IN HERE AND GET WARMED UP!
NOW!!

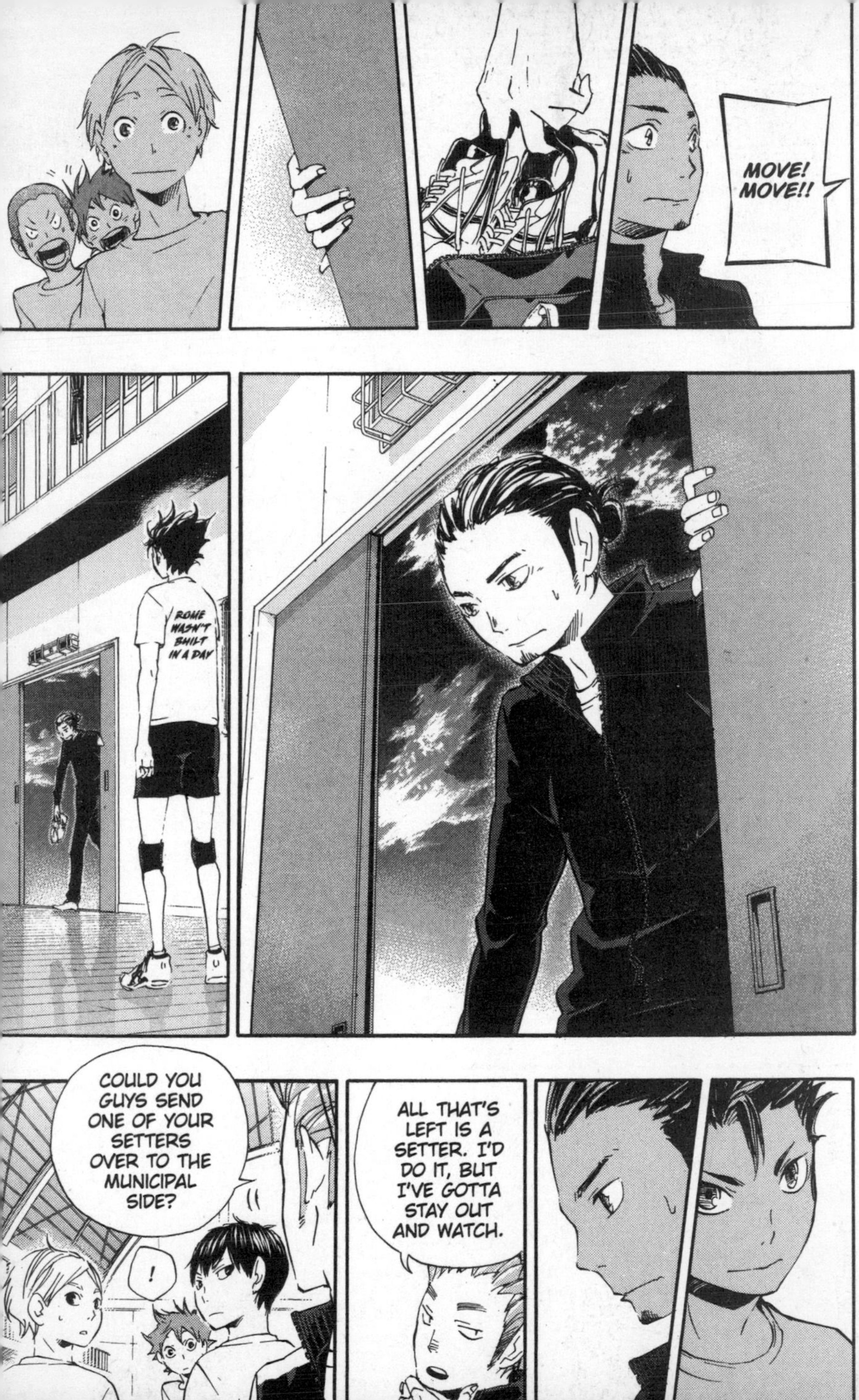
MOVE! MOVE!!
ROME WASN'T BUILT IN A DAY
ALL THAT'S LEFT IS A SETTER. I'D DO IT, BUT I'VE GOTTA STAY OUT AND WATCH.
COULD YOU GUYS SEND ONE OF YOUR SETTERS OVER TO THE MUNICIPAL SIDE?
!

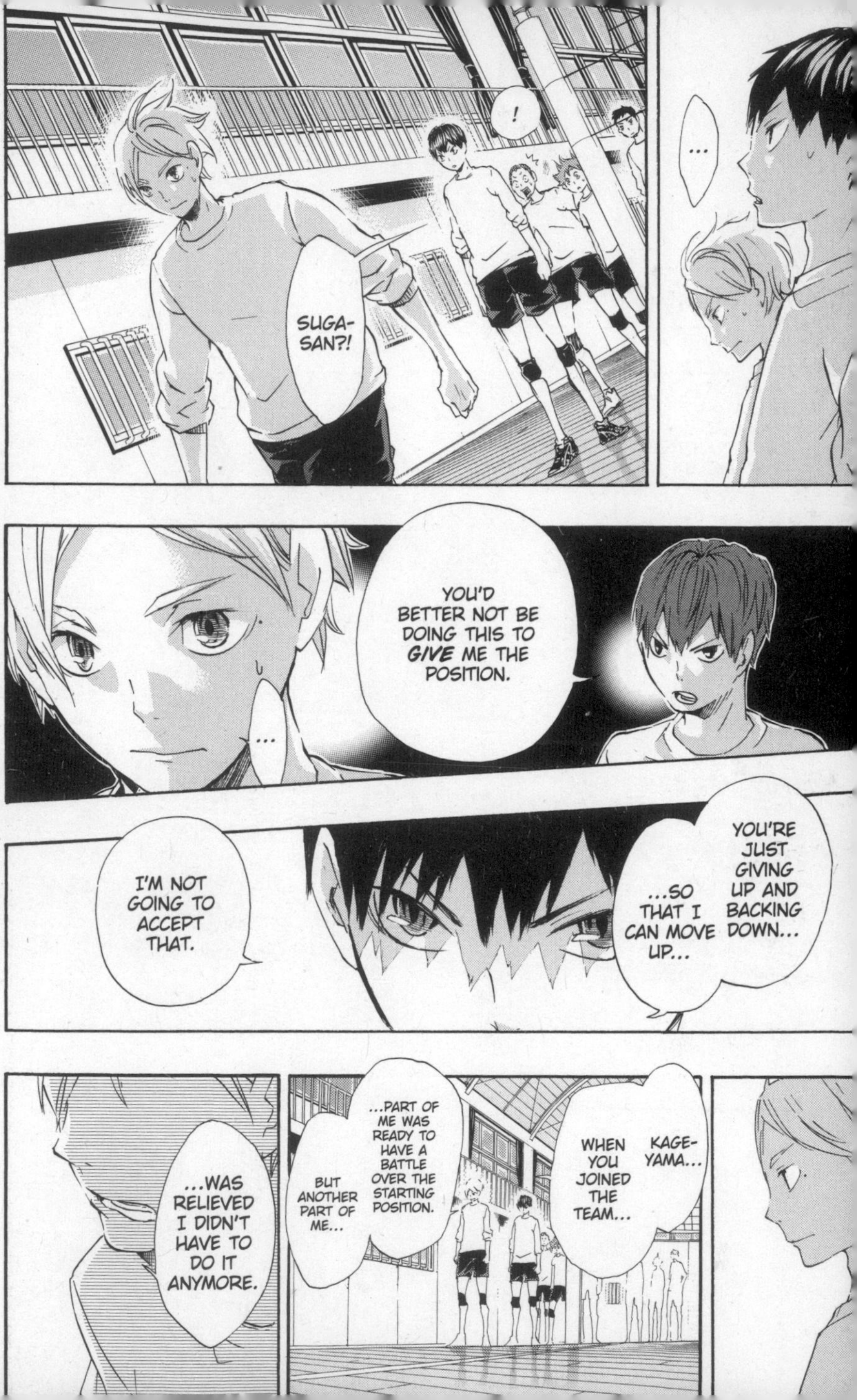
...
!
SUGA-SAN?!
YOU'D BETTER NOT BE DOING THIS TO *GIVE* ME THE POSITION.
...
YOU'RE JUST GIVING UP AND BACKING DOWN...
...SO THAT I CAN MOVE UP...
I'M NOT GOING TO ACCEPT THAT.
KAGE-YAMA...
WHEN YOU JOINED THE TEAM...
...PART OF ME WAS READY TO HAVE A BATTLE OVER THE STARTING POSITION.
BUT ANOTHER PART OF ME...
...WAS RELIEVED I DIDN'T HAVE TO DO IT ANYMORE.

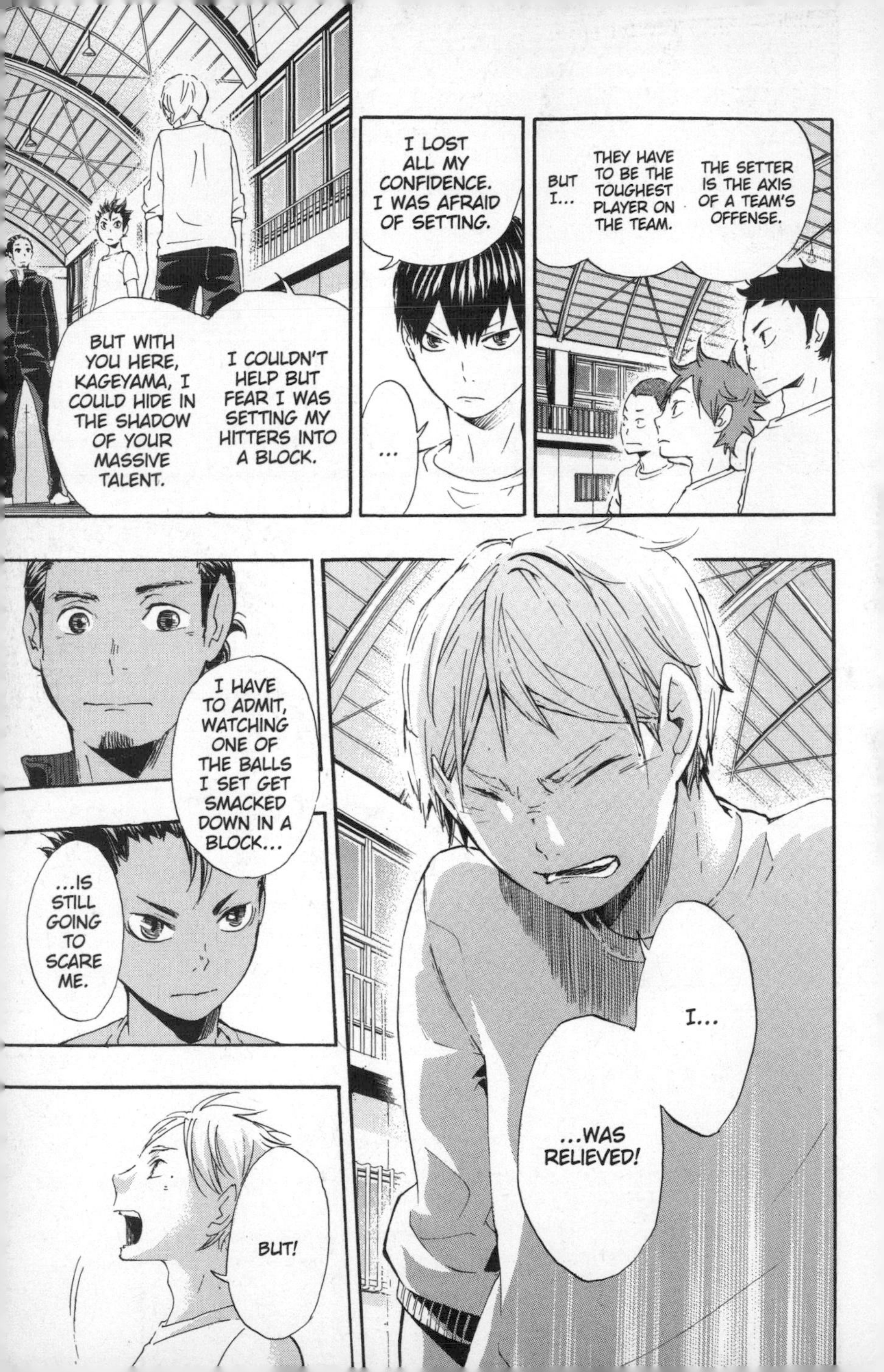
THE SETTER IS THE AXIS OF A TEAM'S OFFENSE.
THEY HAVE TO BE THE TOUGHEST PLAYER ON THE TEAM.
BUT I...
I LOST ALL MY CONFIDENCE. I WAS AFRAID OF SETTING.
...
I COULDN'T HELP BUT FEAR I WAS SETTING MY HITTERS INTO A BLOCK.
BUT WITH YOU HERE, KAGEYAMA, I COULD HIDE IN THE SHADOW OF YOUR MASSIVE TALENT.
I...
...WAS RELIEVED!
I HAVE TO ADMIT, WATCHING ONE OF THE BALLS I SET GET SMACKED DOWN IN A BLOCK...
...IS STILL GOING TO SCARE ME.
BUT!

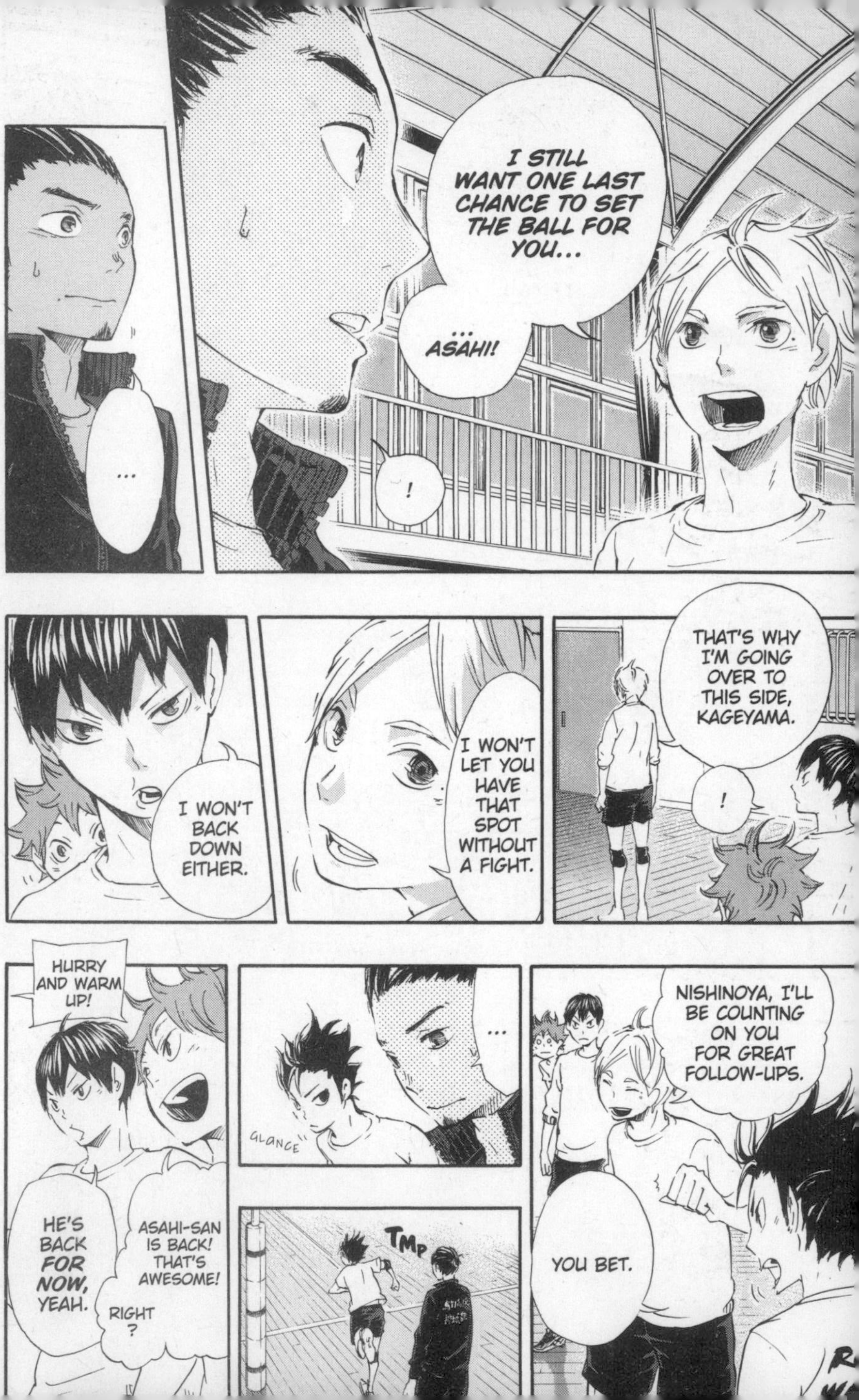
I STILL WANT ONE LAST CHANCE TO SET THE BALL FOR YOU...
...ASAHI!
!
...
THAT'S WHY I'M GOING OVER TO THIS SIDE, KAGEYAMA.
!
I WON'T LET YOU HAVE THAT SPOT WITHOUT A FIGHT.
I WON'T BACK DOWN EITHER.
NISHINOYA, I'LL BE COUNTING ON YOU FOR GREAT FOLLOW-UPS.
YOU BET.
...
GLANCE
TMP
HURRY AND WARM UP!
ASAHI-SAN IS BACK! THAT'S AWESOME!
HE'S BACK FOR NOW, YEAH.
RIGHT?

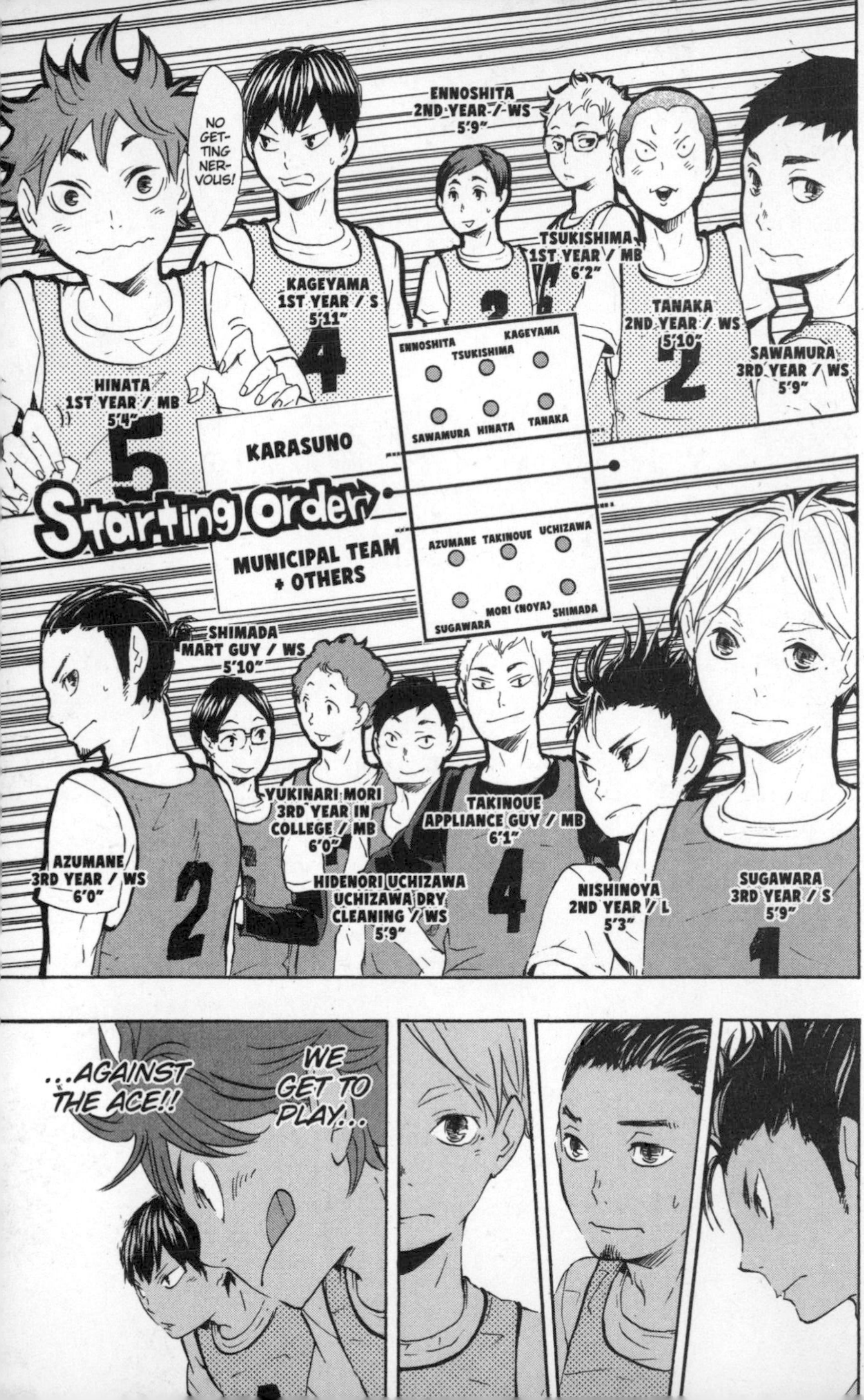
SAWAMURA
3RD YEAR / WS
5'9"
TANAKA
2ND YEAR / WS
5'10"
TSUKISHIMA
1ST YEAR / MB
6'2"
ENNOSHITA
2ND YEAR / WS
5'9"
KAGEYAMA
1ST YEAR / S
5'11"
NO GETTING NERVOUS!
HINATA
1ST YEAR / MB
5'4"
Starting Order
KARASUNO
ENNOSHITA TSUKISHIMA KAGEYAMA
SAWAMURA HINATA TANAKA
MUNICIPAL TEAM + OTHERS
AZUMANE TAKINOUE UCHIZAWA
SUGAWARA MORI (NOYA) SHIMADA
SUGAWARA
3RD YEAR / S
5'9"
NISHINOYA
2ND YEAR / L
5'3"
TAKINOUE
APPLIANCE GUY / MB
6'1"
HIDENORI UCHIZAWA
UCHIZAWA DRY CLEANING / WS
5'9"
YUKINARI MORI
3RD YEAR IN COLLEGE / MB
6'0"
SHIMADA
MART GUY / WS
5'10"
AZUMANE
3RD YEAR / WS
6'0"
WE GET TO PLAY...
...AGAINST THE ACE!!

YUSUKE TAKINOUE
(TAKINOUE APPLIANCE, 26 YEARS OLD)

KARASUNO VOLLEYBALL TEAM ALUMNUS

HEIGHT: 6'1"

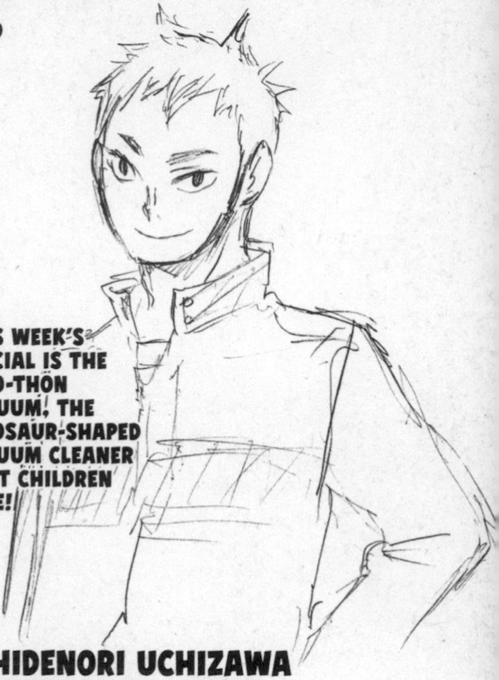

ABILITY PARAMETERS (5-POINT SCALE)

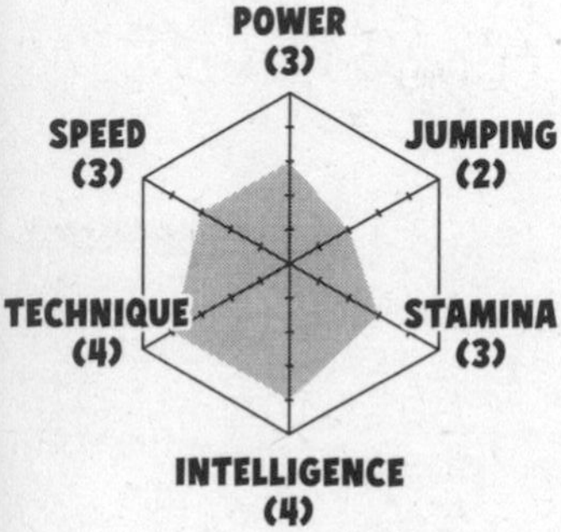
POWER (3)
JUMPING (2)
STAMINA (3)
INTELLIGENCE (4)
TECHNIQUE (4)
SPEED (3)

THIS WEEK'S SPECIAL IS THE DINO-THON VACUUM, THE DINOSAUR-SHAPED VACUUM CLEANER THAT CHILDREN LOVE!

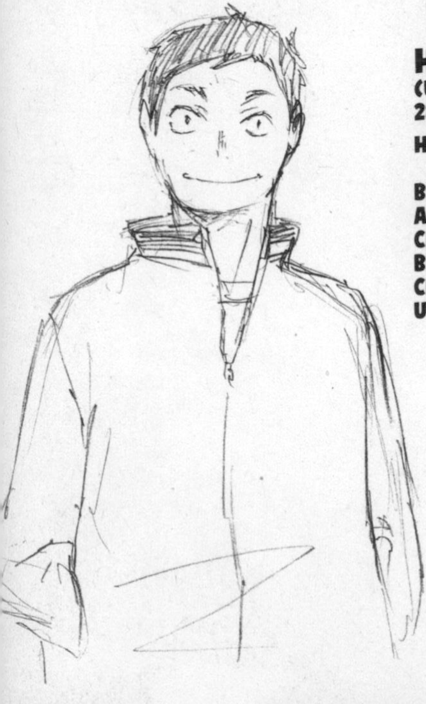

HIDENORI UCHIZAWA
(UCHIZAWA DRY CLEANING, 28 YEARS OLD)

HEIGHT: 5'9"

BEFORE YOU PACK AWAY ALL YOUR SUMMER CLOTHES FOR THE WINTER, BRING THEM IN FOR DRY CLEANING! WE ALSO PICK UP AND DELIVER!

ABILITY PARAMETERS (5-POINT SCALE)

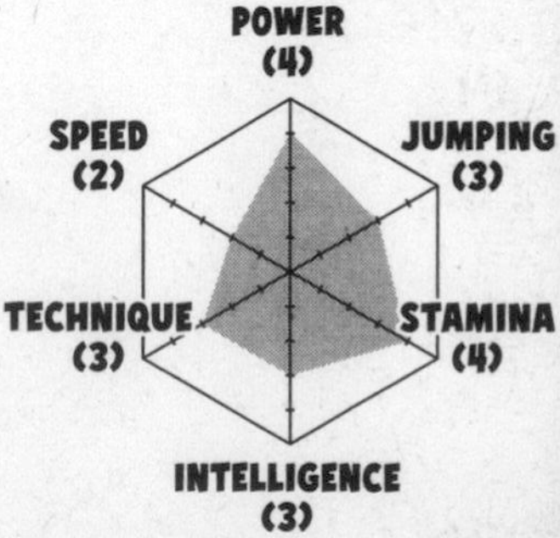
POWER (4)
JUMPING (3)
STAMINA (4)
INTELLIGENCE (3)
TECHNIQUE (3)
SPEED (2)

CHAPTER 20: Guardian Deity

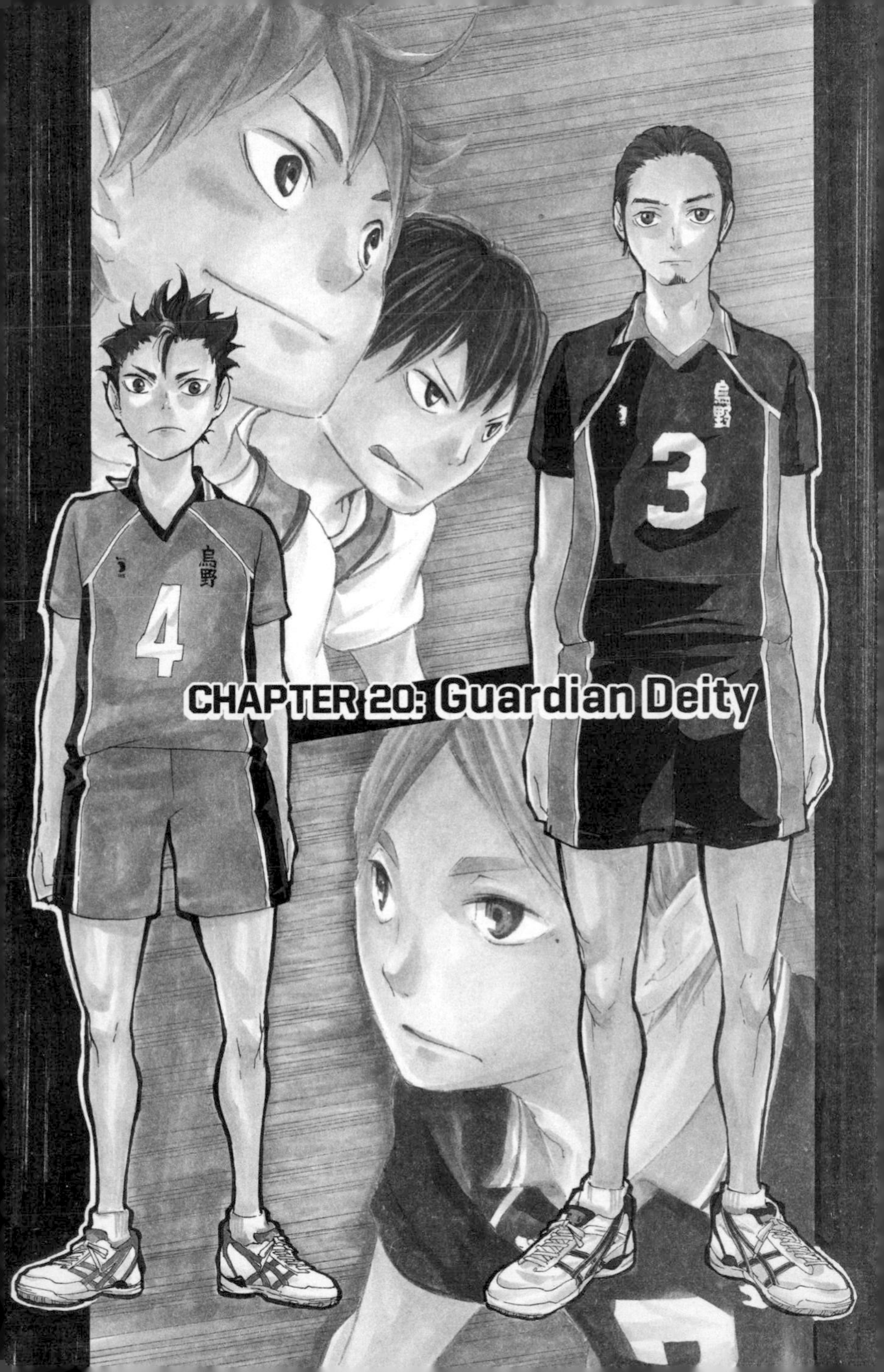

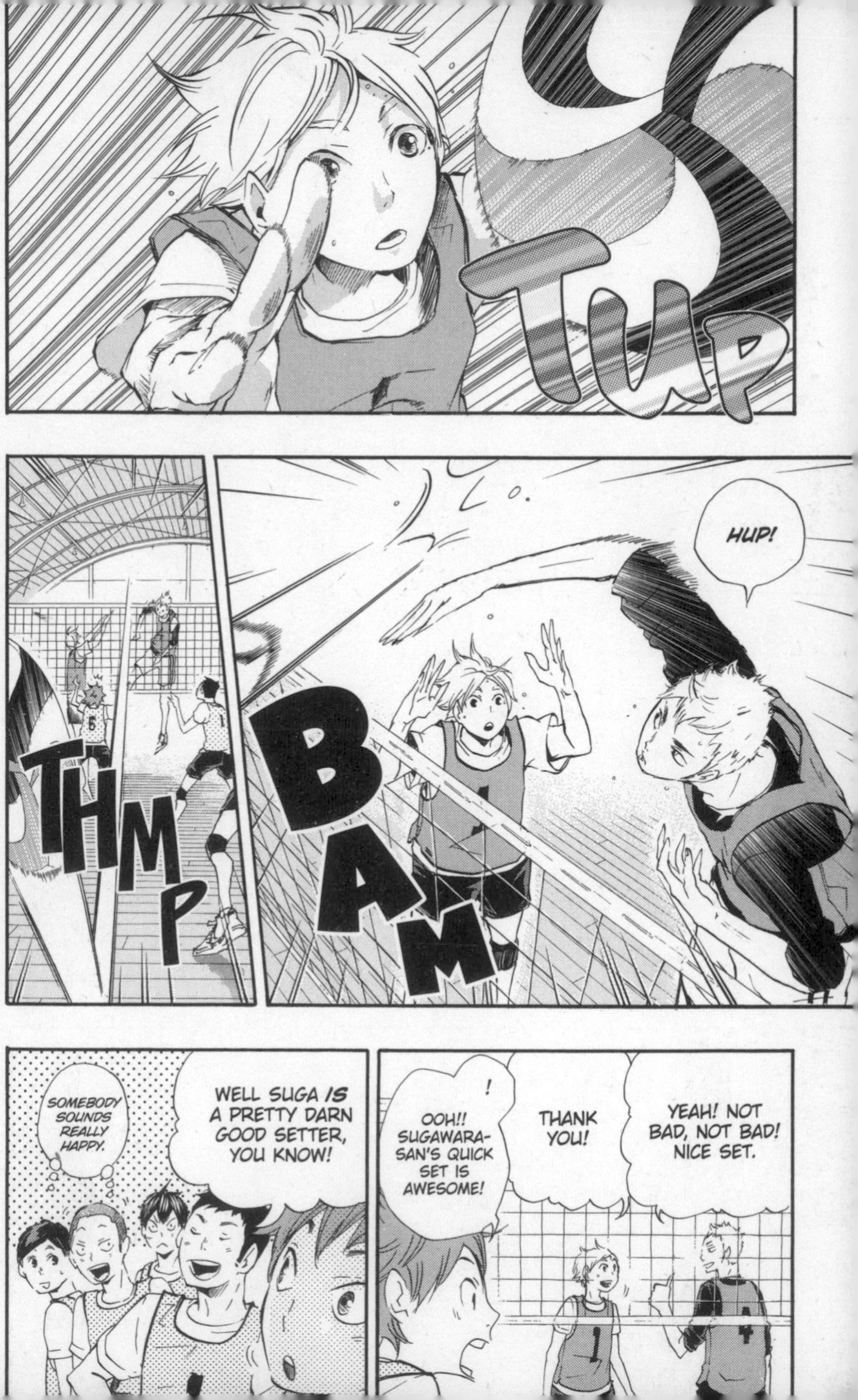
TUP
HUP!
BAM
THMP
YEAH! NOT BAD, NOT BAD! NICE SET.
THANK YOU!
!
OOH!! SUGAWARA-SAN'S QUICK SET IS AWESOME!
WELL SUGA *IS* A PRETTY DARN GOOD SETTER, YOU KNOW!
SOMEBODY SOUNDS REALLY HAPPY.

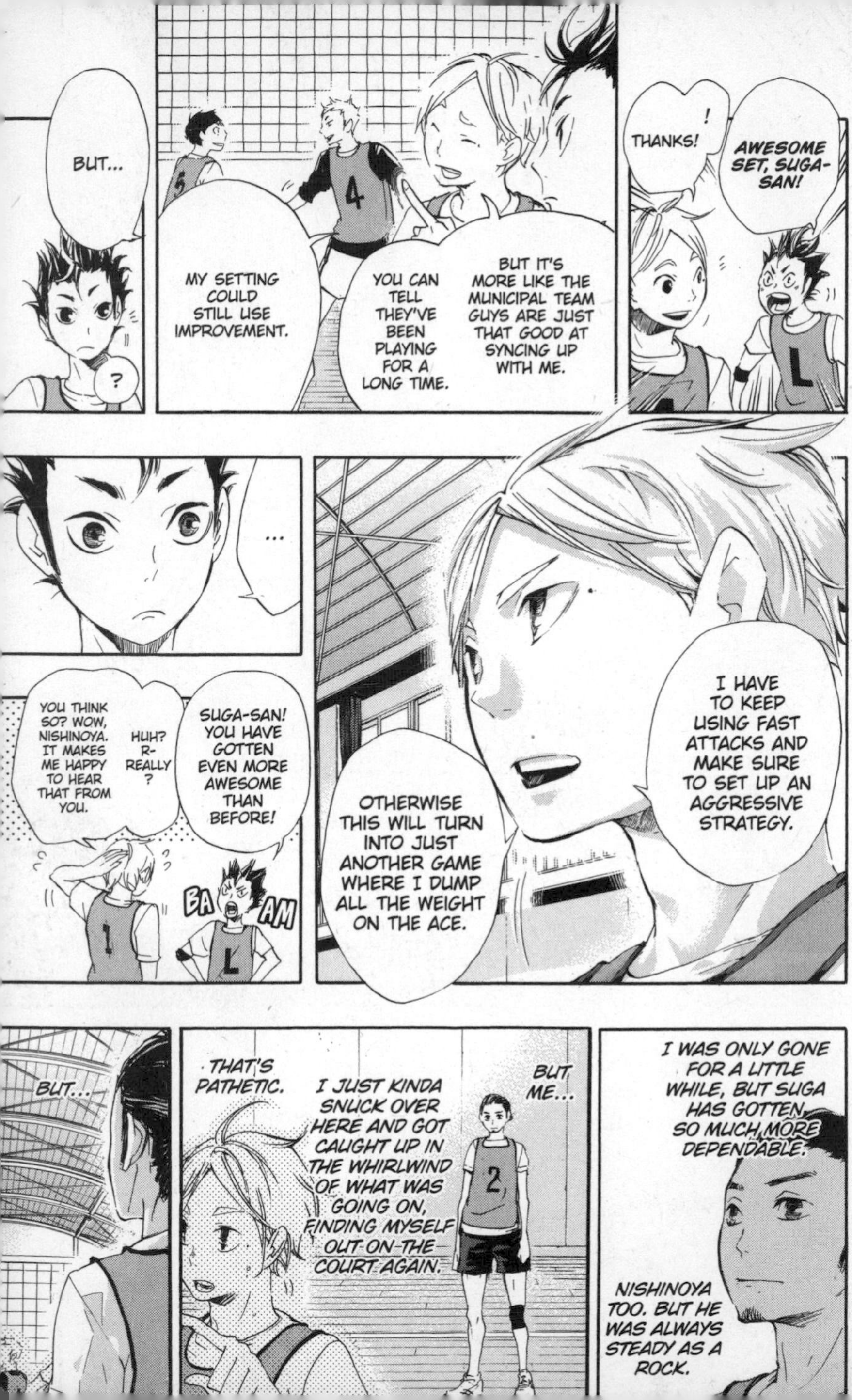
AWESOME SET, SUGA-SAN!
!
THANKS!
BUT IT'S MORE LIKE THE MUNICIPAL TEAM GUYS ARE JUST THAT GOOD AT SYNCING UP WITH ME.
YOU CAN TELL THEY'VE BEEN PLAYING FOR A LONG TIME.
MY SETTING COULD STILL USE IMPROVEMENT.
BUT...
?
I HAVE TO KEEP USING FAST ATTACKS AND MAKE SURE TO SET UP AN AGGRESSIVE STRATEGY.
OTHERWISE THIS WILL TURN INTO JUST ANOTHER GAME WHERE I DUMP ALL THE WEIGHT ON THE ACE.
...
SUGA-SAN! YOU HAVE GOTTEN EVEN MORE AWESOME THAN BEFORE!
BA AM
HUH? R-REALLY?
YOU THINK SO? WOW, NISHINOYA. IT MAKES ME HAPPY TO HEAR THAT FROM YOU.
I WAS ONLY GONE FOR A LITTLE WHILE, BUT SUGA HAS GOTTEN SO MUCH MORE DEPENDABLE.
NISHINOYA TOO. BUT HE WAS ALWAYS STEADY AS A ROCK.
BUT ME...
I JUST KINDA SNUCK OVER HERE AND GOT CAUGHT UP IN THE WHIRLWIND OF WHAT WAS GOING ON, FINDING MYSELF OUT ON THE COURT AGAIN.
THAT'S PATHETIC.
BUT...

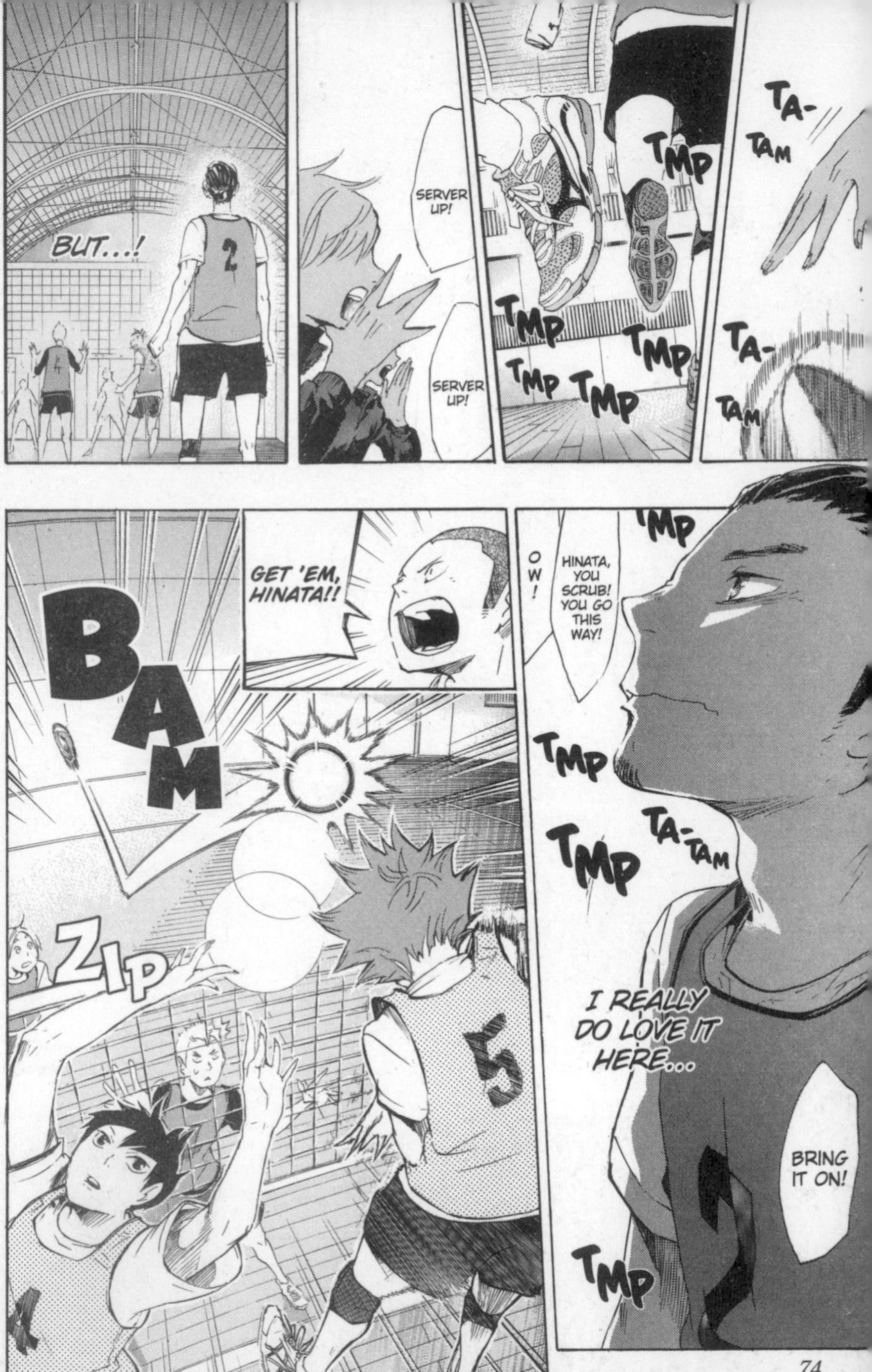
TA-TAM
TA-TAM
TMP
TMP
TMP
TMP
TMP
SERVER UP!
SERVER UP!
BUT...!
TMP
HINATA, YOU SCRUB! YOU GO THIS WAY!
OW!
TMP
TA-TAM
TMP
I REALLY DO LOVE IT HERE...
BRING IT ON!
TMP
GET 'EM, HINATA!!
BAM
ZIP

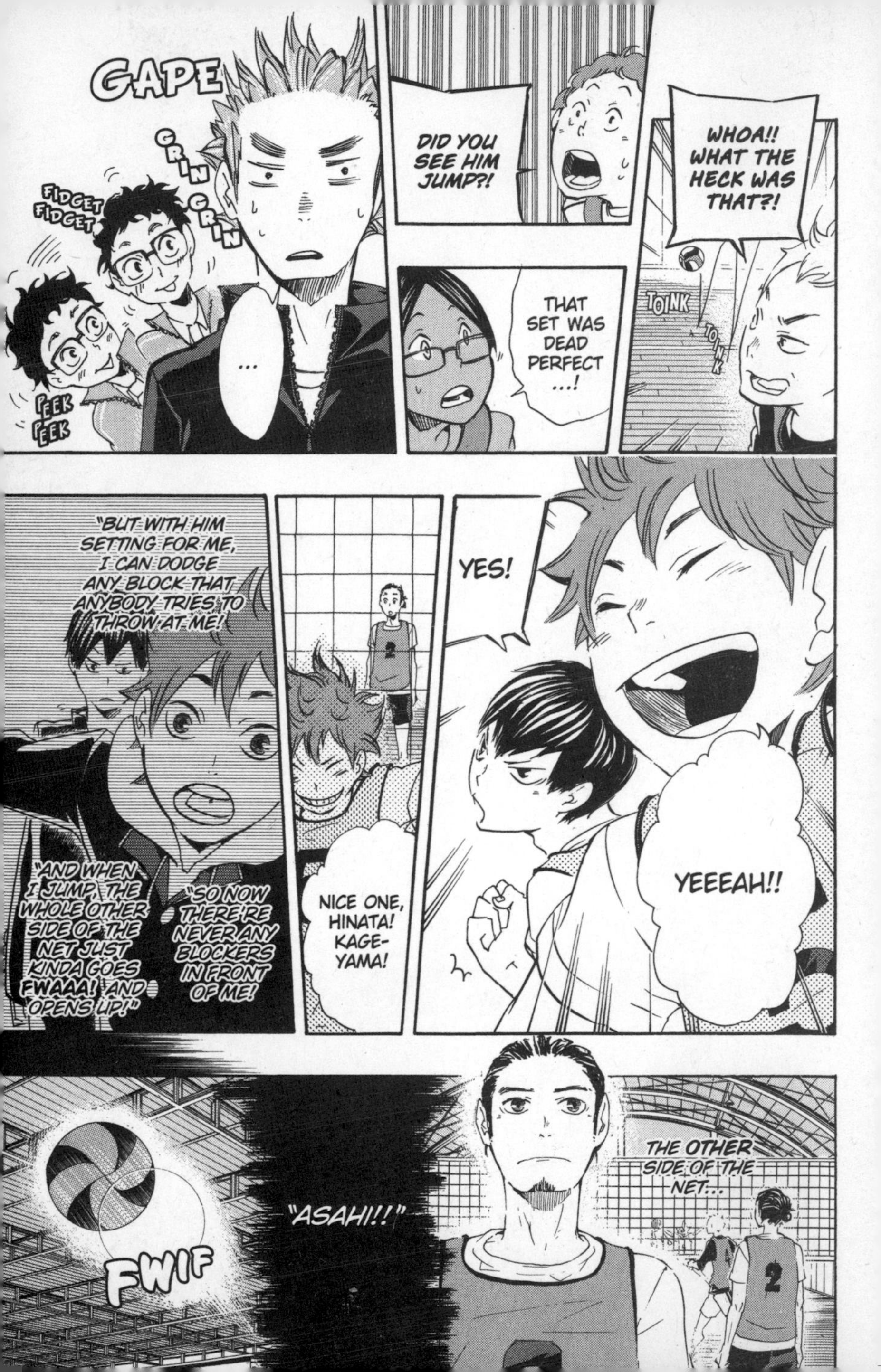
WHOA!! WHAT THE HECK WAS THAT?!
TOINK
TOINK
DID YOU SEE HIM JUMP?!
THAT SET WAS DEAD PERFECT ...!
GAPE
GRIN GRIN
FIDGET FIDGET
...
PEEK PEEK
YES!
YEEEAH!!
NICE ONE, HINATA! KAGE-YAMA!
"BUT WITH HIM SETTING FOR ME, I CAN DODGE ANY BLOCK THAT ANYBODY TRIES TO THROW AT ME!
"SO NOW THERE'RE NEVER ANY BLOCKERS IN FRONT OF ME!
"AND WHEN I JUMP, THE WHOLE OTHER SIDE OF THE NET JUST KINDA GOES FWAAA! AND OPENS UP!"
THE OTHER SIDE OF THE NET...
"ASAHI!!"
FWIF

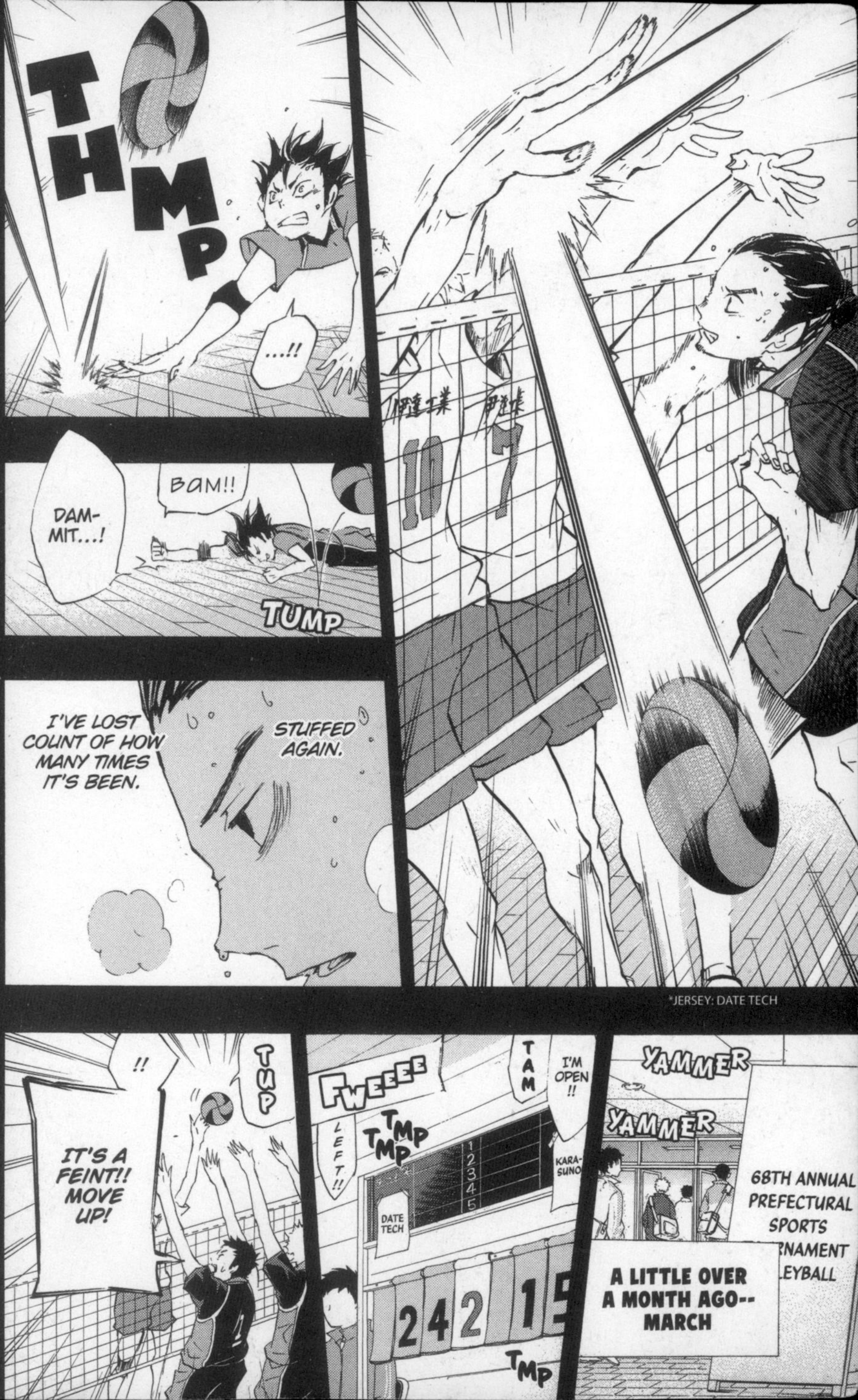
伊達工業
伊達工業
THMP
...!!
BAM!!
DAM-MIT...!
TUMP
STUFFED AGAIN.
I'VE LOST COUNT OF HOW MANY TIMES IT'S BEEN.
YAMMER
YAMMER
68TH ANNUAL PREFECTURAL SPORTS
RNAMENT
LEYBALL
A LITTLE OVER A MONTH AGO--MARCH
TAM
I'M OPEN!!
FWEEEE
LEFT!!
TMP TMP
KARA-SUNO
DATE TECH
TMP
TUP
!!
IT'S A FEINT!! MOVE UP!

*JERSEY: DATE TECH

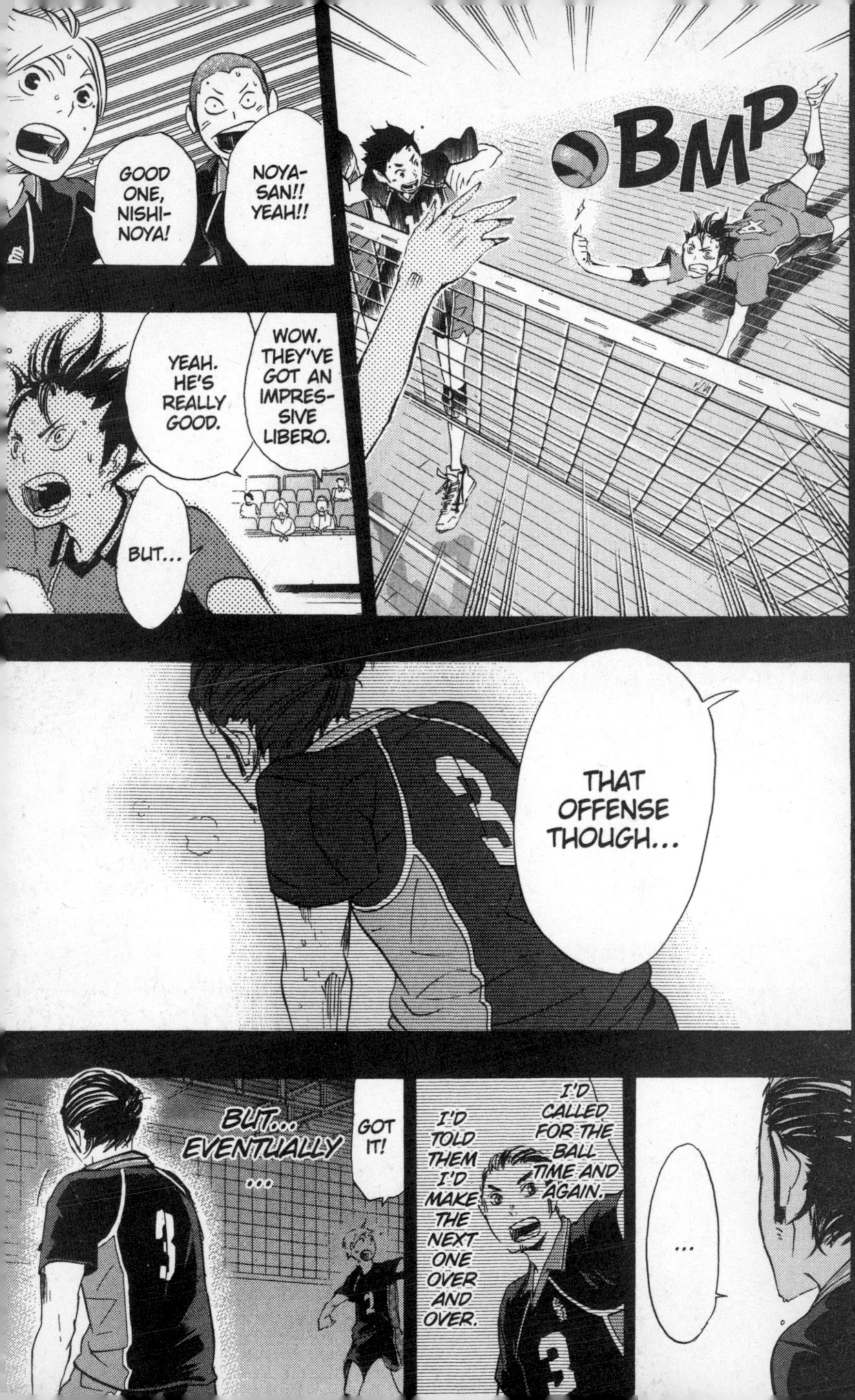
BMP
NOYA-SAN!! YEAH!!
GOOD ONE, NISHI-NOYA!
WOW. THEY'VE GOT AN IMPRES-SIVE LIBERO.
YEAH. HE'S REALLY GOOD.
BUT...
THAT OFFENSE THOUGH...
...
I'D CALLED FOR THE BALL TIME AND AGAIN.
I'D TOLD THEM I'D MAKE THE NEXT ONE OVER AND OVER.
GOT IT!
BUT... EVENTUALLY ...

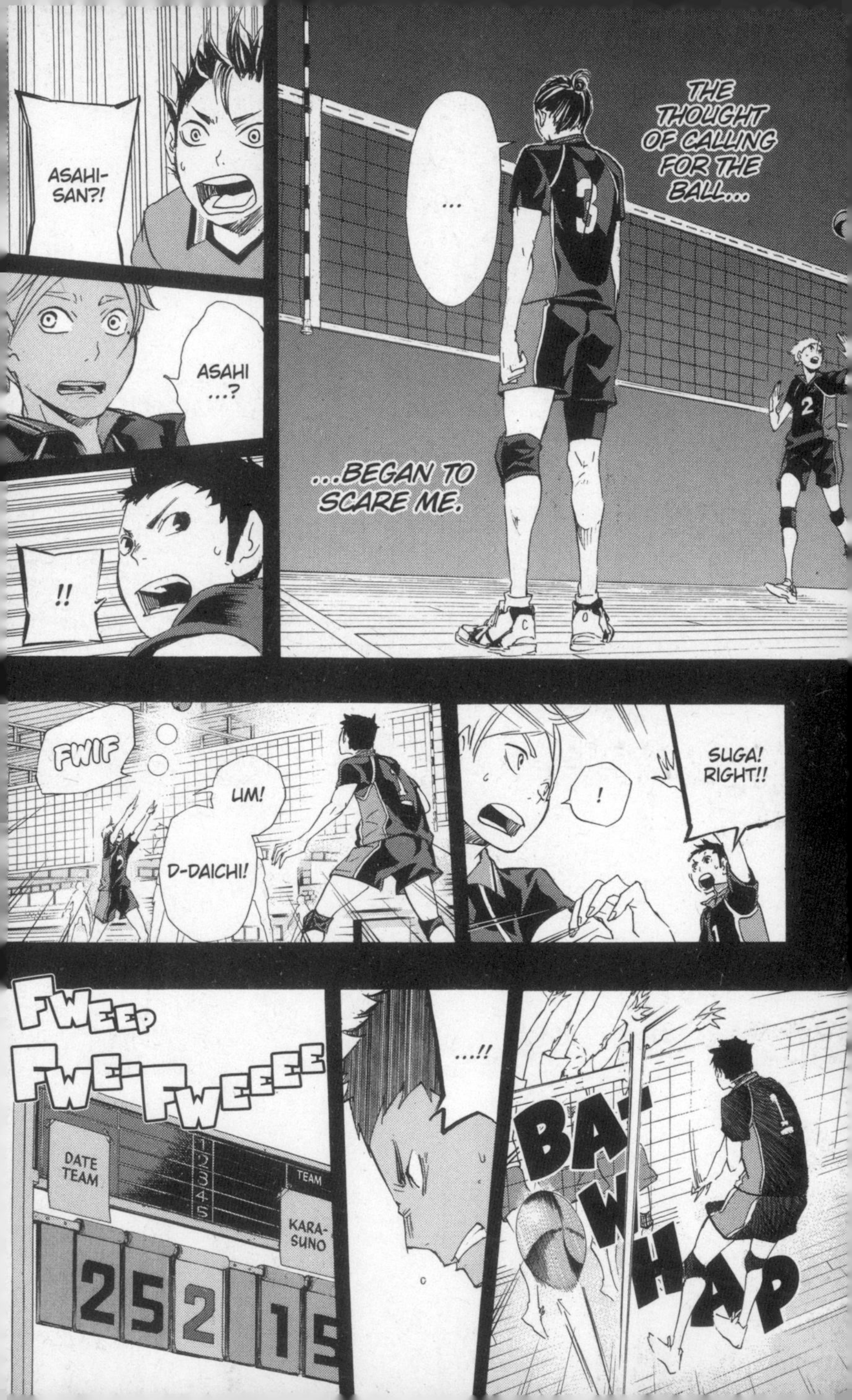
THE THOUGHT OF CALLING FOR THE BALL...
...
...BEGAN TO SCARE ME.
ASAHI-SAN?!
ASAHI ...?
!!
SUGA! RIGHT!!
!
FWIF
UM!
D-DAICHI!
BA-WHAP
...!!
FWEEP
FWE-FWEEEE
DATE TEAM
TEAM
KARA-SUNO

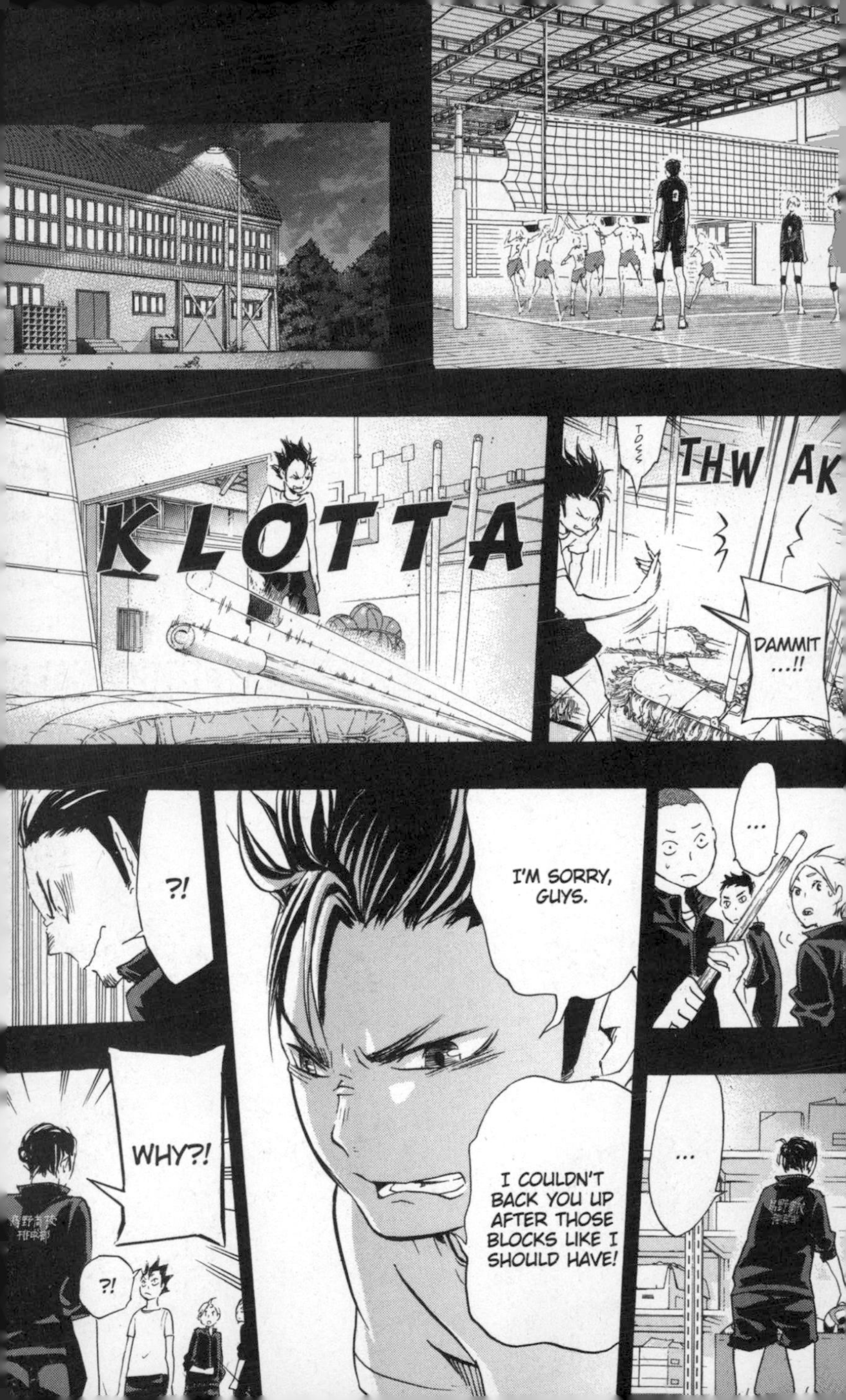
TOSS
THW AK
DAMMIT ...!!
KLOTTA
...
...
I'M SORRY, GUYS.
I COULDN'T BACK YOU UP AFTER THOSE BLOCKS LIKE I SHOULD HAVE!
?!
WHY?!
?!

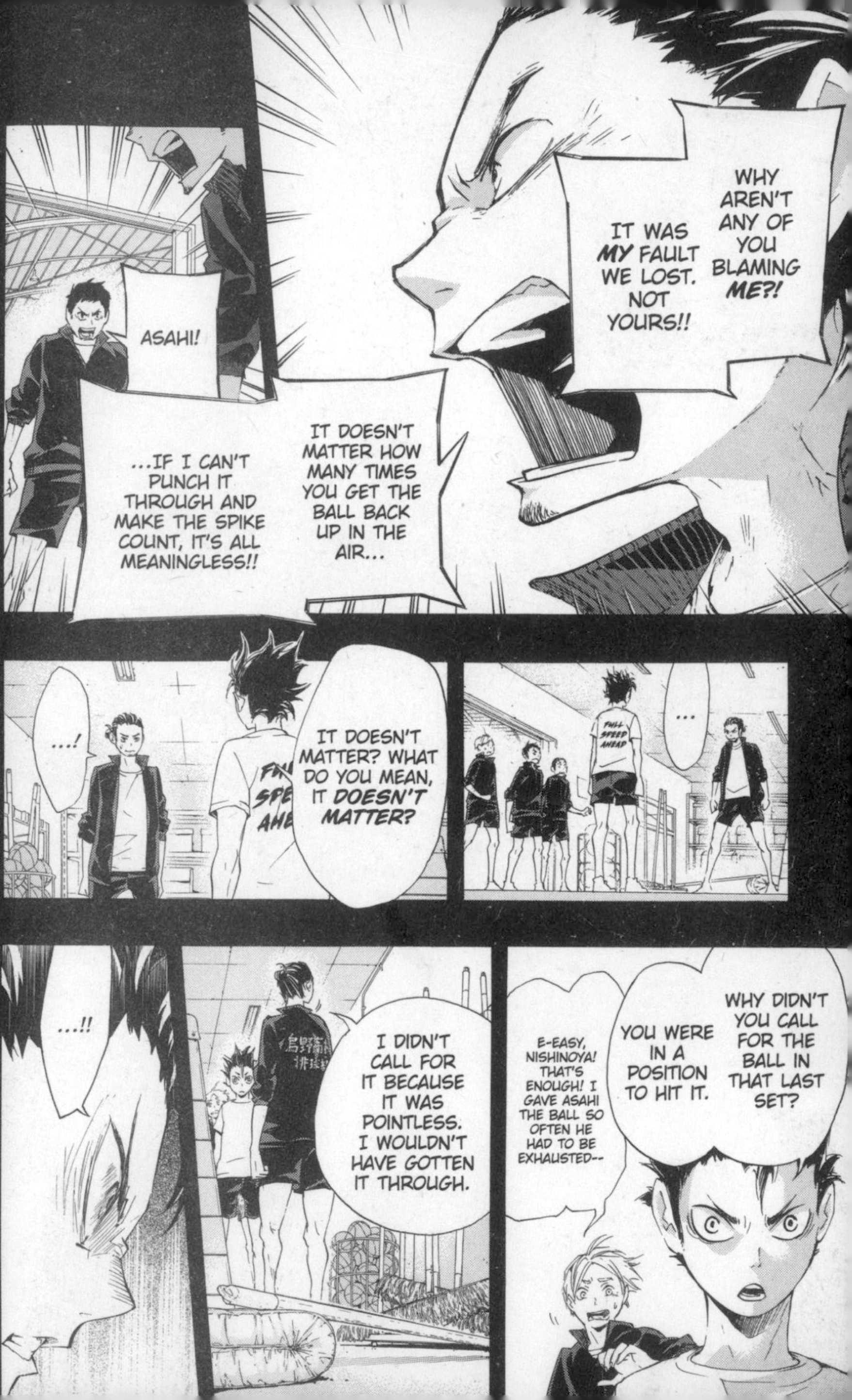
WHY AREN'T ANY OF YOU BLAMING *ME?!*
IT WAS *MY* FAULT WE LOST. NOT YOURS!!
IT DOESN'T MATTER HOW MANY TIMES YOU GET THE BALL BACK UP IN THE AIR...
...IF I CAN'T PUNCH IT THROUGH AND MAKE THE SPIKE COUNT, IT'S ALL MEANINGLESS!!
ASAHI!
...
FULL SPEED AHEAD
IT DOESN'T MATTER? WHAT DO YOU MEAN, IT *DOESN'T MATTER?*
...!
WHY DIDN'T YOU CALL FOR THE BALL IN THAT LAST SET?
YOU WERE IN A POSITION TO HIT IT.
E-EASY, NISHINOYA! THAT'S ENOUGH! I GAVE ASAHI THE BALL SO OFTEN HE HAD TO BE EXHAUSTED--
I DIDN'T CALL FOR IT BECAUSE IT WAS POINTLESS. I WOULDN'T HAVE GOTTEN IT THROUGH.
...!!

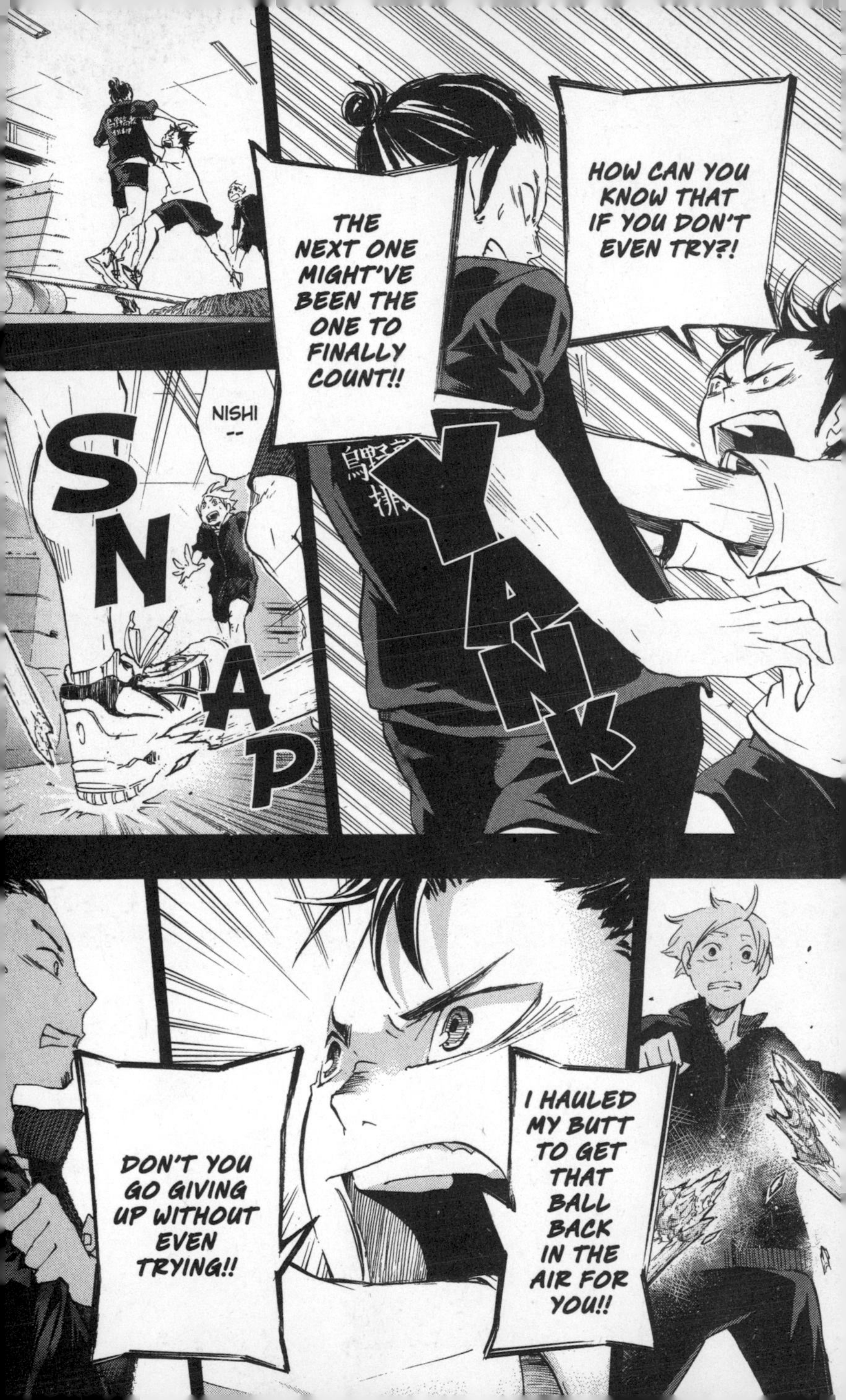
HOW CAN YOU KNOW THAT IF YOU DON'T EVEN TRY?!
THE NEXT ONE MIGHT'VE BEEN THE ONE TO FINALLY COUNT!!
YANK
NISHI --
SNAP
I HAULED MY BUTT TO GET THAT BALL BACK IN THE AIR FOR YOU!!
DON'T YOU GO GIVING UP WITHOUT EVEN TRYING!!

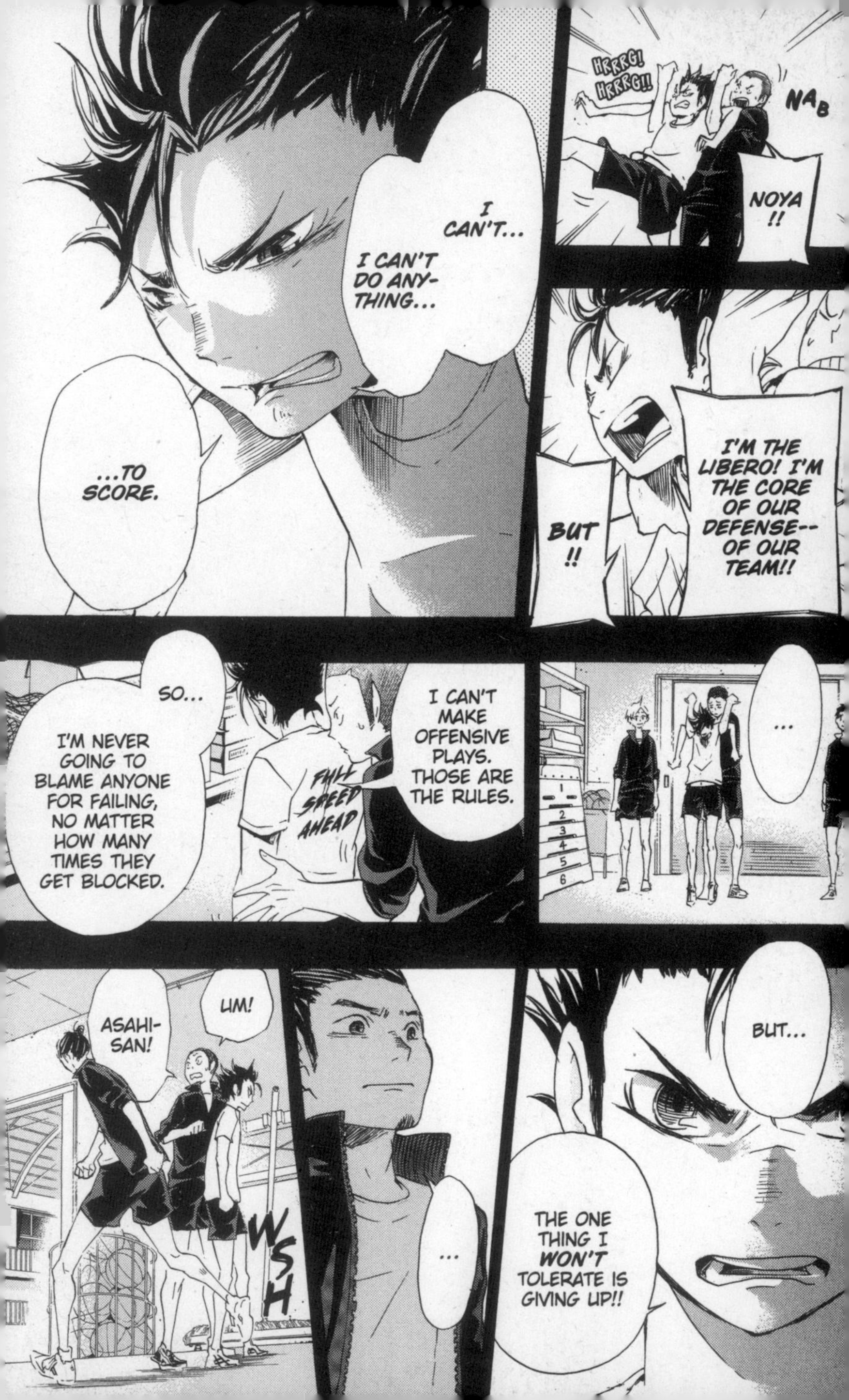
NAB
HRRRG! HRRRG!!
NOYA!!
I'M THE LIBERO! I'M THE CORE OF OUR DEFENSE--OF OUR TEAM!!
BUT!!
I CAN'T...
I CAN'T DO ANYTHING...
...TO SCORE.
...
I CAN'T MAKE OFFENSIVE PLAYS. THOSE ARE THE RULES.
FULL SPEED AHEAD
SO...
I'M NEVER GOING TO BLAME ANYONE FOR FAILING, NO MATTER HOW MANY TIMES THEY GET BLOCKED.
BUT...
THE ONE THING I *WON'T* TOLERATE IS GIVING UP!!
...
UM!
ASAHI-SAN!
WSH

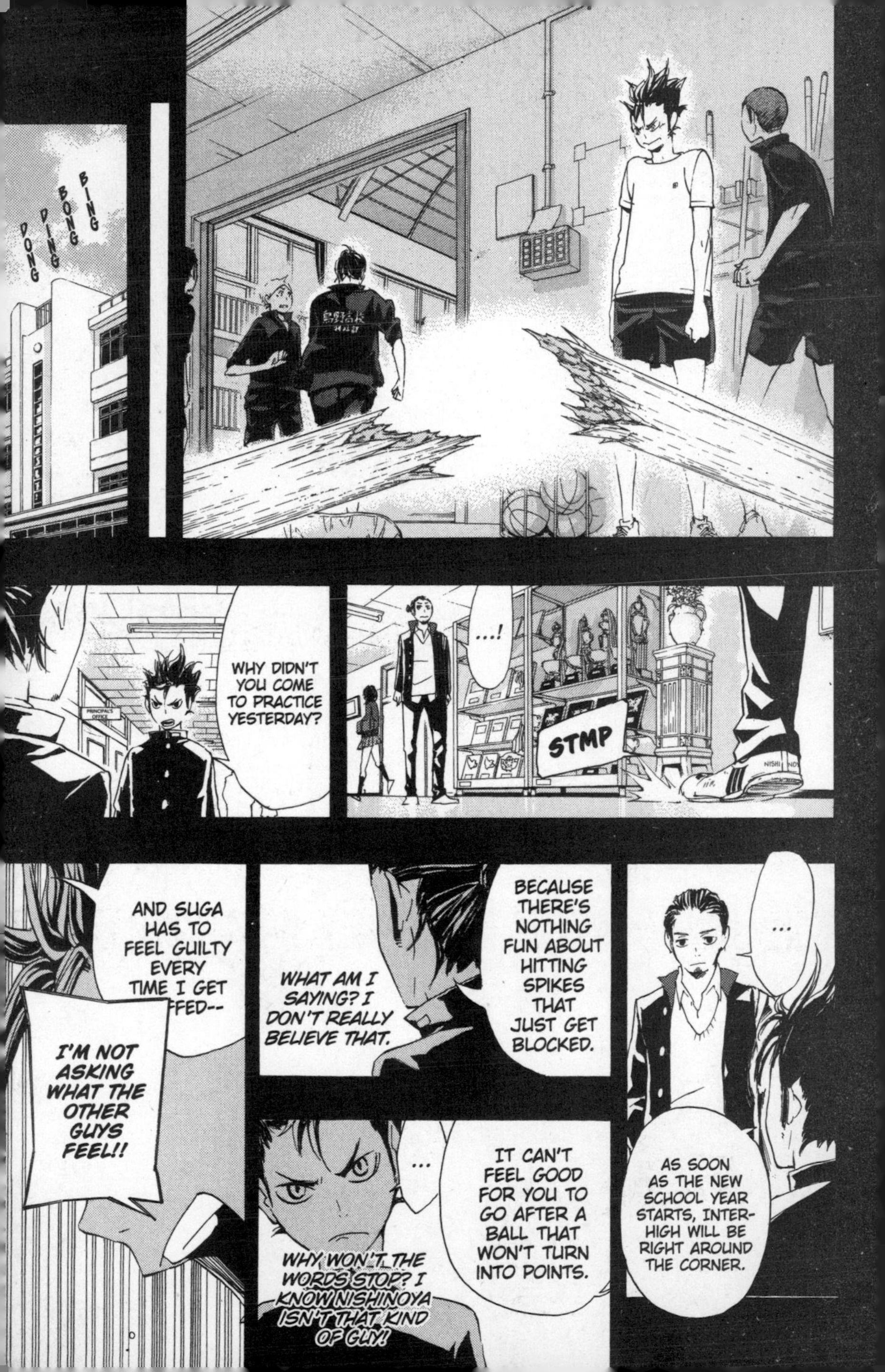
BING BONG DING DONG
...!
STMP
WHY DIDN'T YOU COME TO PRACTICE YESTERDAY?
PRINCIPAL'S OFFICE
...
AS SOON AS THE NEW SCHOOL YEAR STARTS, INTER-HIGH WILL BE RIGHT AROUND THE CORNER.
BECAUSE THERE'S NOTHING FUN ABOUT HITTING SPIKES THAT JUST GET BLOCKED.
WHAT AM I SAYING? I DON'T REALLY BELIEVE THAT.
IT CAN'T FEEL GOOD FOR YOU TO GO AFTER A BALL THAT WON'T TURN INTO POINTS.
...
WHY WON'T THE WORDS STOP? I KNOW NISHINOYA ISN'T THAT KIND OF GUY!
AND SUGA HAS TO FEEL GUILTY EVERY TIME I GET FFED--
I'M NOT ASKING WHAT THE OTHER GUYS FEEL!!

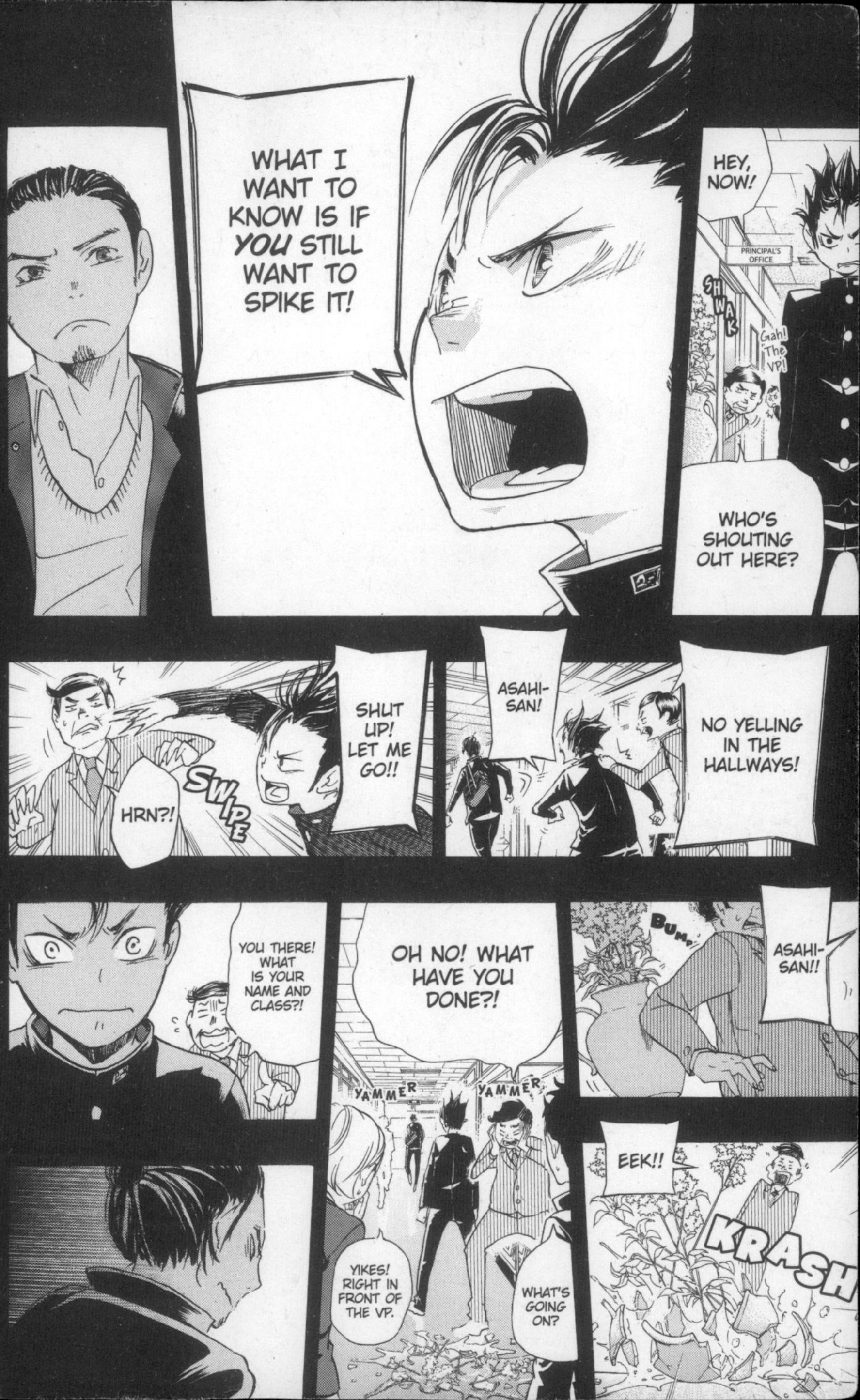
HEY, NOW!
PRINCIPAL'S OFFICE
SHWAK
Gah! The VP!
WHO'S SHOUTING OUT HERE?
WHAT I WANT TO KNOW IS IF *YOU* STILL WANT TO SPIKE IT!
NO YELLING IN THE HALLWAYS!
ASAHI-SAN!
SHUT UP! LET ME GO!!
SWIPE
HRN?!
BUMP
ASAHI-SAN!!
EEK!!
KRASH
OH NO! WHAT HAVE YOU DONE?!
YAMMER
YAMMER
WHAT'S GOING ON?
YIKES! RIGHT IN FRONT OF THE VP.
YOU THERE! WHAT IS YOUR NAME AND CLASS?!

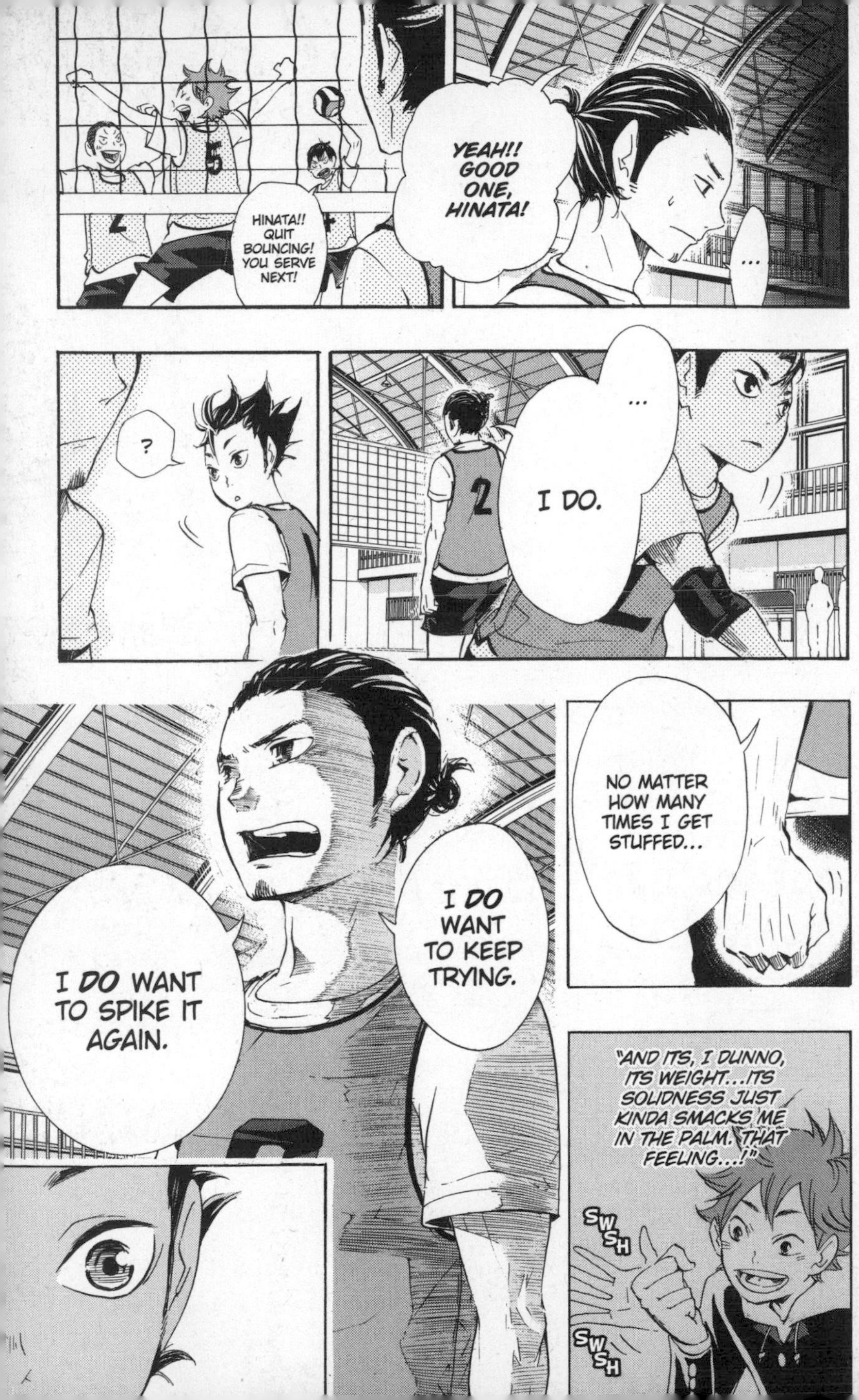
...
YEAH!! GOOD ONE, HINATA!
HINATA!! QUIT BOUNCING! YOU SERVE NEXT!
...
I DO.
?
NO MATTER HOW MANY TIMES I GET STUFFED...
"AND ITS, I DUNNO, ITS WEIGHT...ITS SOLIDNESS JUST KINDA SMACKS ME IN THE PALM. THAT FEELING...!"
SWSH
SWSH
I *DO* WANT TO KEEP TRYING.
I *DO* WANT TO SPIKE IT AGAIN.

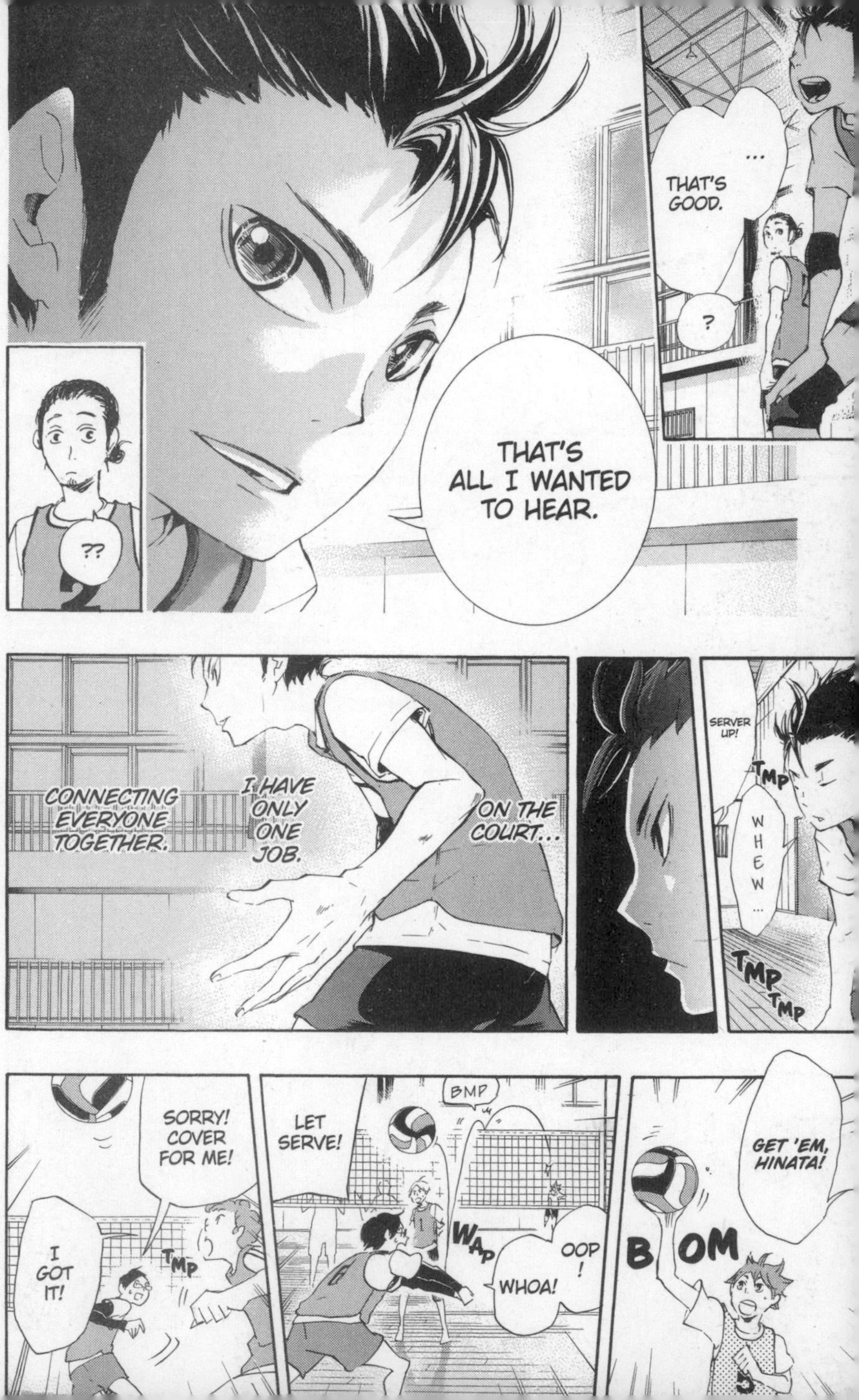
...
THAT'S GOOD.
?
THAT'S ALL I WANTED TO HEAR.
??
SERVER UP!
TMP
WHEW...
TMP TMP
ON THE COURT...
I HAVE ONLY ONE JOB.
CONNECTING EVERYONE TOGETHER.
GET 'EM, HINATA!
BOOM
BMP
LET SERVE!
WAP
OOP!
WHOA!
SORRY! COVER FOR ME!
TMP
I GOT IT!

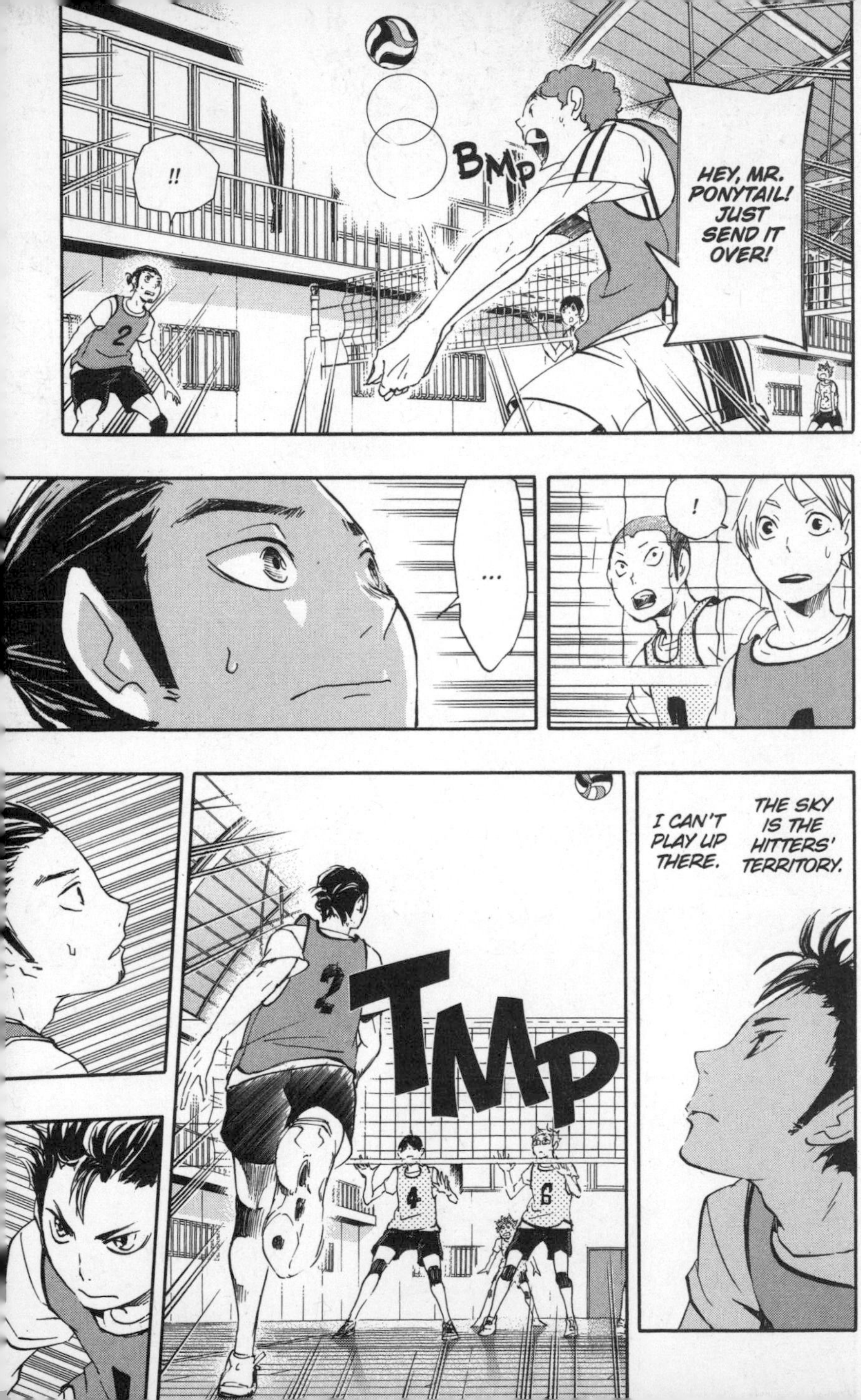
HEY, MR. PONYTAIL! JUST SEND IT OVER!
BMP
!!
!
...
THE SKY IS THE HITTERS' TERRITORY.
I CAN'T PLAY UP THERE.
TMP

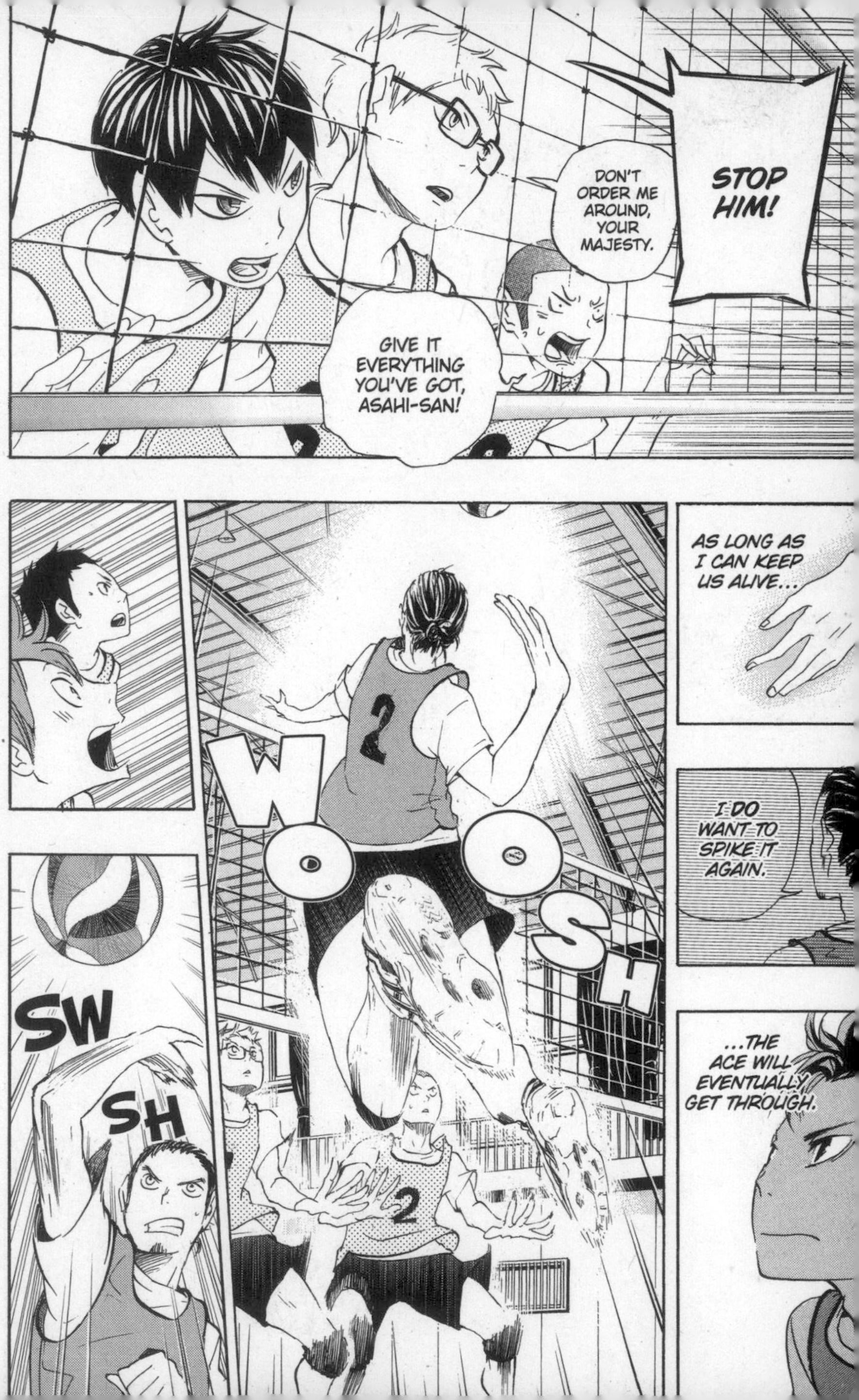
STOP HIM!
DON'T ORDER ME AROUND, YOUR MAJESTY.
GIVE IT EVERYTHING YOU'VE GOT, ASAHI-SAN!
AS LONG AS I CAN KEEP US ALIVE...
I DO WANT TO SPIKE IT AGAIN.
...THE ACE WILL EVENTUALLY GET THROUGH.
WOOSH
SWSH

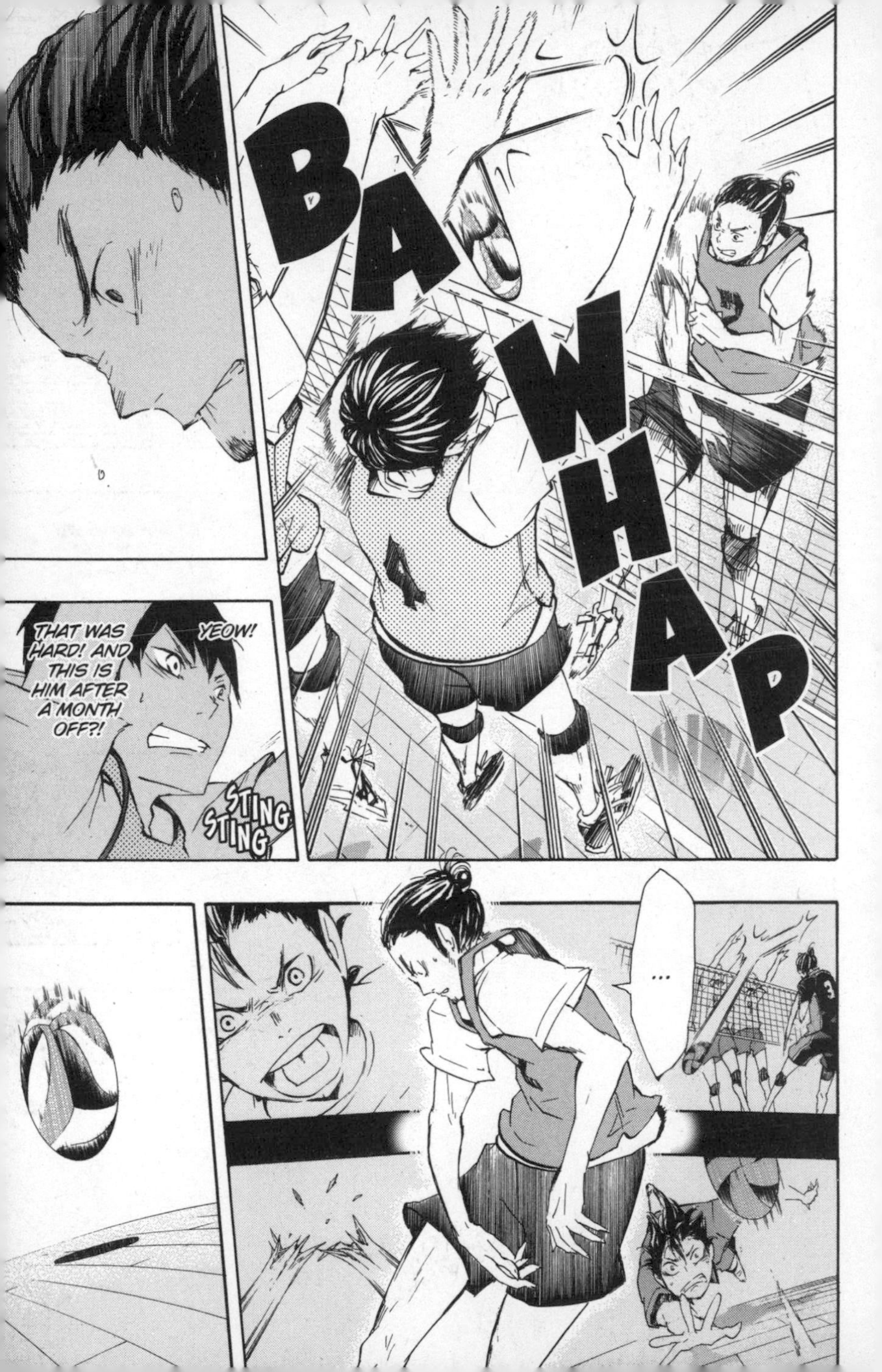
BAWHAP
YEOW!
THAT WAS HARD! AND THIS IS HIM AFTER A MONTH OFF?!
STING STING
...

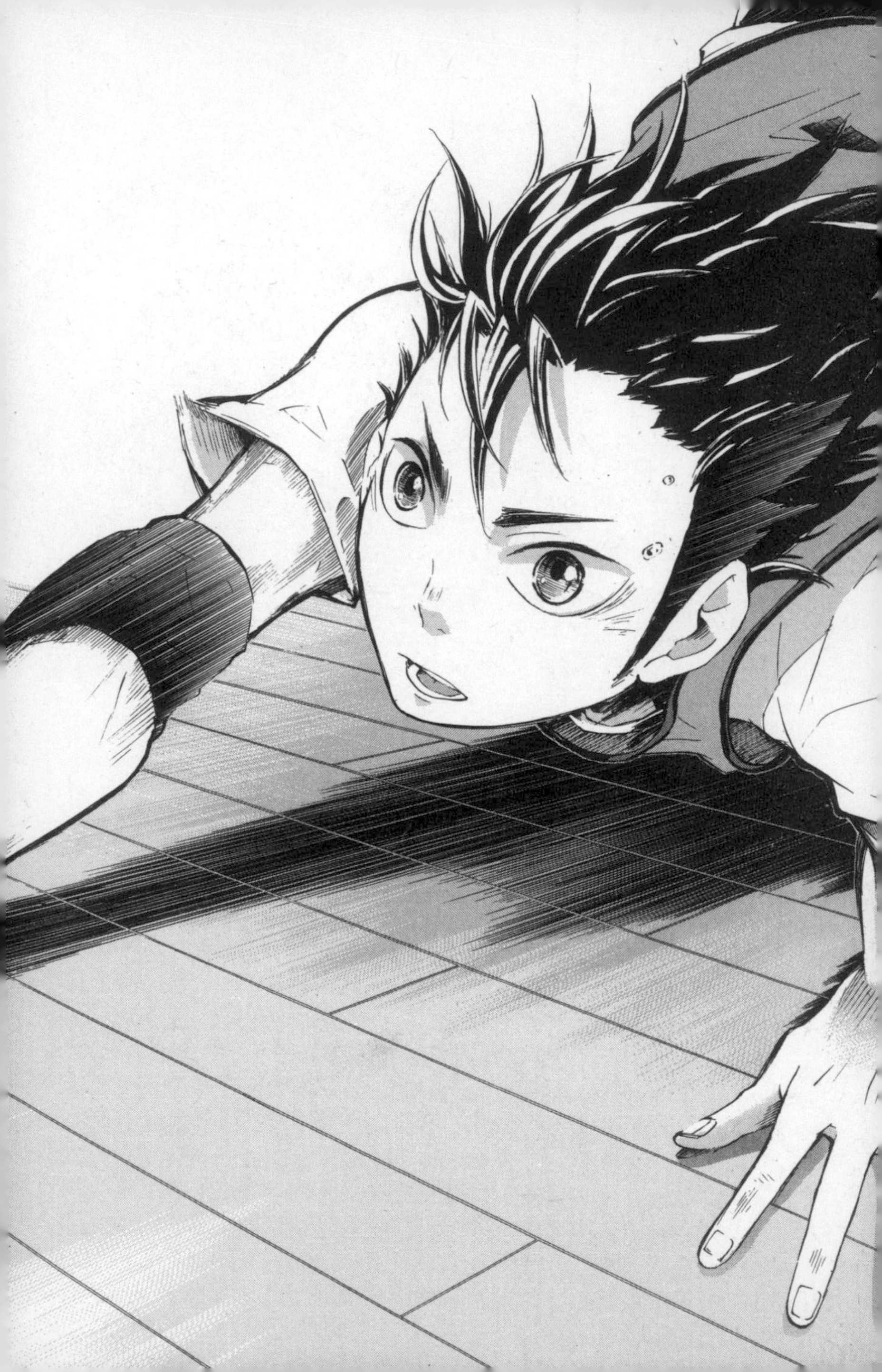

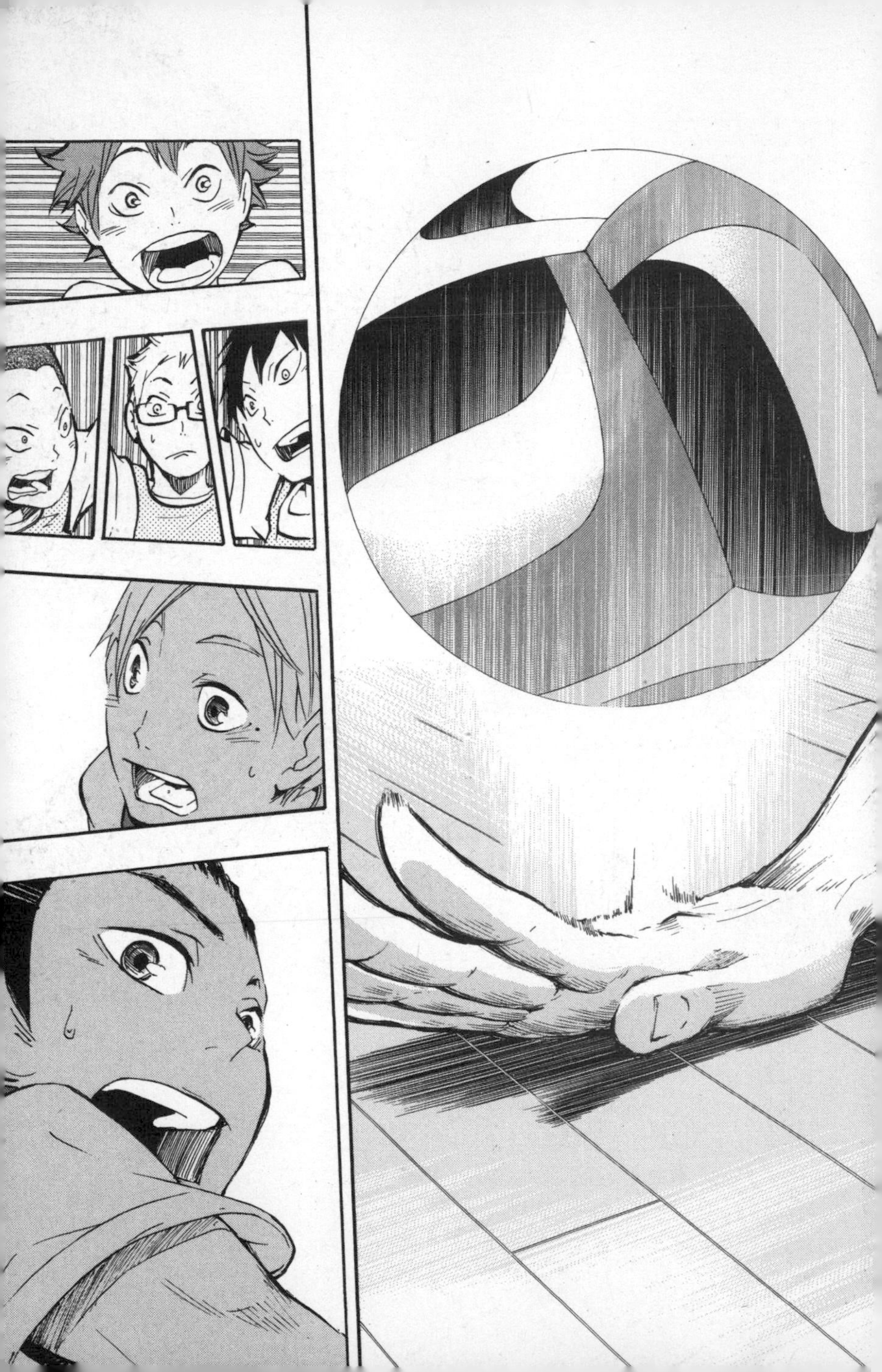

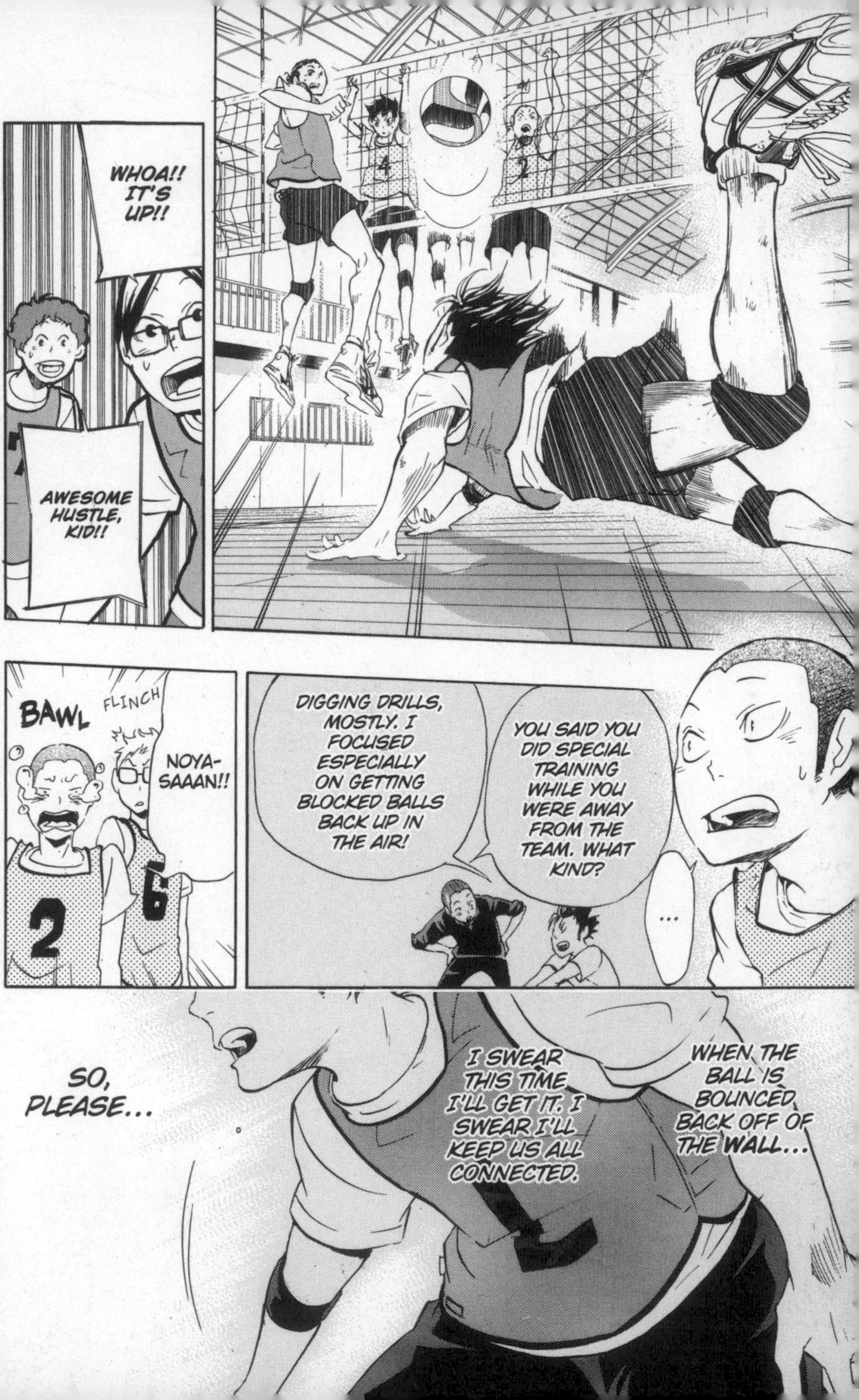
WHOA!! IT'S UP!!
AWESOME HUSTLE, KID!!
YOU SAID YOU DID SPECIAL TRAINING WHILE YOU WERE AWAY FROM THE TEAM. WHAT KIND?
DIGGING DRILLS, MOSTLY. I FOCUSED ESPECIALLY ON GETTING BLOCKED BALLS BACK UP IN THE AIR!
...
NOYA-SAAAN!!
FLINCH
BAWL
WHEN THE BALL IS BOUNCED BACK OFF OF THE WALL...
I SWEAR THIS TIME I'LL GET IT. I SWEAR I'LL KEEP US ALL CONNECTED.
SO, PLEASE...

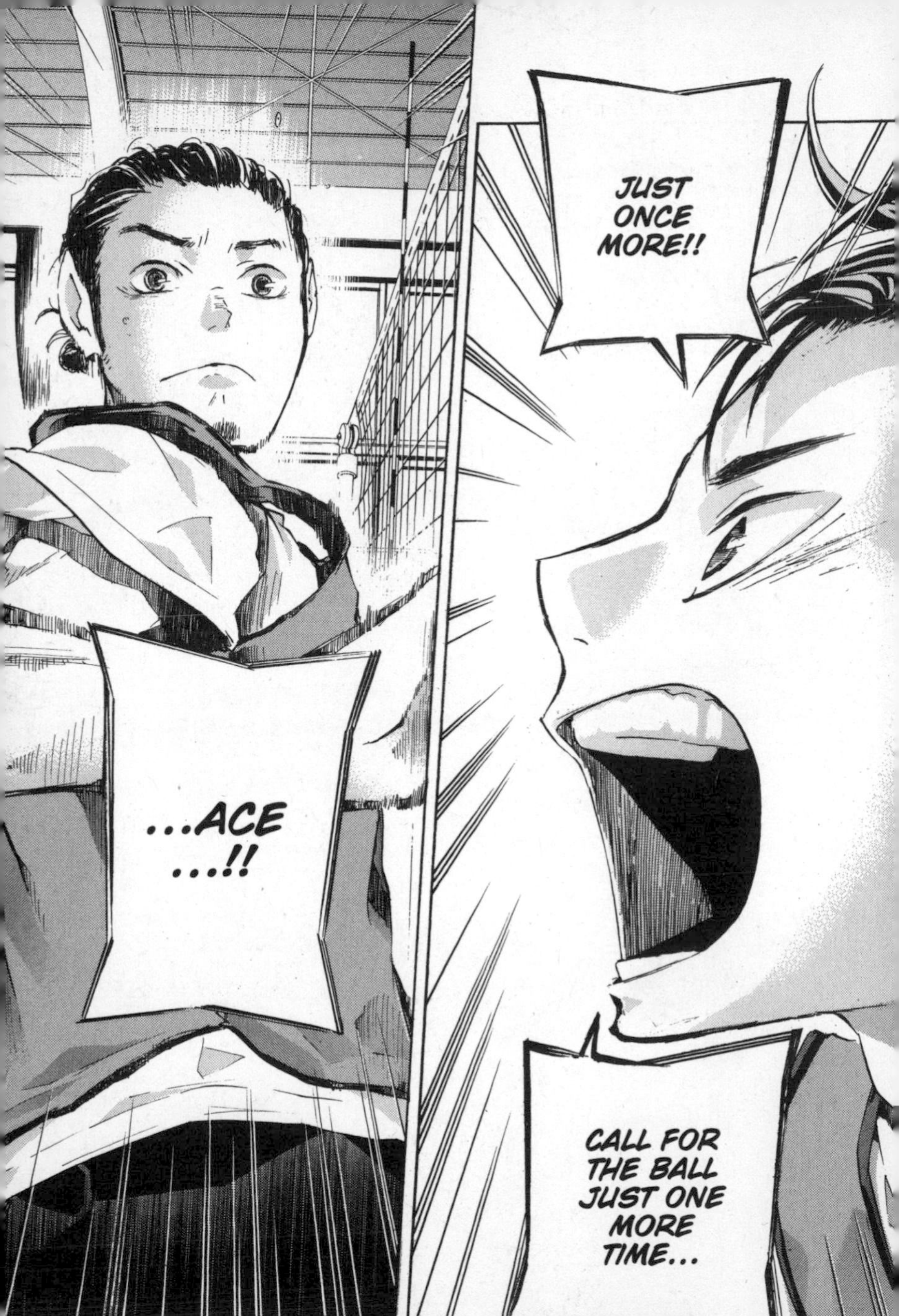
JUST ONCE MORE!!
CALL FOR THE BALL JUST ONE MORE TIME...
...ACE ...!!

MAKOTO SHIMADA
(SHIMADA MART, 26 YEARS OLD)

KARASUNO VOLLEYBALL TEAM ALUMNUS

HEIGHT: 5'10"

TODAY'S SPECIALS ARE EGGS! ONLY 99 YEN A PACK! AND PORK BELLY IS DOWN TO 98 YEN PER 100 GRAMS!

ABILITY PARAMETERS
(5-POINT SCALE)

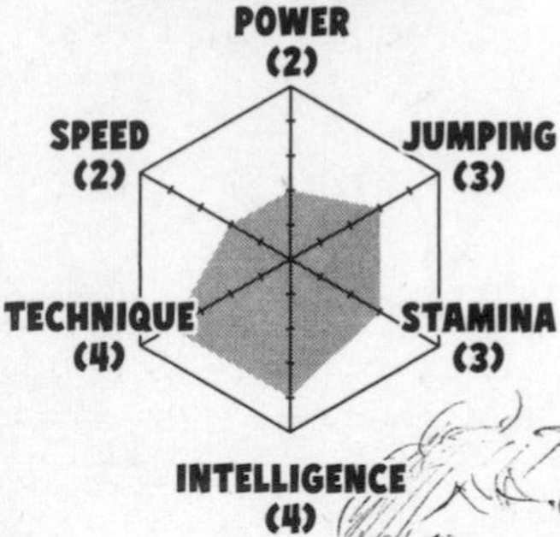
POWER (2)
JUMPING (3)
STAMINA (3)
INTELLIGENCE (4)
TECHNIQUE (4)
SPEED (2)

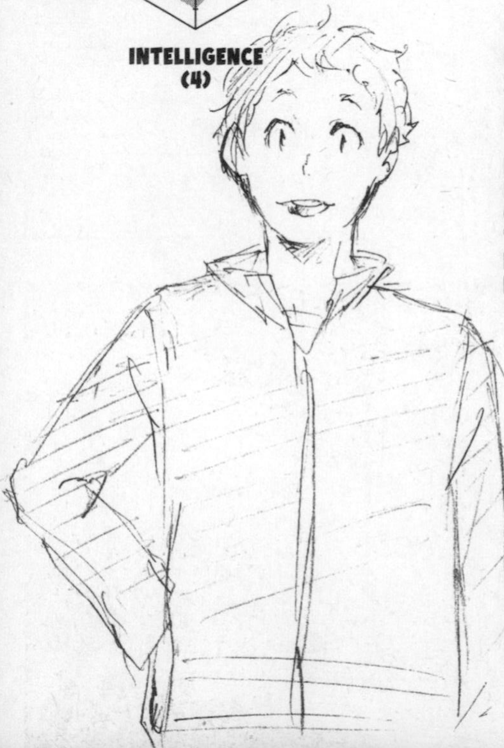

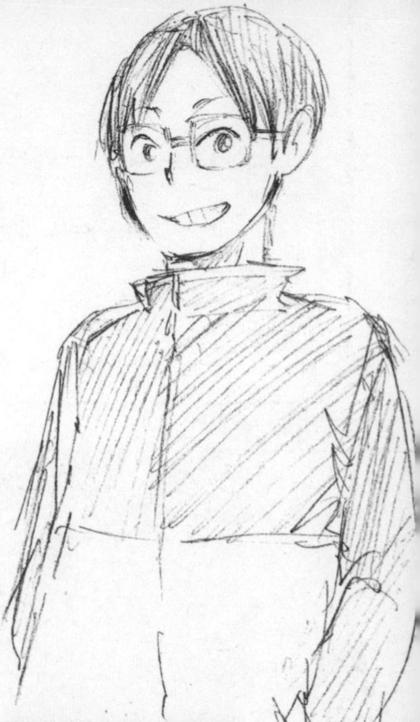

YUKINARI MORI
NORTHEASTERN BUSINESS COLLEGE 3RD YEAR

HEIGHT: 6'0"

HIS RECENT CONCERN IS HOW ALL THE OLDER GUYS ON THE MUNICIPAL TEAM ALWAYS INSIST ON DRAGGING HIM OUT TO GO DRINKING WITH THEM.

ABILITY PARAMETERS
(5-POINT SCALE)

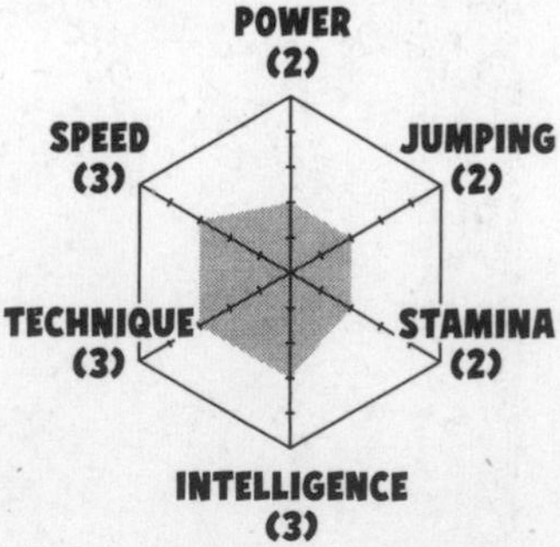
POWER (2)
JUMPING (2)
STAMINA (2)
INTELLIGENCE (3)
TECHNIQUE (3)
SPEED (3)

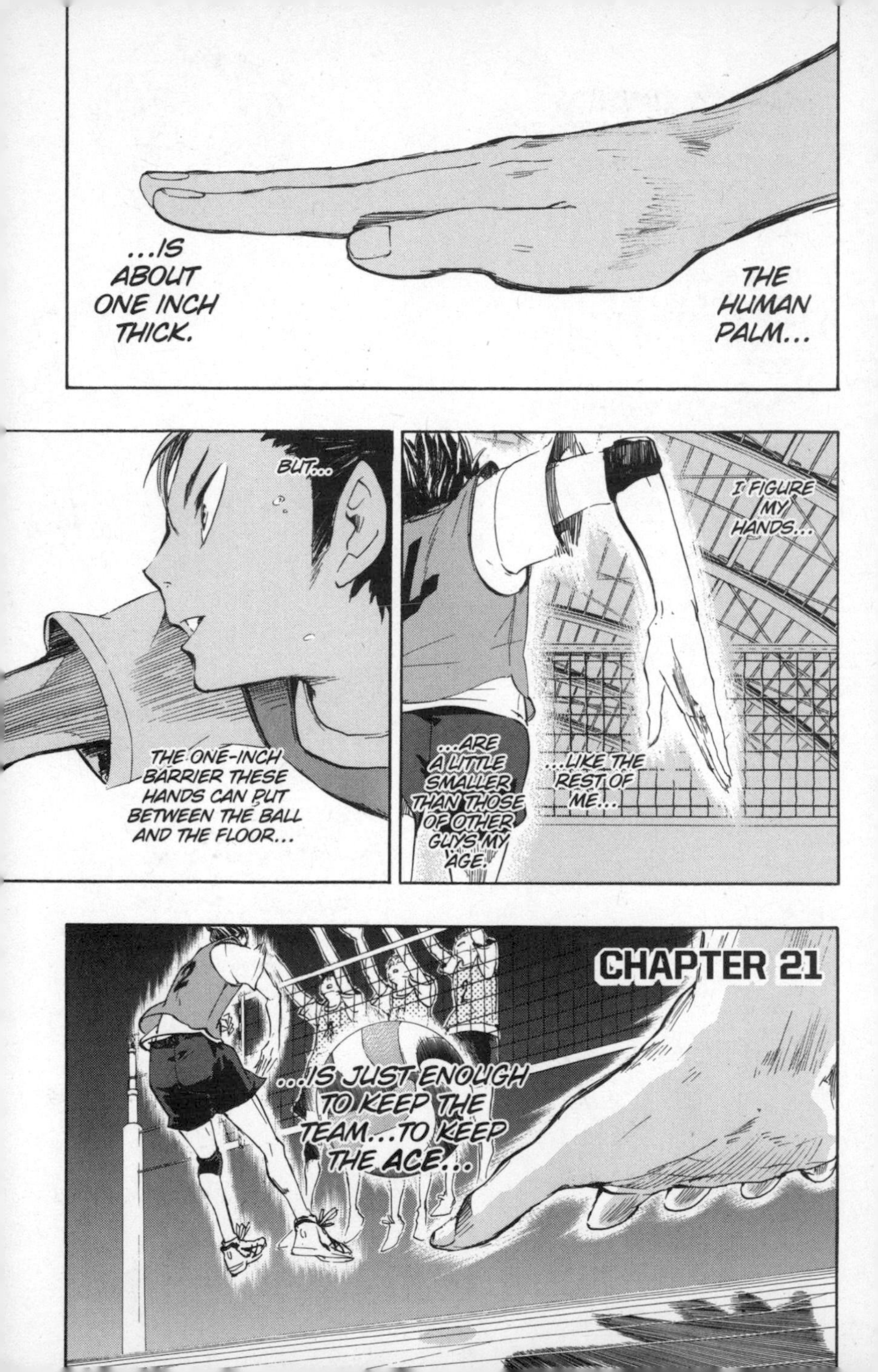
THE HUMAN PALM...
...IS ABOUT ONE INCH THICK.
I FIGURE MY HANDS...
...LIKE THE REST OF ME...
...ARE A LITTLE SMALLER THAN THOSE OF OTHER GUYS MY AGE.
BUT...
THE ONE-INCH BARRIER THESE HANDS CAN PUT BETWEEN THE BALL AND THE FLOOR...
CHAPTER 21
...IS JUST ENOUGH TO KEEP THE TEAM...TO KEEP THE ACE...

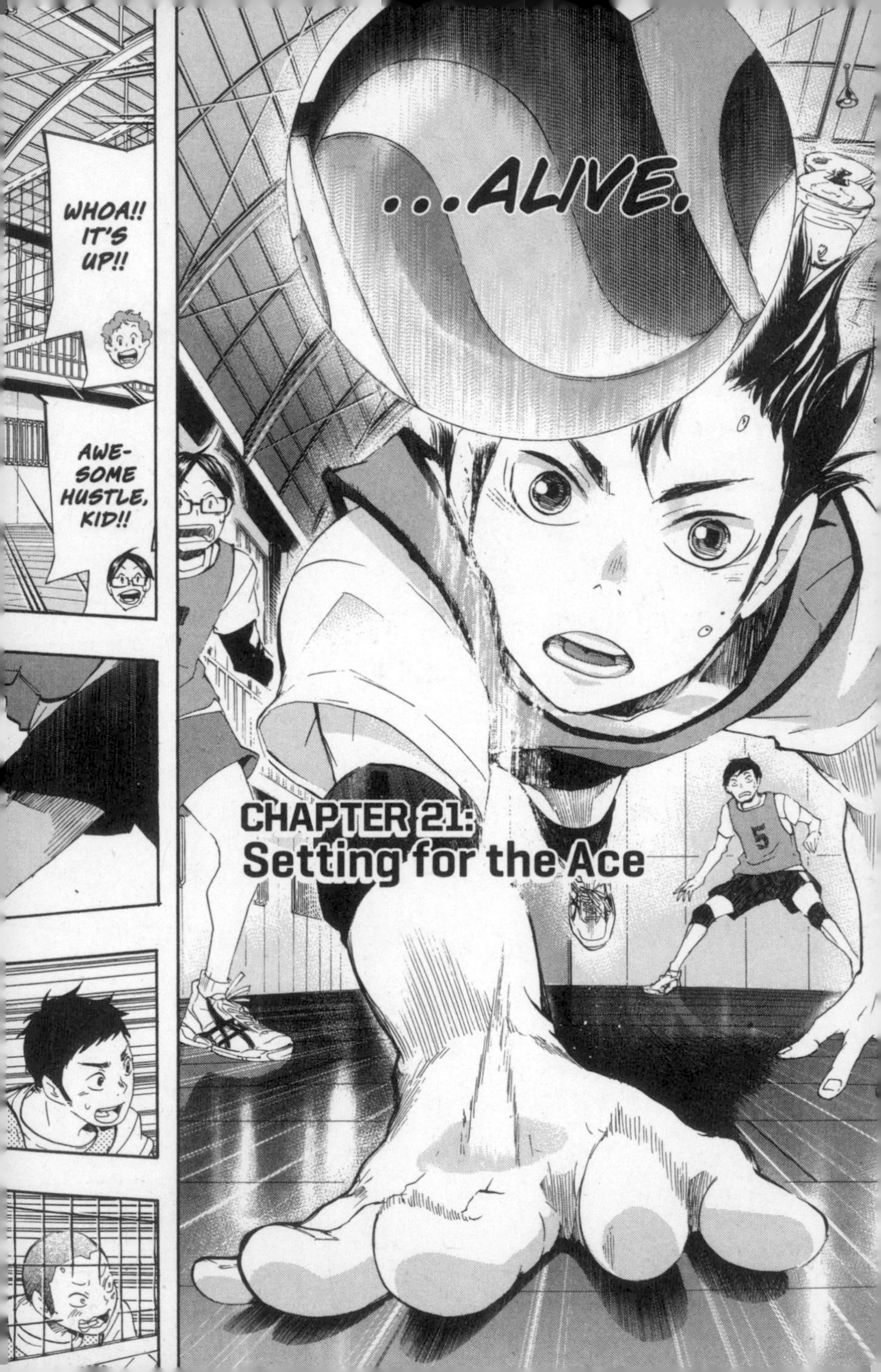
...ALIVE.
CHAPTER 21:
Setting for the Ace
WHOA!! IT'S UP!!
AWE-SOME HUSTLE, KID!!

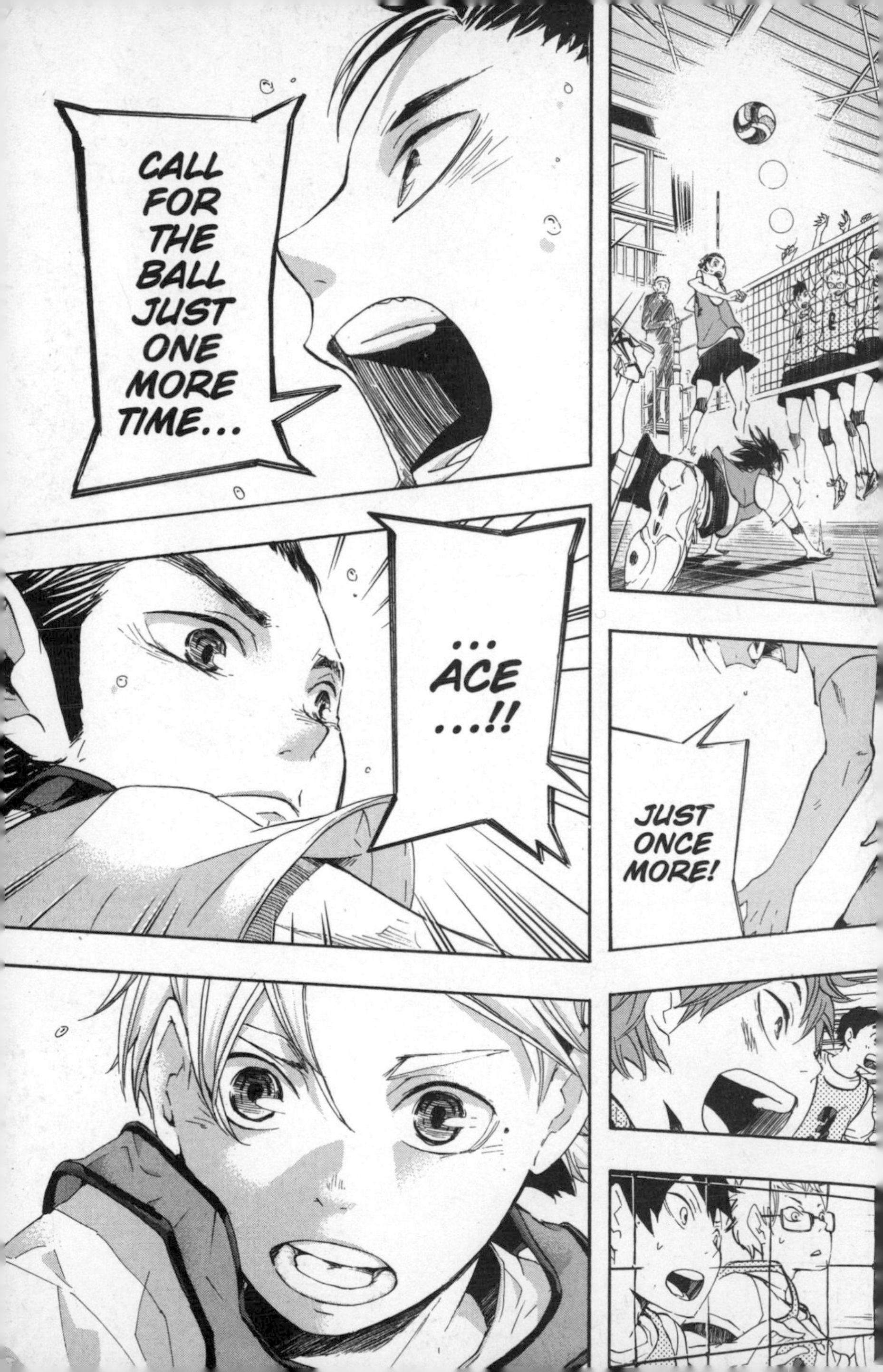
CALL FOR THE BALL JUST ONE MORE TIME...
JUST ONCE MORE!
...ACE...!!

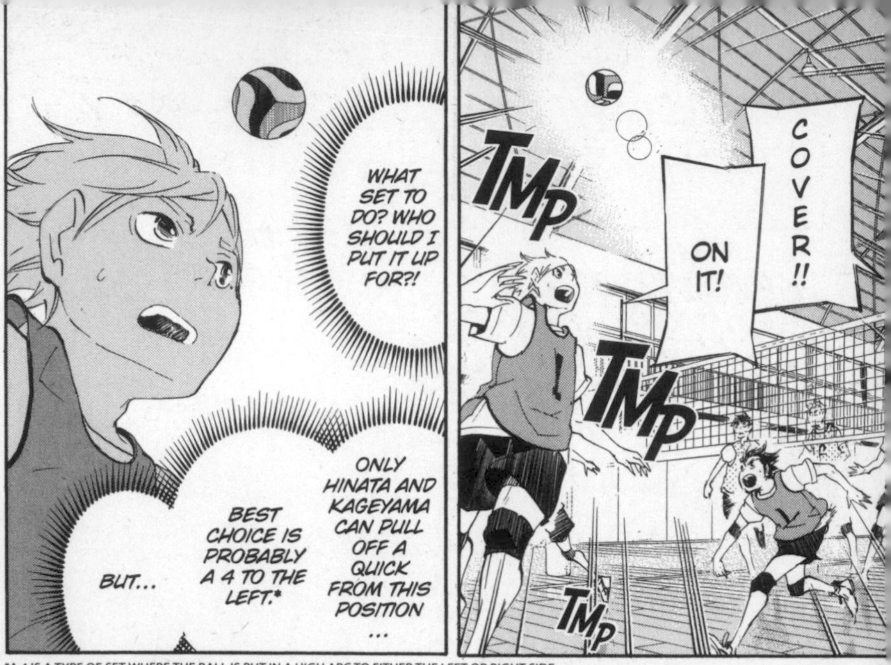
COVER!!
ON IT!
TMP
TMP
TMP
WHAT SET TO DO? WHO SHOULD I PUT IT UP FOR?!
ONLY HINATA AND KAGEYAMA CAN PULL OFF A QUICK FROM THIS POSITION ...
BEST CHOICE IS PROBABLY A 4 TO THE LEFT.*
BUT...

*A 4 IS A TYPE OF SET WHERE THE BALL IS PUT IN A HIGH ARC TO EITHER THE LEFT OR RIGHT SIDE.

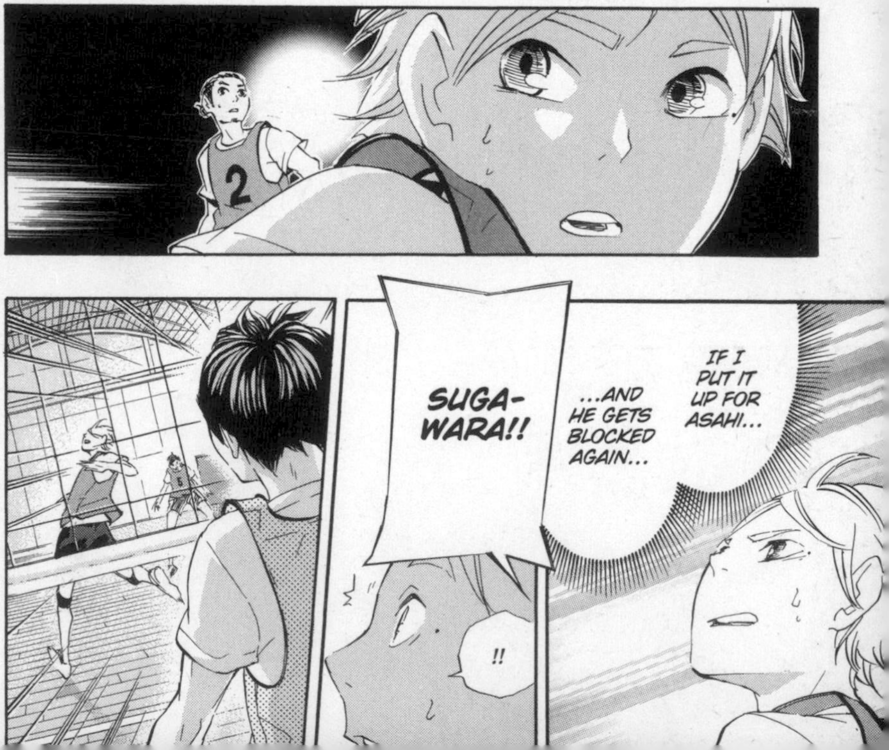
IF I PUT IT UP FOR ASAHI...
...AND HE GETS BLOCKED AGAIN...
SUGA-WARA!!
!!

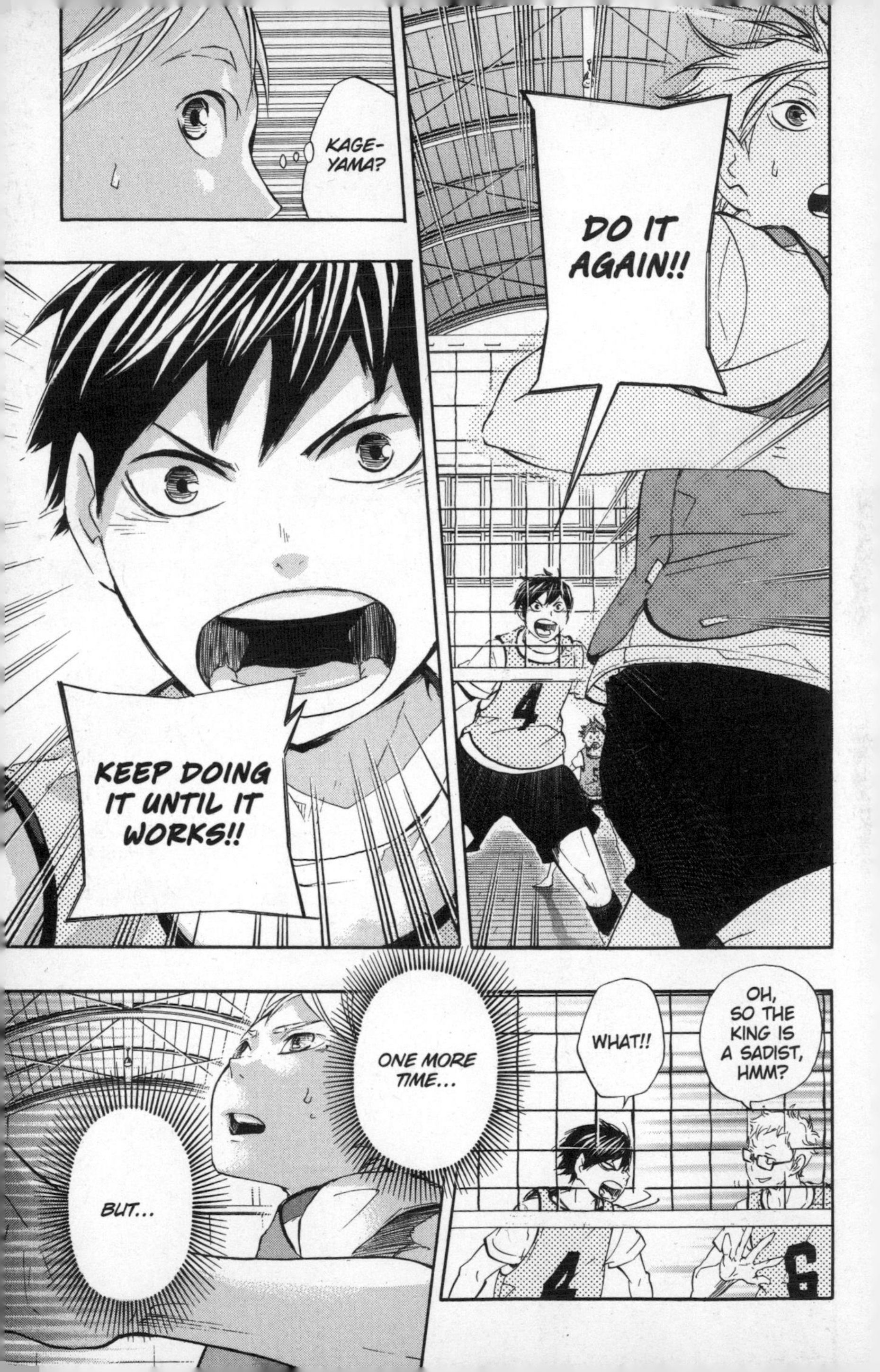
DO IT AGAIN!!
KAGE-YAMA?
KEEP DOING IT UNTIL IT WORKS!!
OH, SO THE KING IS A SADIST, HMM?
WHAT!!
ONE MORE TIME...
BUT...

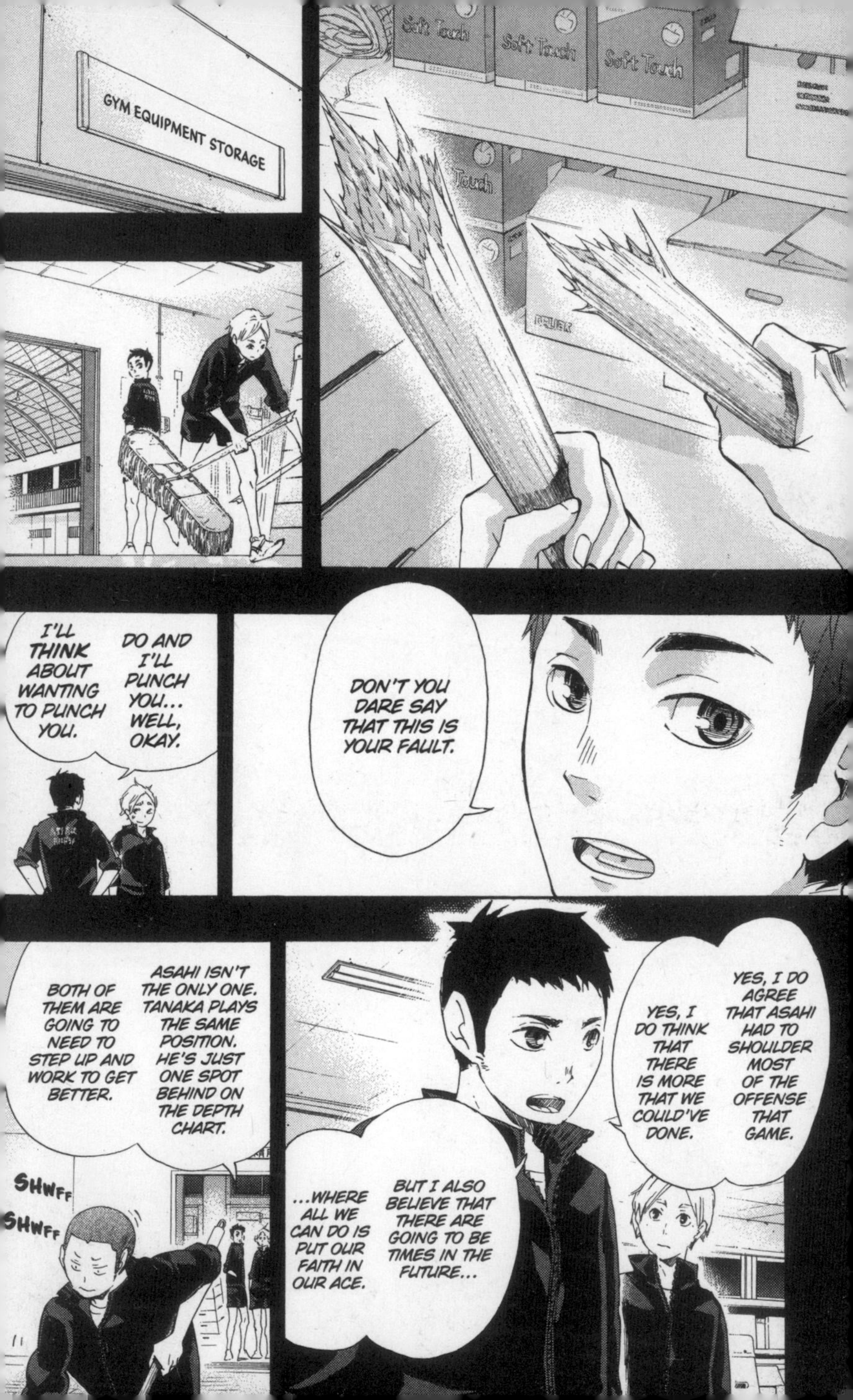
Soft Touch
Soft Touch
Soft Touch
Touch
GYM EQUIPMENT STORAGE
DON'T YOU DARE SAY THAT THIS IS YOUR FAULT.
DO AND I'LL PUNCH YOU... WELL, OKAY.
I'LL THINK ABOUT WANTING TO PUNCH YOU.
YES, I DO AGREE THAT ASAHI HAD TO SHOULDER MOST OF THE OFFENSE THAT GAME.
YES, I DO THINK THAT THERE IS MORE THAT WE COULD'VE DONE.
BUT I ALSO BELIEVE THAT THERE ARE GOING TO BE TIMES IN THE FUTURE...
...WHERE ALL WE CAN DO IS PUT OUR FAITH IN OUR ACE.
ASAHI ISN'T THE ONLY ONE. TANAKA PLAYS THE SAME POSITION. HE'S JUST ONE SPOT BEHIND ON THE DEPTH CHART.
BOTH OF THEM ARE GOING TO NEED TO STEP UP AND WORK TO GET BETTER.
SHWFF
SHWFF

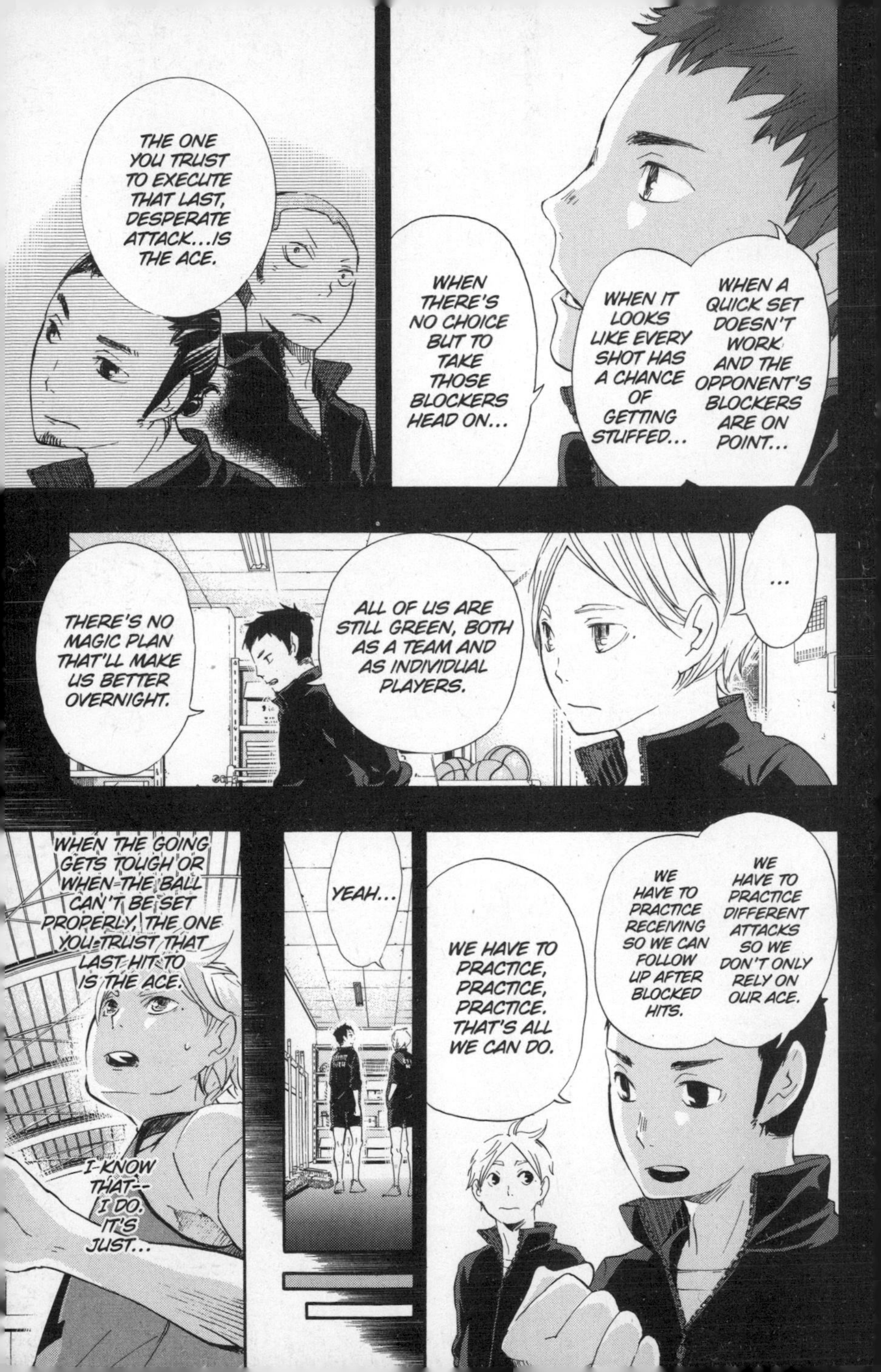
WHEN A QUICK SET DOESN'T WORK AND THE OPPONENT'S BLOCKERS ARE ON POINT...
WHEN IT LOOKS LIKE EVERY SHOT HAS A CHANCE OF GETTING STUFFED...
WHEN THERE'S NO CHOICE BUT TO TAKE THOSE BLOCKERS HEAD ON...
THE ONE YOU TRUST TO EXECUTE THAT LAST, DESPERATE ATTACK...IS THE ACE.
...
ALL OF US ARE STILL GREEN, BOTH AS A TEAM AND AS INDIVIDUAL PLAYERS.
THERE'S NO MAGIC PLAN THAT'LL MAKE US BETTER OVERNIGHT.
WE HAVE TO PRACTICE DIFFERENT ATTACKS SO WE DON'T ONLY RELY ON OUR ACE.
WE HAVE TO PRACTICE RECEIVING SO WE CAN FOLLOW UP AFTER BLOCKED HITS.
WE HAVE TO PRACTICE, PRACTICE, PRACTICE. THAT'S ALL WE CAN DO.
YEAH...
WHEN THE GOING GETS TOUGH OR WHEN THE BALL CAN'T BE SET PROPERLY, THE ONE YOU TRUST THAT LAST HIT TO IS THE ACE.
I-KNOW THAT-- I DO. IT'S JUST...

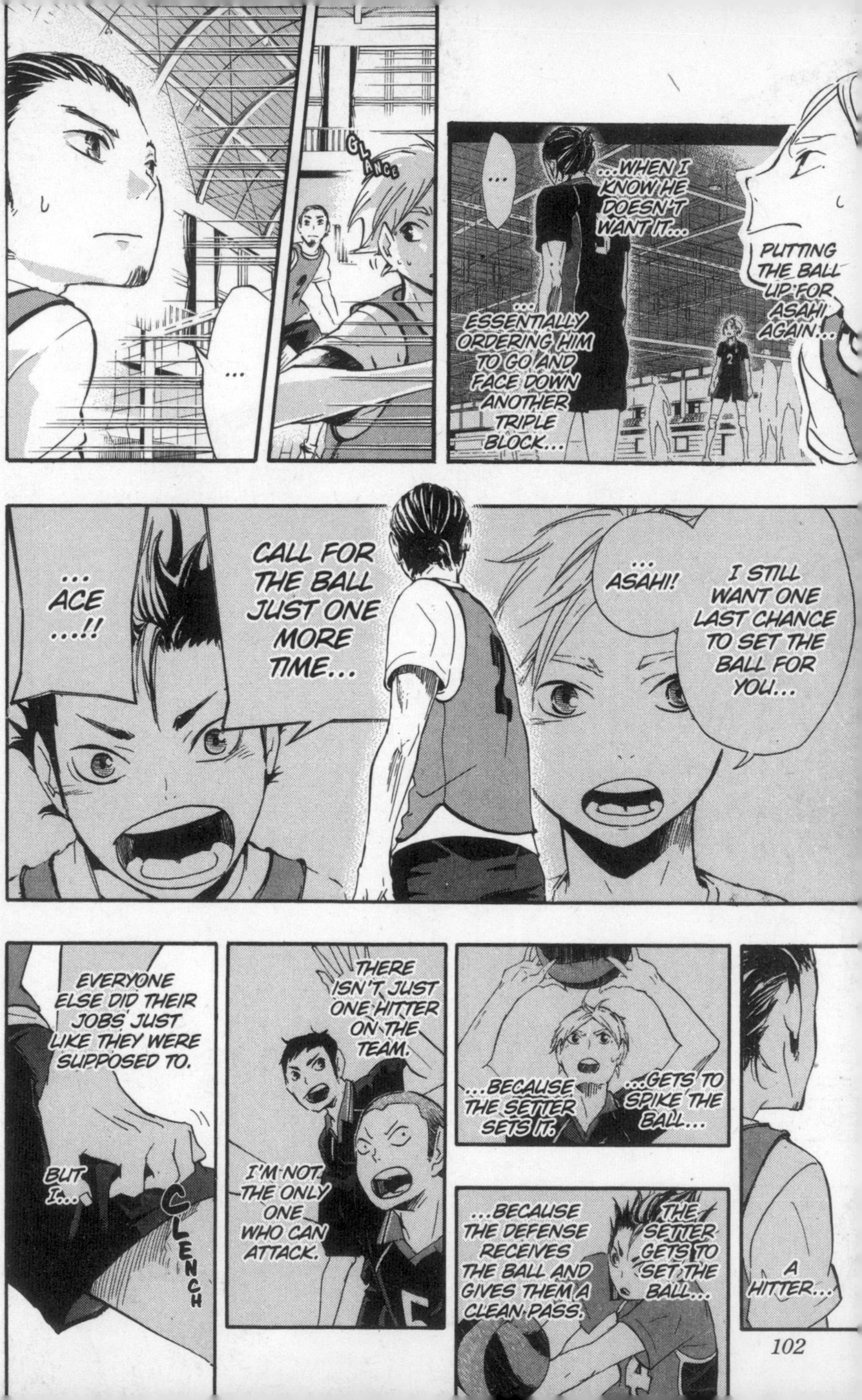
PUTTING THE BALL UP FOR ASAHI AGAIN...
...
...WHEN I KNOW HE DOESN'T WANT IT...
...ESSENTIALLY ORDERING HIM TO GO AND FACE DOWN ANOTHER TRIPLE BLOCK...
GLANCE
...
I STILL WANT ONE LAST CHANCE TO SET THE BALL FOR YOU...
...ASAHI!
CALL FOR THE BALL JUST ONE MORE TIME...
...ACE ...!!
A HITTER...
...GETS TO SPIKE THE BALL...
...BECAUSE THE SETTER SETS IT.
THE SETTER GETS TO SET THE BALL...
...BECAUSE THE DEFENSE RECEIVES THE BALL AND GIVES THEM A CLEAN PASS.
THERE ISN'T JUST ONE HITTER ON THE TEAM.
I'M NOT THE ONLY ONE WHO CAN ATTACK.
EVERYONE ELSE DID THEIR JOBS JUST LIKE THEY WERE SUPPOSED TO.
BUT I...
CLENCH

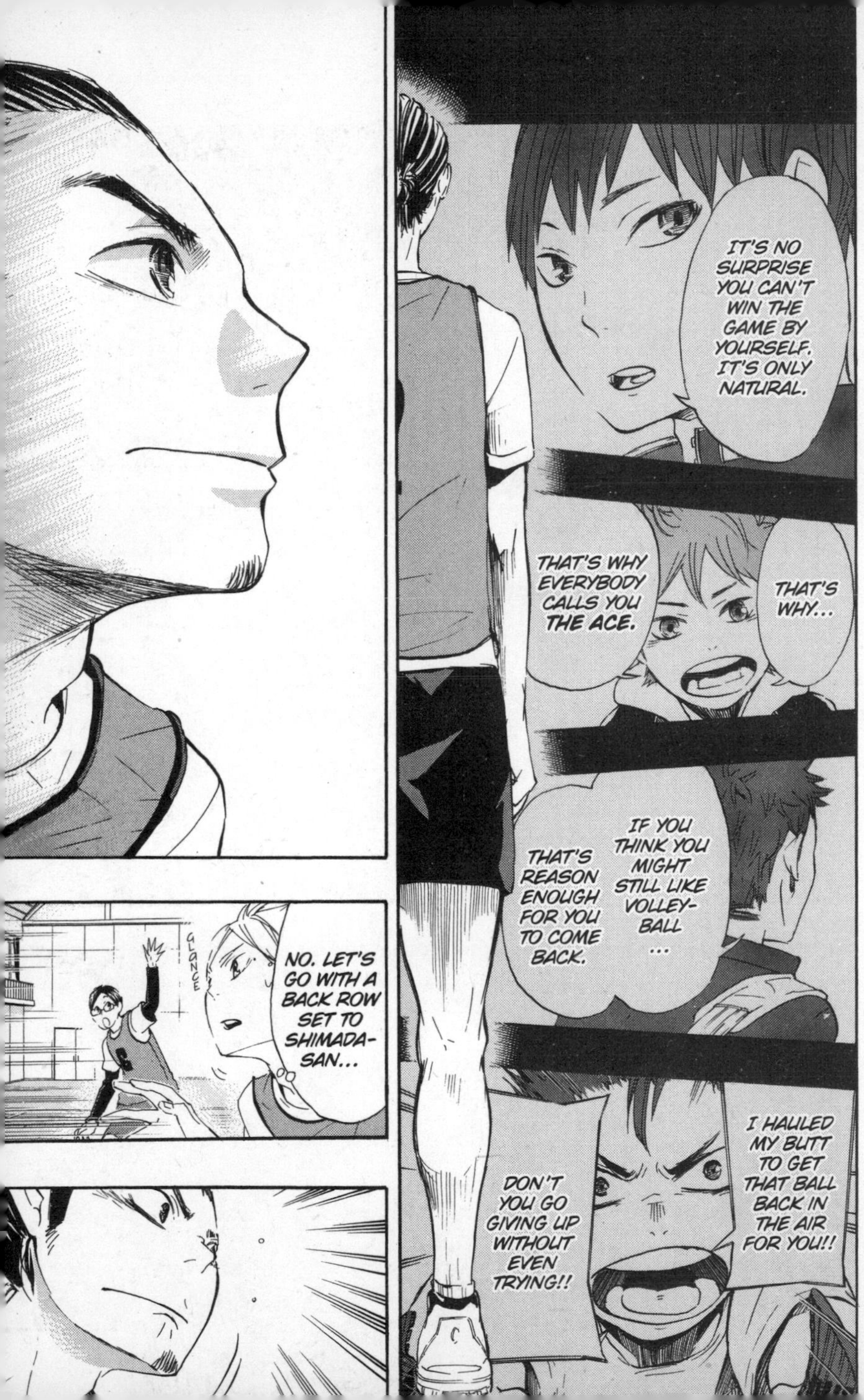
IT'S NO SURPRISE YOU CAN'T WIN THE GAME BY YOURSELF. IT'S ONLY NATURAL.
THAT'S WHY...
THAT'S WHY EVERYBODY CALLS YOU THE ACE.
IF YOU THINK YOU MIGHT STILL LIKE VOLLEY-BALL ...
THAT'S REASON ENOUGH FOR YOU TO COME BACK.
I HAULED MY BUTT TO GET THAT BALL BACK IN THE AIR FOR YOU!!
DON'T YOU GO GIVING UP WITHOUT EVEN TRYING!!
GLANCE
NO. LET'S GO WITH A BACK ROW SET TO SHIMADA-SAN...

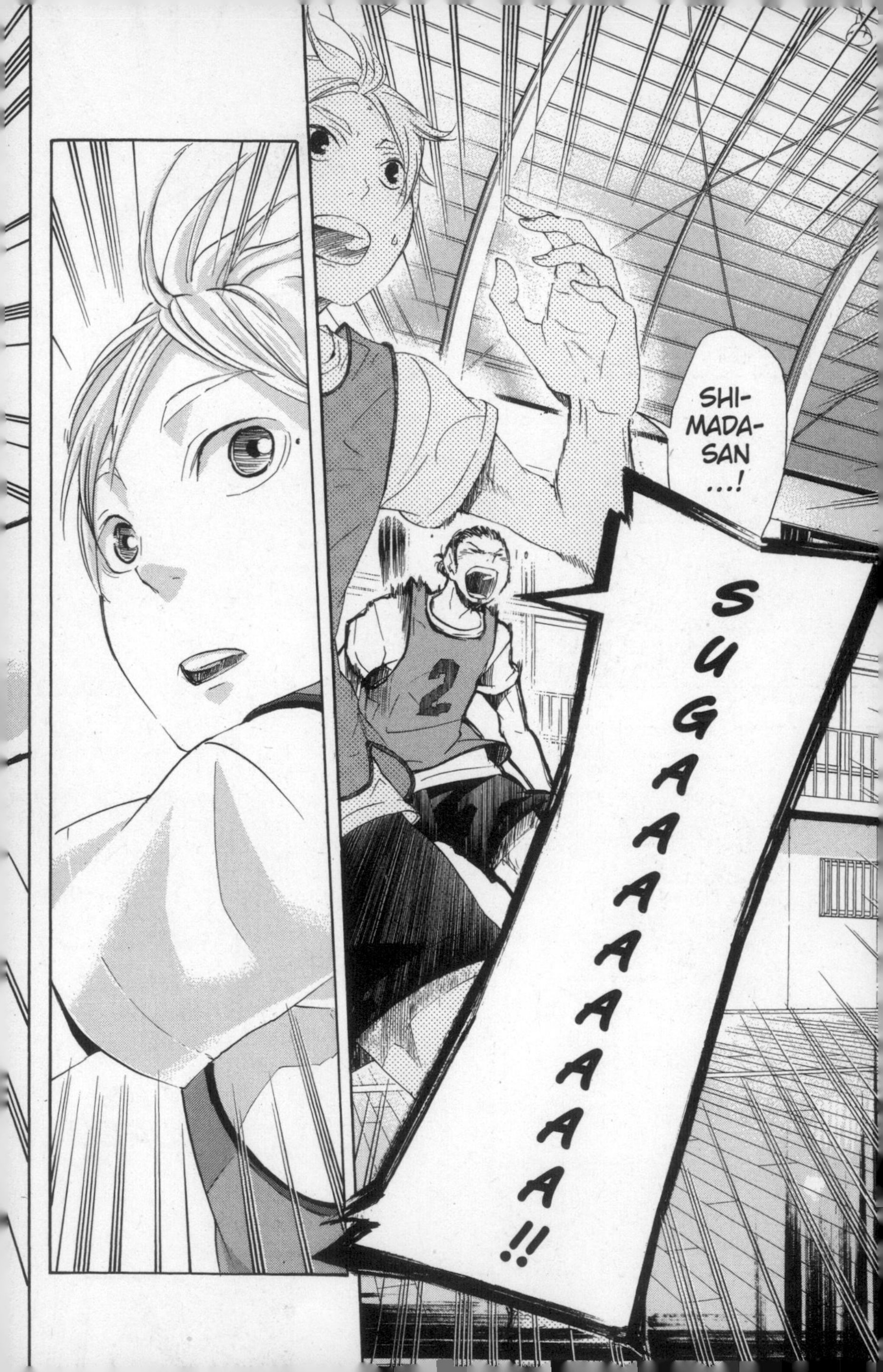
SHI-MADA-SAN ...!
SUGAAAAAAAAAAA!!

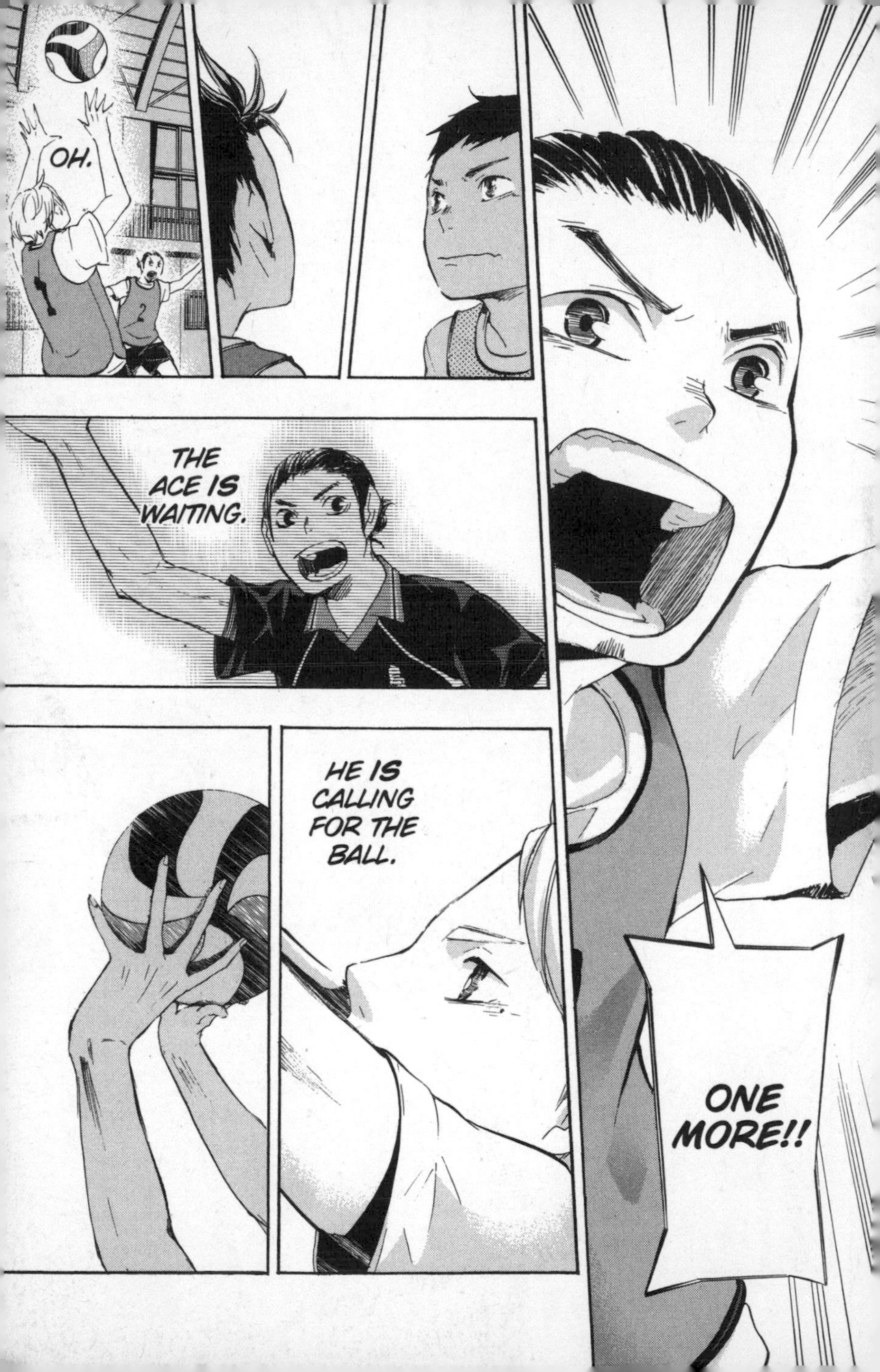
ONE MORE!!
OH.
THE ACE IS WAITING.
HE IS CALLING FOR THE BALL.

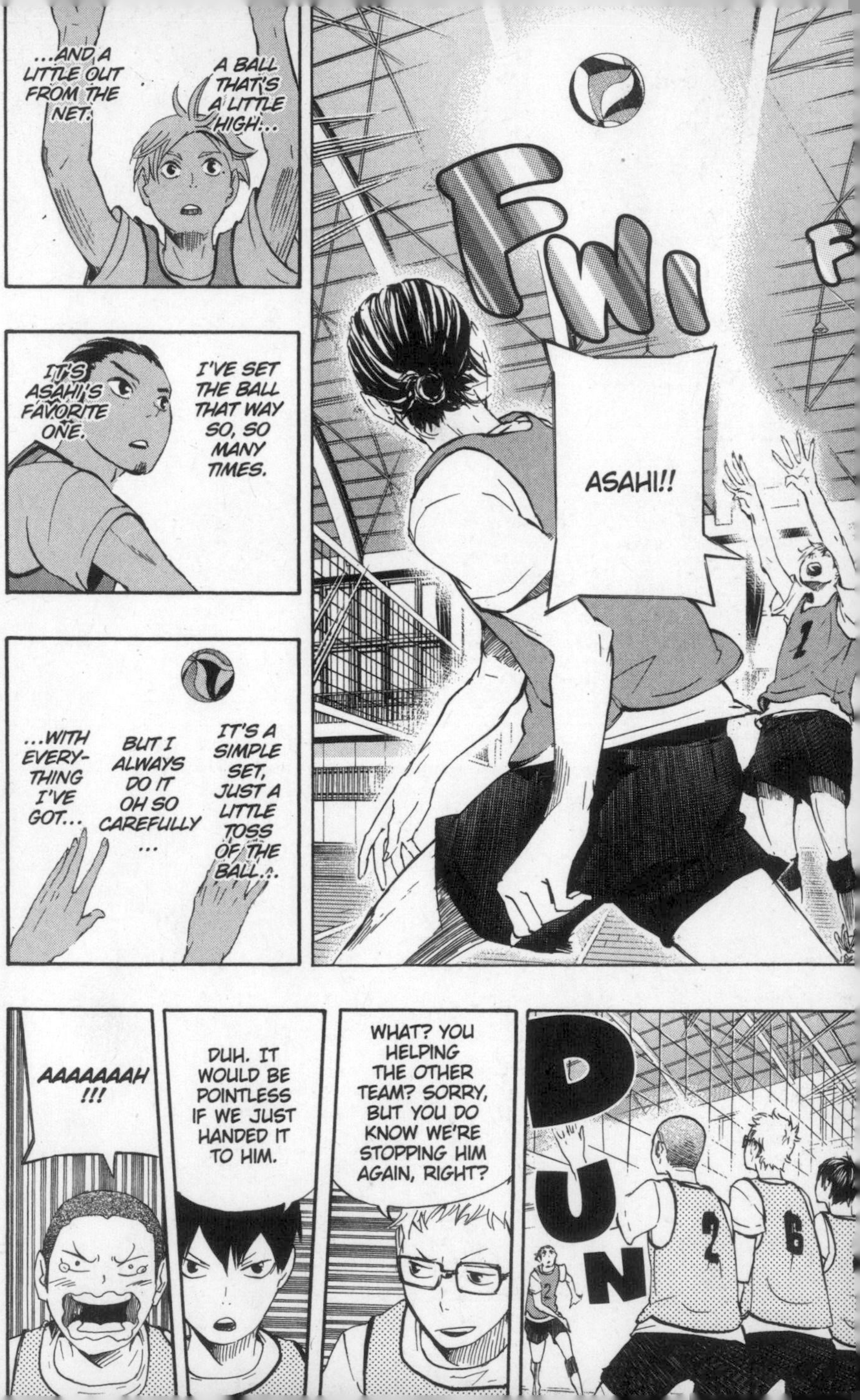
F
FWI
ASAHI!!
A BALL THAT'S A LITTLE HIGH...
...AND A LITTLE OUT FROM THE NET.
I'VE SET THE BALL THAT WAY SO, SO MANY TIMES.
IT'S ASAHI'S FAVORITE ONE.
IT'S A SIMPLE SET, JUST A LITTLE TOSS OF THE BALL...
BUT I ALWAYS DO IT OH SO CAREFULLY...
...WITH EVERYTHING I'VE GOT...
DUN
WHAT? YOU HELPING THE OTHER TEAM? SORRY, BUT YOU DO KNOW WE'RE STOPPING HIM AGAIN, RIGHT?
DUH. IT WOULD BE POINTLESS IF WE JUST HANDED IT TO HIM.
AAAAAAAH!!!

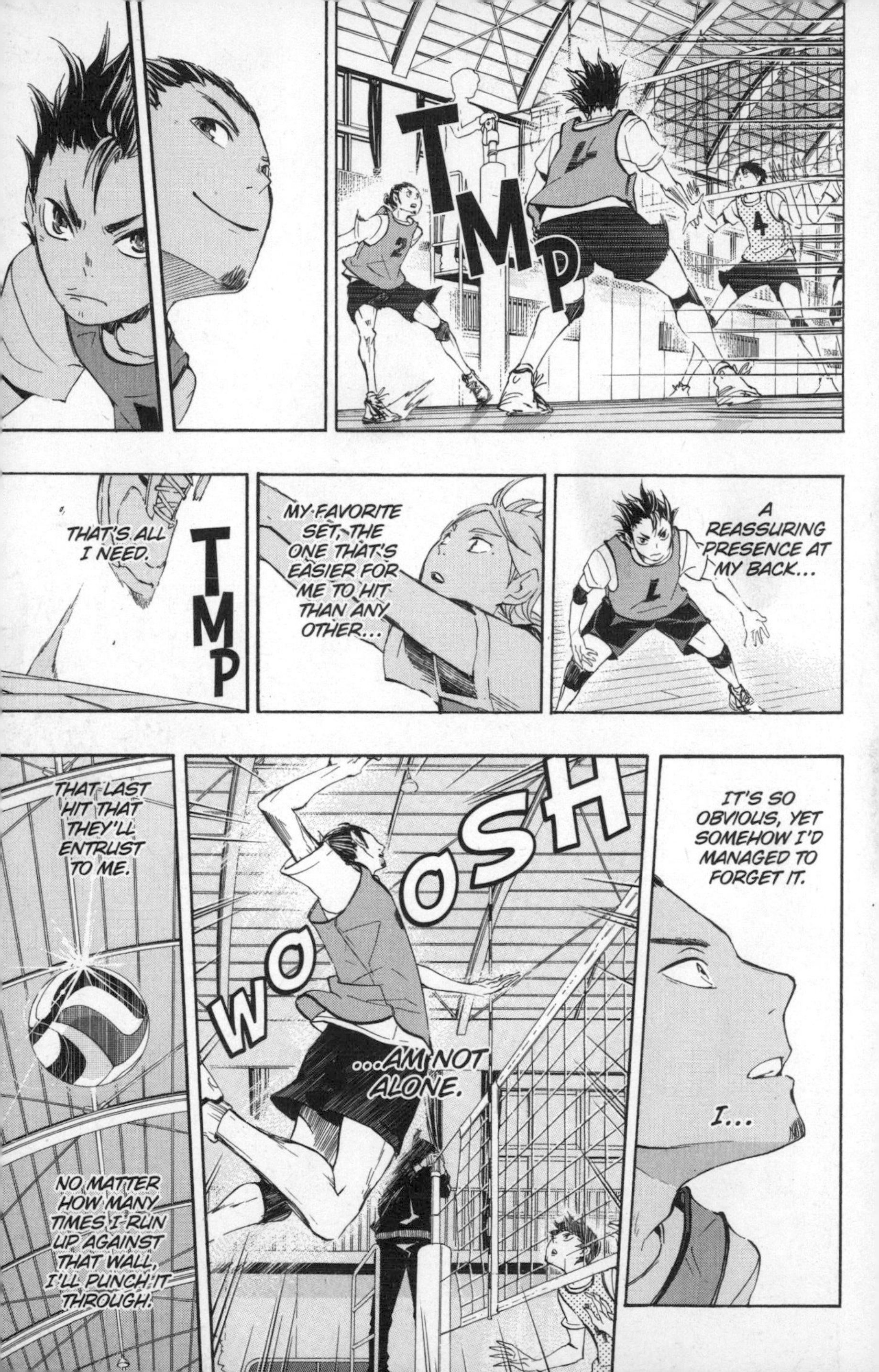
TMP
A REASSURING PRESENCE AT MY BACK...
MY FAVORITE SET, THE ONE THAT'S EASIER FOR ME TO HIT THAN ANY OTHER...
THAT'S ALL I NEED.
TMP
IT'S SO OBVIOUS, YET SOMEHOW I'D MANAGED TO FORGET IT.
I...
WOOSH
...AM NOT ALONE.
THAT LAST HIT THAT THEY'LL ENTRUST TO ME.
NO MATTER HOW MANY TIMES I RUN UP AGAINST THAT WALL, I'LL PUNCH IT THROUGH.

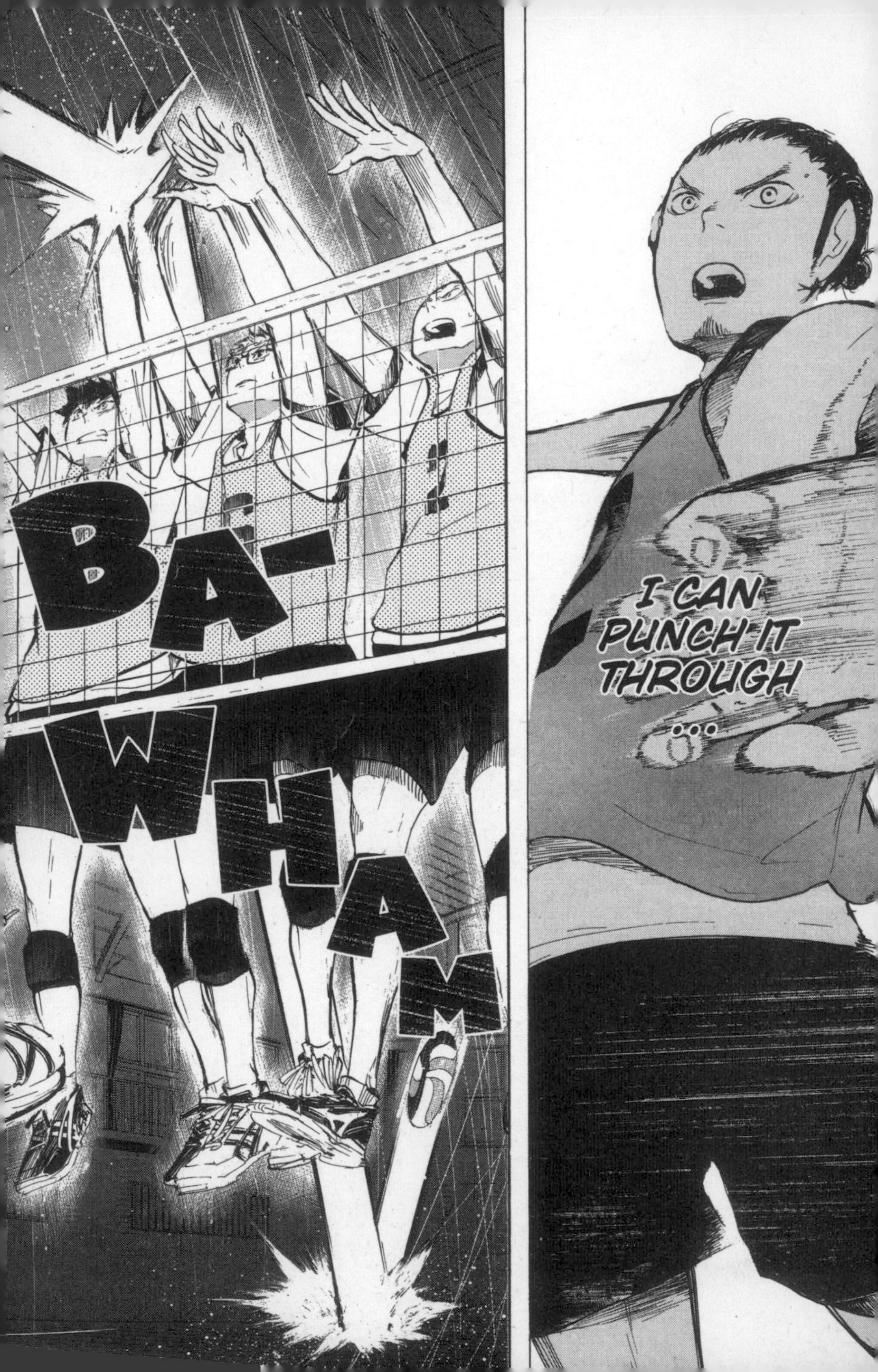
I CAN PUNCH IT THROUGH ...
BA-WHAM

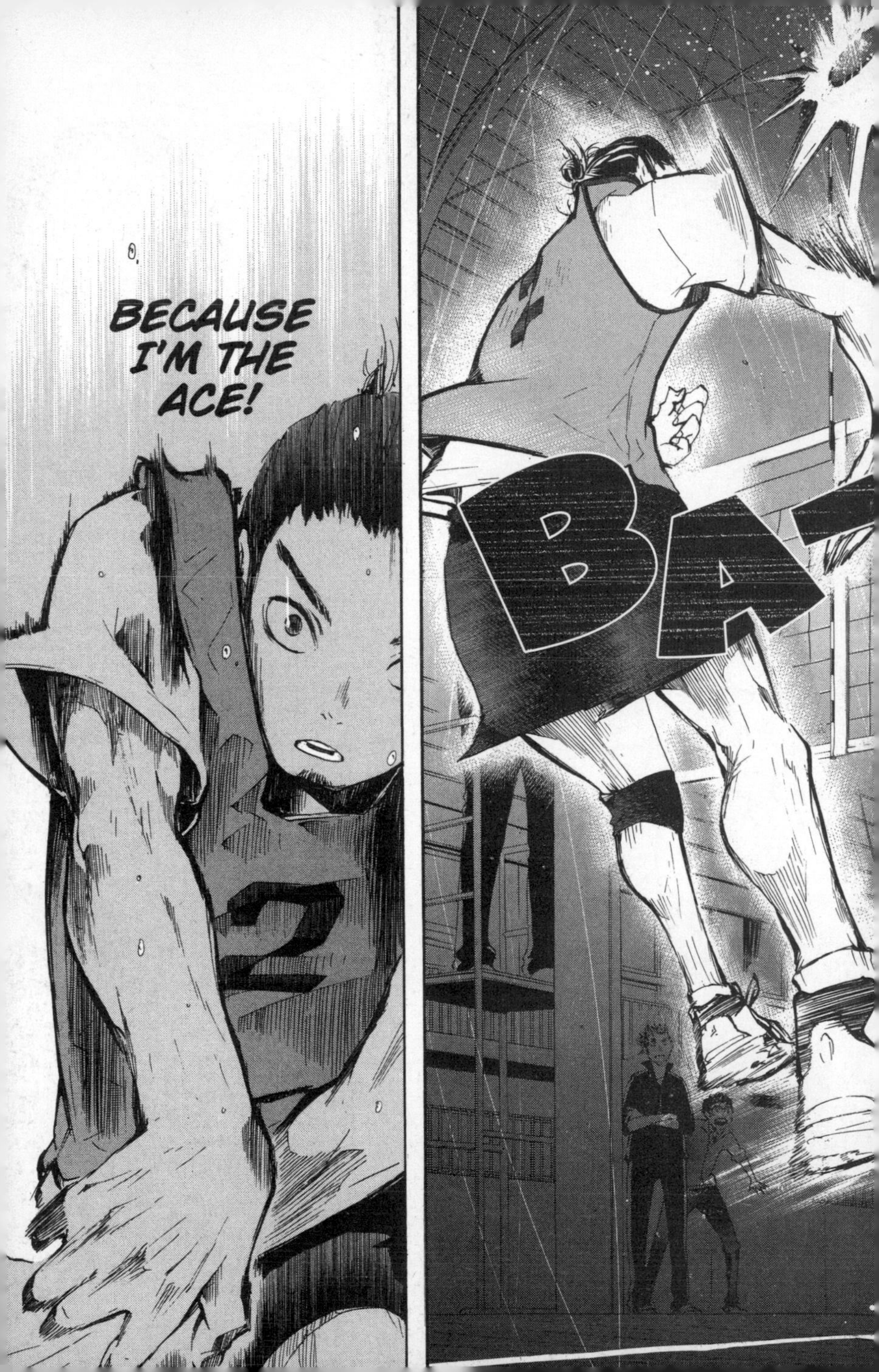
BA
BECAUSE I'M THE ACE!

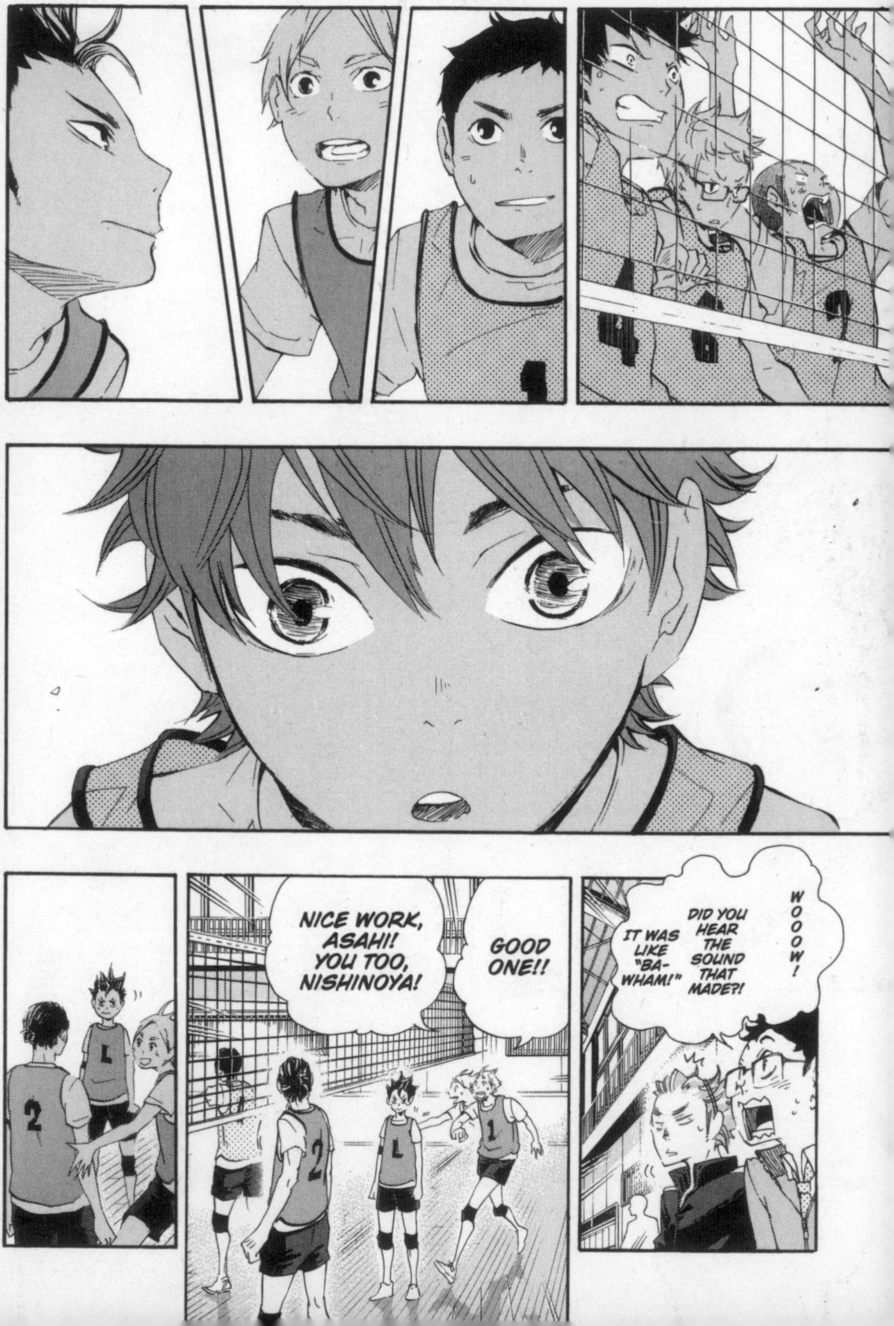
WOOOOW!
DID YOU HEAR THE SOUND THAT MADE?!
IT WAS LIKE "BA-WHAM!"
GOOD ONE!!
NICE WORK, ASAHI! YOU TOO, NISHINOYA!

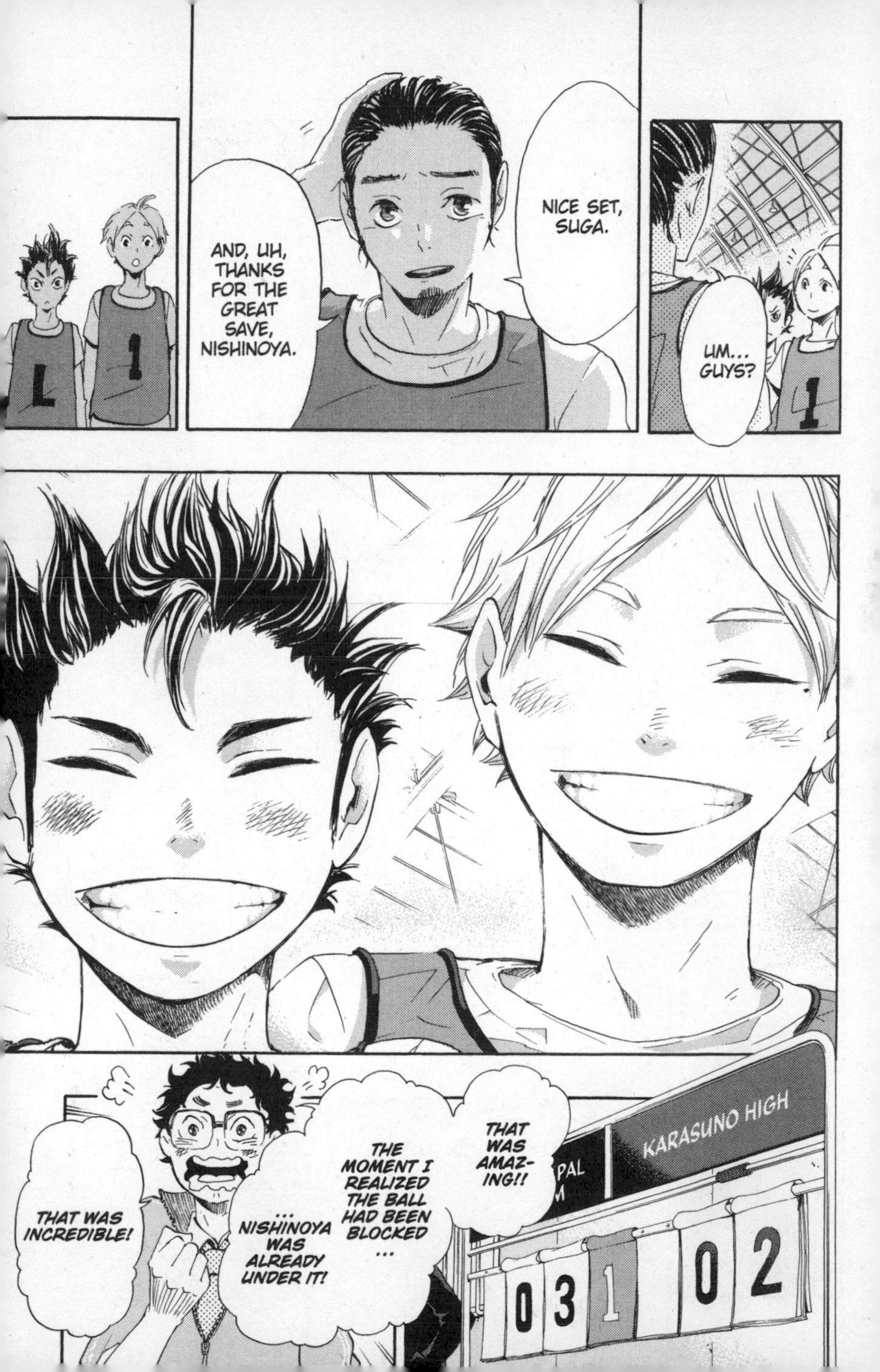
UM... GUYS?
NICE SET, SUGA.
AND, UH, THANKS FOR THE GREAT SAVE, NISHINOYA.
THAT WAS AMAZ-ING!!
THE MOMENT I REALIZED THE BALL HAD BEEN BLOCKED ...
... NISHINOYA WAS ALREADY UNDER IT!
THAT WAS INCREDIBLE!
KARASUNO HIGH
03 1 02

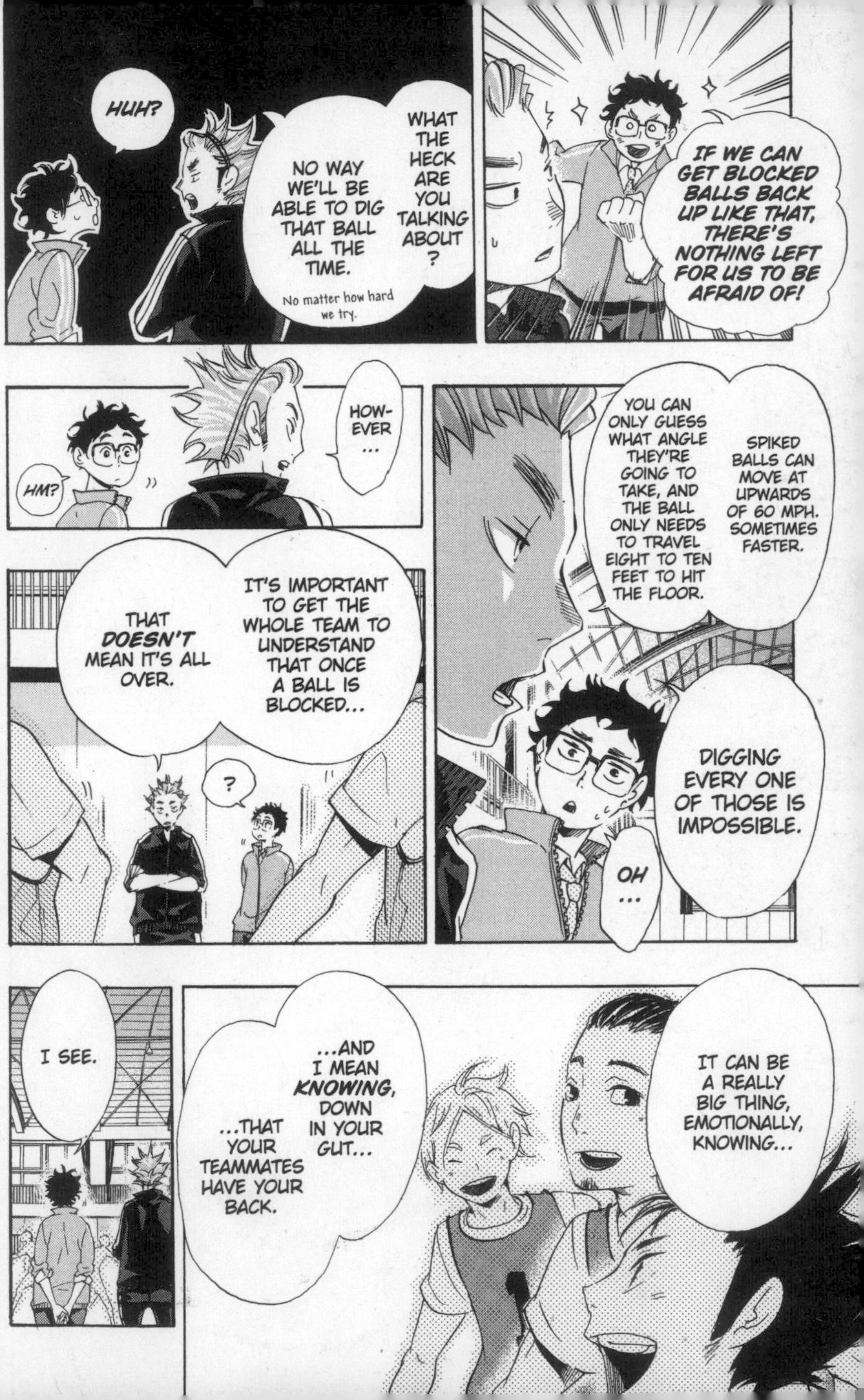

IF WE CAN GET BLOCKED BALLS BACK UP LIKE THAT, THERE'S NOTHING LEFT FOR US TO BE AFRAID OF!
WHAT THE HECK ARE YOU TALKING ABOUT?
NO WAY WE'LL BE ABLE TO DIG THAT BALL ALL THE TIME.
No matter how hard we try.
HUH?
HOW-EVER...
HM?
SPIKED BALLS CAN MOVE AT UPWARDS OF 60 MPH. SOMETIMES FASTER.
YOU CAN ONLY GUESS WHAT ANGLE THEY'RE GOING TO TAKE, AND THE BALL ONLY NEEDS TO TRAVEL EIGHT TO TEN FEET TO HIT THE FLOOR.
DIGGING EVERY ONE OF THOSE IS IMPOSSIBLE.
OH...
IT'S IMPORTANT TO GET THE WHOLE TEAM TO UNDERSTAND THAT ONCE A BALL IS BLOCKED...
THAT DOESN'T MEAN IT'S ALL OVER.
?
IT CAN BE A REALLY BIG THING, EMOTIONALLY, KNOWING...
...AND I MEAN KNOWING, DOWN IN YOUR GUT...
...THAT YOUR TEAMMATES HAVE YOUR BACK.
I SEE.

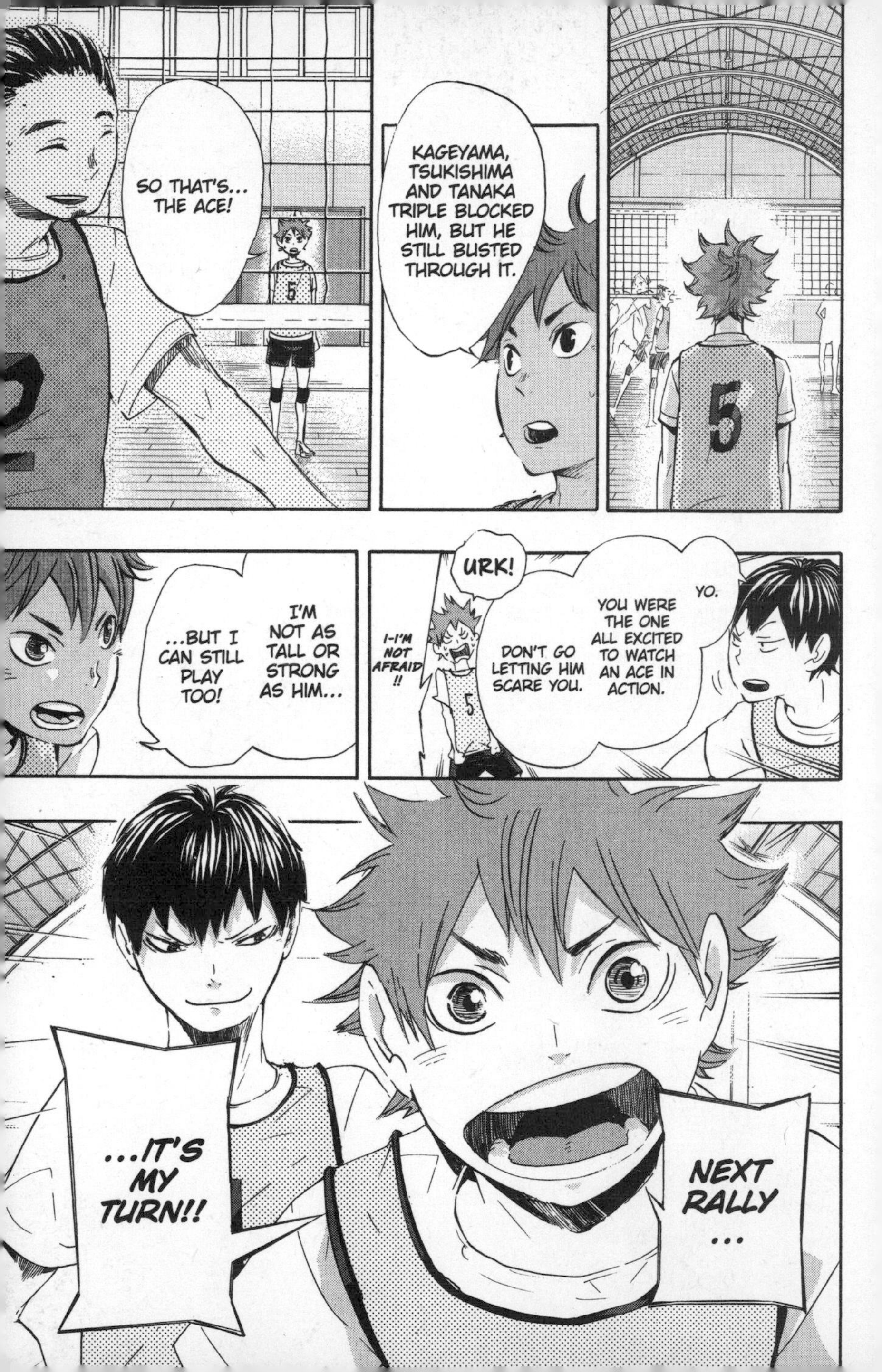
KAGEYAMA, TSUKISHIMA AND TANAKA TRIPLE BLOCKED HIM, BUT HE STILL BUSTED THROUGH IT.
SO THAT'S... THE ACE!
YO.
YOU WERE THE ONE ALL EXCITED TO WATCH AN ACE IN ACTION.
DON'T GO LETTING HIM SCARE YOU.
URK!
I-I'M NOT AFRAID!!
I'M NOT AS TALL OR STRONG AS HIM...
...BUT I CAN STILL PLAY TOO!
NEXT RALLY...
...IT'S MY TURN!!

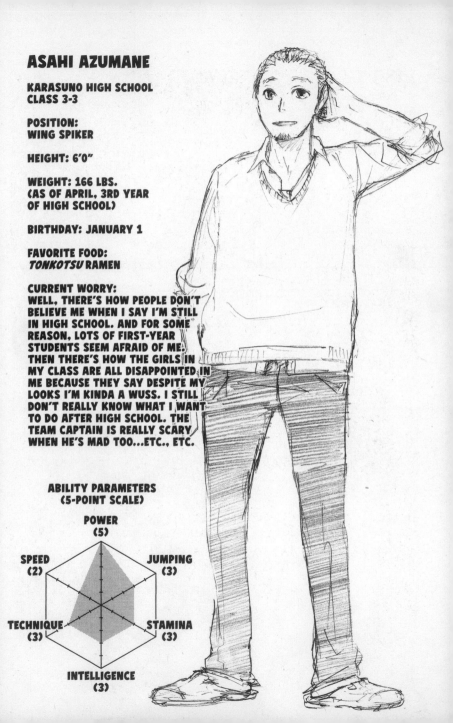

ASAHI AZUMANE

KARASUNO HIGH SCHOOL
CLASS 3-3

POSITION:
WING SPIKER

HEIGHT: 6'0"

WEIGHT: 166 LBS.
(AS OF APRIL, 3RD YEAR OF HIGH SCHOOL)

BIRTHDAY: JANUARY 1

FAVORITE FOOD:
***TONKOTSU* RAMEN**

CURRENT WORRY:
WELL, THERE'S HOW PEOPLE DON'T BELIEVE ME WHEN I SAY I'M STILL IN HIGH SCHOOL. AND FOR SOME REASON, LOTS OF FIRST-YEAR STUDENTS SEEM AFRAID OF ME. THEN THERE'S HOW THE GIRLS IN MY CLASS ARE ALL DISAPPOINTED IN ME BECAUSE THEY SAY DESPITE MY LOOKS I'M KINDA A WUSS. I STILL DON'T REALLY KNOW WHAT I WANT TO DO AFTER HIGH SCHOOL. THE TEAM CAPTAIN IS REALLY SCARY WHEN HE'S MAD TOO...ETC., ETC.

ABILITY PARAMETERS
(5-POINT SCALE)

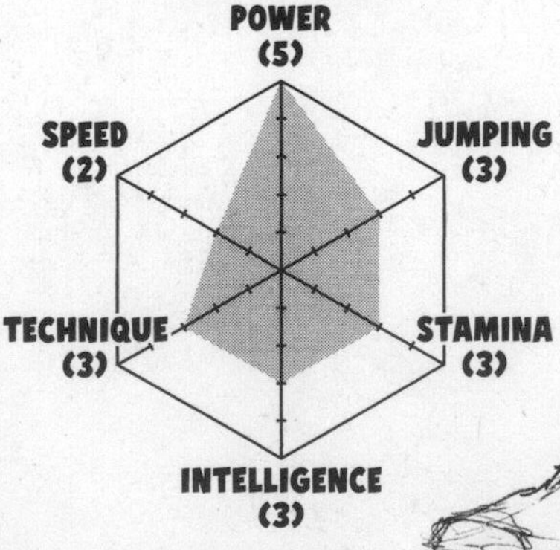
POWER (5)
JUMPING (3)
STAMINA (3)
INTELLIGENCE (3)
TECHNIQUE (3)
SPEED (2)

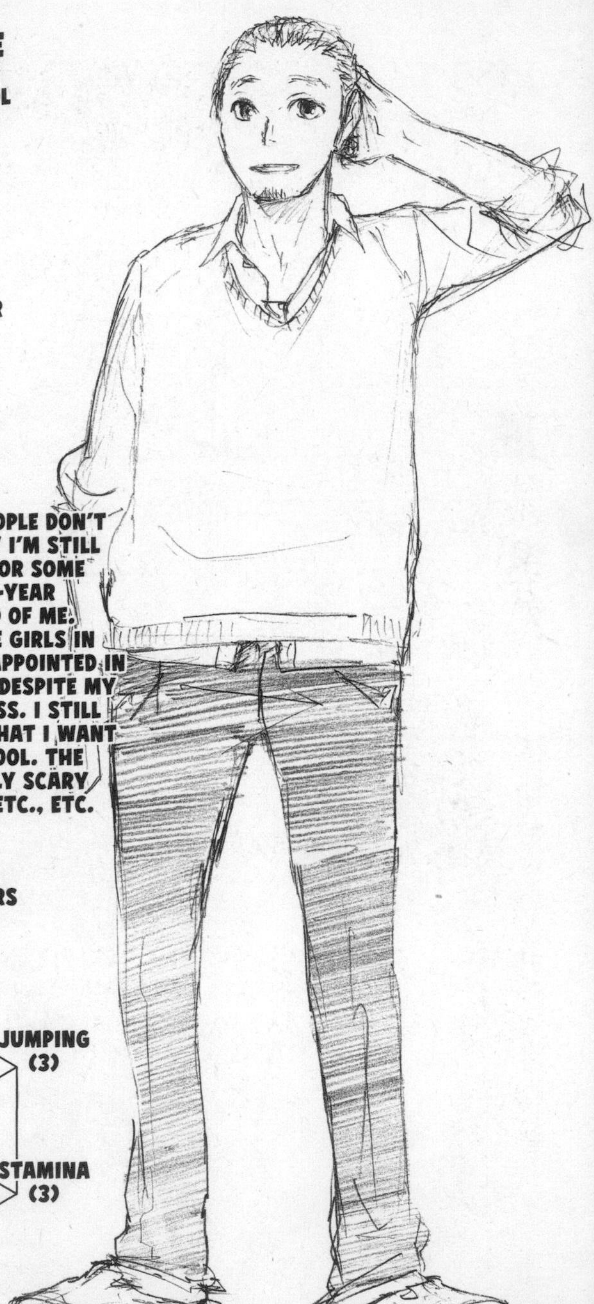

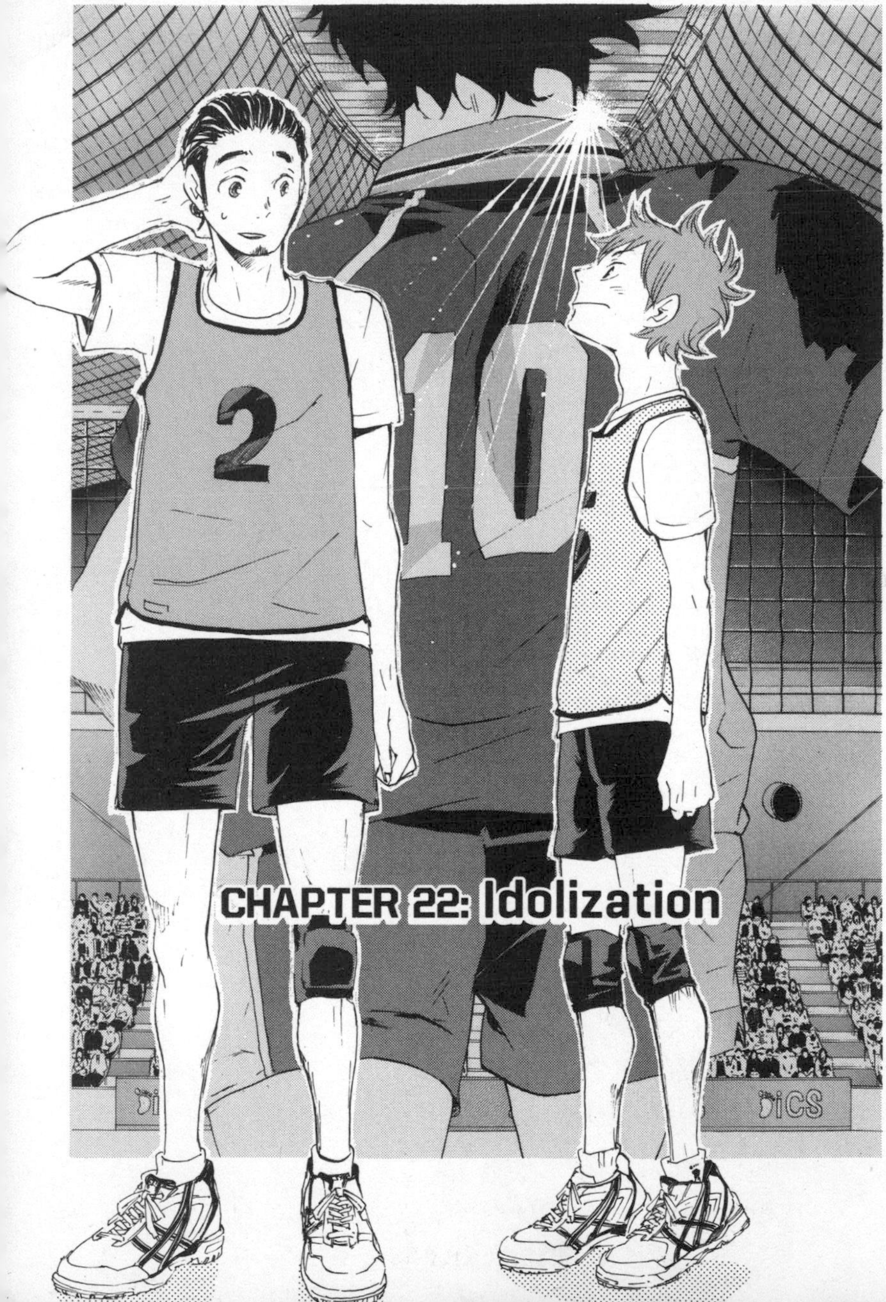
CHAPTER 22: Idolization

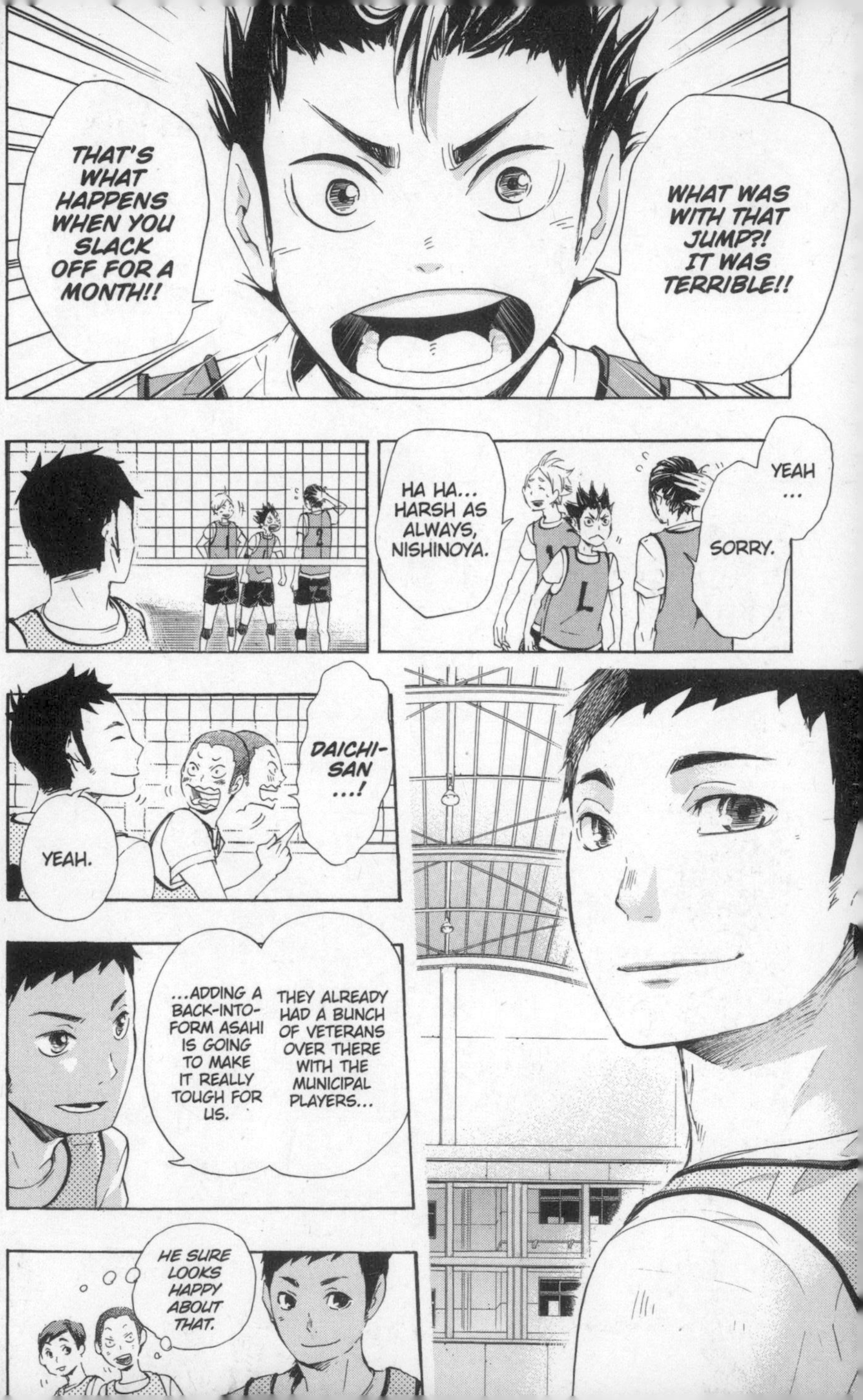
WHAT WAS WITH THAT JUMP?! IT WAS TERRIBLE!!
THAT'S WHAT HAPPENS WHEN YOU SLACK OFF FOR A MONTH!!
YEAH ... SORRY.
HA HA... HARSH AS ALWAYS, NISHINOYA.
DAICHI-SAN ...!
YEAH.
THEY ALREADY HAD A BUNCH OF VETERANS OVER THERE WITH THE MUNICIPAL PLAYERS...
...ADDING A BACK-INTO-FORM ASAHI IS GOING TO MAKE IT REALLY TOUGH FOR US.
HE SURE LOOKS HAPPY ABOUT THAT.

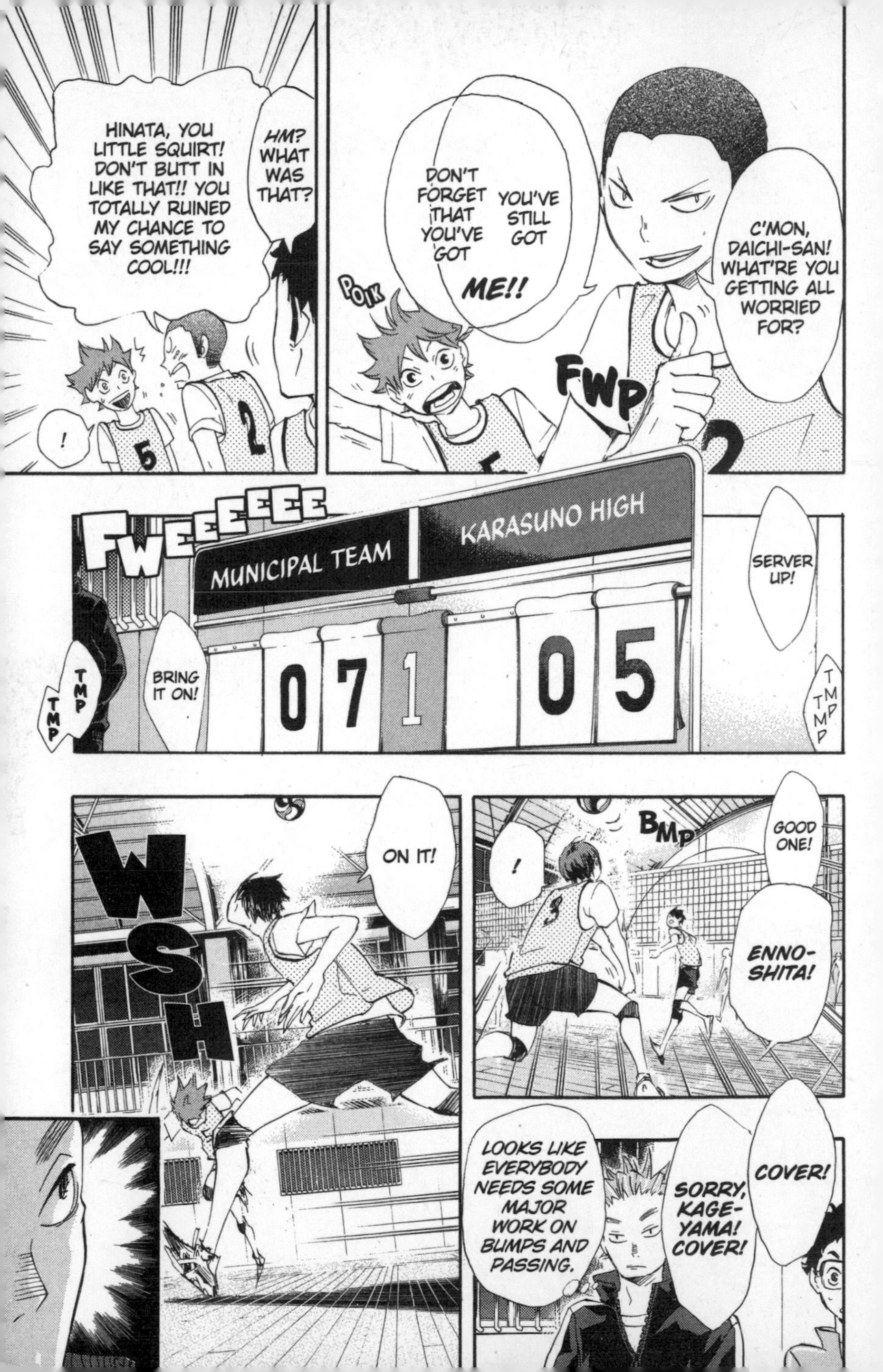
C'MON, DAICHI-SAN! WHAT'RE YOU GETTING ALL WORRIED FOR?
FWP
YOU'VE STILL GOT
DON'T FORGET THAT YOU'VE GOT
ME!!
POIK
HM? WHAT WAS THAT?
HINATA, YOU LITTLE SQUIRT! DON'T BUTT IN LIKE THAT!! YOU TOTALLY RUINED MY CHANCE TO SAY SOMETHING COOL!!!
!
SERVER UP!
TMP TMP
KARASUNO HIGH
MUNICIPAL TEAM
07 1 05
FWEEEEEE
BRING IT ON!
TMP TMP
GOOD ONE!
BMP
!
ENNO-SHITA!
ON IT!
WSSH
COVER!
SORRY, KAGE-YAMA! COVER!
LOOKS LIKE EVERYBODY NEEDS SOME MAJOR WORK ON BUMPS AND PASSING.

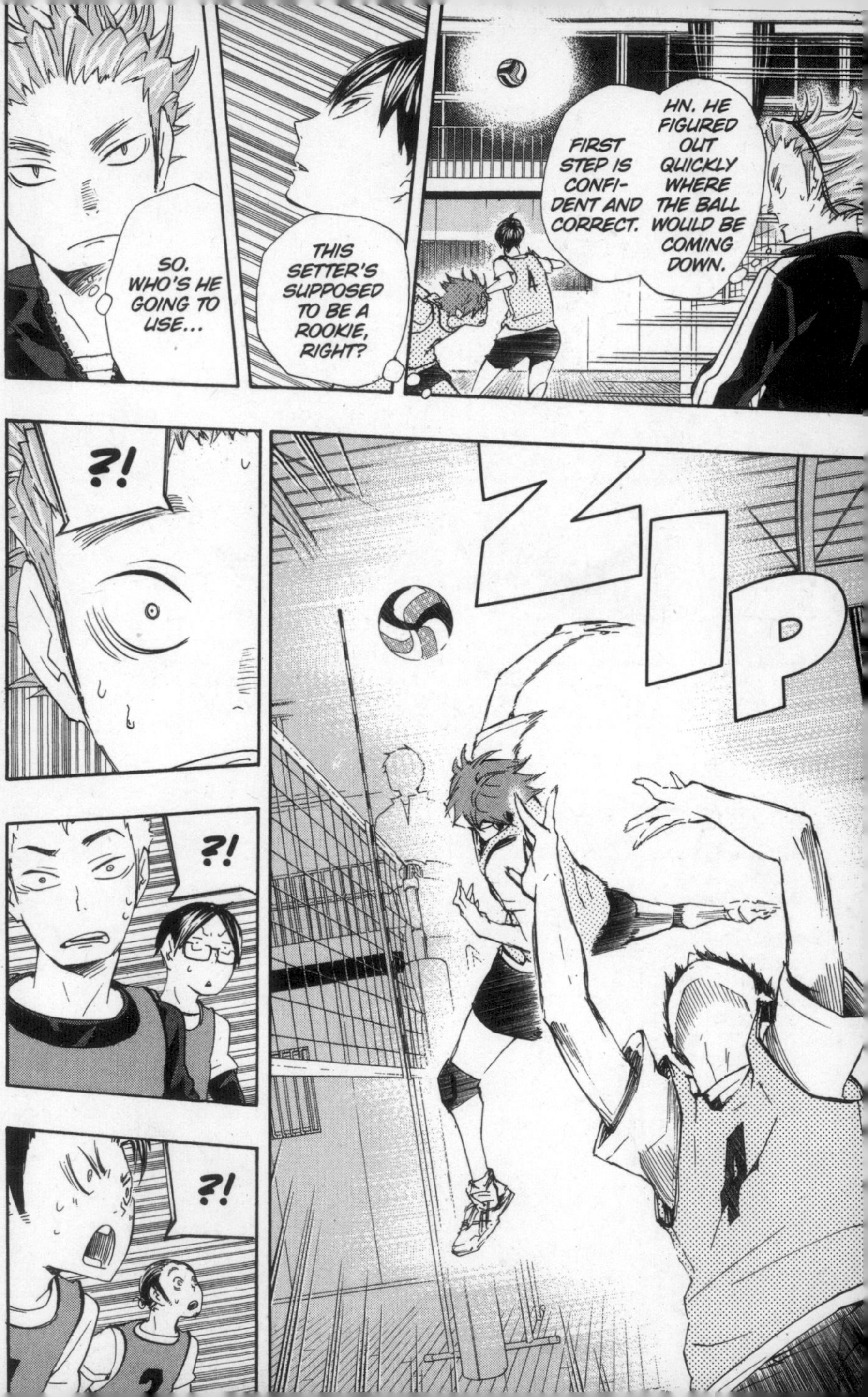
HN. HE FIGURED OUT QUICKLY WHERE THE BALL WOULD BE COMING DOWN.
FIRST STEP IS CONFI-DENT AND CORRECT.
THIS SETTER'S SUPPOSED TO BE A ROOKIE, RIGHT?
SO. WHO'S HE GOING TO USE...
ZIP
?!
?!
?!

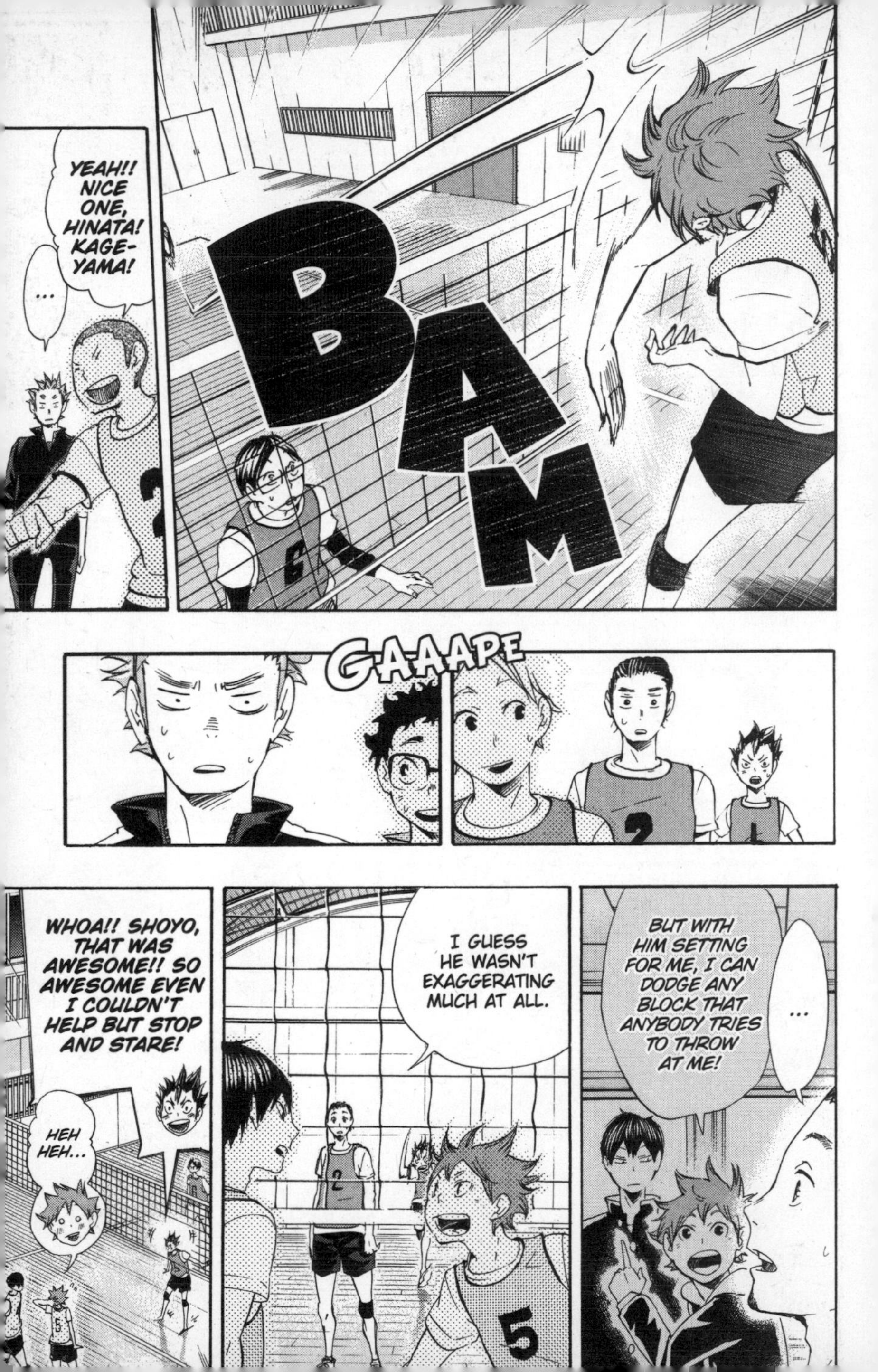
BAM
YEAH!! NICE ONE, HINATA! KAGE-YAMA!
...
GAAAPE
...
BUT WITH HIM SETTING FOR ME, I CAN DODGE ANY BLOCK THAT ANYBODY TRIES TO THROW AT ME!
I GUESS HE WASN'T EXAGGERATING MUCH AT ALL.
WHOA!! SHOYO, THAT WAS AWESOME!! SO AWESOME EVEN I COULDN'T HELP BUT STOP AND STARE!
HEH HEH...

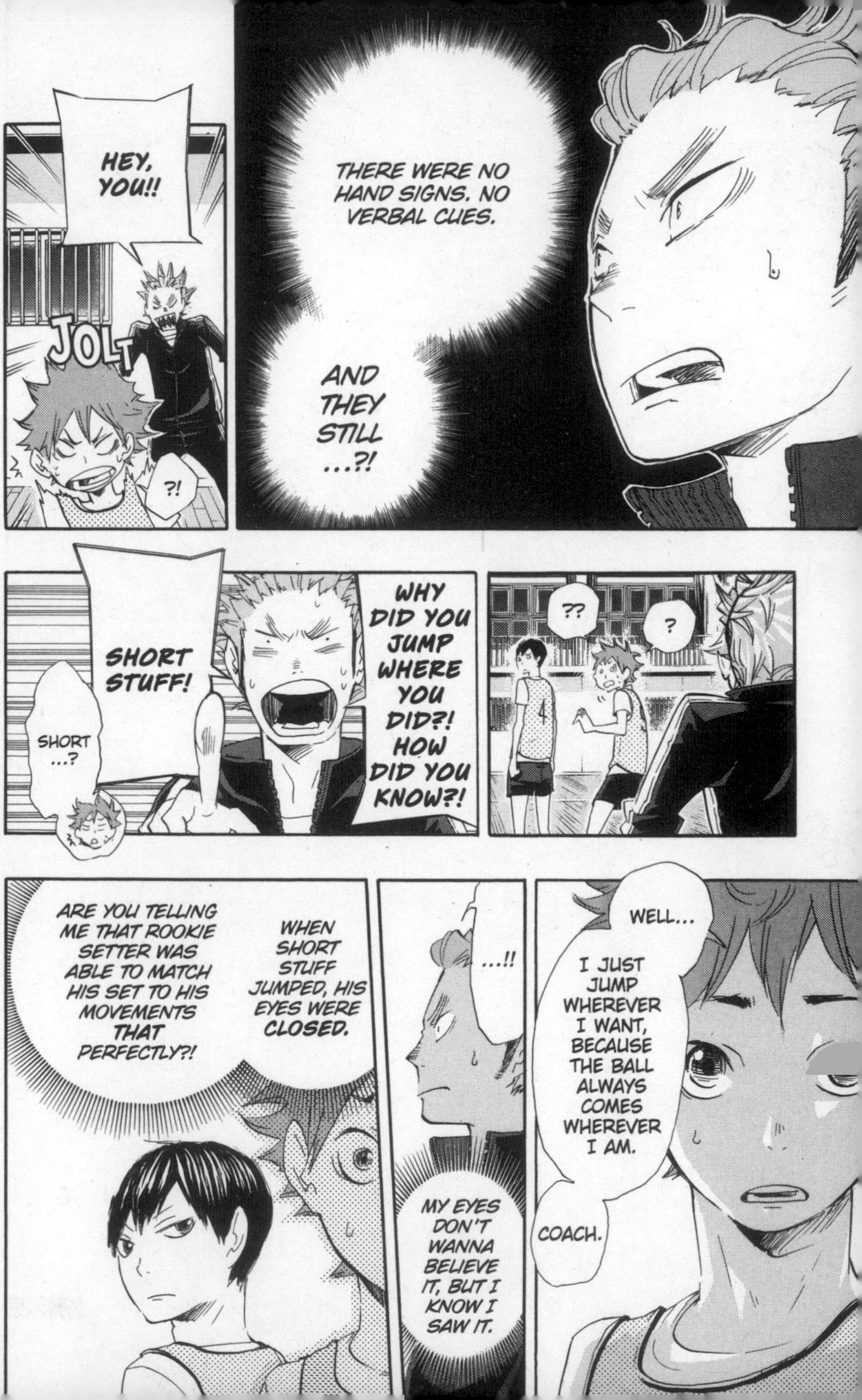
THERE WERE NO HAND SIGNS. NO VERBAL CUES.
AND THEY STILL ...?!
HEY, YOU!!
JOLT
?!
??
?
WHY DID YOU JUMP WHERE YOU DID?! HOW DID YOU KNOW?!
SHORT STUFF!
SHORT ...?
WELL...
I JUST JUMP WHEREVER I WANT, BECAUSE THE BALL ALWAYS COMES WHEREVER I AM.
COACH.
...!!
MY EYES DON'T WANNA BELIEVE IT, BUT I KNOW I SAW IT.
WHEN SHORT STUFF JUMPED, HIS EYES WERE CLOSED.
ARE YOU TELLING ME THAT ROOKIE SETTER WAS ABLE TO MATCH HIS SET TO HIS MOVEMENTS THAT PERFECTLY?!

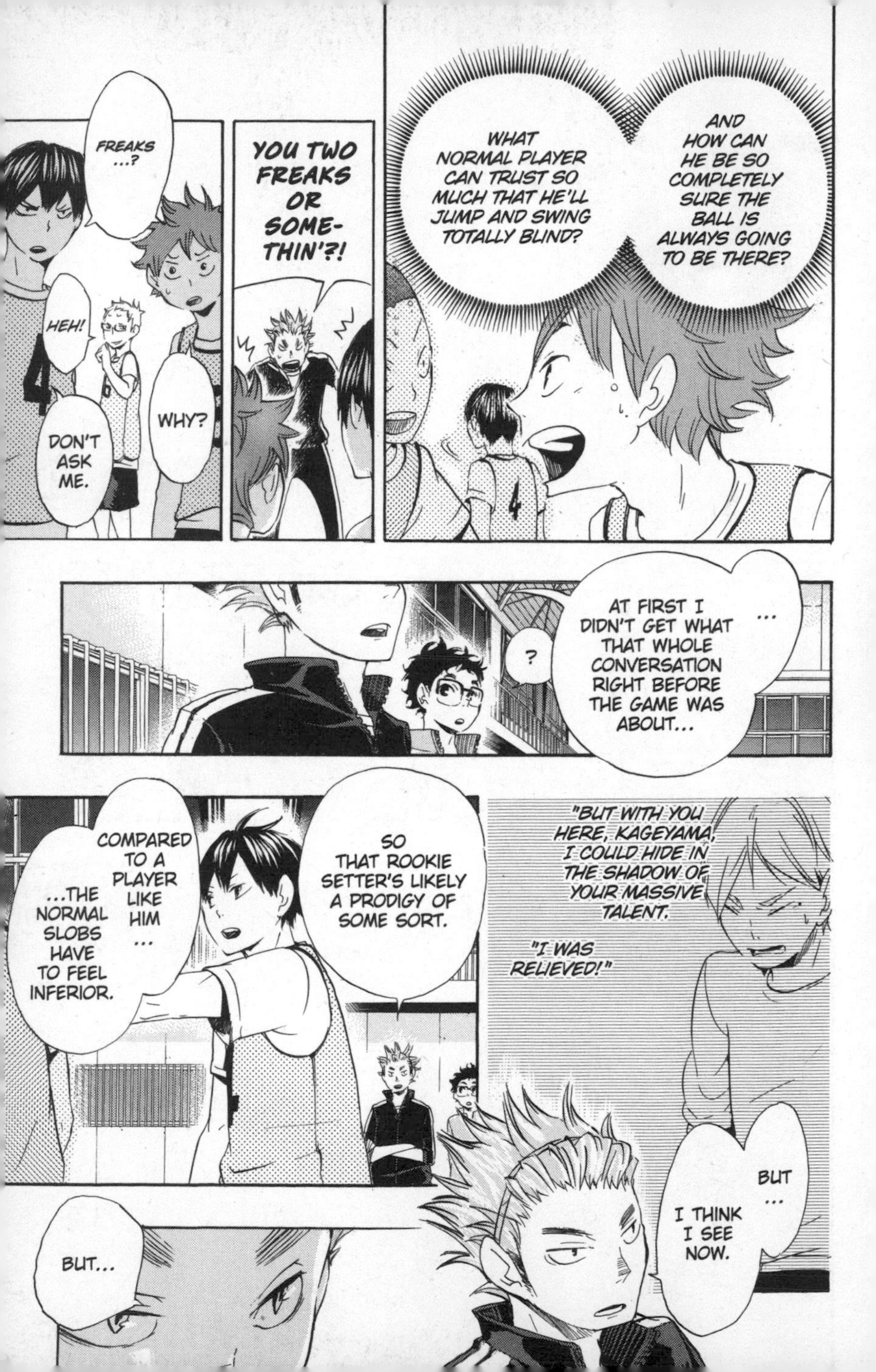
WHAT NORMAL PLAYER CAN TRUST SO MUCH THAT HE'LL JUMP AND SWING TOTALLY BLIND?
AND HOW CAN HE BE SO COMPLETELY SURE THE BALL IS ALWAYS GOING TO BE THERE?
YOU TWO FREAKS OR SOME-THIN'?!
FREAKS ...?
HEH!
WHY?
DON'T ASK ME.
...
AT FIRST I DIDN'T GET WHAT THAT WHOLE CONVERSATION RIGHT BEFORE THE GAME WAS ABOUT...
?
"BUT WITH YOU HERE, KAGEYAMA, I COULD HIDE IN THE SHADOW OF YOUR MASSIVE TALENT.
"I WAS RELIEVED!"
SO THAT ROOKIE SETTER'S LIKELY A PRODIGY OF SOME SORT.
COMPARED TO A PLAYER LIKE HIM ...
...THE NORMAL SLOBS HAVE TO FEEL INFERIOR.
BUT ... I THINK I SEE NOW.
BUT...

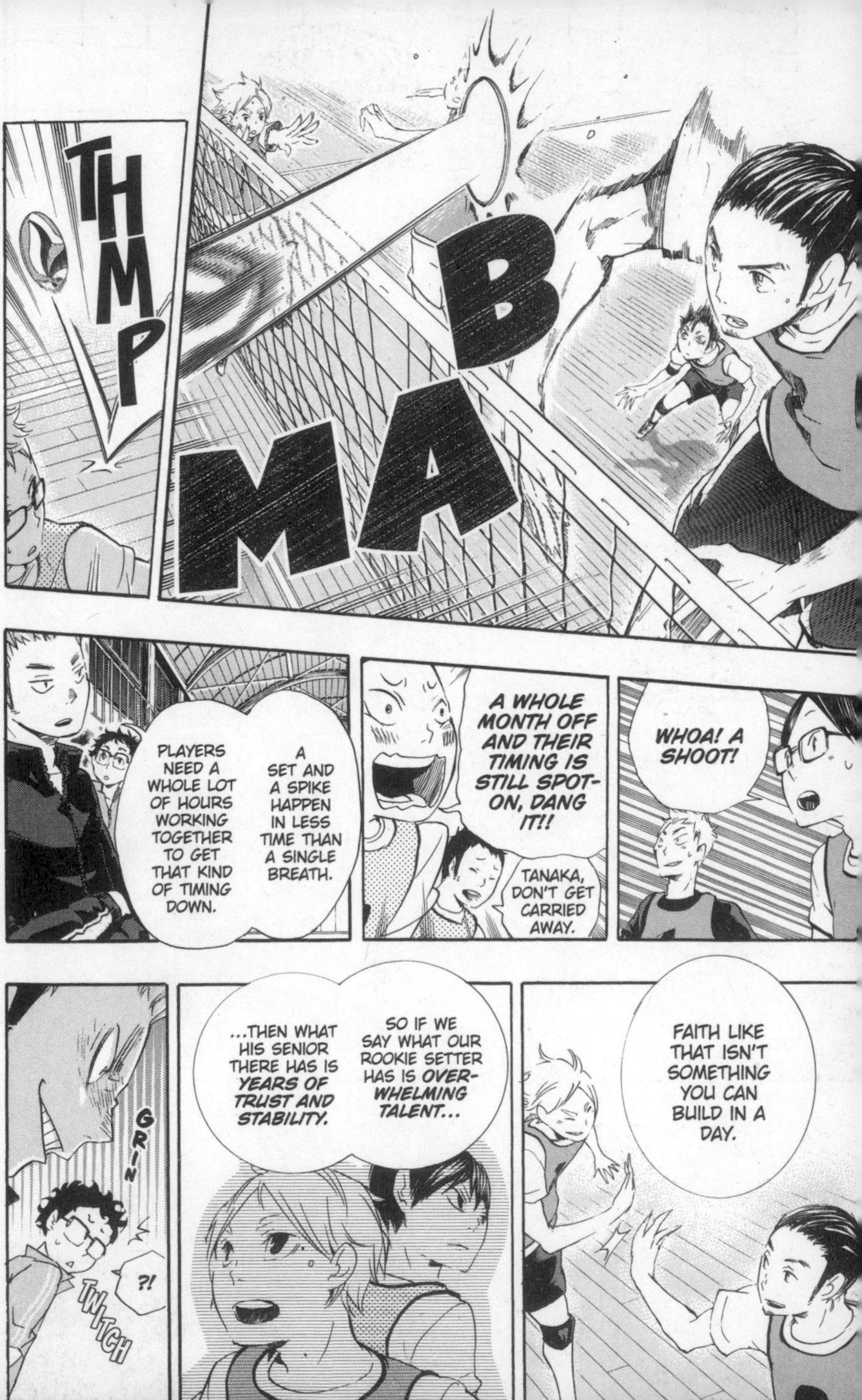
BAM
THMP
WHOA! A SHOOT!
A WHOLE MONTH OFF AND THEIR TIMING IS STILL SPOT-ON, DANG IT!!
TANAKA, DON'T GET CARRIED AWAY.
A SET AND A SPIKE HAPPEN IN LESS TIME THAN A SINGLE BREATH.
PLAYERS NEED A WHOLE LOT OF HOURS WORKING TOGETHER TO GET THAT KIND OF TIMING DOWN.
FAITH LIKE THAT ISN'T SOMETHING YOU CAN BUILD IN A DAY.
SO IF WE SAY WHAT OUR ROOKIE SETTER HAS IS OVER-WHELMING TALENT...
...THEN WHAT HIS SENIOR THERE HAS IS YEARS OF TRUST AND STABILITY.
GRIN
?!
TWITCH

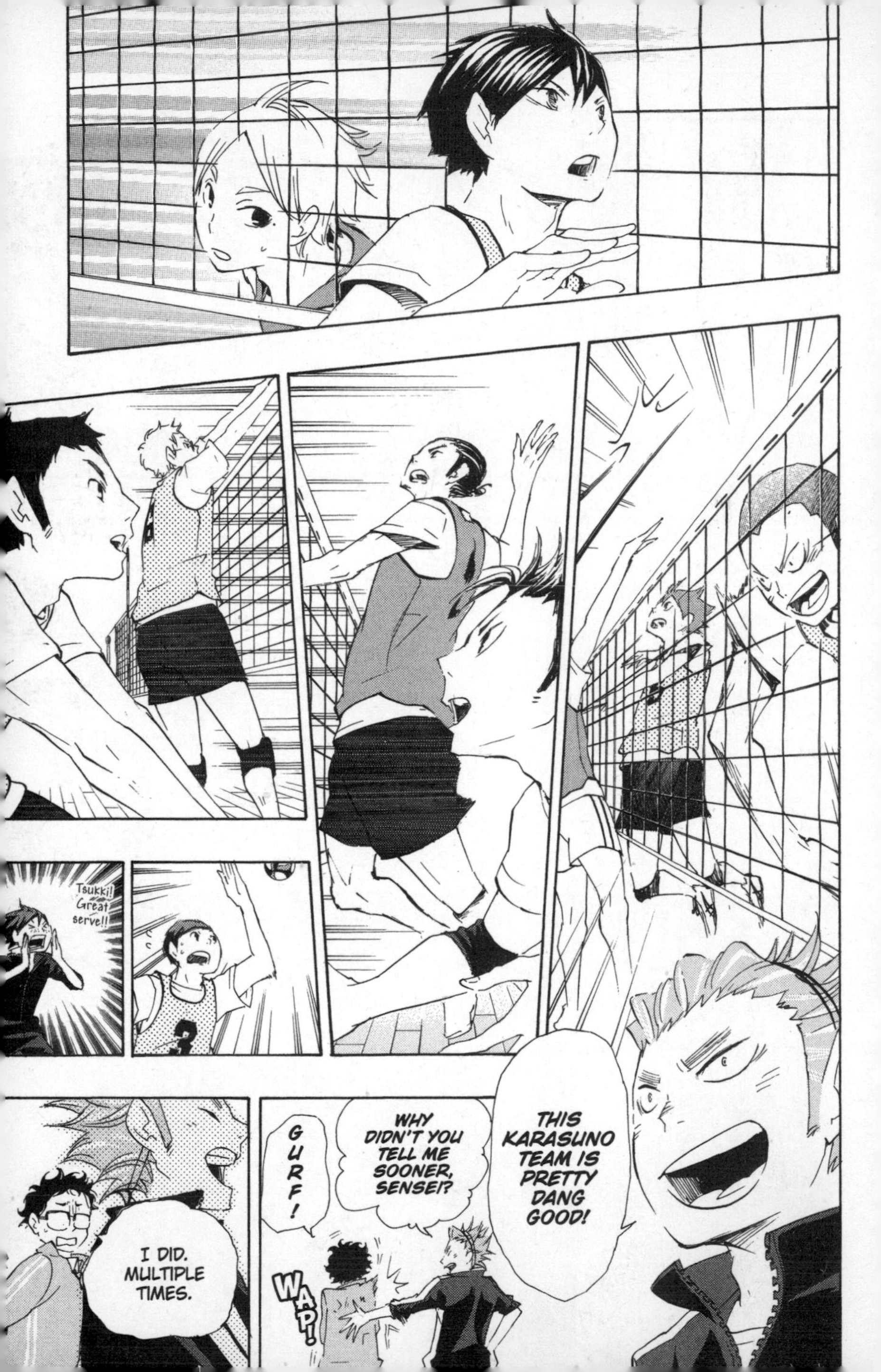
Tsukki! Great serve!!
THIS KARASUNO TEAM IS PRETTY DANG GOOD!
WHY DIDN'T YOU TELL ME SOONER, SENSEI?
GURF!
WAP!
I DID. MULTIPLE TIMES.

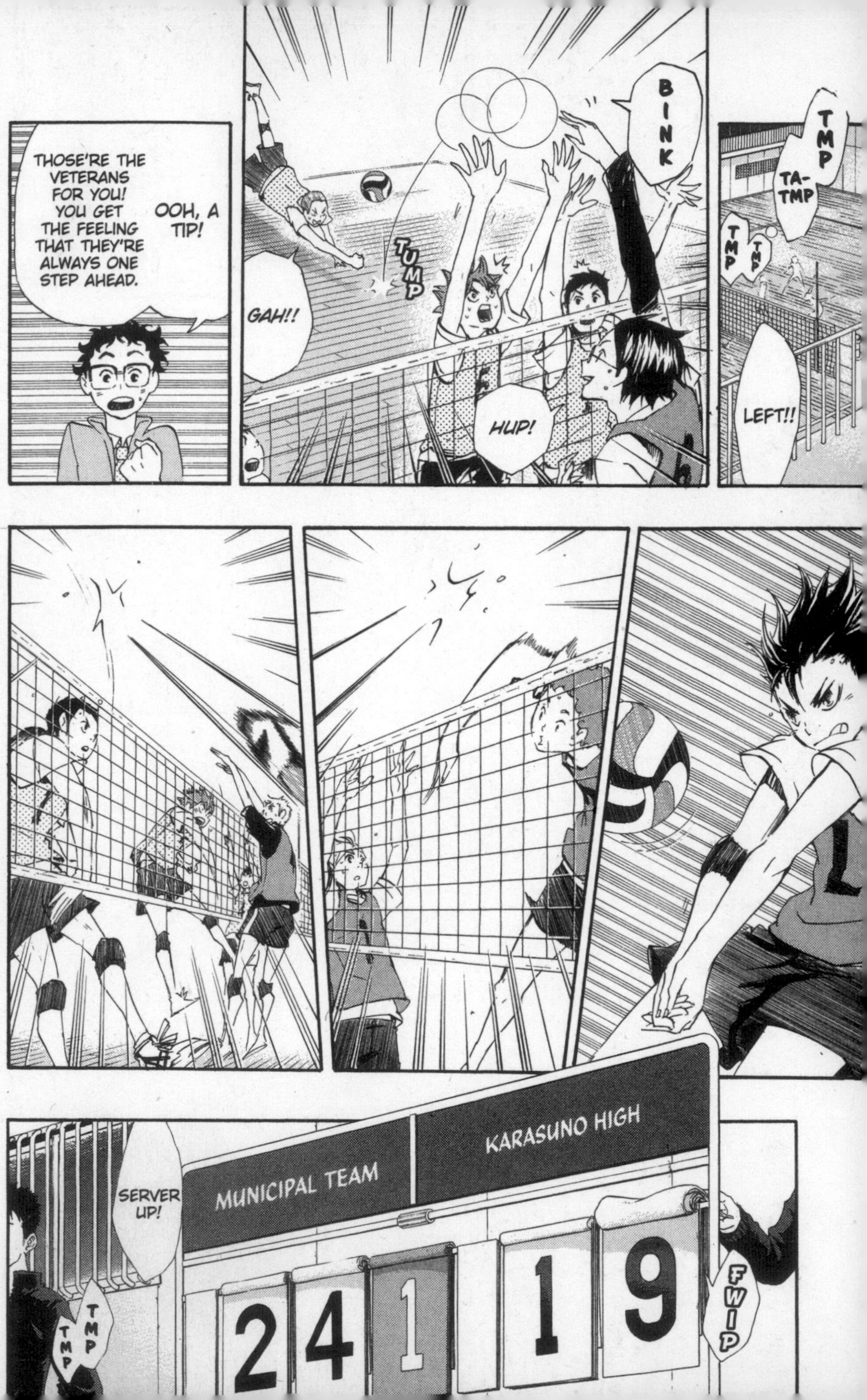
TMP
TA-TMP
TMP
TMP
LEFT!!
BINK
TUMP
GAH!!
HUP!
OOH, A TIP!
THOSE'RE THE VETERANS FOR YOU! YOU GET THE FEELING THAT THEY'RE ALWAYS ONE STEP AHEAD.
FWIP
KARASUNO HIGH
MUNICIPAL TEAM
SERVER UP!
24 1 19
TMP
TMP

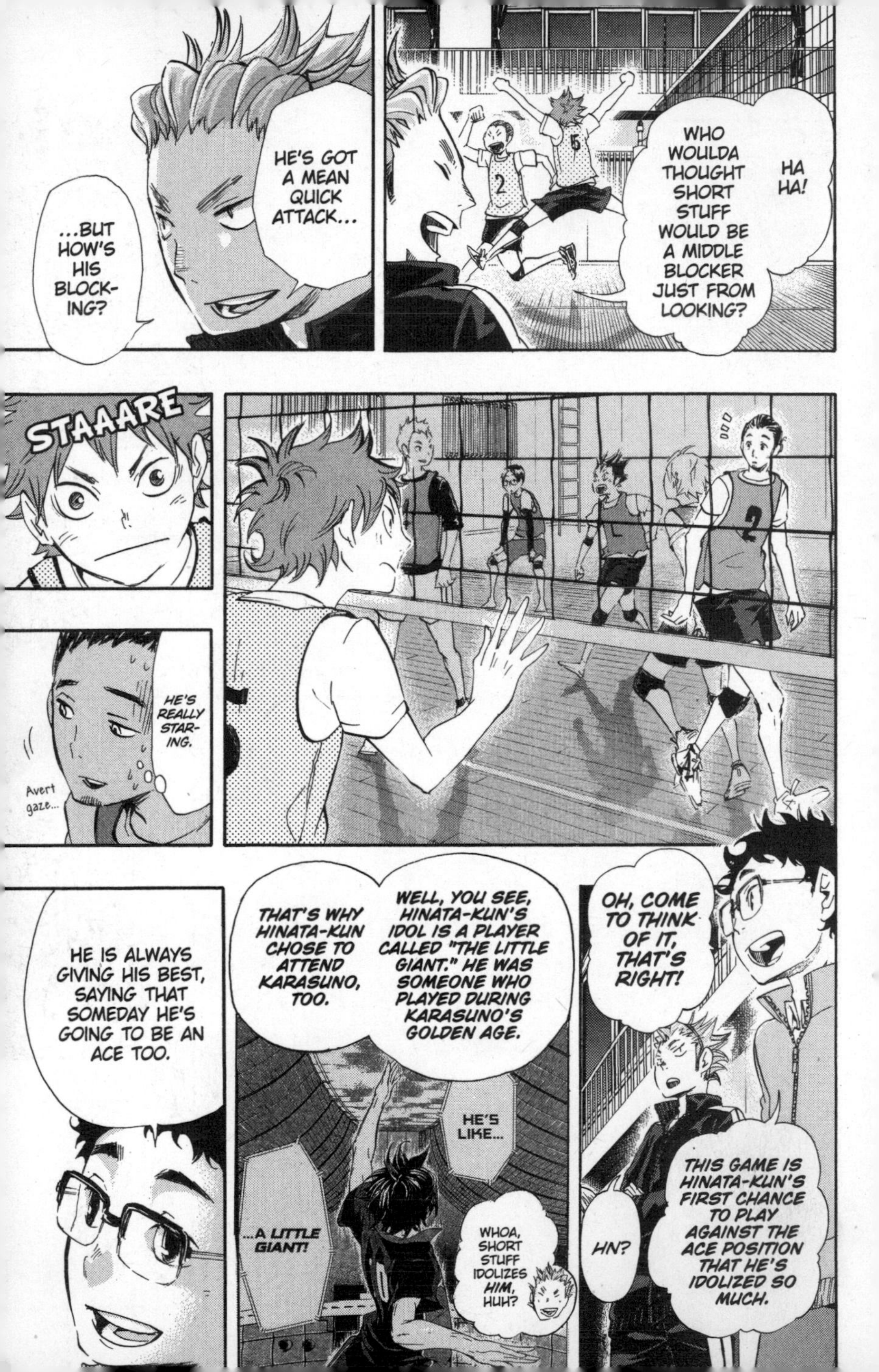
HA HA!
WHO WOULDA THOUGHT SHORT STUFF WOULD BE A MIDDLE BLOCKER JUST FROM LOOKING?
HE'S GOT A MEAN QUICK ATTACK...
...BUT HOW'S HIS BLOCKING?
STAAARE
HE'S REALLY STARING.
Avert gaze...
OH, COME TO THINK OF IT, THAT'S RIGHT!
HN?
THIS GAME IS HINATA-KUN'S FIRST CHANCE TO PLAY AGAINST THE ACE POSITION THAT HE'S IDOLIZED SO MUCH.
WELL, YOU SEE, HINATA-KUN'S IDOL IS A PLAYER CALLED "THE LITTLE GIANT." HE WAS SOMEONE WHO PLAYED DURING KARASUNO'S GOLDEN AGE.
THAT'S WHY HINATA-KUN CHOSE TO ATTEND KARASUNO, TOO.
HE'S LIKE...
...A LITTLE GIANT!
WHOA, SHORT STUFF IDOLIZES HIM, HUH?
HE IS ALWAYS GIVING HIS BEST, SAYING THAT SOMEDAY HE'S GOING TO BE AN ACE TOO.

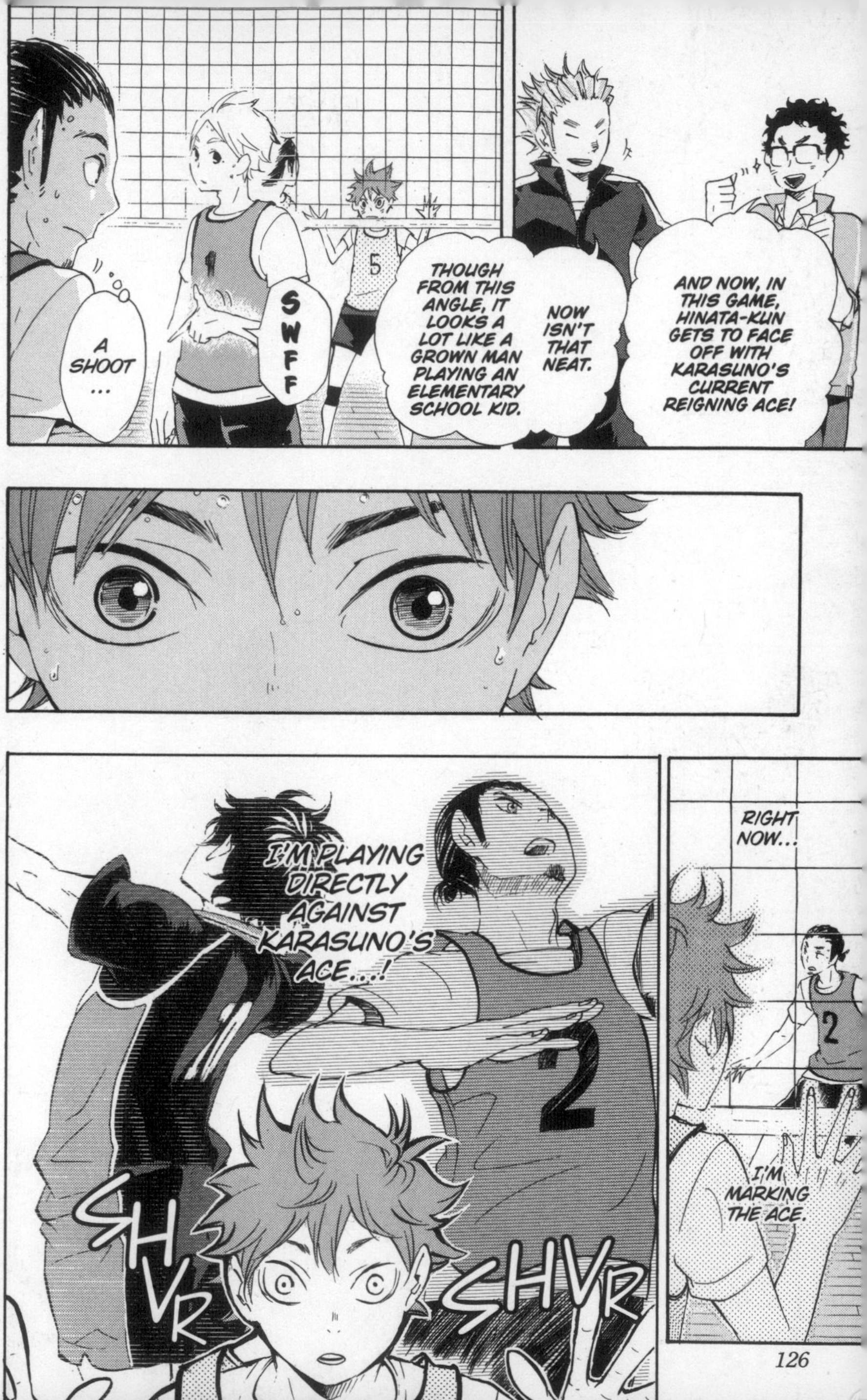
AND NOW, IN THIS GAME, HINATA-KUN GETS TO FACE OFF WITH KARASUNO'S CURRENT REIGNING ACE!
NOW ISN'T THAT NEAT.
THOUGH FROM THIS ANGLE, IT LOOKS A LOT LIKE A GROWN MAN PLAYING AN ELEMENTARY SCHOOL KID.
SWFF
A SHOOT ...
RIGHT NOW...
I'M MARKING THE ACE.
I'M PLAYING DIRECTLY AGAINST KARASUNO'S ACE...!
SHVR
SHVR

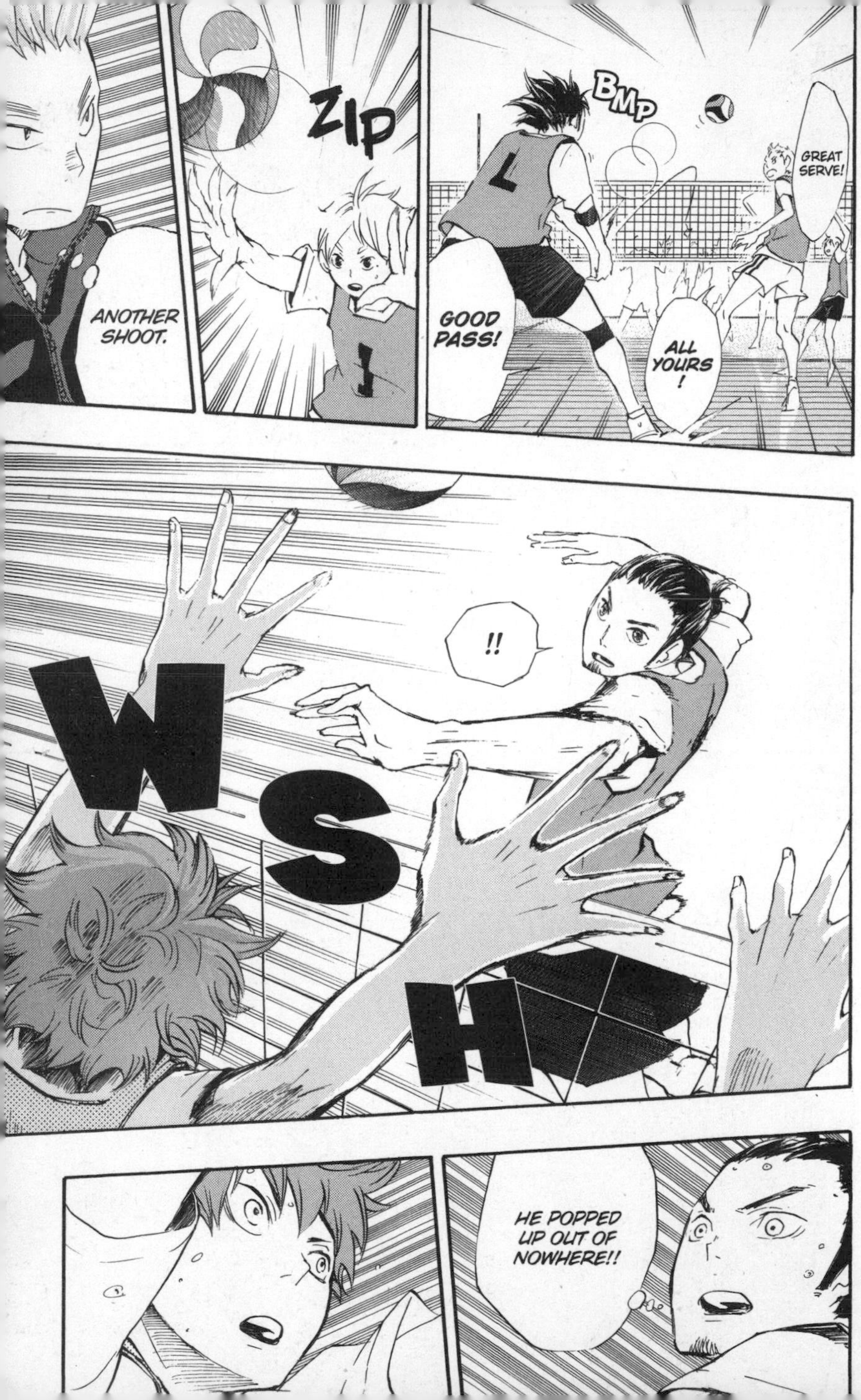
GREAT SERVE!
BMP
ALL YOURS!
GOOD PASS!
ZIP
ANOTHER SHOOT.
!!
WSH
HE POPPED UP OUT OF NOWHERE!!

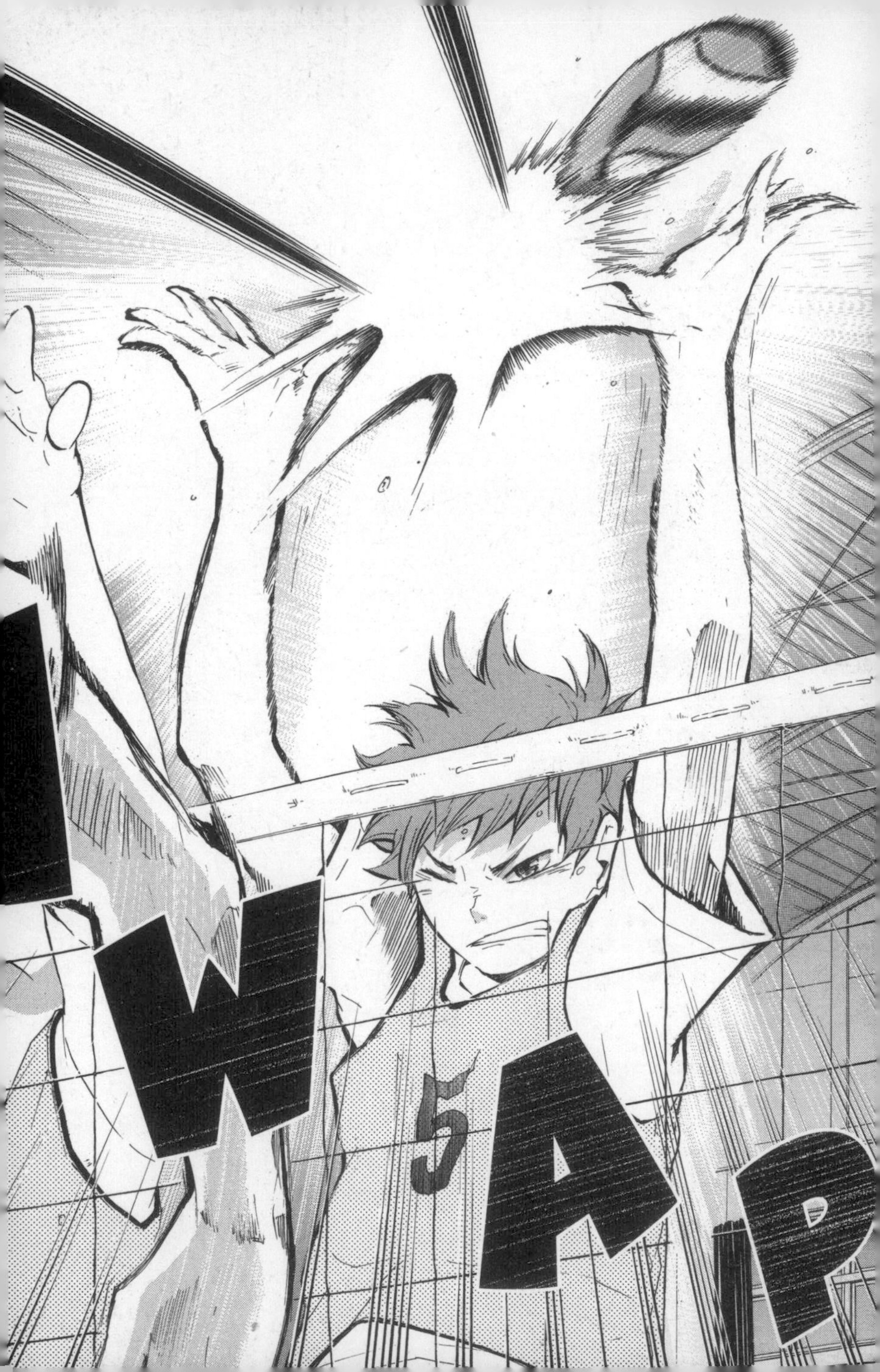
WHAP

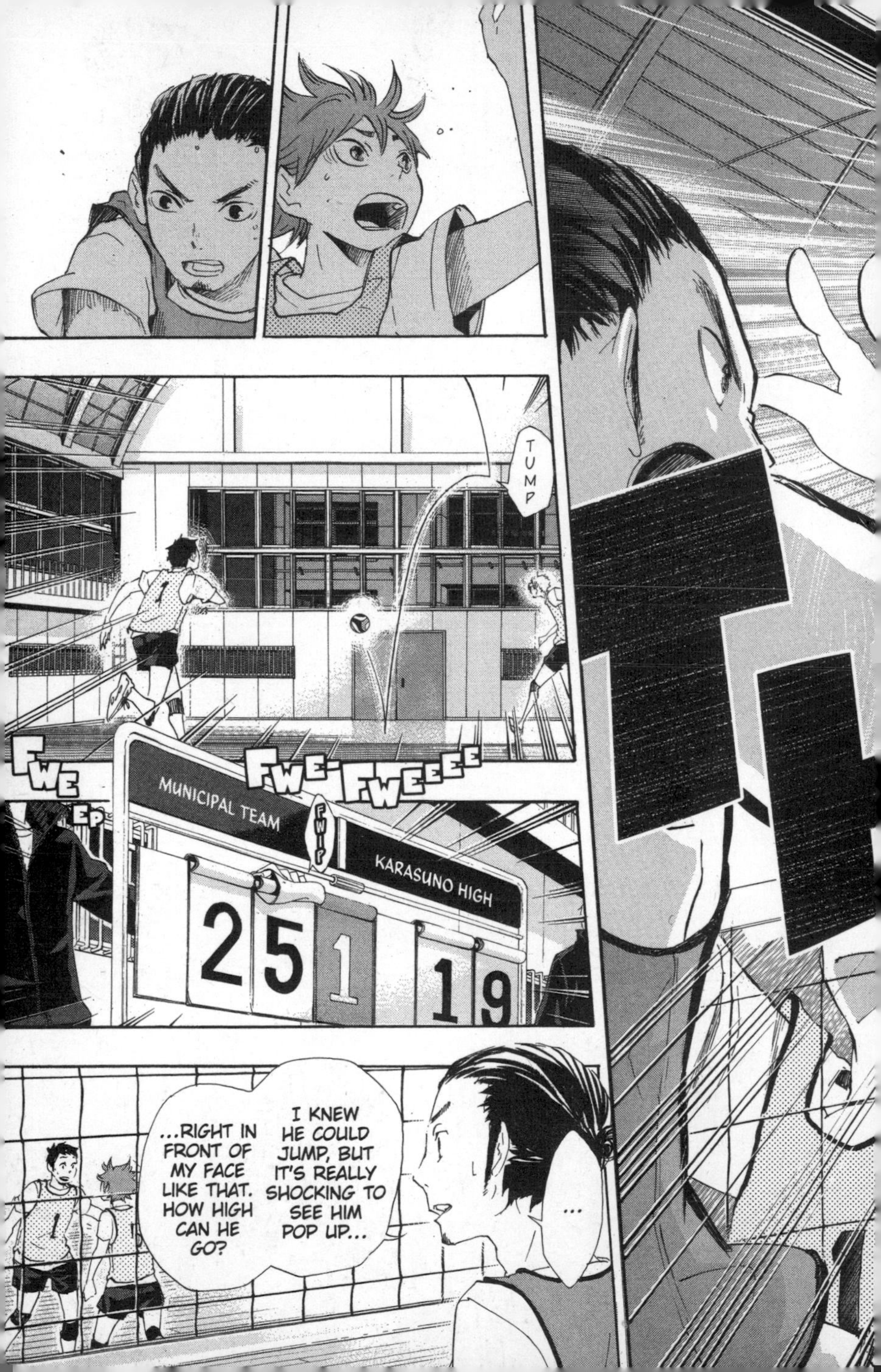
TUMP
FWE-FWEEEE
FWEEP
MUNICIPAL TEAM
KARASUNO HIGH
FWIP
25 1 19
...
I KNEW HE COULD JUMP, BUT IT'S REALLY SHOCKING TO SEE HIM POP UP...
...RIGHT IN FRONT OF MY FACE LIKE THAT. HOW HIGH CAN HE GO?

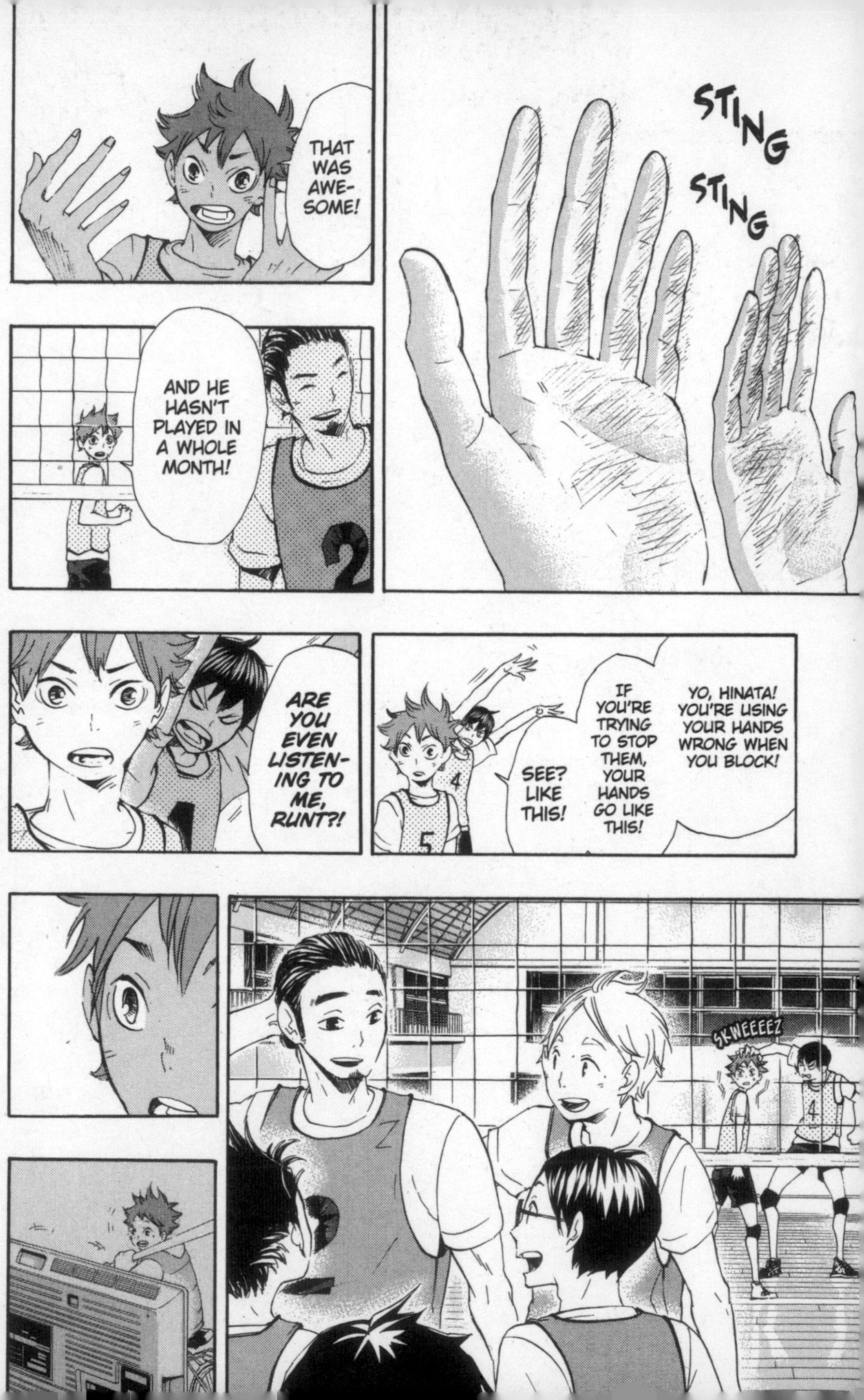
STING
STING
THAT WAS AWESOME!
AND HE HASN'T PLAYED IN A WHOLE MONTH!
YO, HINATA! YOU'RE USING YOUR HANDS WRONG WHEN YOU BLOCK!
IF YOU'RE TRYING TO STOP THEM, YOUR HANDS GO LIKE THIS!
SEE? LIKE THIS!
ARE YOU EVEN LISTENING TO ME, RUNT?!
SKWEEEEZ

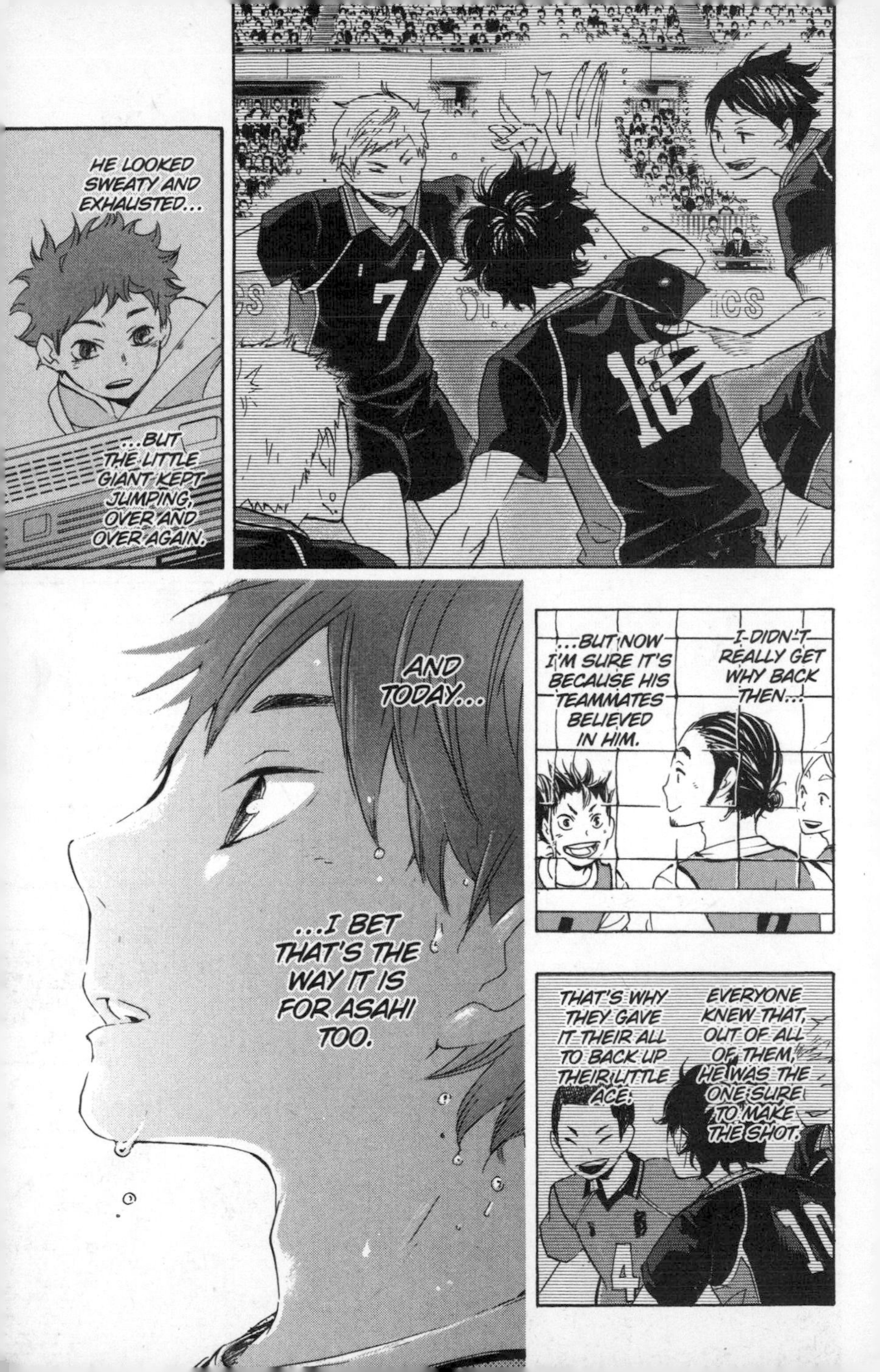

HE LOOKED SWEATY AND EXHAUSTED...
...BUT THE LITTLE GIANT KEPT JUMPING, OVER AND OVER AGAIN.
I DIDN'T REALLY GET WHY BACK THEN...
...BUT NOW I'M SURE IT'S BECAUSE HIS TEAMMATES BELIEVED IN HIM.
EVERYONE KNEW THAT, OUT OF ALL OF THEM, HE WAS THE ONE SURE TO MAKE THE SHOT.
THAT'S WHY THEY GAVE IT THEIR ALL TO BACK UP THEIR LITTLE ACE.
AND TODAY...
...I BET THAT'S THE WAY IT IS FOR ASAHI TOO.

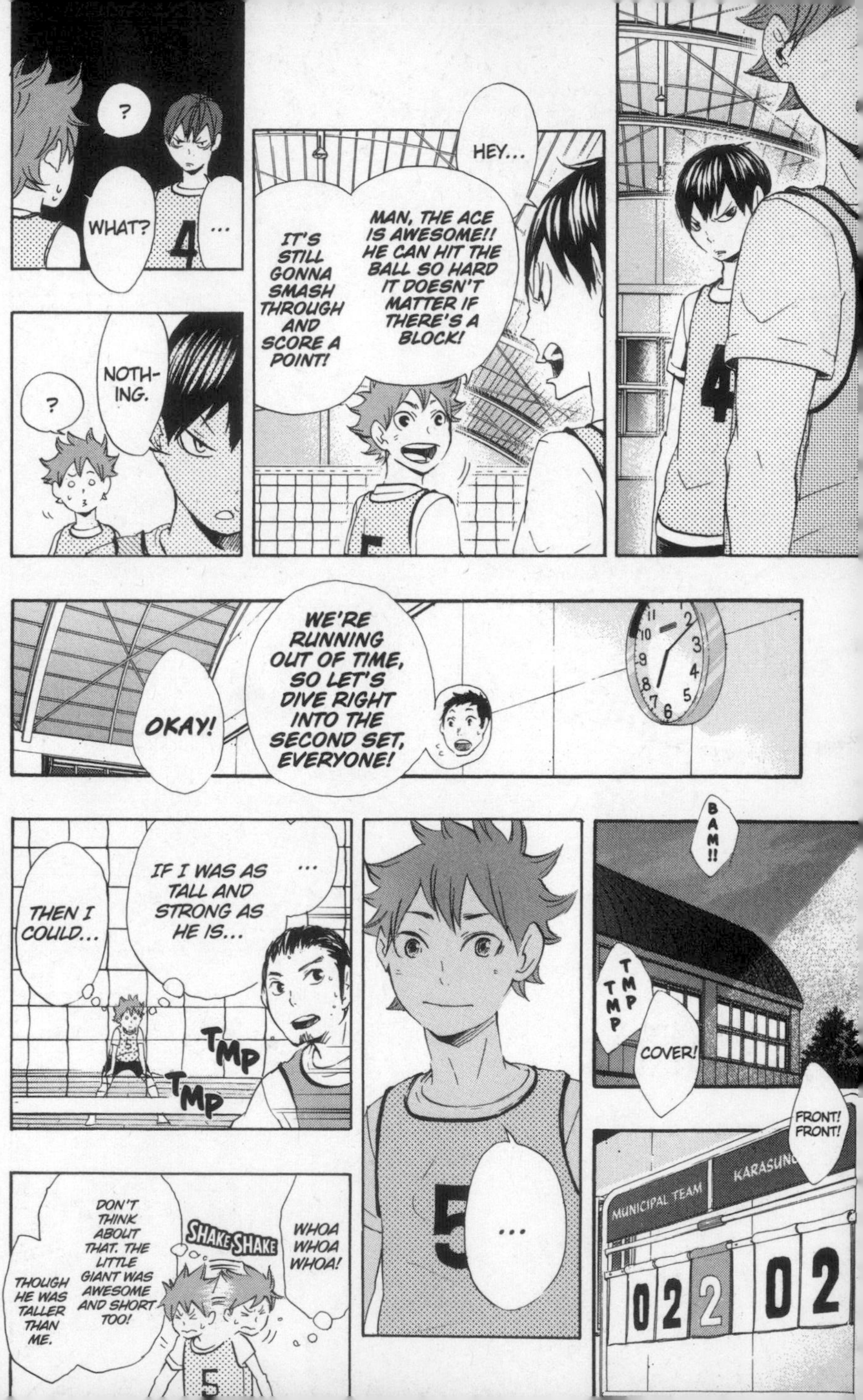
HEY...
MAN, THE ACE IS AWESOME!! HE CAN HIT THE BALL SO HARD IT DOESN'T MATTER IF THERE'S A BLOCK!
IT'S STILL GONNA SMASH THROUGH AND SCORE A POINT!
?
...
WHAT?
NOTHING.
?
WE'RE RUNNING OUT OF TIME, SO LET'S DIVE RIGHT INTO THE SECOND SET, EVERYONE!
OKAY!
BAM!!
TMP TMP TMP
COVER!
FRONT! FRONT!
KARASUN
MUNICIPAL TEAM
02 2 02
...
...
IF I WAS AS TALL AND STRONG AS HE IS...
THEN I COULD...
TMP
TMP
WHOA WHOA WHOA!
SHAKE SHAKE
DON'T THINK ABOUT THAT. THE LITTLE GIANT WAS AWESOME AND SHORT TOO!
THOUGH HE WAS TALLER THAN ME.

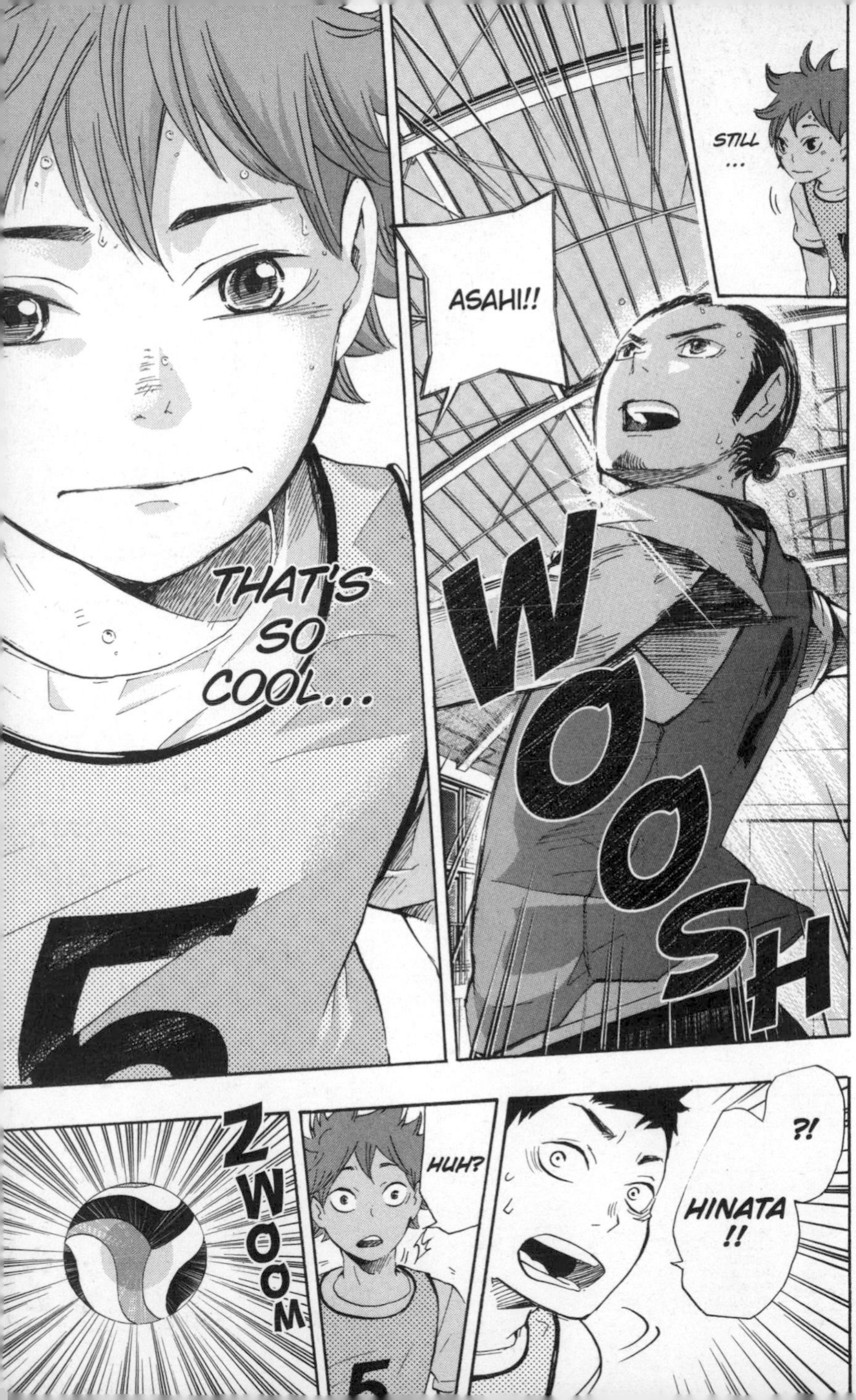
STILL
...
ASAHI!!
WOOSH
THAT'S SO COOL...
?!
HINATA!!
HUH?
ZWOOM

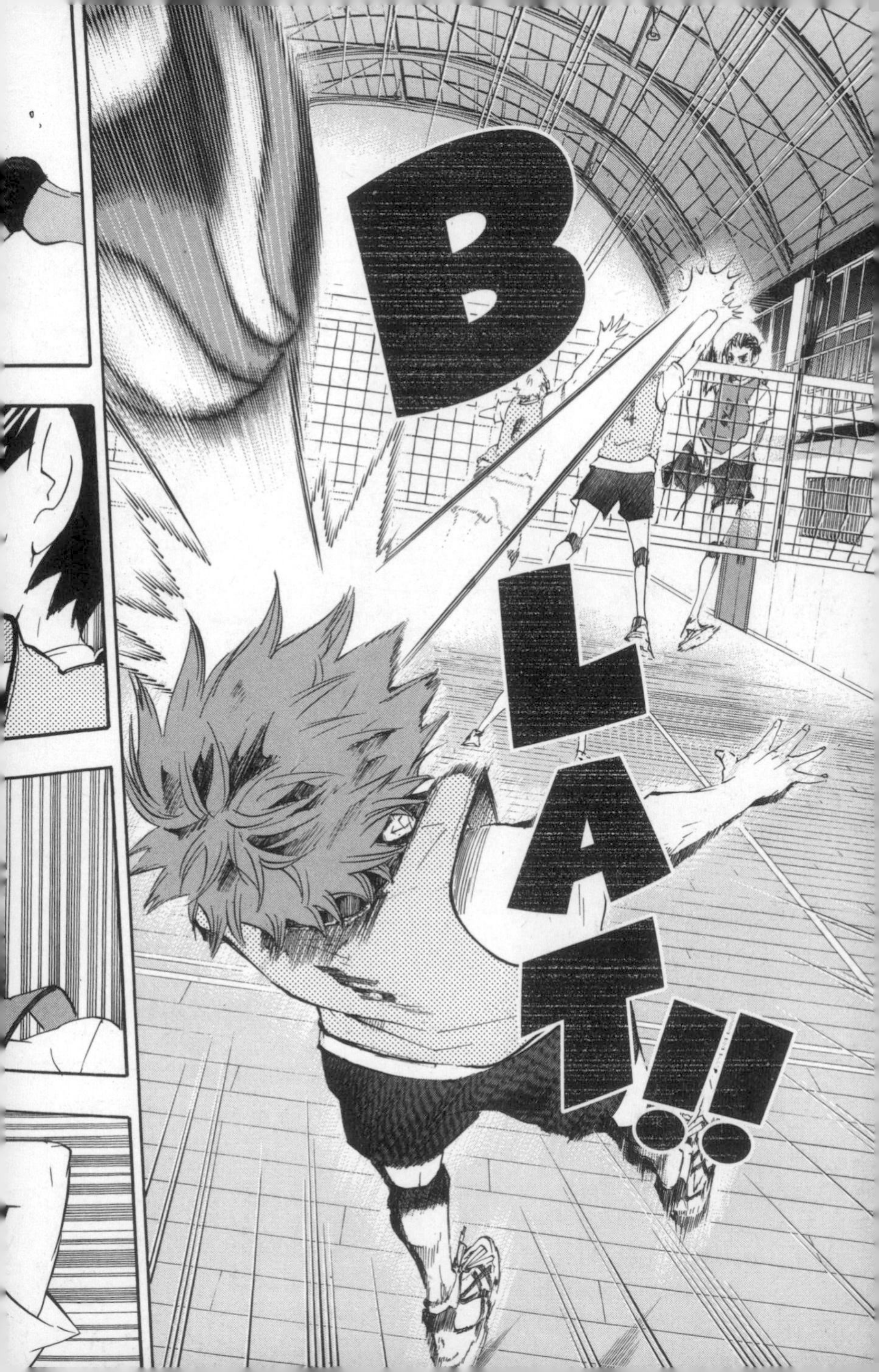
BLAM!!

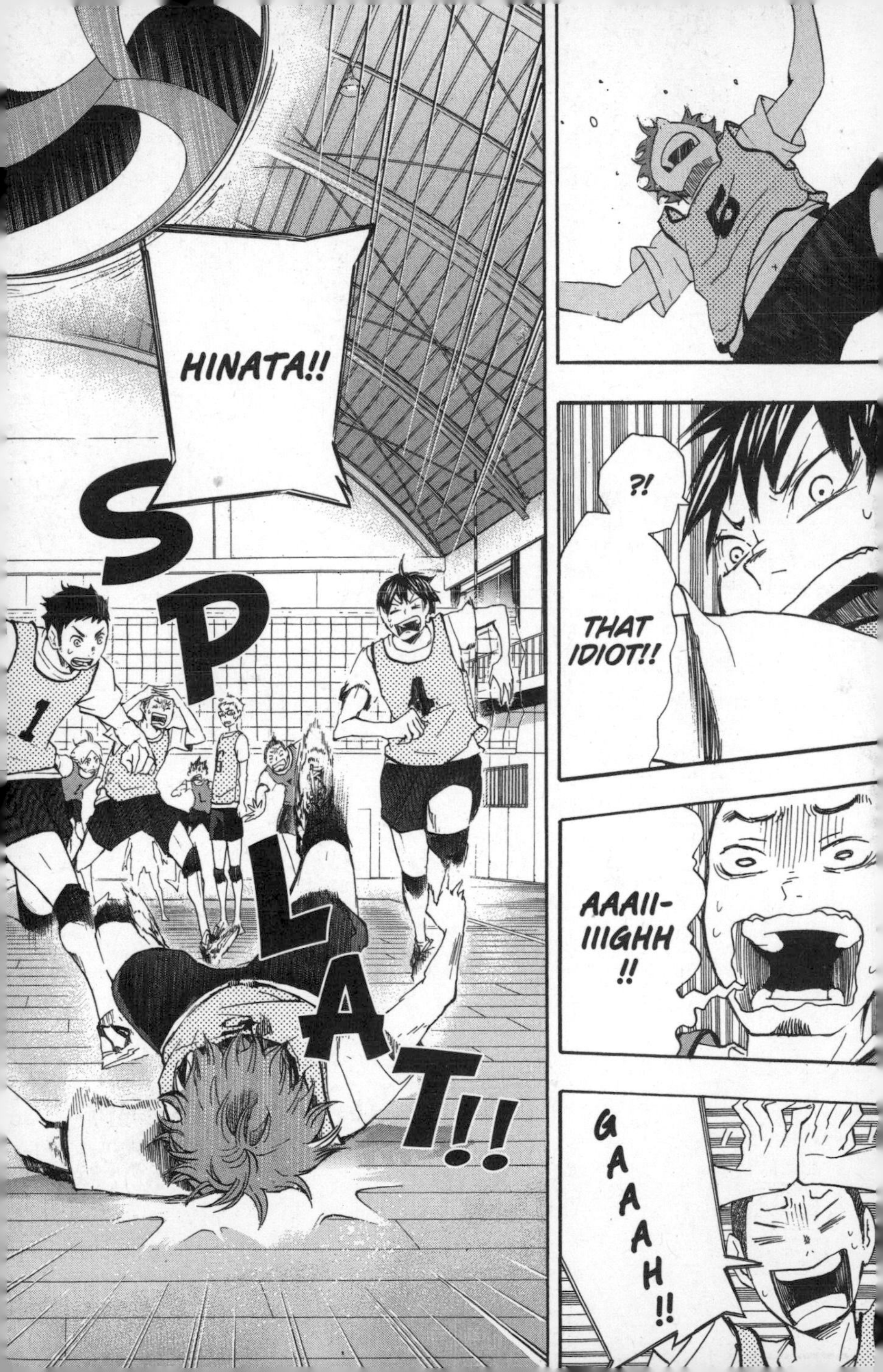
?!
THAT IDIOT!!
AAAII-IIIGHH!!
GAAAAH!!
HINATA!!
SPLAT!!

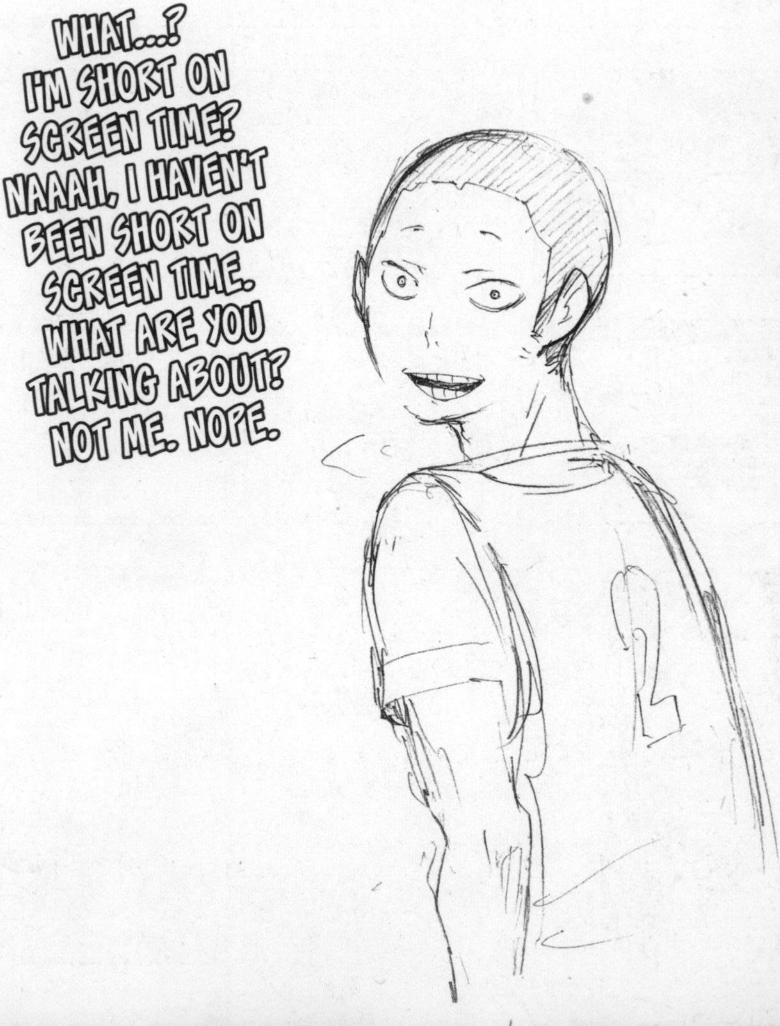
WHAT...?
I'M SHORT ON SCREEN TIME?
NAAAH, I HAVEN'T BEEN SHORT ON SCREEN TIME.
WHAT ARE YOU TALKING ABOUT?
NOT ME. NOPE.

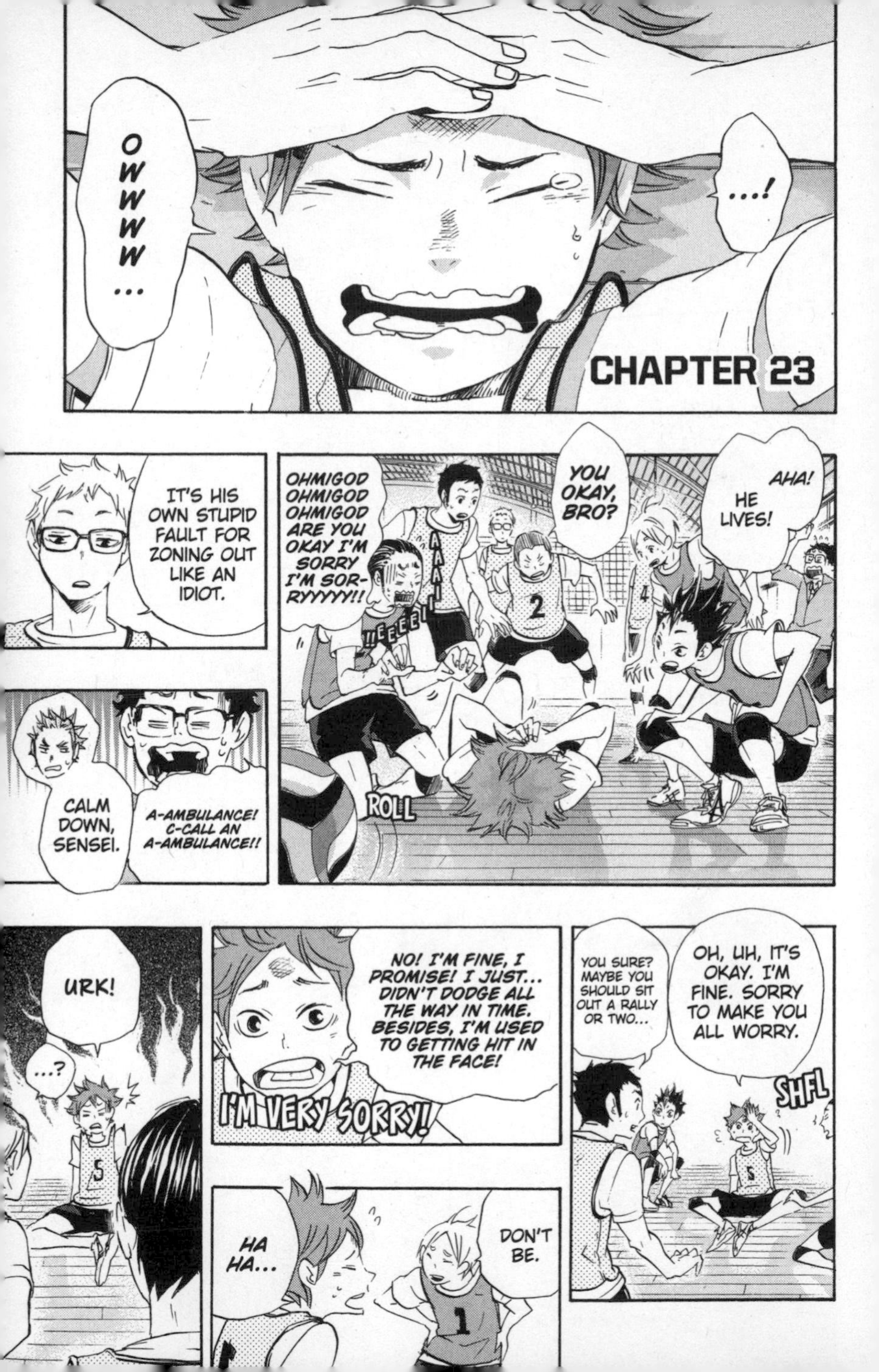
...!
OWWWW...
CHAPTER 23
AHA! HE LIVES!
YOU OKAY, BRO?
OHMIGOD OHMIGOD OHMIGOD ARE YOU OKAY I'M SORRY I'M SORRYYYYY!!
ROLL
IT'S HIS OWN STUPID FAULT FOR ZONING OUT LIKE AN IDIOT.
A-AMBULANCE! C-CALL AN A-AMBULANCE!!
CALM DOWN, SENSEI.
OH, UH, IT'S OKAY. I'M FINE. SORRY TO MAKE YOU ALL WORRY.
YOU SURE? MAYBE YOU SHOULD SIT OUT A RALLY OR TWO...
SHFL
NO! I'M FINE, I PROMISE! I JUST... DIDN'T DODGE ALL THE WAY IN TIME. BESIDES, I'M USED TO GETTING HIT IN THE FACE!
I'M VERY SORRY!
DON'T BE.
HA HA...
URK!
...?

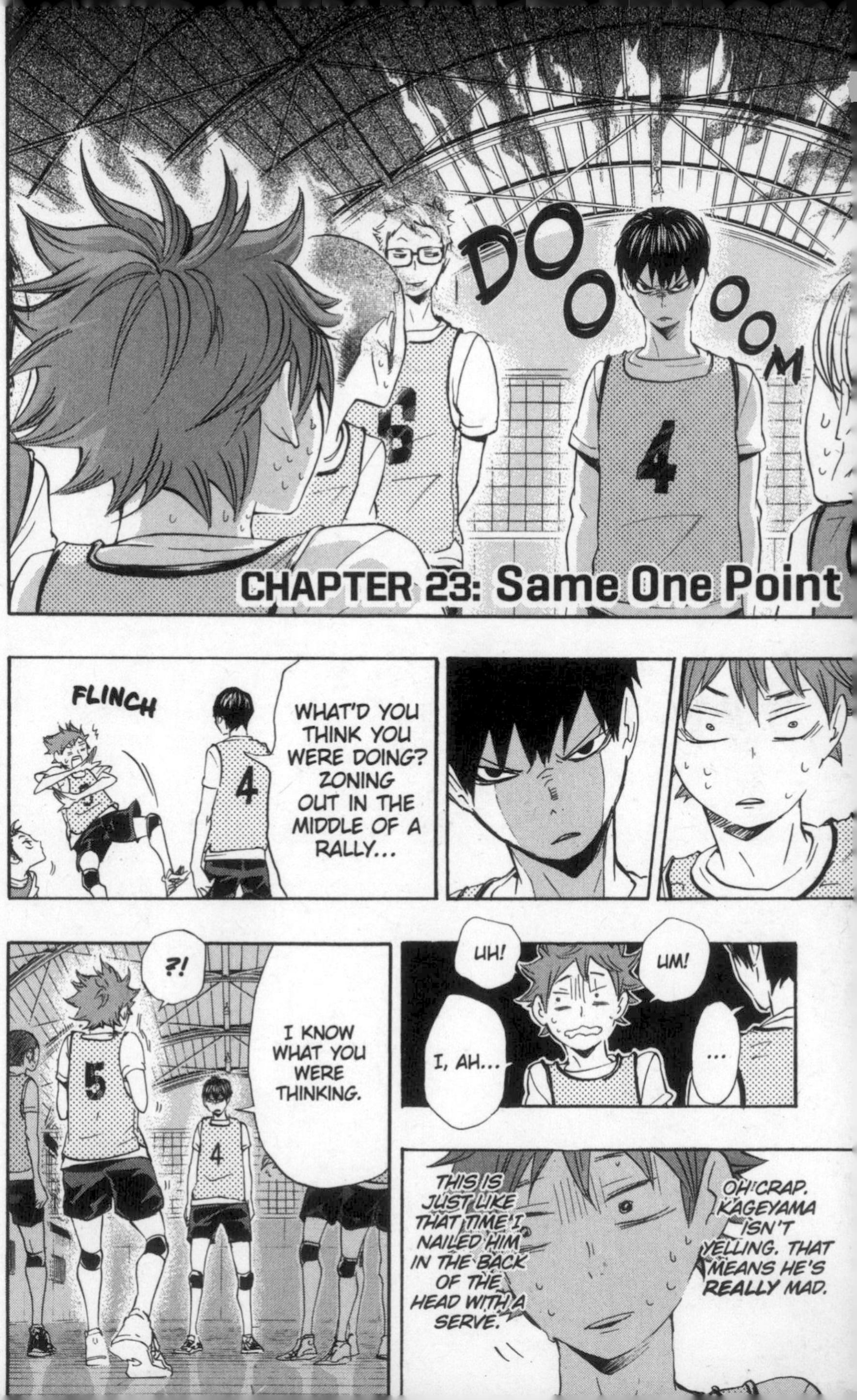
DOOOOOM
CHAPTER 23: Same One Point
FLINCH
WHAT'D YOU THINK YOU WERE DOING? ZONING OUT IN THE MIDDLE OF A RALLY...
UM!
UH!
...
I, AH...
OH CRAP. KAGEYAMA ISN'T YELLING. THAT MEANS HE'S REALLY MAD.
THIS IS JUST LIKE THAT TIME I NAILED HIM IN THE BACK OF THE HEAD WITH A SERVE.
?!
I KNOW WHAT YOU WERE THINKING.

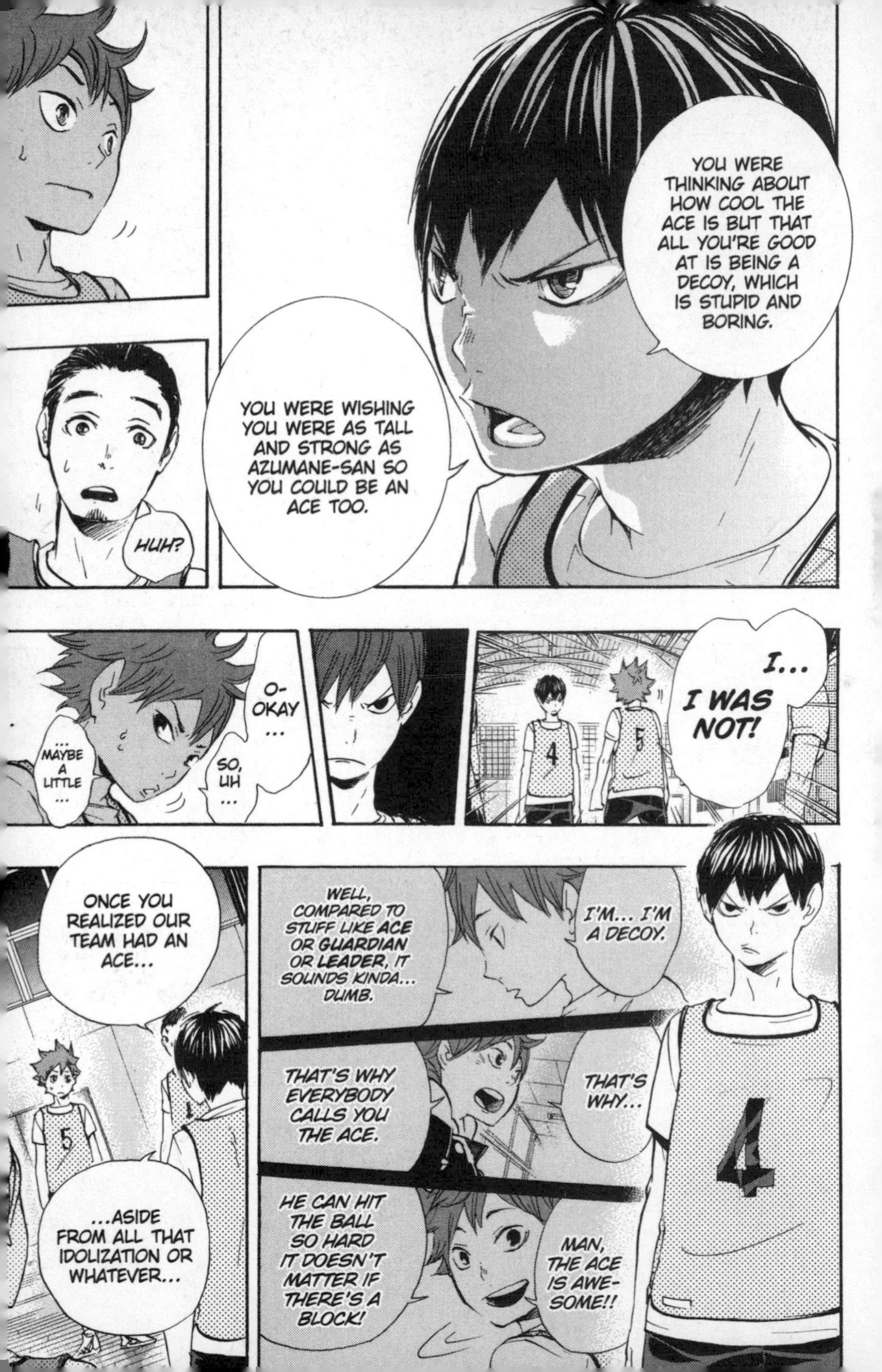
YOU WERE THINKING ABOUT HOW COOL THE ACE IS BUT THAT ALL YOU'RE GOOD AT IS BEING A DECOY, WHICH IS STUPID AND BORING.
YOU WERE WISHING YOU WERE AS TALL AND STRONG AS AZUMANE-SAN SO YOU COULD BE AN ACE TOO.
HUH?
I... I WAS NOT!
O-OKAY ...
SO, UH ...
... MAYBE A LITTLE ...
I'M... I'M A DECOY.
WELL, COMPARED TO STUFF LIKE ACE OR GUARDIAN OR LEADER, IT SOUNDS KINDA... DUMB.
THAT'S WHY...
THAT'S WHY EVERYBODY CALLS YOU THE ACE.
MAN, THE ACE IS AWE-SOME!!
HE CAN HIT THE BALL SO HARD IT DOESN'T MATTER IF THERE'S A BLOCK!
ONCE YOU REALIZED OUR TEAM HAD AN ACE...
...ASIDE FROM ALL THAT IDOLIZATION OR WHATEVER...

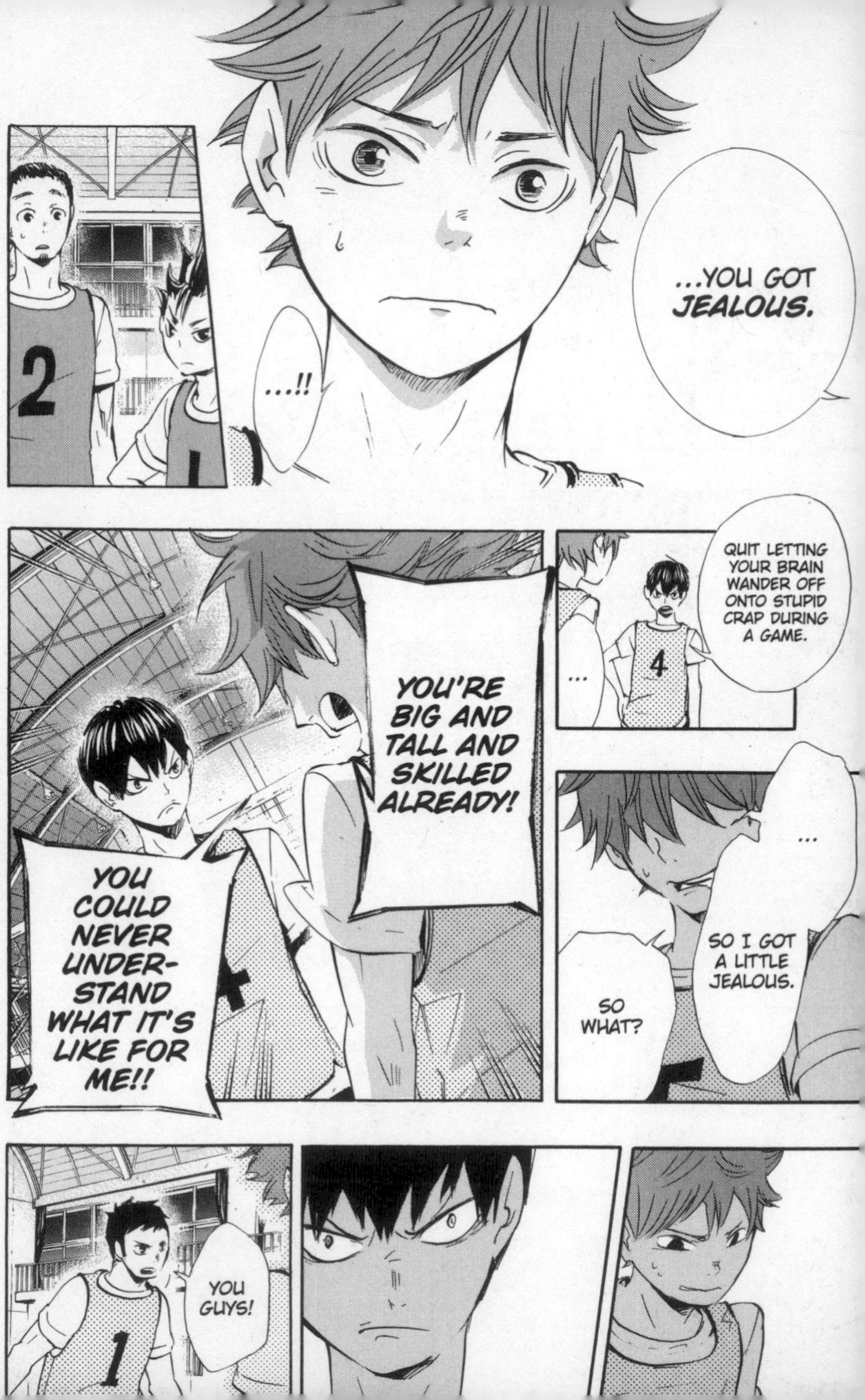
...YOU GOT JEALOUS.
...!!
QUIT LETTING YOUR BRAIN WANDER OFF ONTO STUPID CRAP DURING A GAME.
...
...
SO I GOT A LITTLE JEALOUS.
SO WHAT?
YOU'RE BIG AND TALL AND SKILLED ALREADY!
YOU COULD NEVER UNDERSTAND WHAT IT'S LIKE FOR ME!!
YOU GUYS!

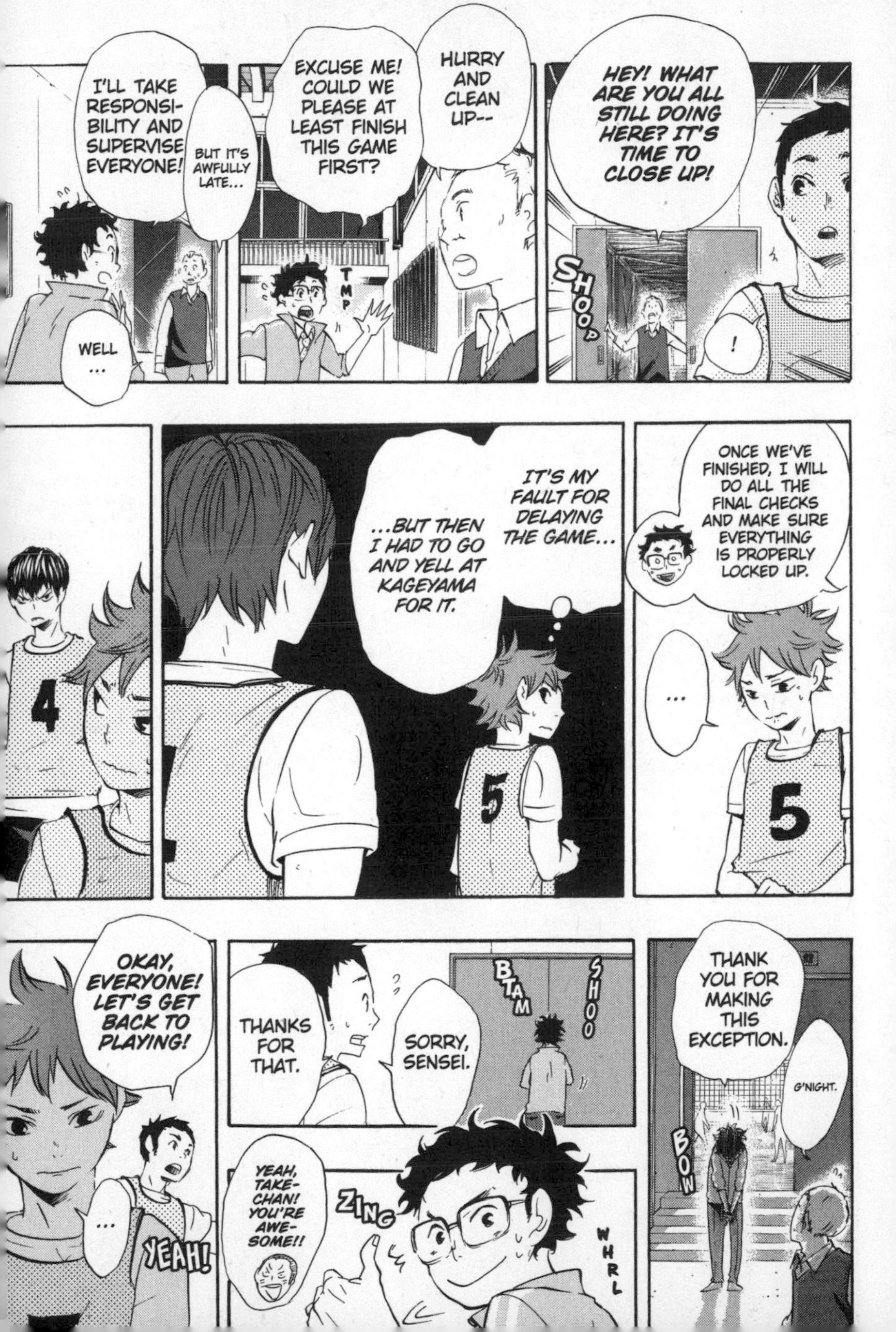
!
HEY! WHAT ARE YOU ALL STILL DOING HERE? IT'S TIME TO CLOSE UP!
SHOOP
HURRY AND CLEAN UP--
EXCUSE ME! COULD WE PLEASE AT LEAST FINISH THIS GAME FIRST?
TMP
BUT IT'S AWFULLY LATE...
I'LL TAKE RESPONSIBILITY AND SUPERVISE EVERYONE!
WELL ...
ONCE WE'VE FINISHED, I WILL DO ALL THE FINAL CHECKS AND MAKE SURE EVERYTHING IS PROPERLY LOCKED UP.
...
IT'S MY FAULT FOR DELAYING THE GAME...
...BUT THEN I HAD TO GO AND YELL AT KAGEYAMA FOR IT.
THANK YOU FOR MAKING THIS EXCEPTION.
G'NIGHT.
BOW
SHOO
BTAM
SORRY, SENSEI.
THANKS FOR THAT.
WHRL
ZING
YEAH, TAKE-CHAN! YOU'RE AWESOME!!
OKAY, EVERYONE! LET'S GET BACK TO PLAYING!
YEAH!
...

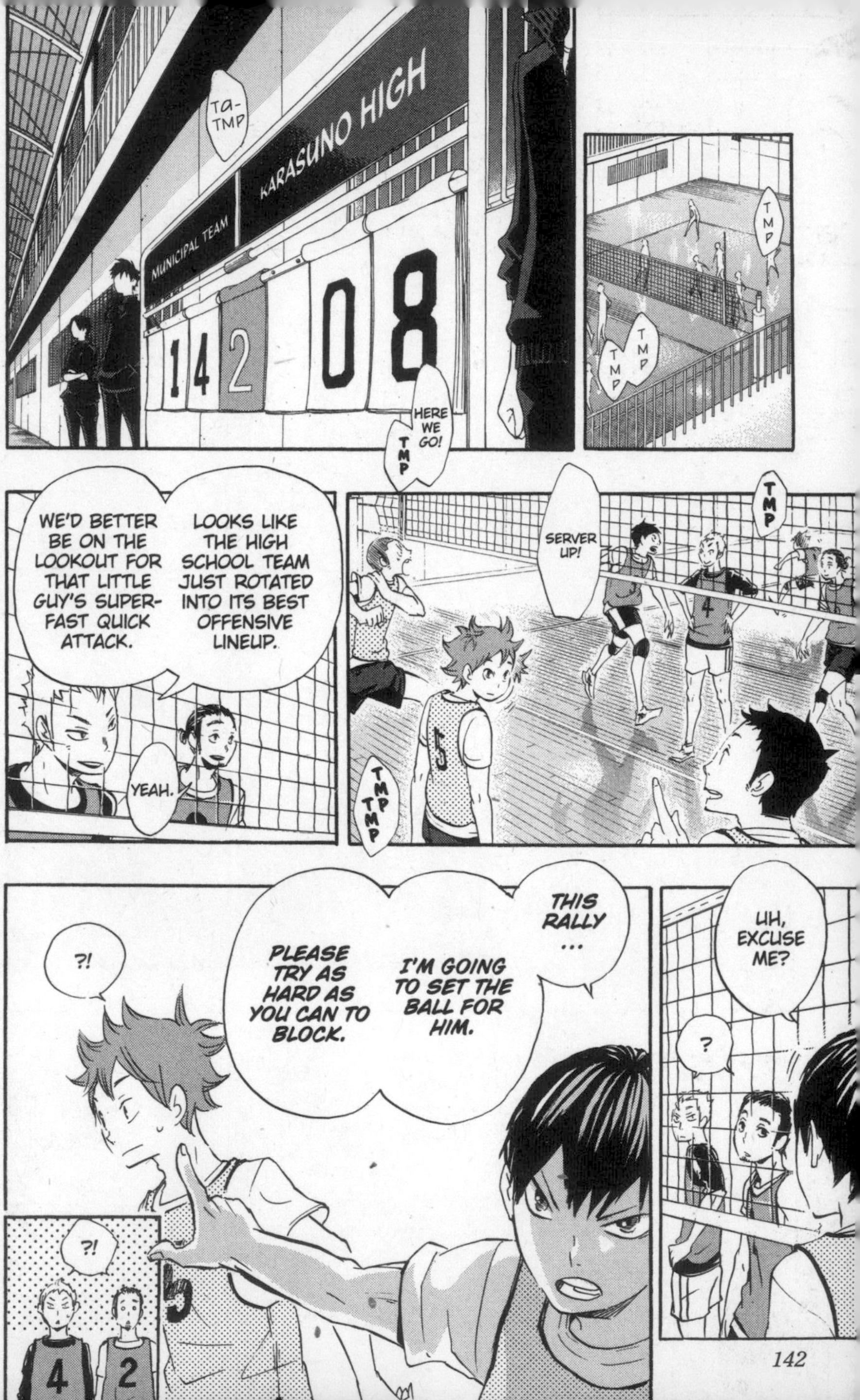
TMP
TMP
TMP
Ta-TMP
KARASUNO HIGH
MUNICIPAL TEAM
14 2 08
HERE WE GO!
TMP
TMP
SERVER UP!
TMP TMP
LOOKS LIKE THE HIGH SCHOOL TEAM JUST ROTATED INTO ITS BEST OFFENSIVE LINEUP.
WE'D BETTER BE ON THE LOOKOUT FOR THAT LITTLE GUY'S SUPER-FAST QUICK ATTACK.
YEAH.
UH, EXCUSE ME?
?
THIS RALLY...
I'M GOING TO SET THE BALL FOR HIM.
PLEASE TRY AS HARD AS YOU CAN TO BLOCK.
?!
?!

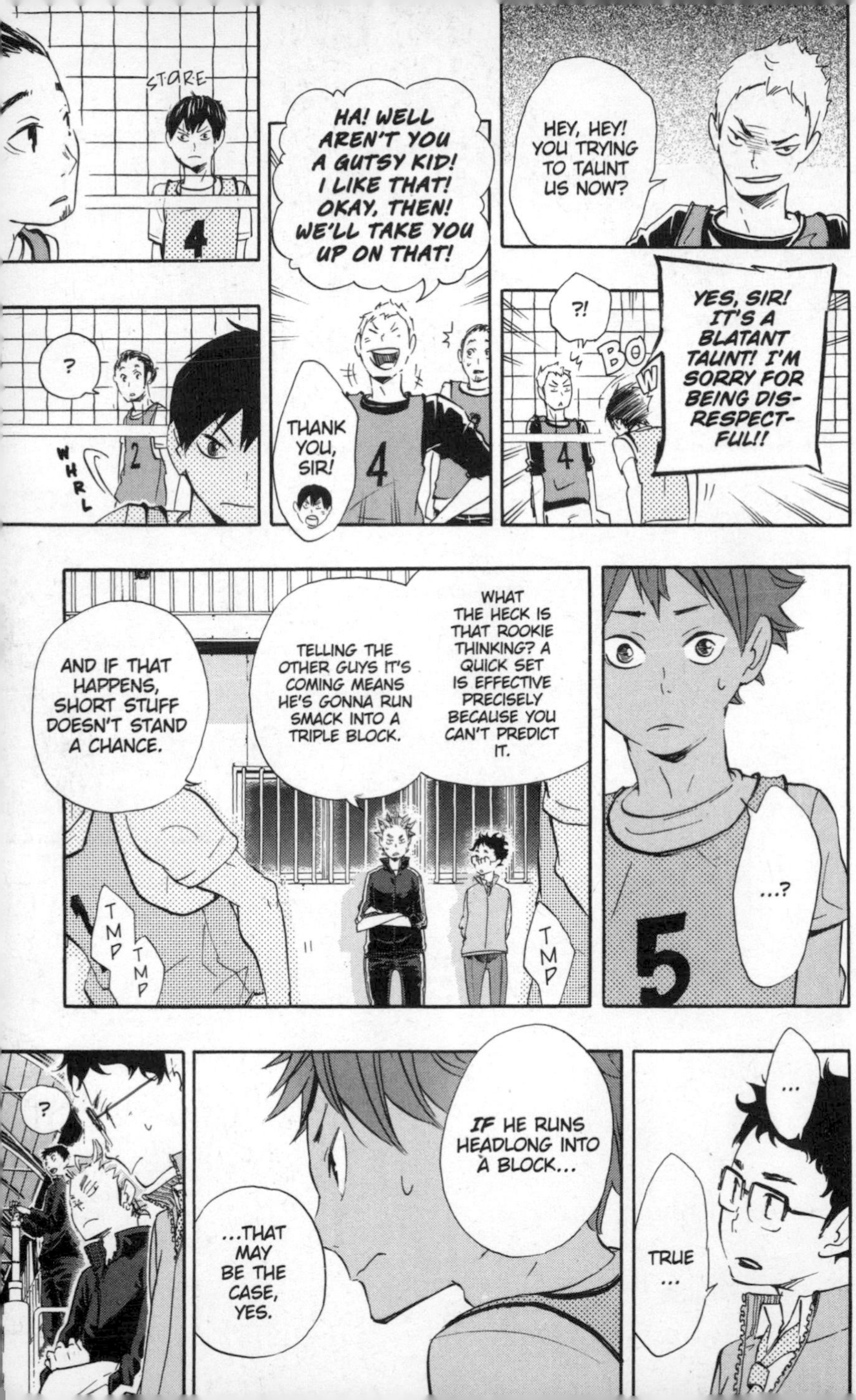
HEY, HEY! YOU TRYING TO TAUNT US NOW?
?!
BOW
YES, SIR! IT'S A BLATANT TAUNT! I'M SORRY FOR BEING DIS-RESPECT-FUL!!
HA! WELL AREN'T YOU A GUTSY KID! I LIKE THAT! OKAY, THEN! WE'LL TAKE YOU UP ON THAT!
THANK YOU, SIR!
STARE
?
WHRL
...?
WHAT THE HECK IS THAT ROOKIE THINKING? A QUICK SET IS EFFECTIVE PRECISELY BECAUSE YOU CAN'T PREDICT IT.
TELLING THE OTHER GUYS IT'S COMING MEANS HE'S GONNA RUN SMACK INTO A TRIPLE BLOCK.
AND IF THAT HAPPENS, SHORT STUFF DOESN'T STAND A CHANCE.
TMP
TMP
TMP
...
TRUE ...
IF HE RUNS HEADLONG INTO A BLOCK...
...THAT MAY BE THE CASE, YES.
?

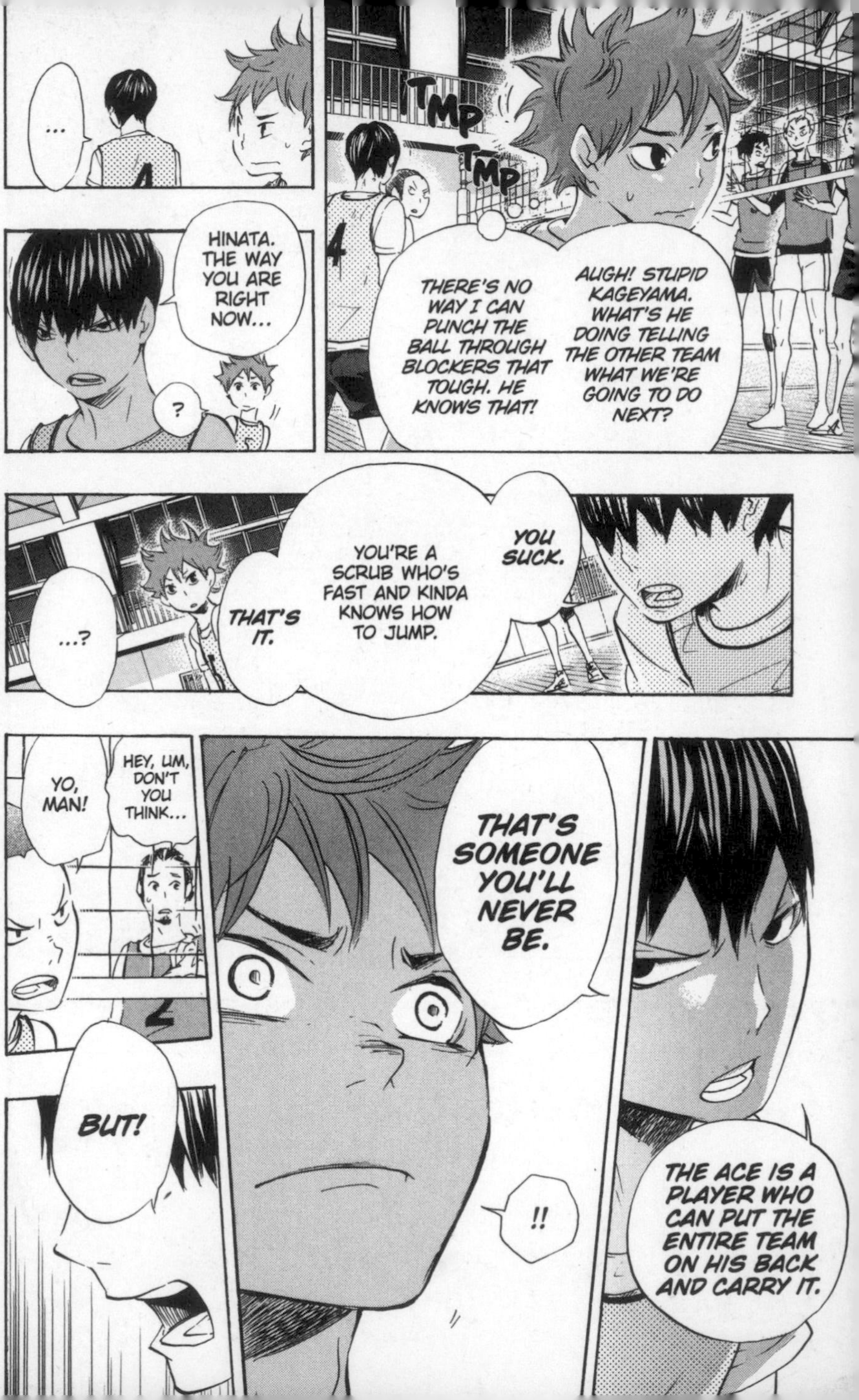
TMP
TMP
AUGH! STUPID KAGEYAMA. WHAT'S HE DOING TELLING THE OTHER TEAM WHAT WE'RE GOING TO DO NEXT?
THERE'S NO WAY I CAN PUNCH THE BALL THROUGH BLOCKERS THAT TOUGH. HE KNOWS THAT!
...
HINATA. THE WAY YOU ARE RIGHT NOW...
?
YOU SUCK.
YOU'RE A SCRUB WHO'S FAST AND KINDA KNOWS HOW TO JUMP.
THAT'S IT.
...?
THE ACE IS A PLAYER WHO CAN PUT THE ENTIRE TEAM ON HIS BACK AND CARRY IT.
THAT'S SOMEONE YOU'LL NEVER BE.
!!
HEY, UM, DON'T YOU THINK...
YO, MAN!
BUT!

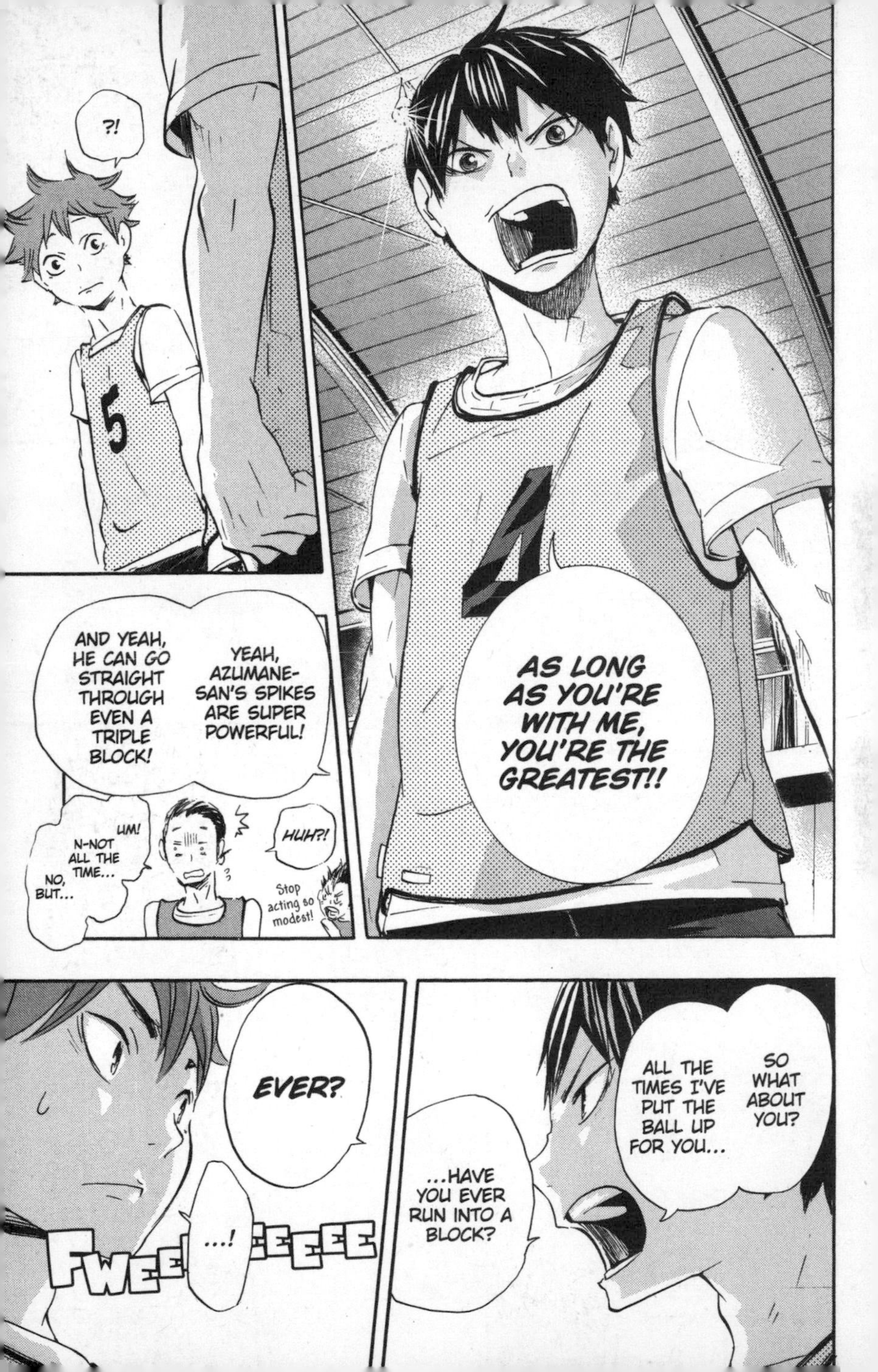
AS LONG AS YOU'RE WITH ME, YOU'RE THE GREATEST!!
?!
YEAH, AZUMANE-SAN'S SPIKES ARE SUPER POWERFUL!
AND YEAH, HE CAN GO STRAIGHT THROUGH EVEN A TRIPLE BLOCK!
HUH?!
Stop acting so modest!
UM! N-NOT ALL THE TIME... NO, BUT...
SO WHAT ABOUT YOU?
ALL THE TIMES I'VE PUT THE BALL UP FOR YOU...
...HAVE YOU EVER RUN INTO A BLOCK?
EVER?
...!
FWEE EEEEE

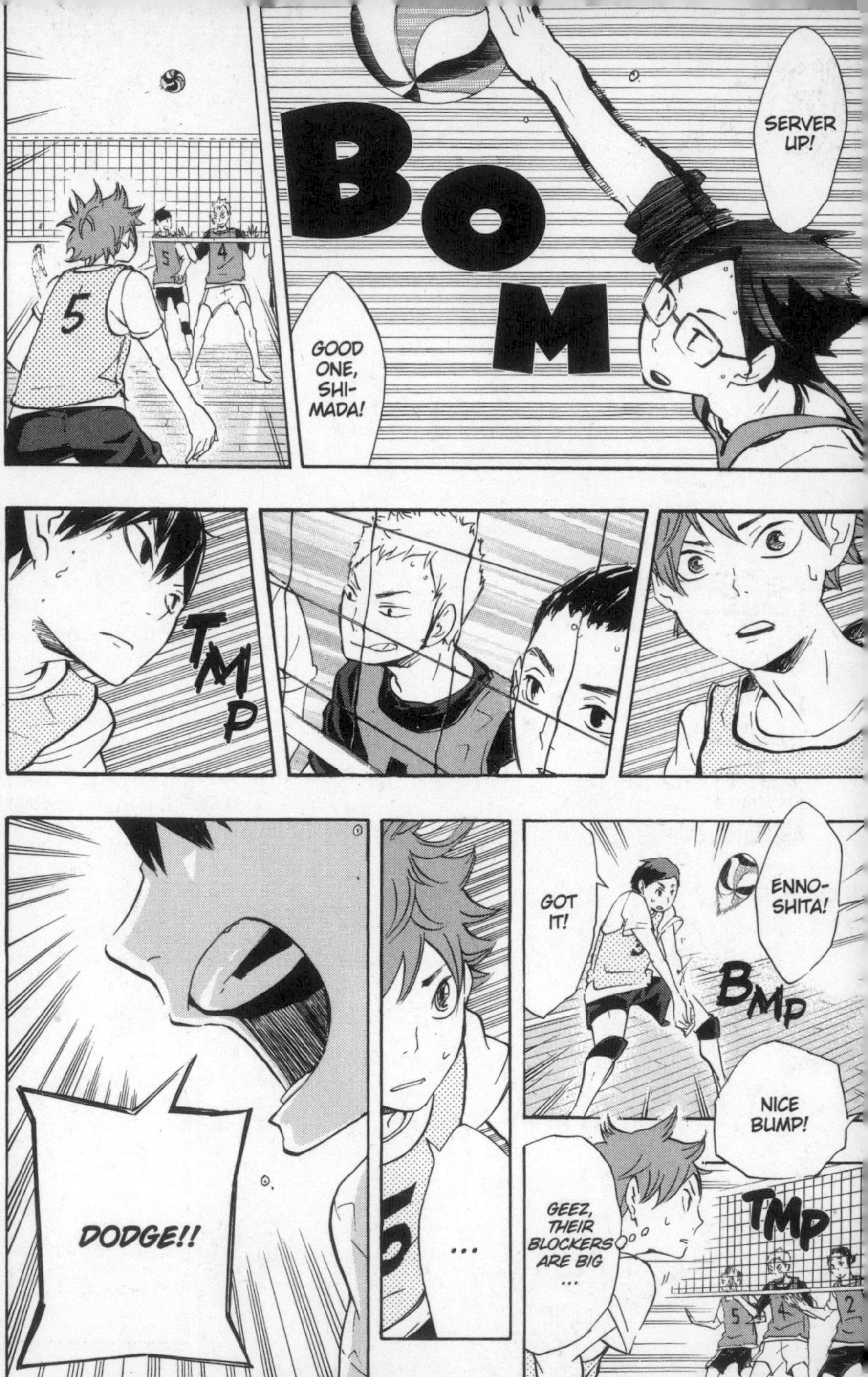
SERVER UP!
BOM
GOOD ONE, SHIMADA!
TMP
ENNOSHITA!
GOT IT!
BMP
NICE BUMP!
TMP
GEEZ, THEIR BLOCKERS ARE BIG ...
...
DODGE!!

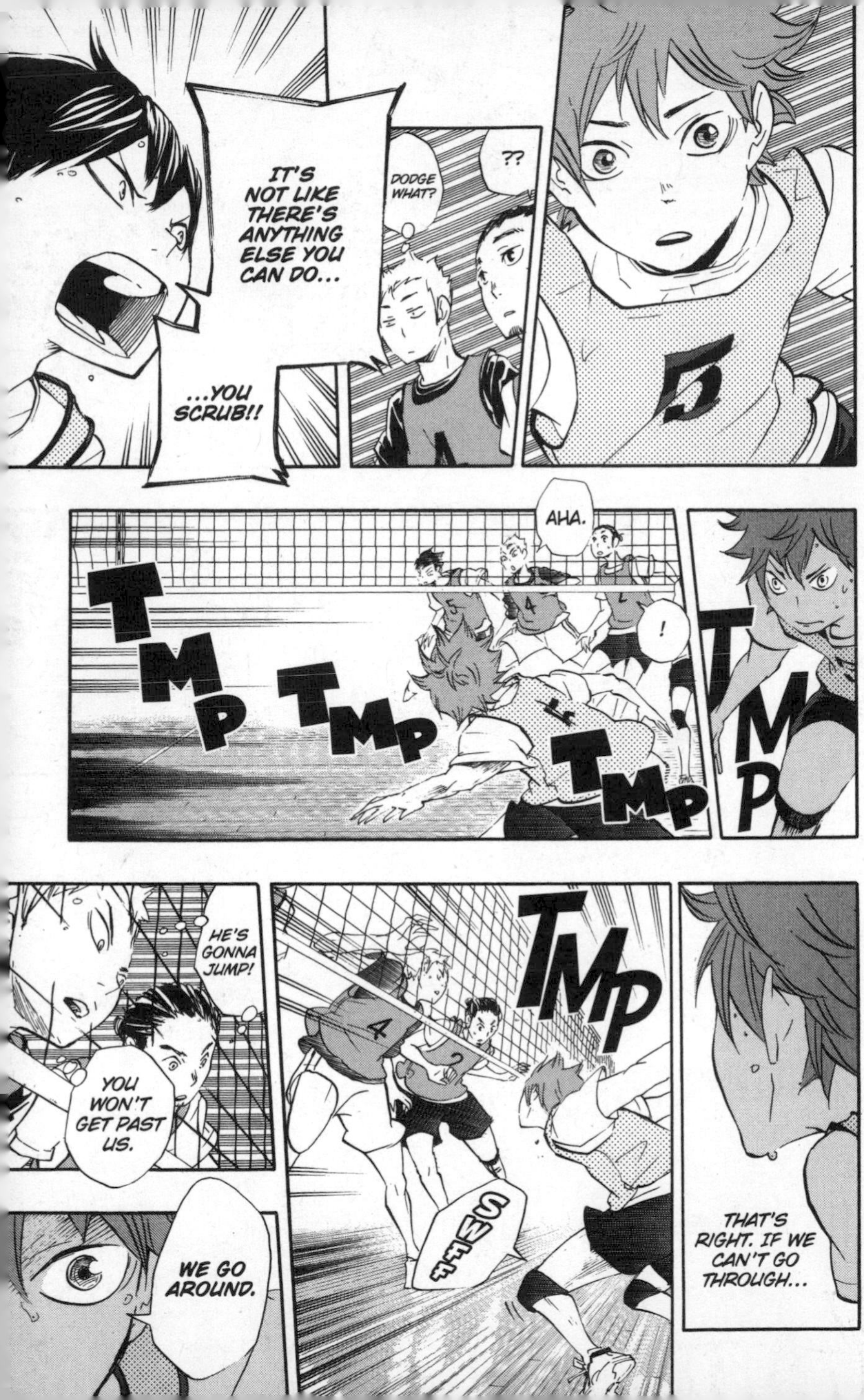
??
DODGE WHAT?
IT'S NOT LIKE THERE'S ANYTHING ELSE YOU CAN DO...
...YOU SCRUB!!
TMP
AHA.
!
TMP TMP TMP
THAT'S RIGHT. IF WE CAN'T GO THROUGH...
TMP
SWFF
HE'S GONNA JUMP!
YOU WON'T GET PAST US.
WE GO AROUND.

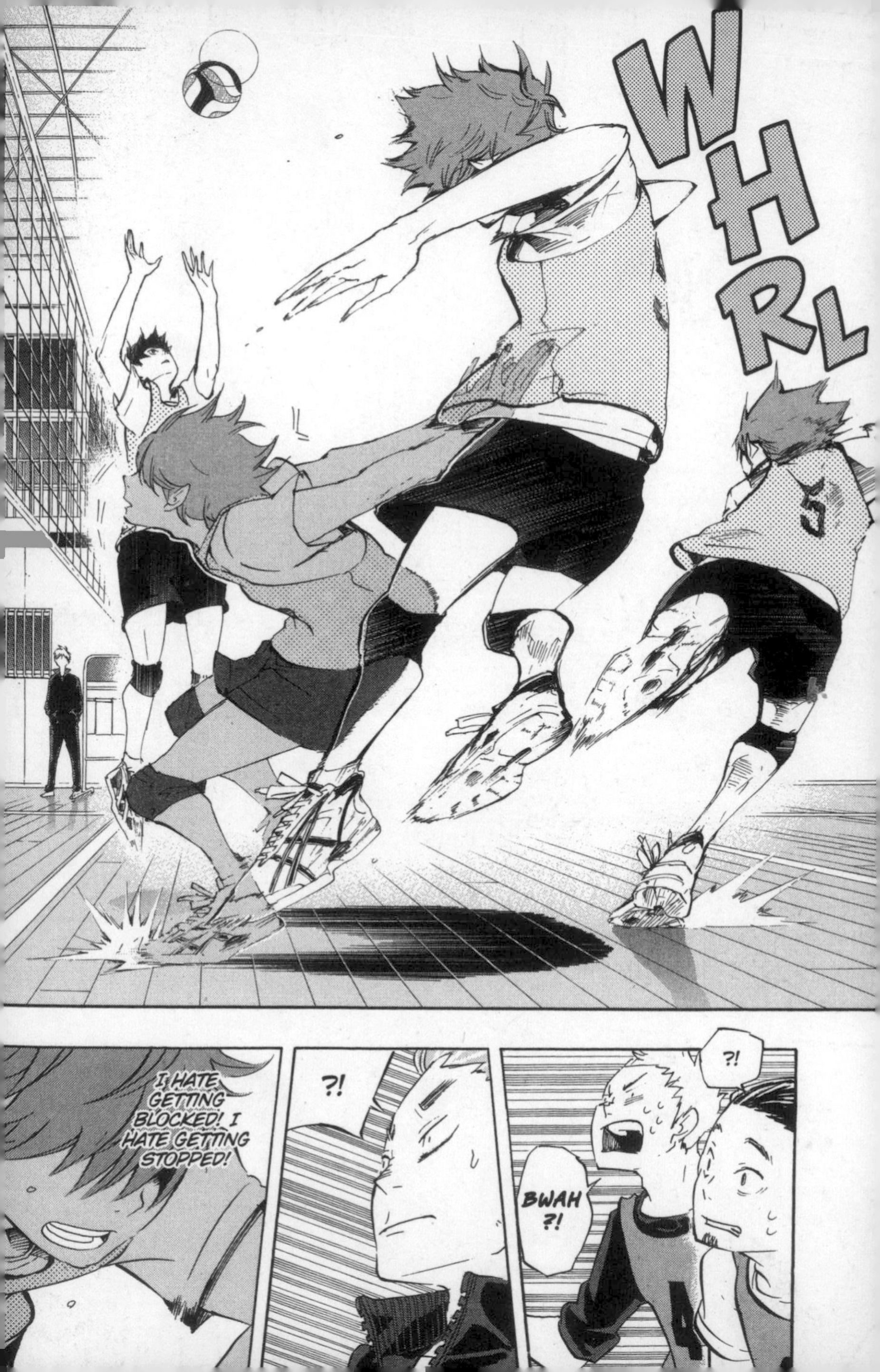
WHRL
?!
BWAH ?!
?!
I HATE GETTING BLOCKED! I HATE GETTING STOPPED!

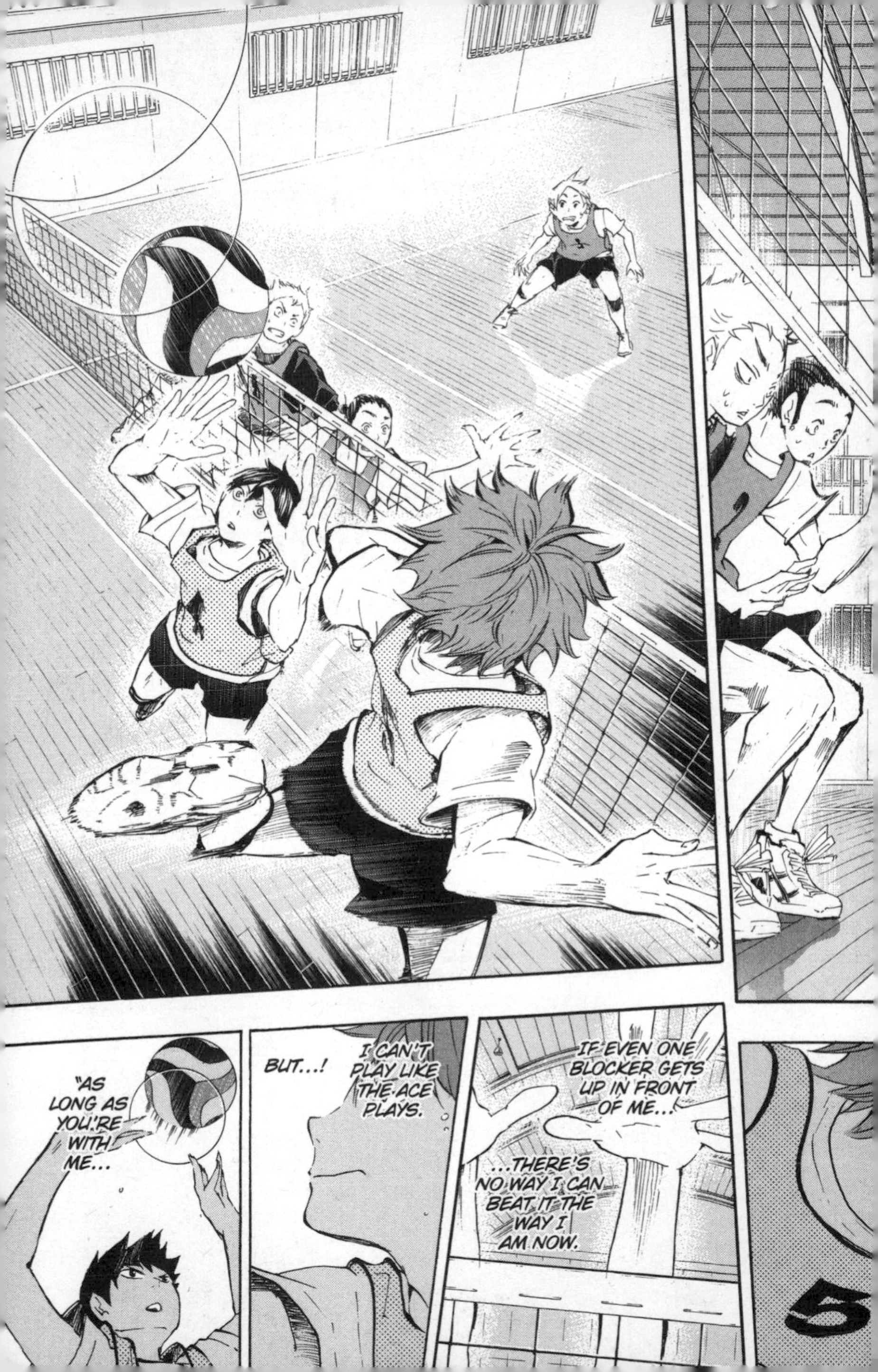
IF EVEN ONE BLOCKER GETS UP IN FRONT OF ME...
...THERE'S NO WAY I CAN BEAT IT THE WAY I AM NOW.
I CAN'T PLAY LIKE THE ACE PLAYS.
BUT...!
"AS LONG AS YOU'RE WITH ME...

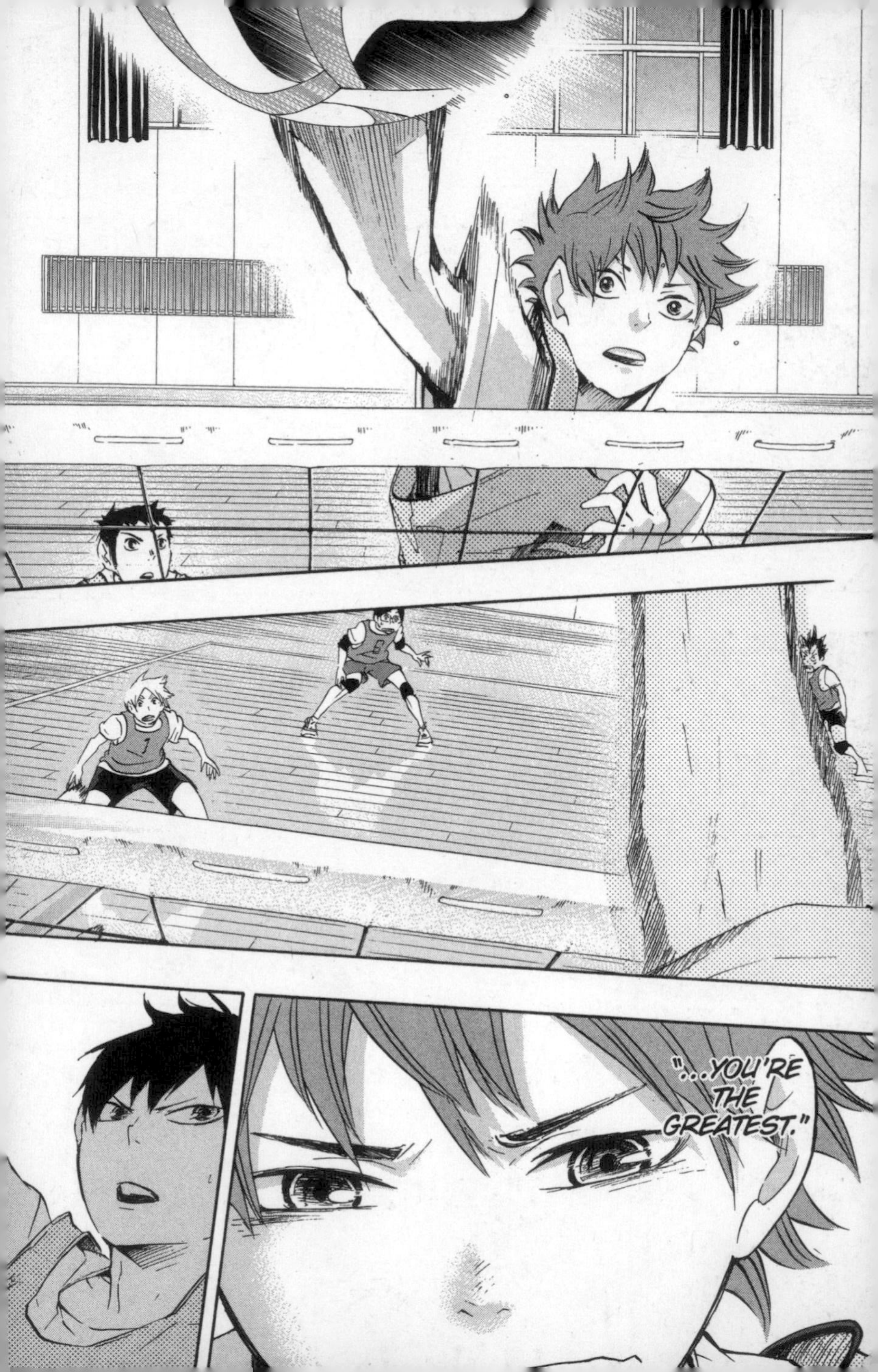
"...YOU'RE THE GREATEST."

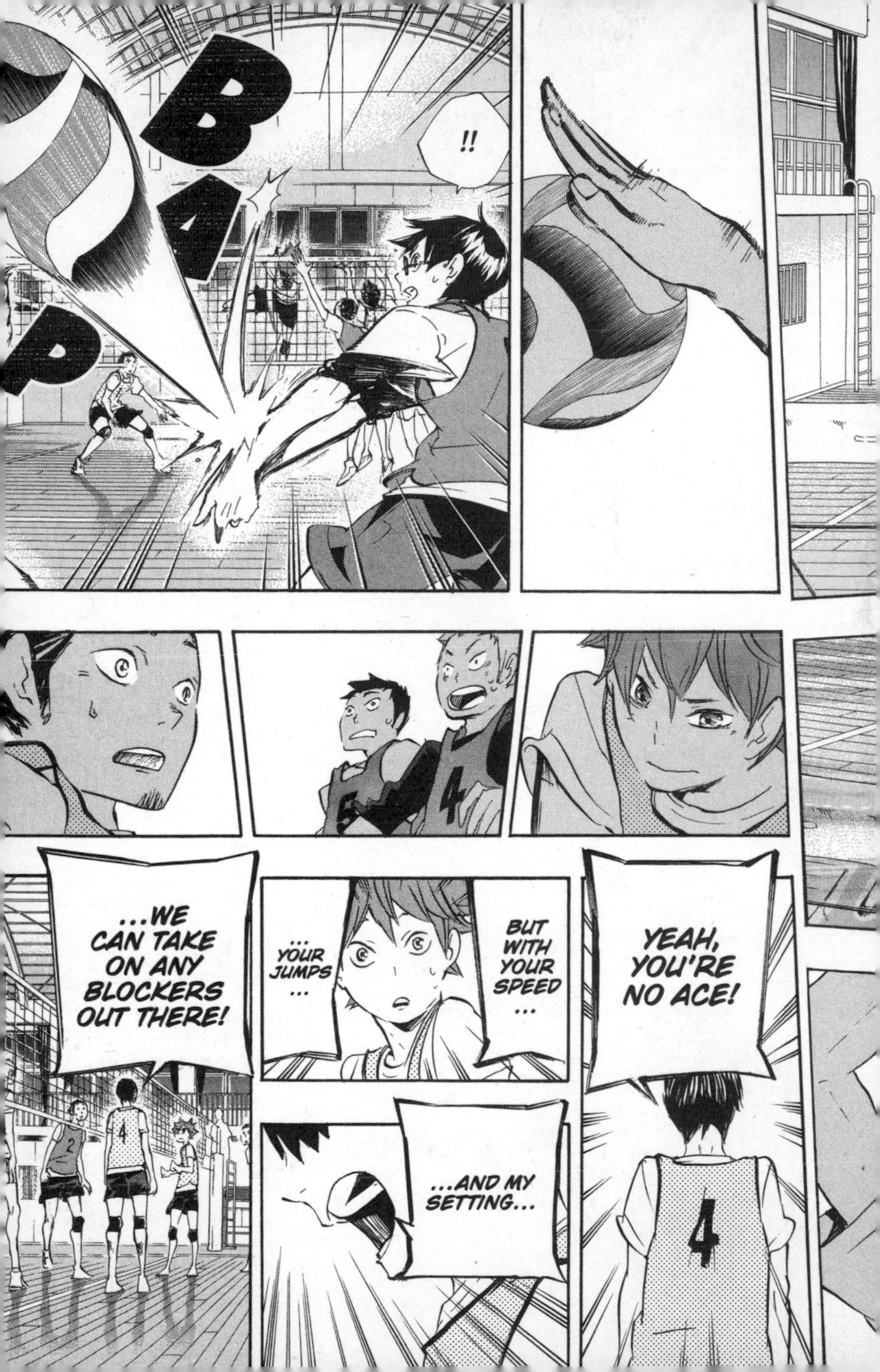
!!
BAP
YEAH, YOU'RE NO ACE!
BUT WITH YOUR SPEED...
...YOUR JUMPS...
...AND MY SETTING...
...WE CAN TAKE ON ANY BLOCKERS OUT THERE!

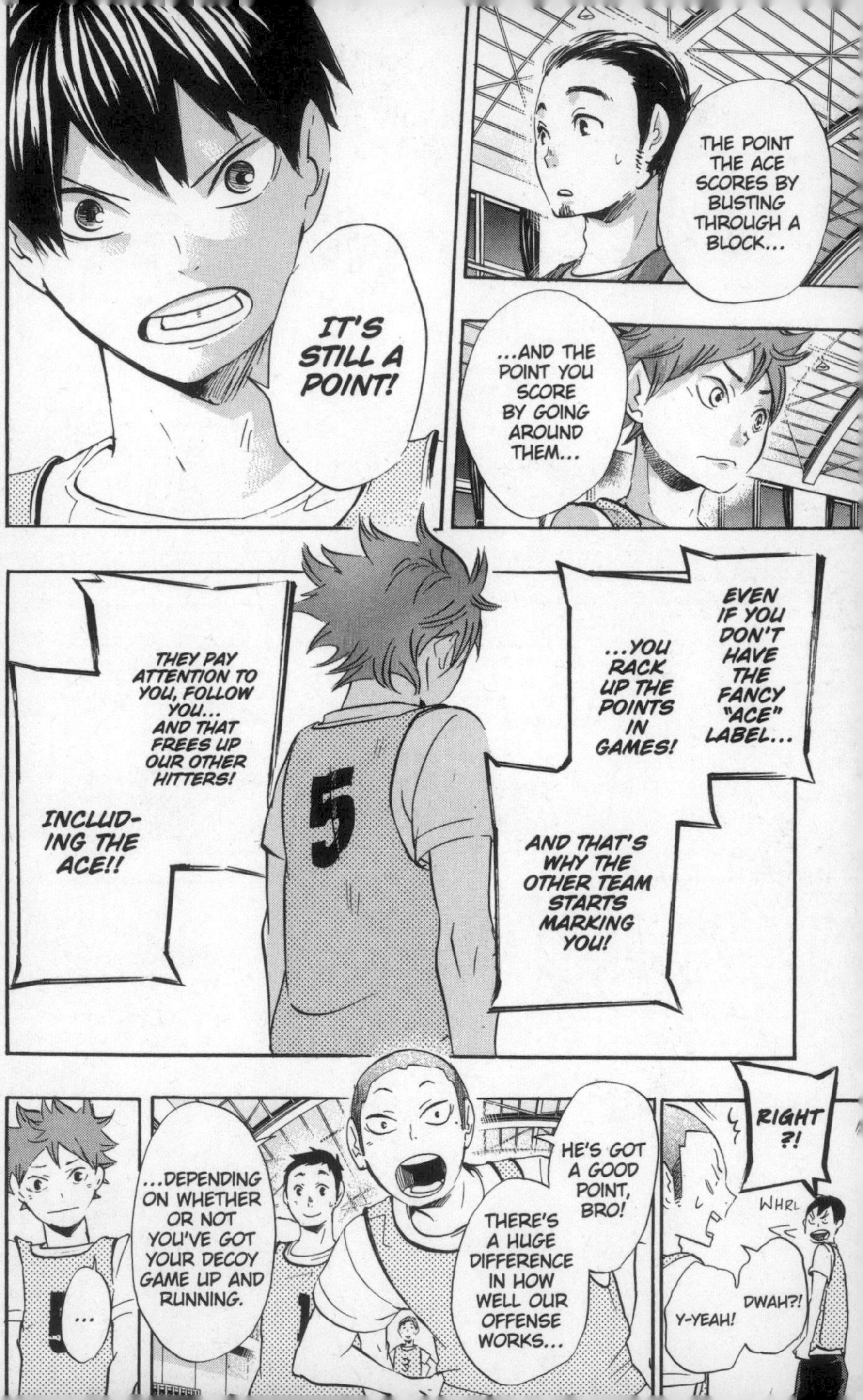
THE POINT THE ACE SCORES BY BUSTING THROUGH A BLOCK...
...AND THE POINT YOU SCORE BY GOING AROUND THEM...
IT'S STILL A POINT!
EVEN IF YOU DON'T HAVE THE FANCY "ACE" LABEL...
...YOU RACK UP THE POINTS IN GAMES!
AND THAT'S WHY THE OTHER TEAM STARTS MARKING YOU!
THEY PAY ATTENTION TO YOU, FOLLOW YOU... AND THAT FREES UP OUR OTHER HITTERS!
INCLUD-ING THE ACE!!
RIGHT?!
WHRL
DWAH?!
Y-YEAH!
HE'S GOT A GOOD POINT, BRO!
THERE'S A HUGE DIFFERENCE IN HOW WELL OUR OFFENSE WORKS...
...DEPENDING ON WHETHER OR NOT YOU'VE GOT YOUR DECOY GAME UP AND RUNNING.
...

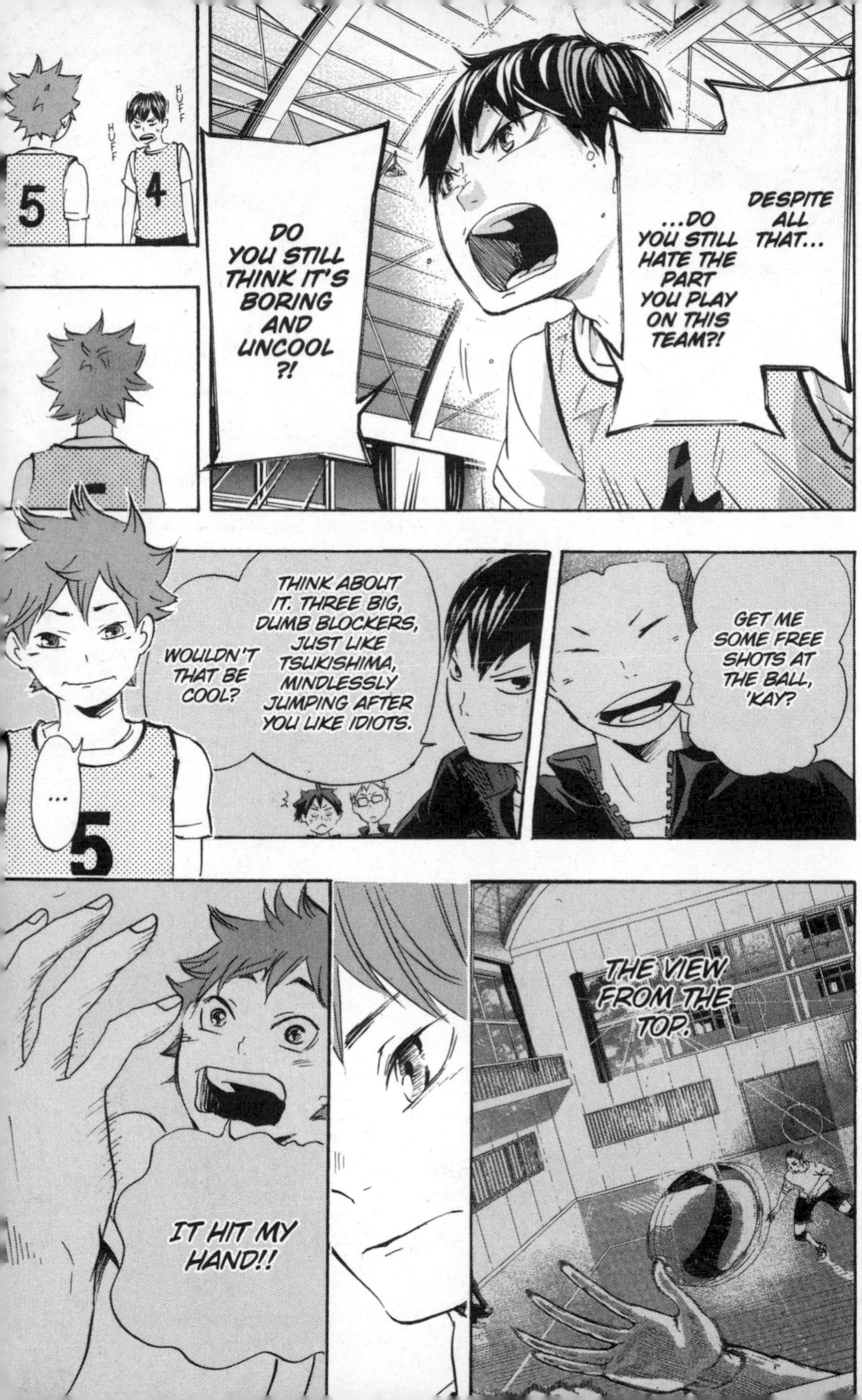
DESPITE ALL THAT...
...DO YOU STILL HATE THE PART YOU PLAY ON THIS TEAM?!
DO YOU STILL THINK IT'S BORING AND UNCOOL ?!
HUFF
HUFF
GET ME SOME FREE SHOTS AT THE BALL, 'KAY?
THINK ABOUT IT. THREE BIG, DUMB BLOCKERS, JUST LIKE TSUKISHIMA, MINDLESSLY JUMPING AFTER YOU LIKE IDIOTS.
WOULDN'T THAT BE COOL?
...
THE VIEW FROM THE TOP.
IT HIT MY HAND!!

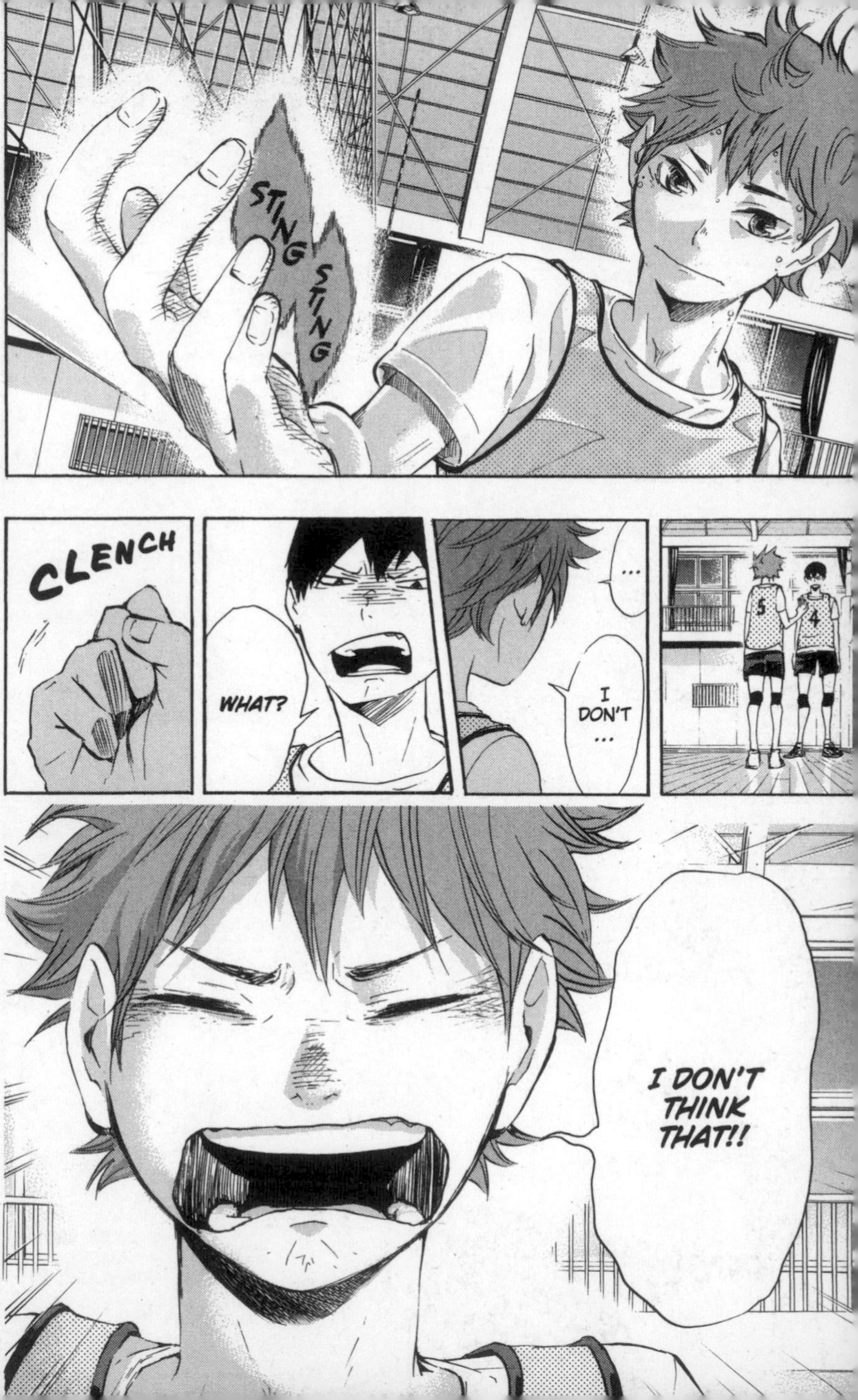
STING
STING
...
I DON'T ...
WHAT?
CLENCH
I DON'T THINK THAT!!

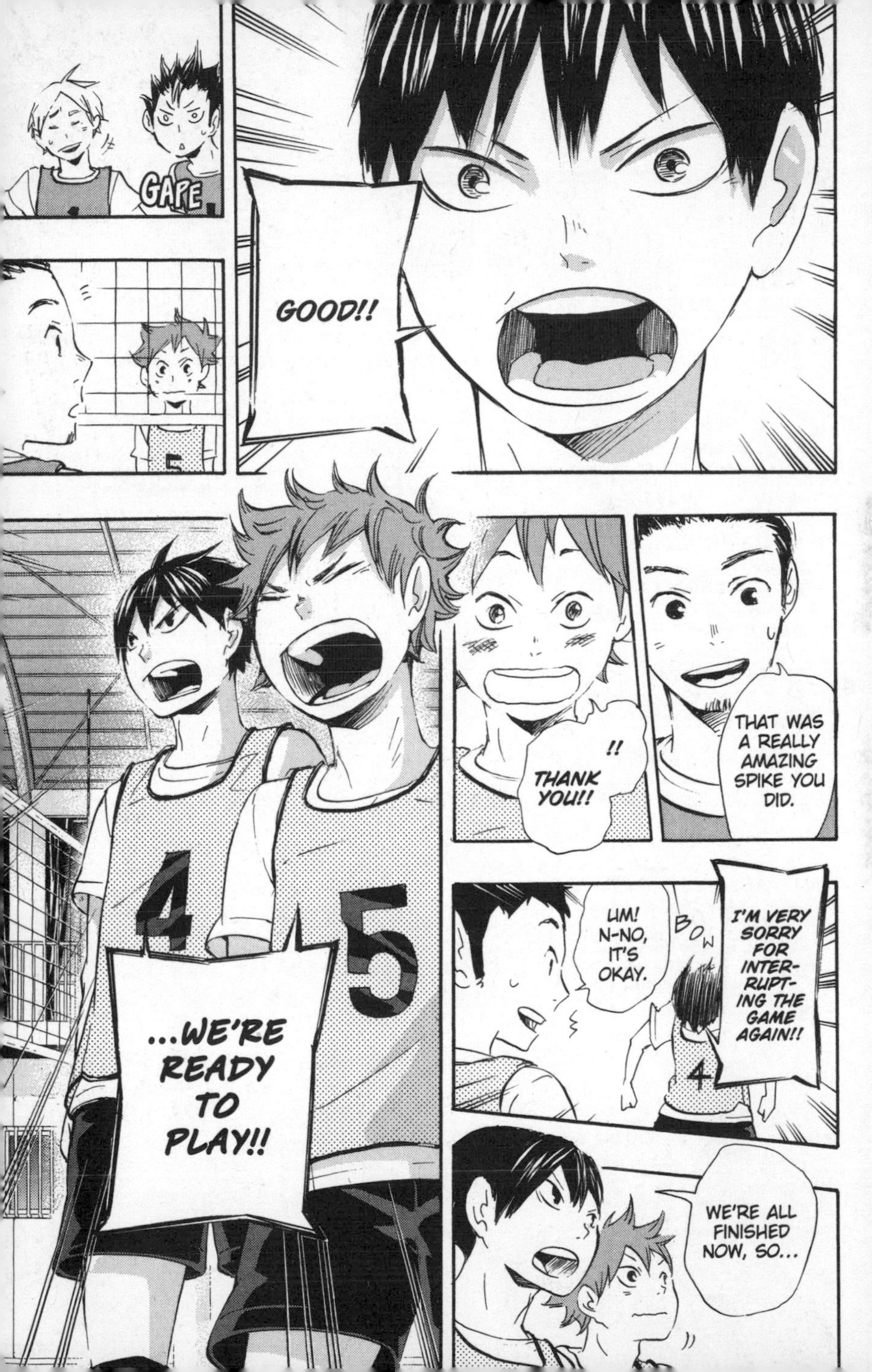
GOOD!!
GAPE
THAT WAS A REALLY AMAZING SPIKE YOU DID.
!!
THANK YOU!!
I'M VERY SORRY FOR INTER-RUPT-ING THE GAME AGAIN!!
BOW
UM! N-NO, IT'S OKAY.
WE'RE ALL FINISHED NOW, SO...
...WE'RE READY TO PLAY!!

KEISHIN UKAI
HEIR TO SAKANOSHITA MARKET

**KARASUNO VOLLEYBALL
TEAM ALUMNUS**

AGE: 26

HEIGHT: 5'10"

WEIGHT: 159 LBS.

BIRTHDAY: APRIL 5

FAVORITE FOOD:
TAMA KONNYAKU YAM
BALLS

CURRENT WORRY:
HE'S NOT EVEN 30, AND
ALREADY EVERYONE IS ON
HIS CASE ABOUT GETTING
MARRIED.

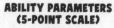

ABILITY PARAMETERS
(5-POINT SCALE)

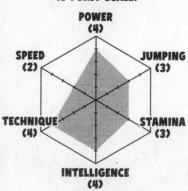

POWER
(4)

SPEED
(2)

JUMPING
(3)

TECHNIQUE
(4)

STAMINA
(3)

INTELLIGENCE
(4)

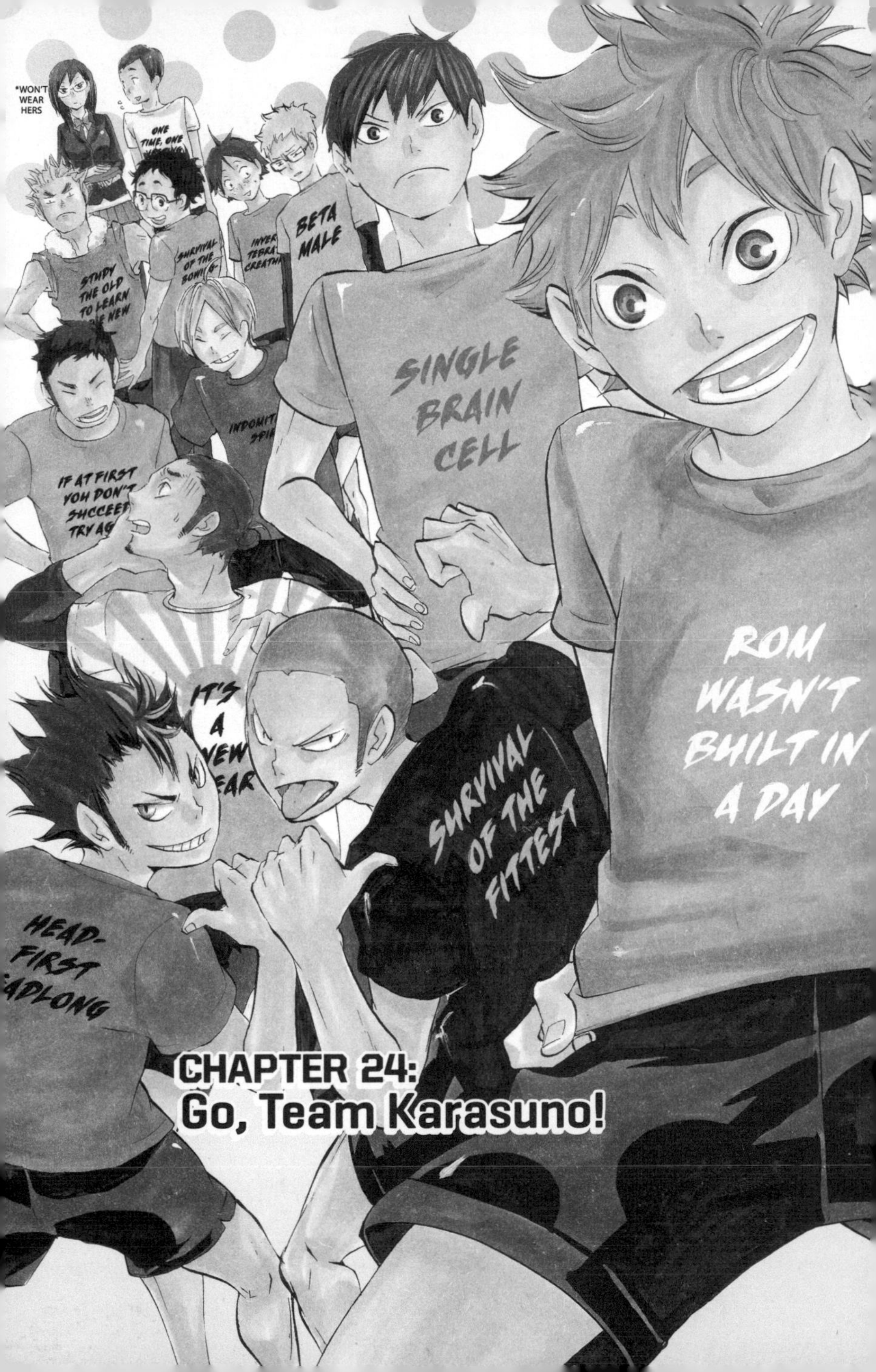
*WON'T WEAR HERS
BETA MALE
STUDY THE OLD TO LEARN
SINGLE BRAIN CELL
ROM WASN'T BUILT IN A DAY
SURVIVAL OF THE FITTEST
HEAD- FIRST

CHAPTER 24: Go, Team Karasuno!

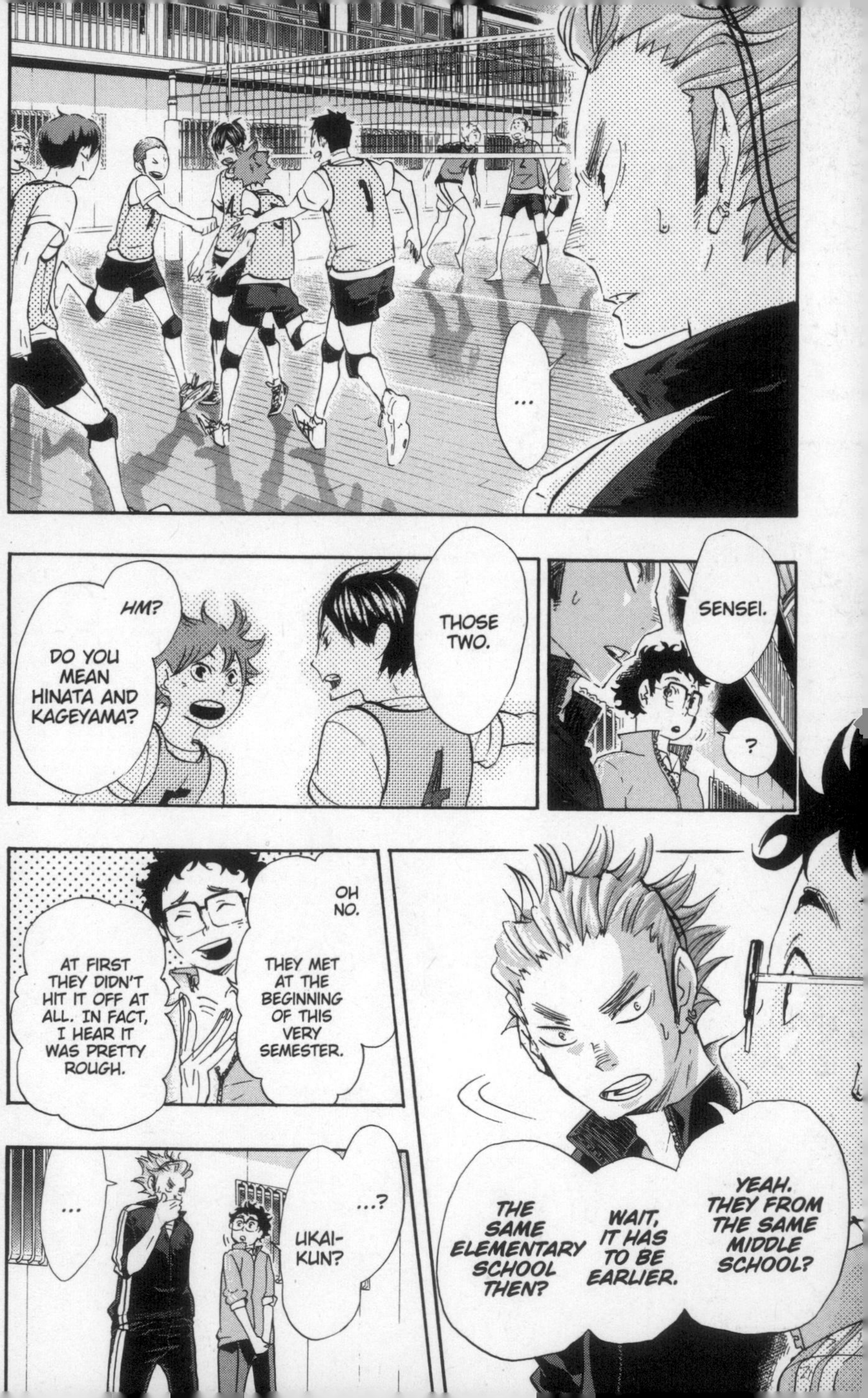
...
SENSEI.
?
THOSE TWO.
HM?
DO YOU MEAN HINATA AND KAGEYAMA?
YEAH. THEY FROM THE SAME MIDDLE SCHOOL?
WAIT, IT HAS TO BE EARLIER.
THE SAME ELEMENTARY SCHOOL THEN?
OH NO.
THEY MET AT THE BEGINNING OF THIS VERY SEMESTER.
AT FIRST THEY DIDN'T HIT IT OFF AT ALL. IN FACT, I HEAR IT WAS PRETTY ROUGH.
...?
UKAI-KUN?
...

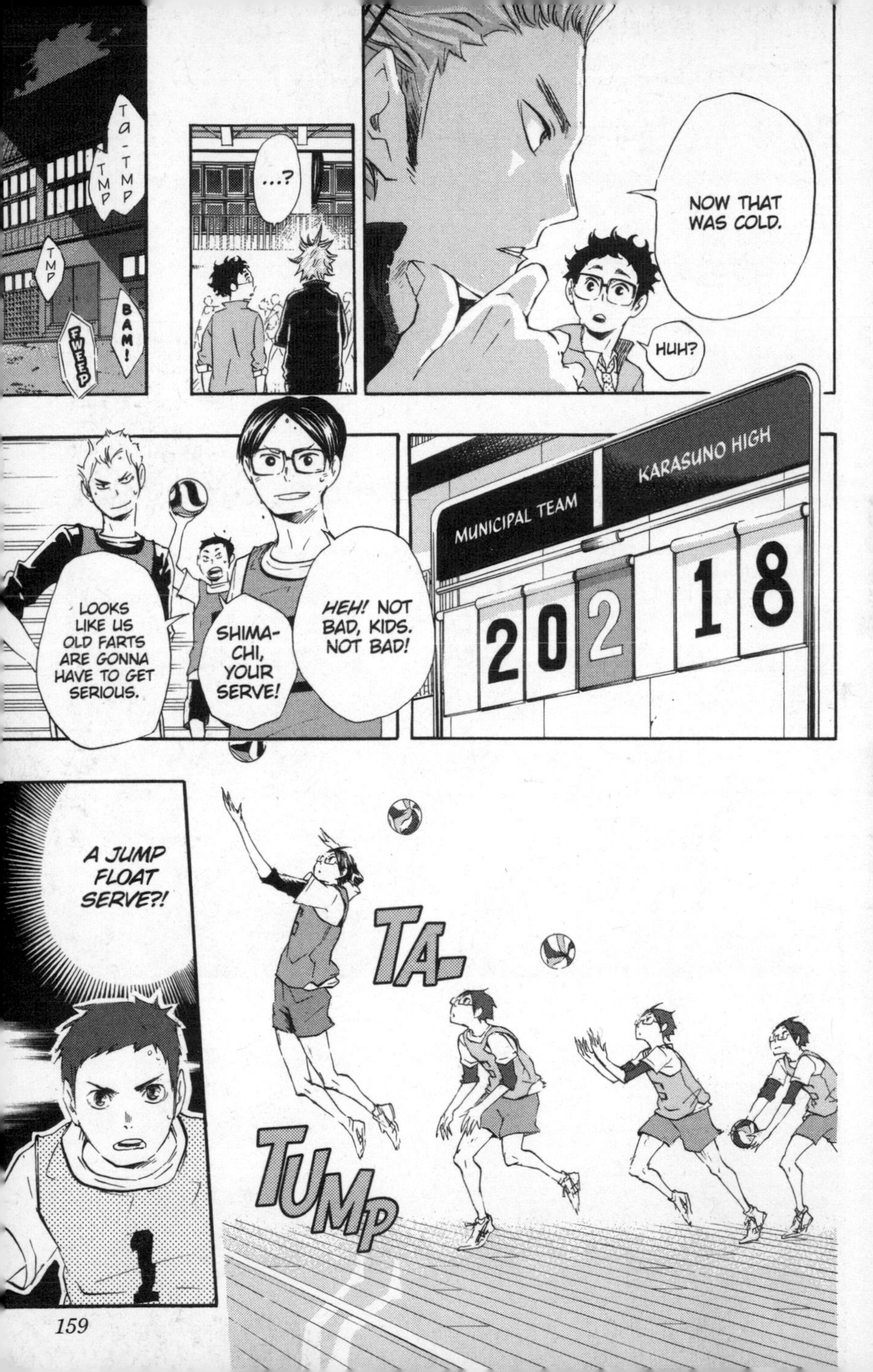
NOW THAT WAS COLD.
HUH?
...?
Ta-TMP
TMP
TMP
BAM!
FWEEP
KARASUNO HIGH
MUNICIPAL TEAM
20
2
18
HEH! NOT BAD, KIDS. NOT BAD!
SHIMA-CHI, YOUR SERVE!
LOOKS LIKE US OLD FARTS ARE GONNA HAVE TO GET SERIOUS.
TA-
TUMP
A JUMP FLOAT SERVE?!

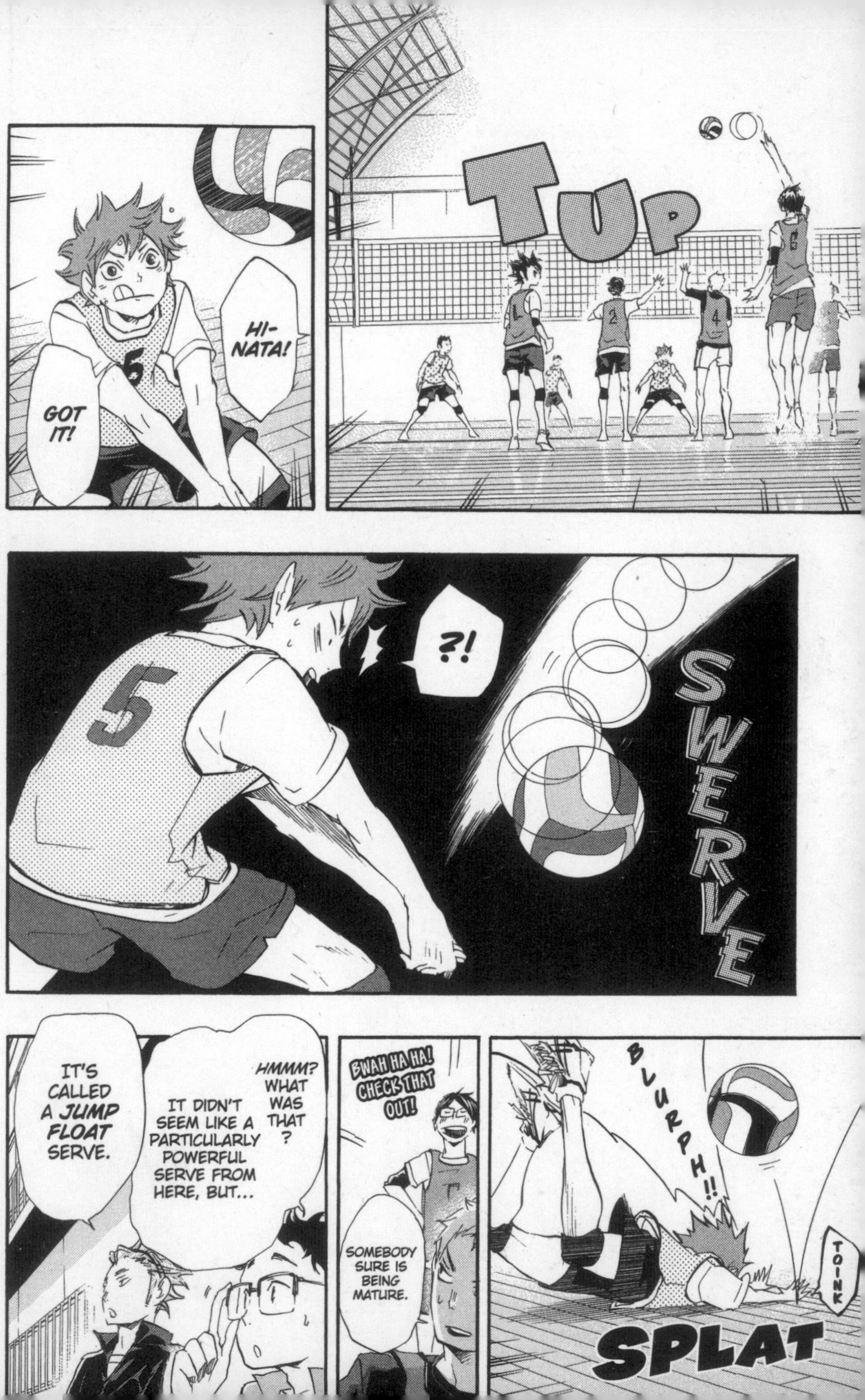
TUP
HI-NATA!
GOT IT!
?!
SWERVE
BLURPH!!
TOINK
SPLAT
BWAH HA HA! CHECK THAT OUT!
SOMEBODY SURE IS BEING MATURE.
HMMM? WHAT WAS THAT?
IT DIDN'T SEEM LIKE A PARTICULARLY POWERFUL SERVE FROM HERE, BUT...
IT'S CALLED A JUMP FLOAT SERVE.

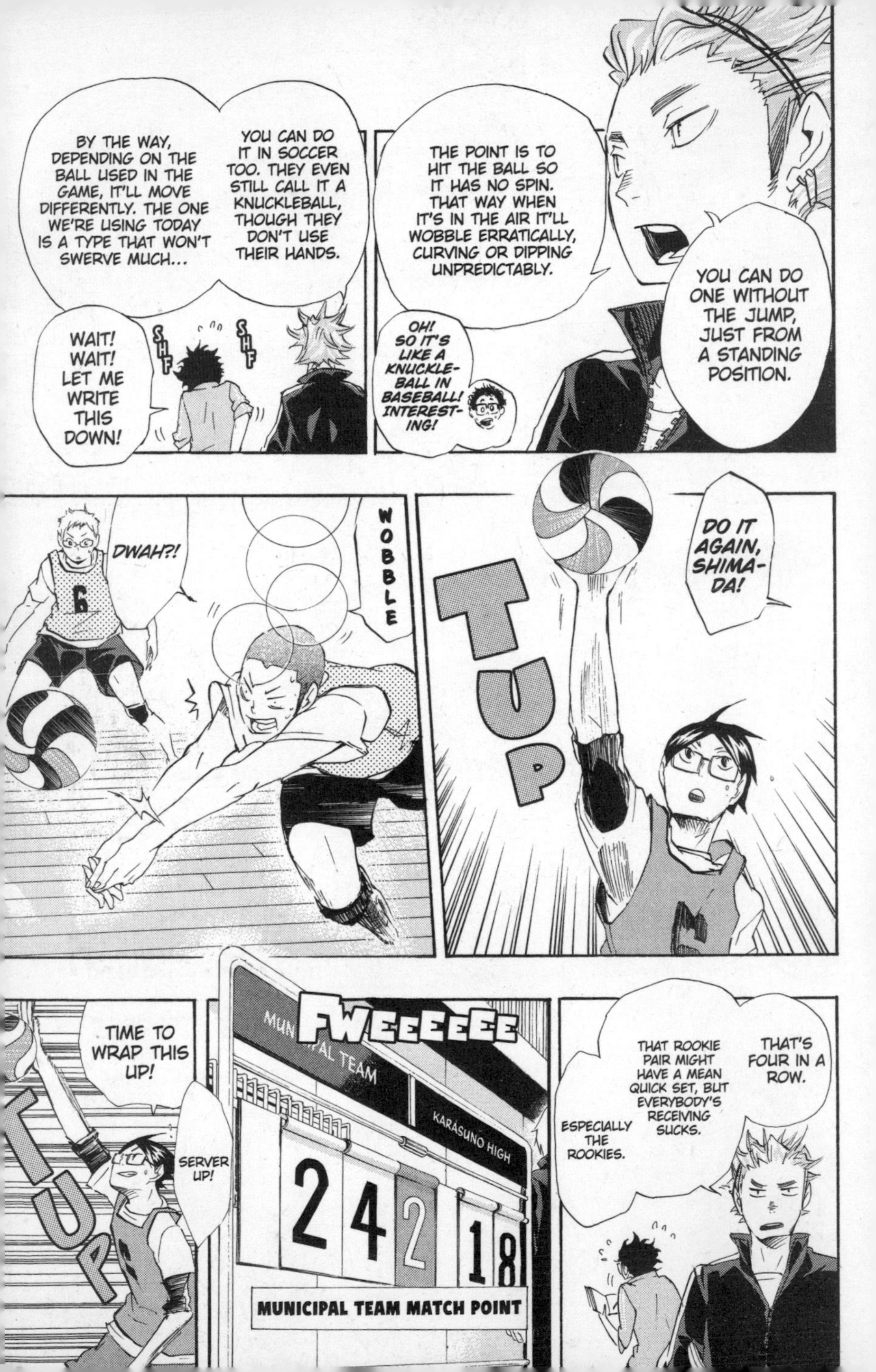
YOU CAN DO ONE WITHOUT THE JUMP, JUST FROM A STANDING POSITION.
THE POINT IS TO HIT THE BALL SO IT HAS NO SPIN. THAT WAY WHEN IT'S IN THE AIR IT'LL WOBBLE ERRATICALLY, CURVING OR DIPPING UNPREDICTABLY.
OH! SO IT'S LIKE A KNUCKLE-BALL IN BASEBALL! INTEREST-ING!
YOU CAN DO IT IN SOCCER TOO. THEY EVEN STILL CALL IT A KNUCKLEBALL, THOUGH THEY DON'T USE THEIR HANDS.
BY THE WAY, DEPENDING ON THE BALL USED IN THE GAME, IT'LL MOVE DIFFERENTLY. THE ONE WE'RE USING TODAY IS A TYPE THAT WON'T SWERVE MUCH...
SHF
SHF
WAIT! WAIT! LET ME WRITE THIS DOWN!
DO IT AGAIN, SHIMA-DA!
TUP
WOBBLE
DWAH?!
THAT'S FOUR IN A ROW.
THAT ROOKIE PAIR MIGHT HAVE A MEAN QUICK SET, BUT EVERYBODY'S RECEIVING SUCKS.
ESPECIALLY THE ROOKIES.
FWEEEEEE
MUNICIPAL TEAM
KARASUNO HIGH
24 2 18
MUNICIPAL TEAM MATCH POINT
TIME TO WRAP THIS UP!
SERVER UP!
TUP

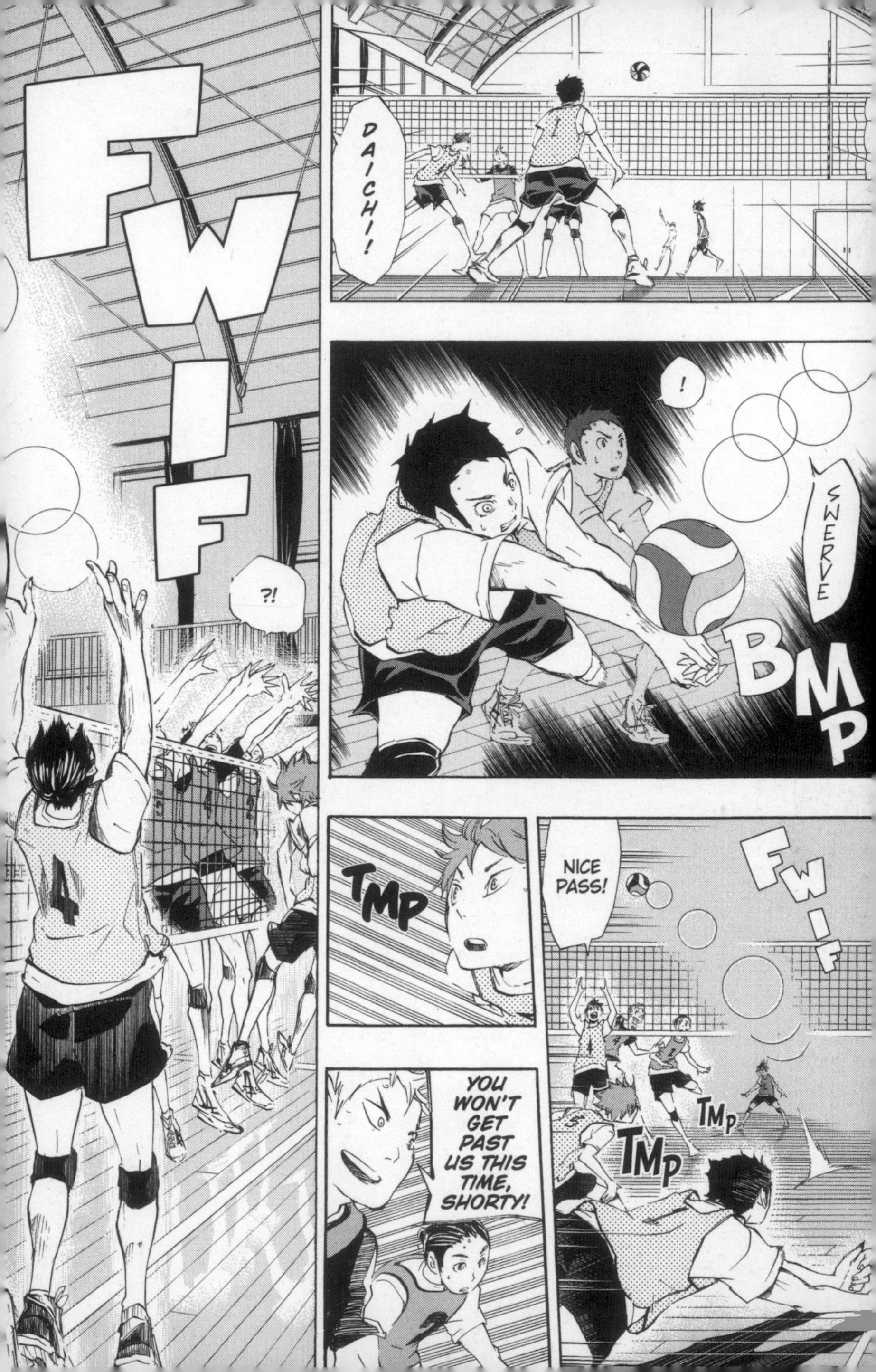
DAICHI!
!
SWERVE
BMP
NICE PASS!
FWIF
TMp
TMp
TMP
YOU WON'T GET PAST US THIS TIME, SHORTY!
FWIFF
?!

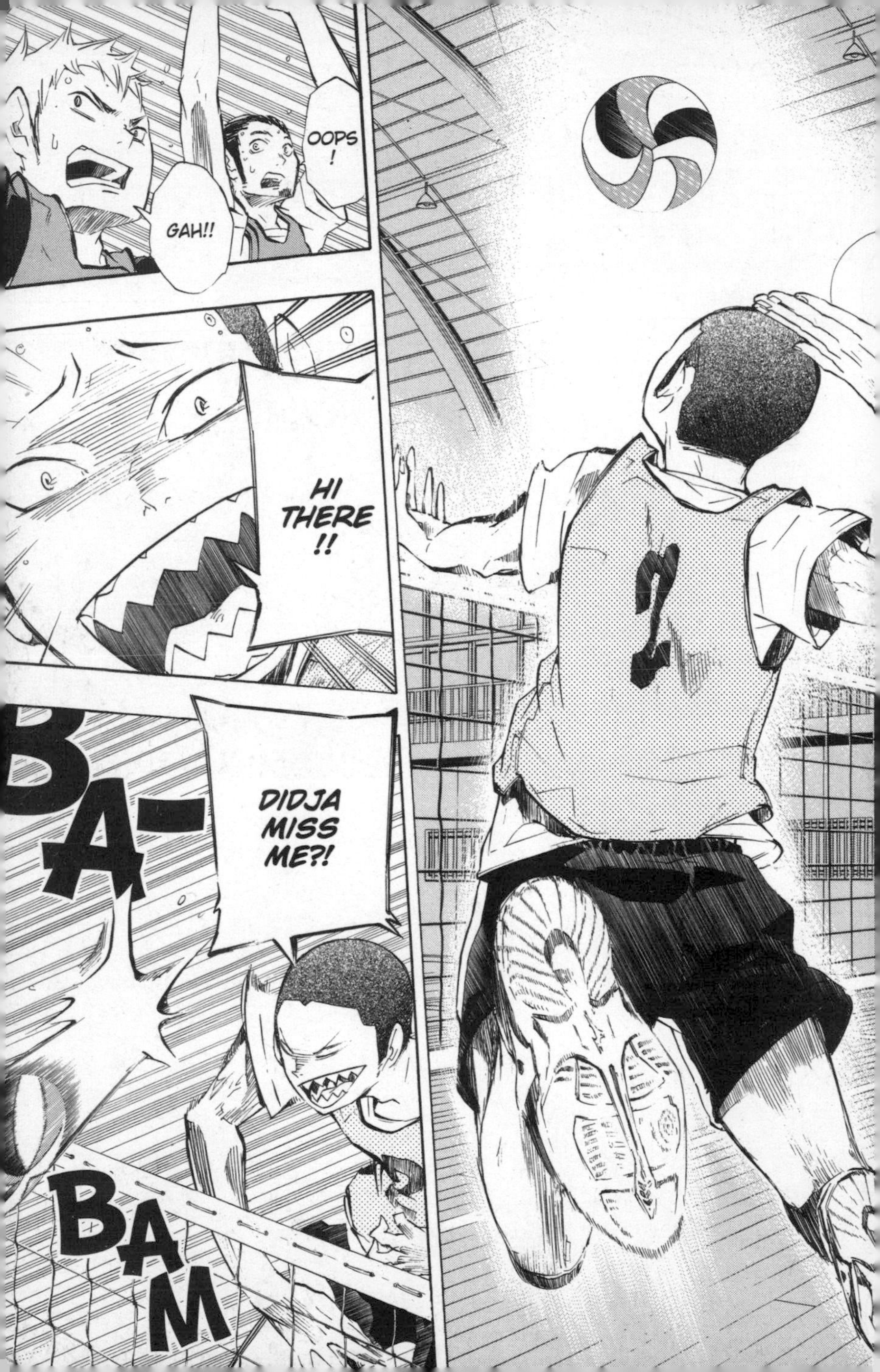
OOPS!
GAH!!
HI THERE!!
DIDJA MISS ME?!
BA-
BAM

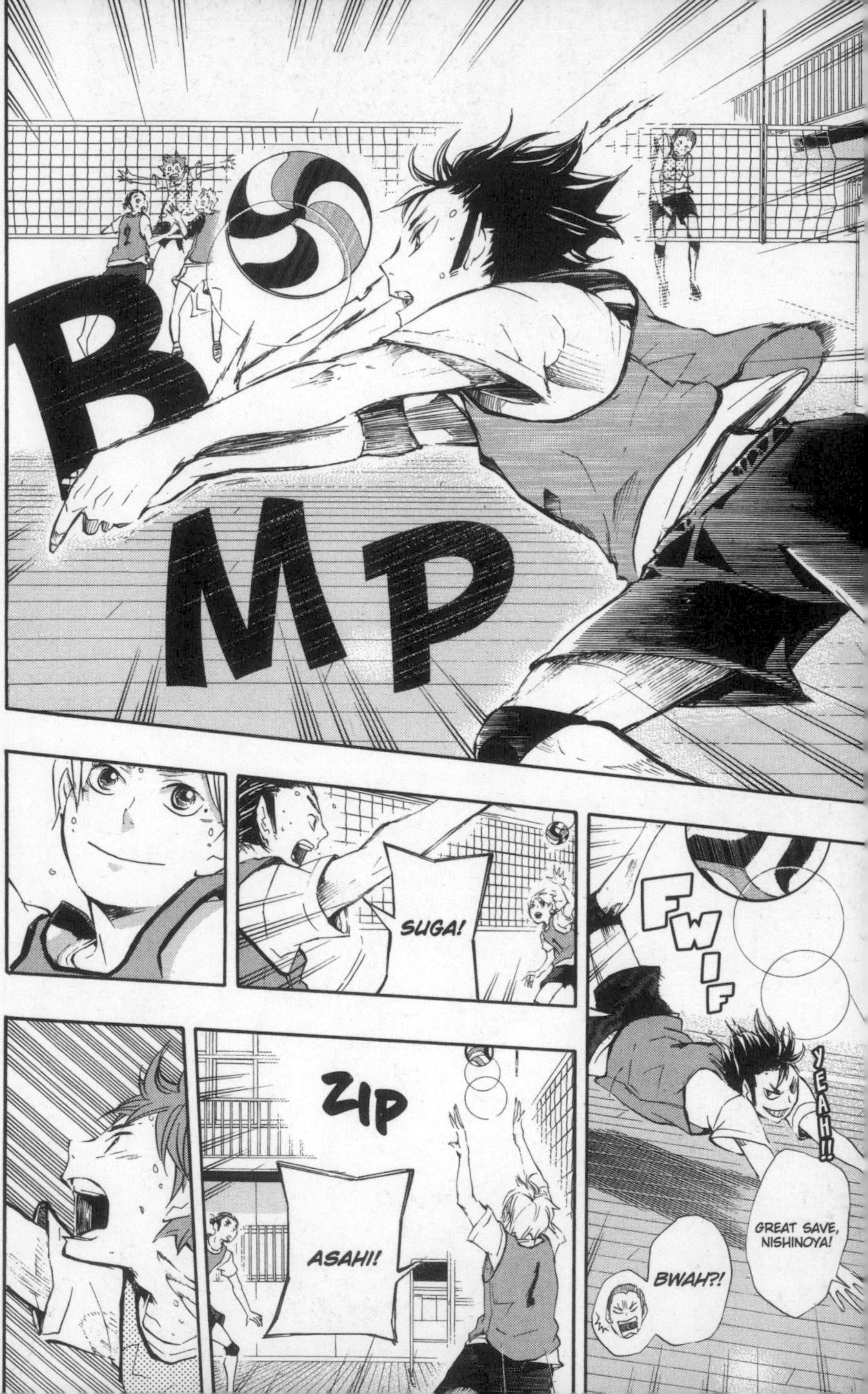
BMP
FWIF
YEAH!!
GREAT SAVE, NISHINOYA!
BWAH?!
SUGA!
ZIP
ASAHI!

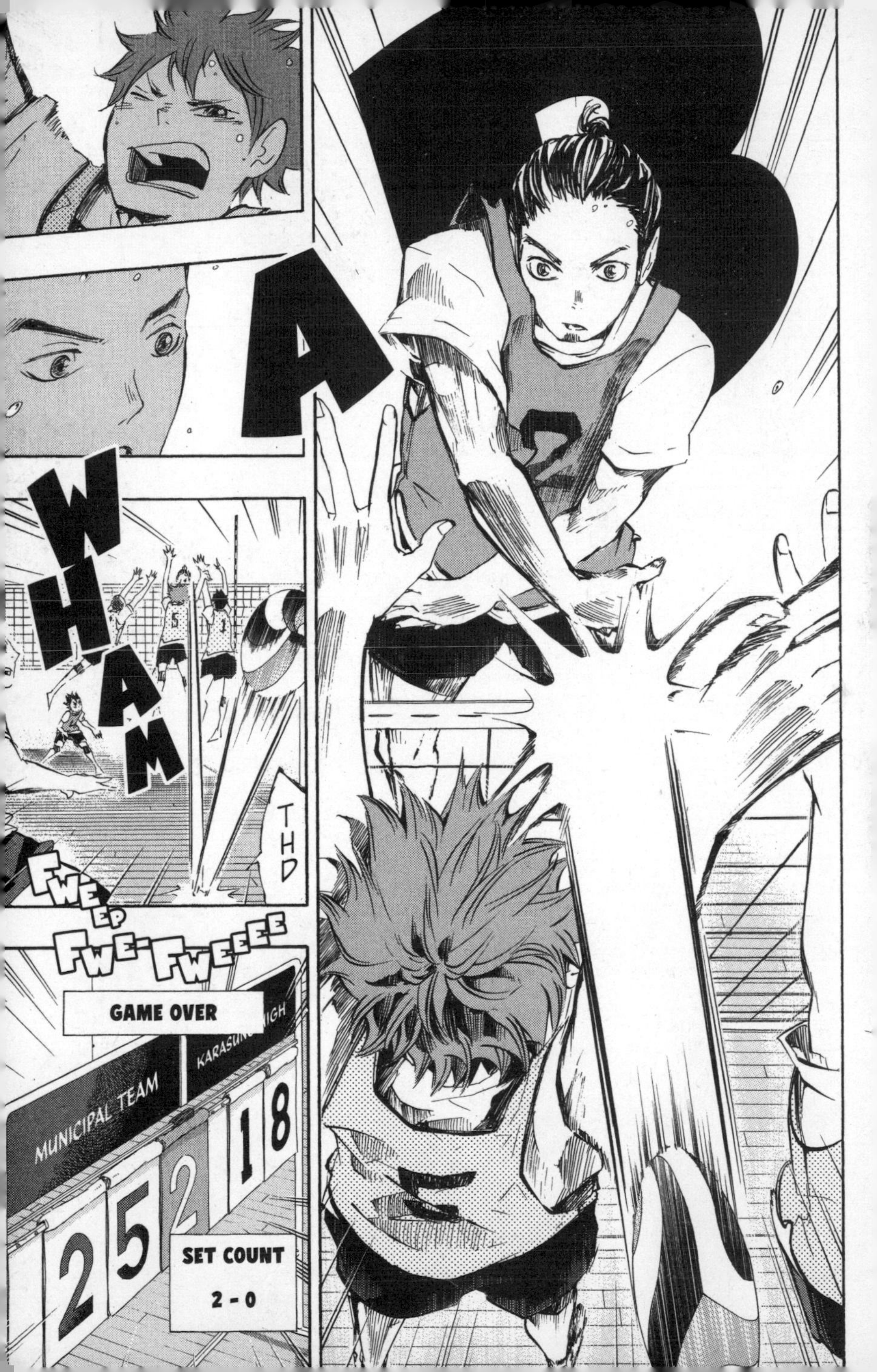
A
WHAM
THD
FWEEP
FWE-FWEEEE
GAME OVER
MUNICIPAL TEAM
KARASUNO
IGH
25
2
18
SET COUNT
2 - 0

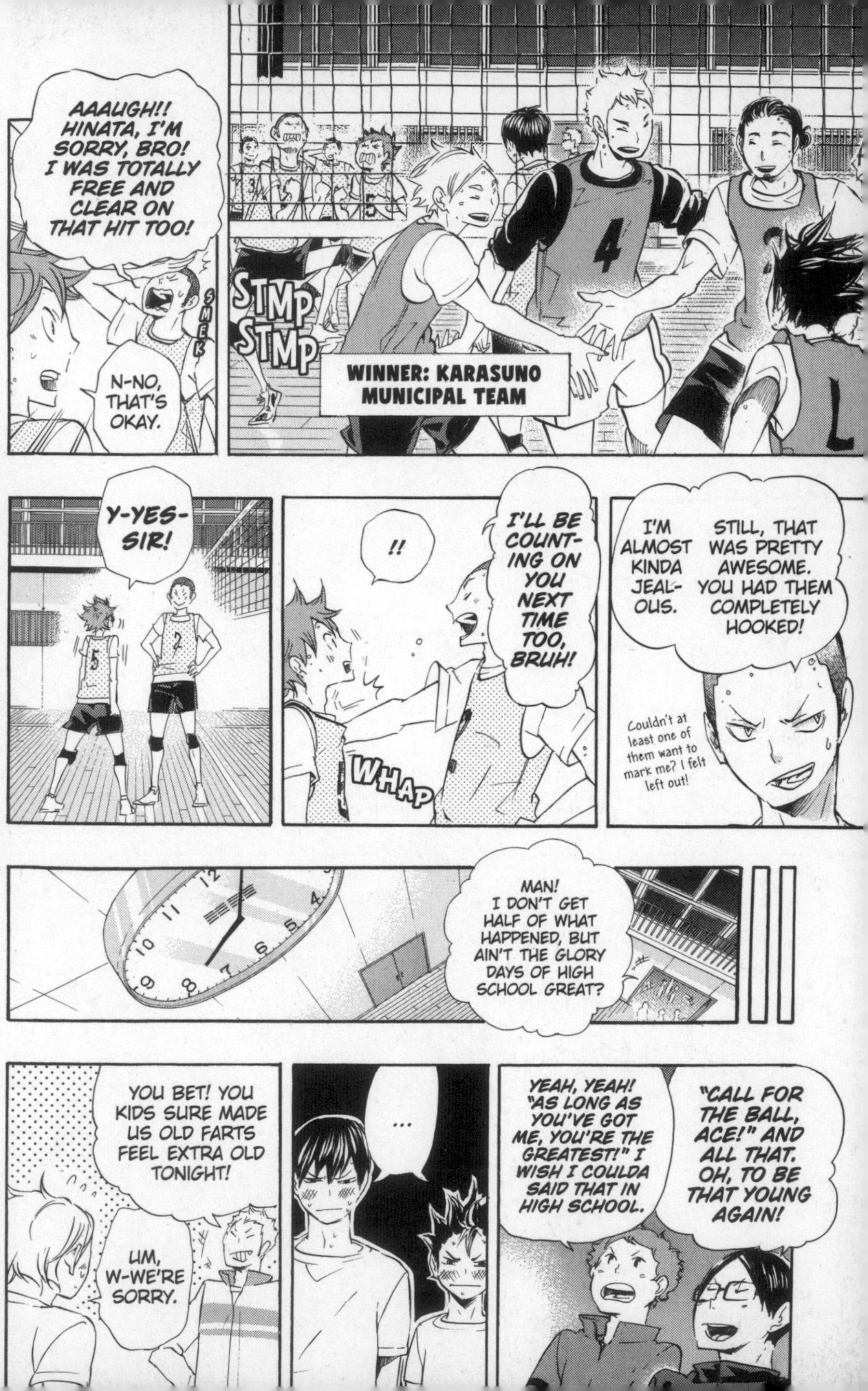
STMP STMP
WINNER: KARASUNO MUNICIPAL TEAM
AAAUGH!! HINATA, I'M SORRY, BRO! I WAS TOTALLY FREE AND CLEAR ON THAT HIT TOO!
SMEK
N-NO, THAT'S OKAY.
STILL, THAT WAS PRETTY AWESOME. YOU HAD THEM COMPLETELY HOOKED!
I'M ALMOST KINDA JEAL-OUS.
Couldn't at least one of them want to mark me? I felt left out!
I'LL BE COUNT-ING ON YOU NEXT TIME TOO, BRUH!
!!
WHAP
Y-YES-SIR!
MAN! I DON'T GET HALF OF WHAT HAPPENED, BUT AIN'T THE GLORY DAYS OF HIGH SCHOOL GREAT?
"CALL FOR THE BALL, ACE!" AND ALL THAT. OH, TO BE THAT YOUNG AGAIN!
YEAH, YEAH! "AS LONG AS YOU'VE GOT ME, YOU'RE THE GREATEST!" I WISH I COULDA SAID THAT IN HIGH SCHOOL.
...
YOU BET! YOU KIDS SURE MADE US OLD FARTS FEEL EXTRA OLD TONIGHT!
UM, W-WE'RE SORRY.

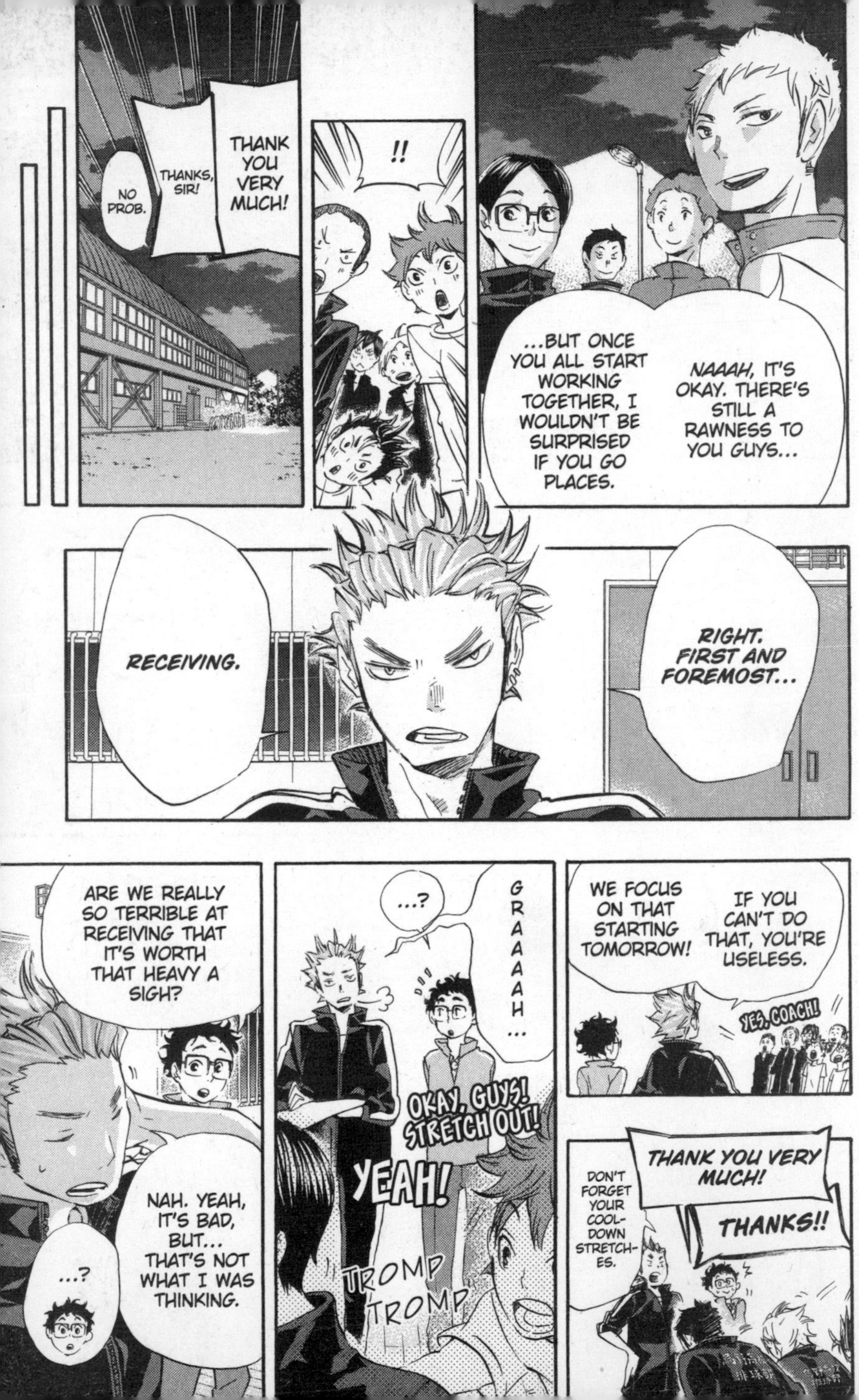
NAAAH, IT'S OKAY. THERE'S STILL A RAWNESS TO YOU GUYS...
...BUT ONCE YOU ALL START WORKING TOGETHER, I WOULDN'T BE SURPRISED IF YOU GO PLACES.
!!
THANK YOU VERY MUCH!
THANKS, SIR!
NO PROB.
RIGHT. FIRST AND FOREMOST...
RECEIVING.
IF YOU CAN'T DO THAT, YOU'RE USELESS.
WE FOCUS ON THAT STARTING TOMORROW!
YES, COACH!
THANK YOU VERY MUCH!
THANKS!!
DON'T FORGET YOUR COOL-DOWN STRETCHES.
GRAAAAH...
...?
OKAY, GUYS! STRETCH OUT!
YEAH!
TROMP TROMP
ARE WE REALLY SO TERRIBLE AT RECEIVING THAT IT'S WORTH THAT HEAVY A SIGH?
NAH. YEAH, IT'S BAD, BUT... THAT'S NOT WHAT I WAS THINKING.
...?

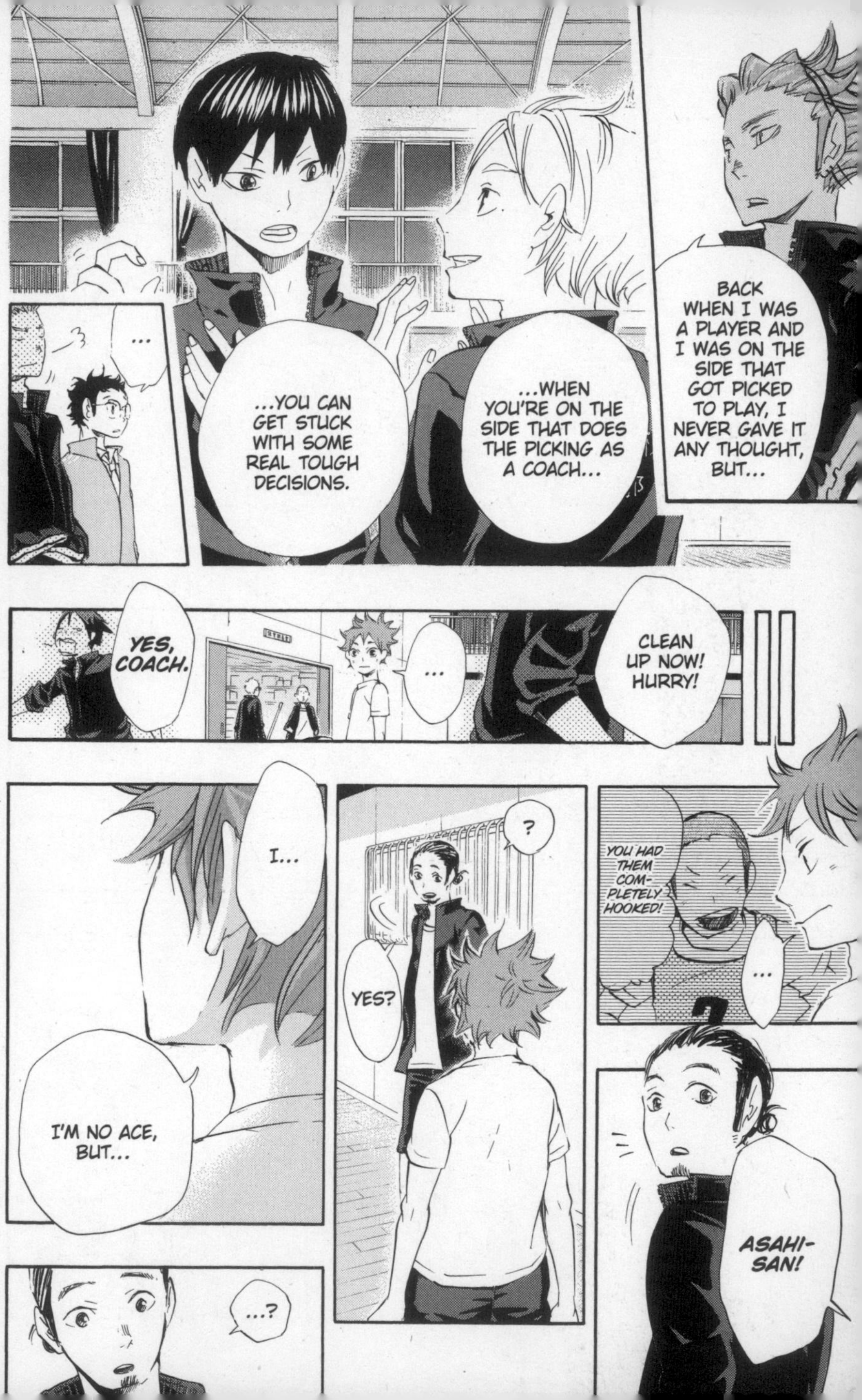
BACK WHEN I WAS A PLAYER AND I WAS ON THE SIDE THAT GOT PICKED TO PLAY, I NEVER GAVE IT ANY THOUGHT, BUT...
...WHEN YOU'RE ON THE SIDE THAT DOES THE PICKING AS A COACH...
...YOU CAN GET STUCK WITH SOME REAL TOUGH DECISIONS.
...
CLEAN UP NOW! HURRY!
...
YES, COACH.
YOU HAD THEM COMPLETELY HOOKED!
...
ASAHI-SAN!
?
YES?
I...
I'M NO ACE, BUT...
...?

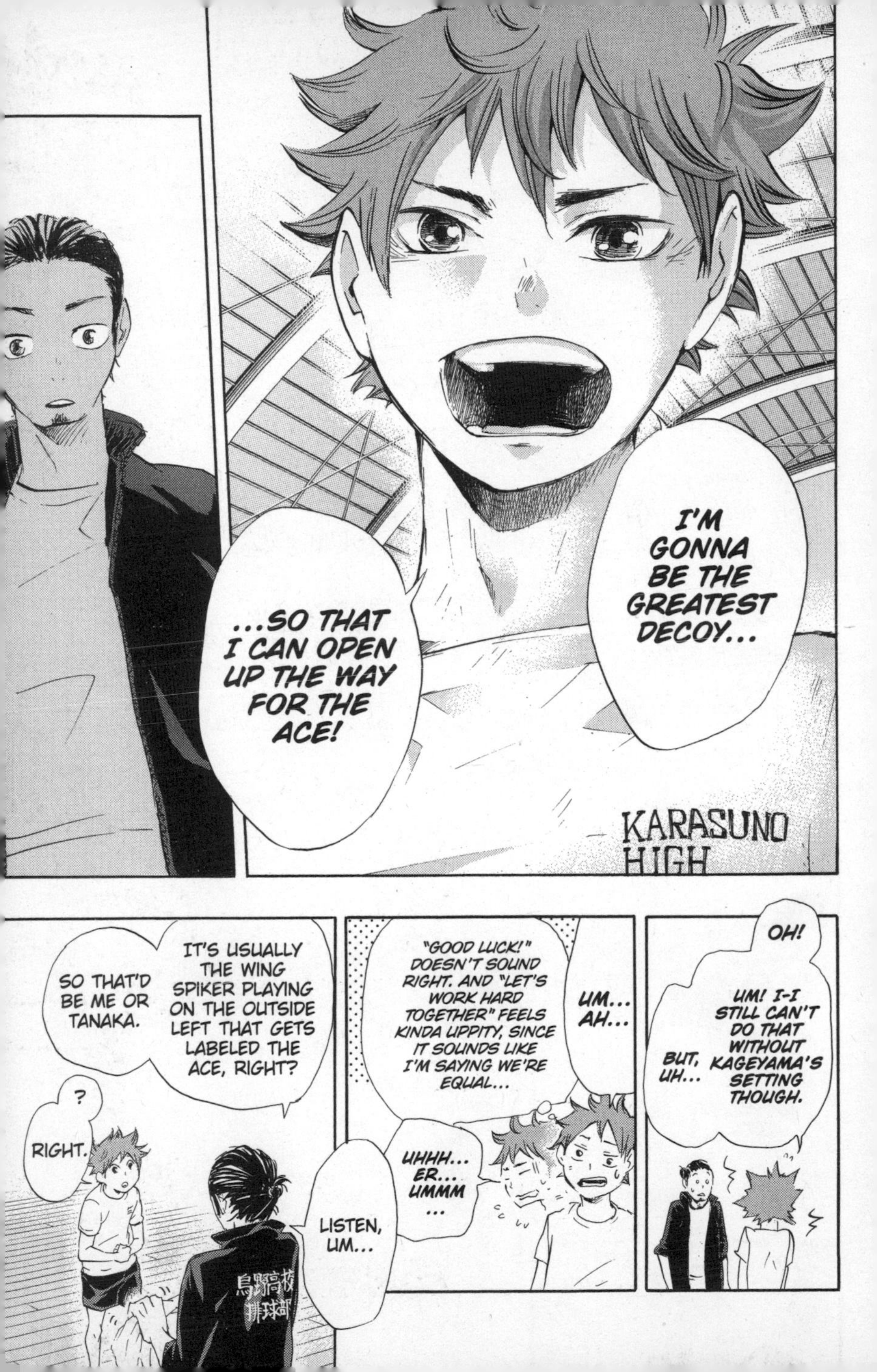
I'M GONNA BE THE GREATEST DECOY...
...SO THAT I CAN OPEN UP THE WAY FOR THE ACE!
KARASUNO HIGH
OH!
UM! I-I STILL CAN'T DO THAT WITHOUT KAGEYAMA'S SETTING THOUGH.
BUT, UH...
UM... AH...
"GOOD LUCK!" DOESN'T SOUND RIGHT. AND "LET'S WORK HARD TOGETHER" FEELS KINDA UPPITY, SINCE IT SOUNDS LIKE I'M SAYING WE'RE EQUAL...
UHHH... ER... UMMM ...
IT'S USUALLY THE WING SPIKER PLAYING ON THE OUTSIDE LEFT THAT GETS LABELED THE ACE, RIGHT?
SO THAT'D BE ME OR TANAKA.
?
RIGHT.
LISTEN, UM...
烏野高校排球部

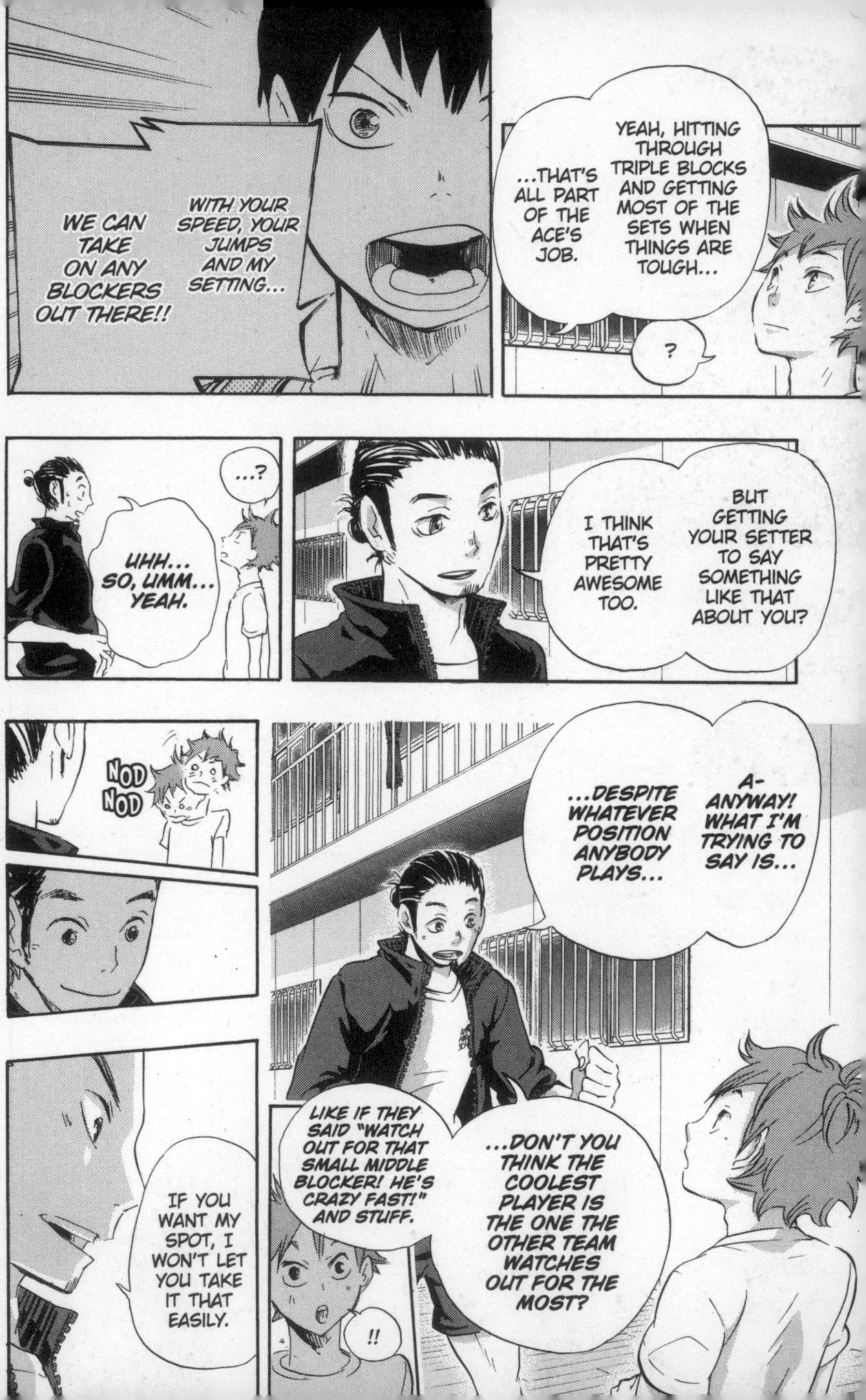
YEAH, HITTING THROUGH TRIPLE BLOCKS AND GETTING MOST OF THE SETS WHEN THINGS ARE TOUGH...
...THAT'S ALL PART OF THE ACE'S JOB.
?
WITH YOUR SPEED, YOUR JUMPS AND MY SETTING...
WE CAN TAKE ON ANY BLOCKERS OUT THERE!!
BUT GETTING YOUR SETTER TO SAY SOMETHING LIKE THAT ABOUT YOU?
I THINK THAT'S PRETTY AWESOME TOO.
...?
UHH... SO, UMM... YEAH.
A- ANYWAY! WHAT I'M TRYING TO SAY IS...
...DESPITE WHATEVER POSITION ANYBODY PLAYS...
...DON'T YOU THINK THE COOLEST PLAYER IS THE ONE THE OTHER TEAM WATCHES OUT FOR THE MOST?
LIKE IF THEY SAID "WATCH OUT FOR THAT SMALL MIDDLE BLOCKER! HE'S CRAZY FAST!" AND STUFF.
!!
NOD NOD
IF YOU WANT MY SPOT, I WON'T LET YOU TAKE IT THAT EASILY.

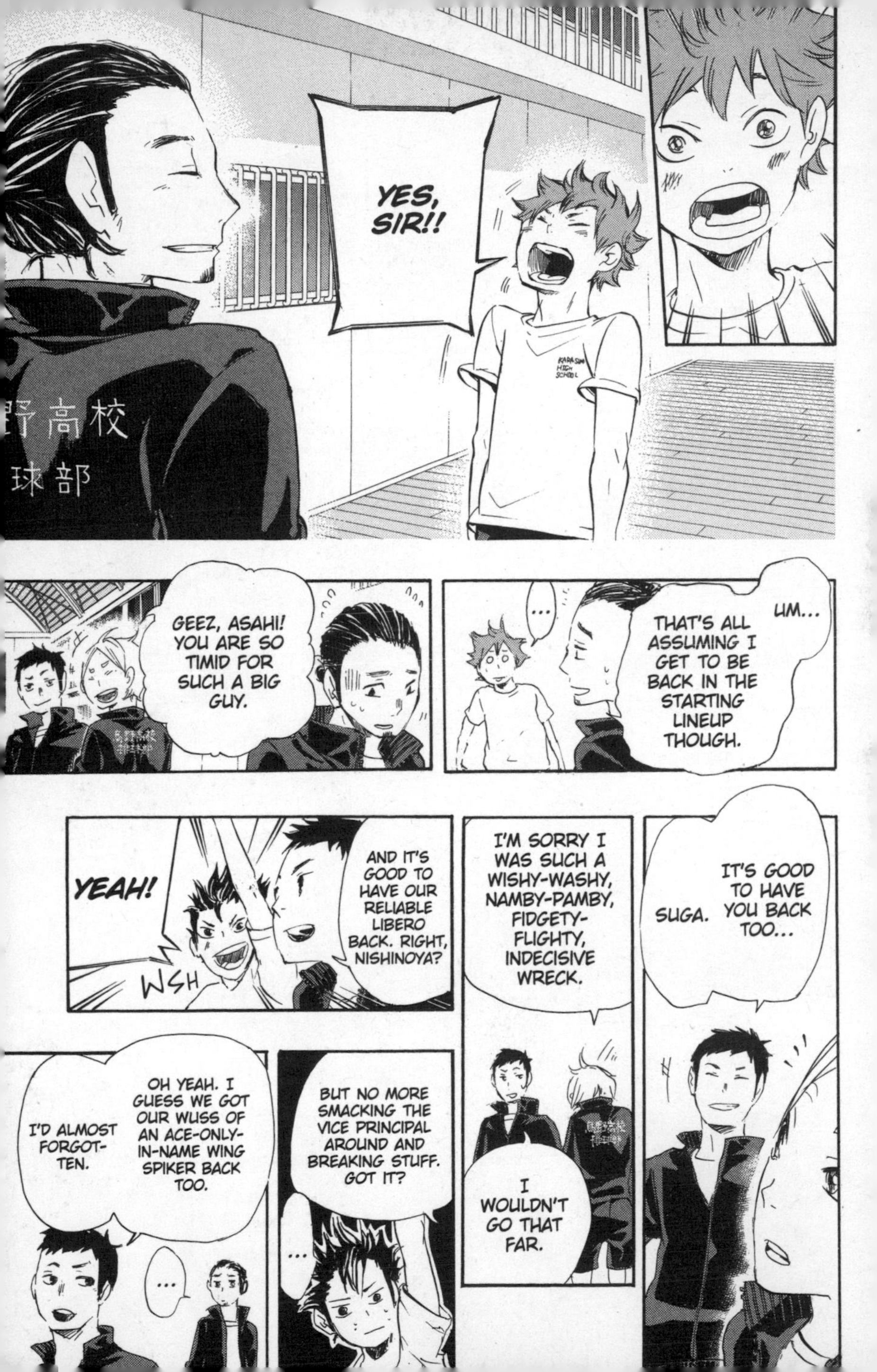
YES, SIR!!
野高校
球部
UM...
THAT'S ALL ASSUMING I GET TO BE BACK IN THE STARTING LINEUP THOUGH.
...
GEEZ, ASAHI! YOU ARE SO TIMID FOR SUCH A BIG GUY.
IT'S GOOD TO HAVE YOU BACK TOO...
SUGA.
I'M SORRY I WAS SUCH A WISHY-WASHY, NAMBY-PAMBY, FIDGETY-FLIGHTY, INDECISIVE WRECK.
I WOULDN'T GO THAT FAR.
AND IT'S GOOD TO HAVE OUR RELIABLE LIBERO BACK. RIGHT, NISHINOYA?
YEAH!
WSH
BUT NO MORE SMACKING THE VICE PRINCIPAL AROUND AND BREAKING STUFF. GOT IT?
...
OH YEAH. I GUESS WE GOT OUR WUSS OF AN ACE-ONLY-IN-NAME WING SPIKER BACK TOO.
I'D ALMOST FORGOT-TEN.
...

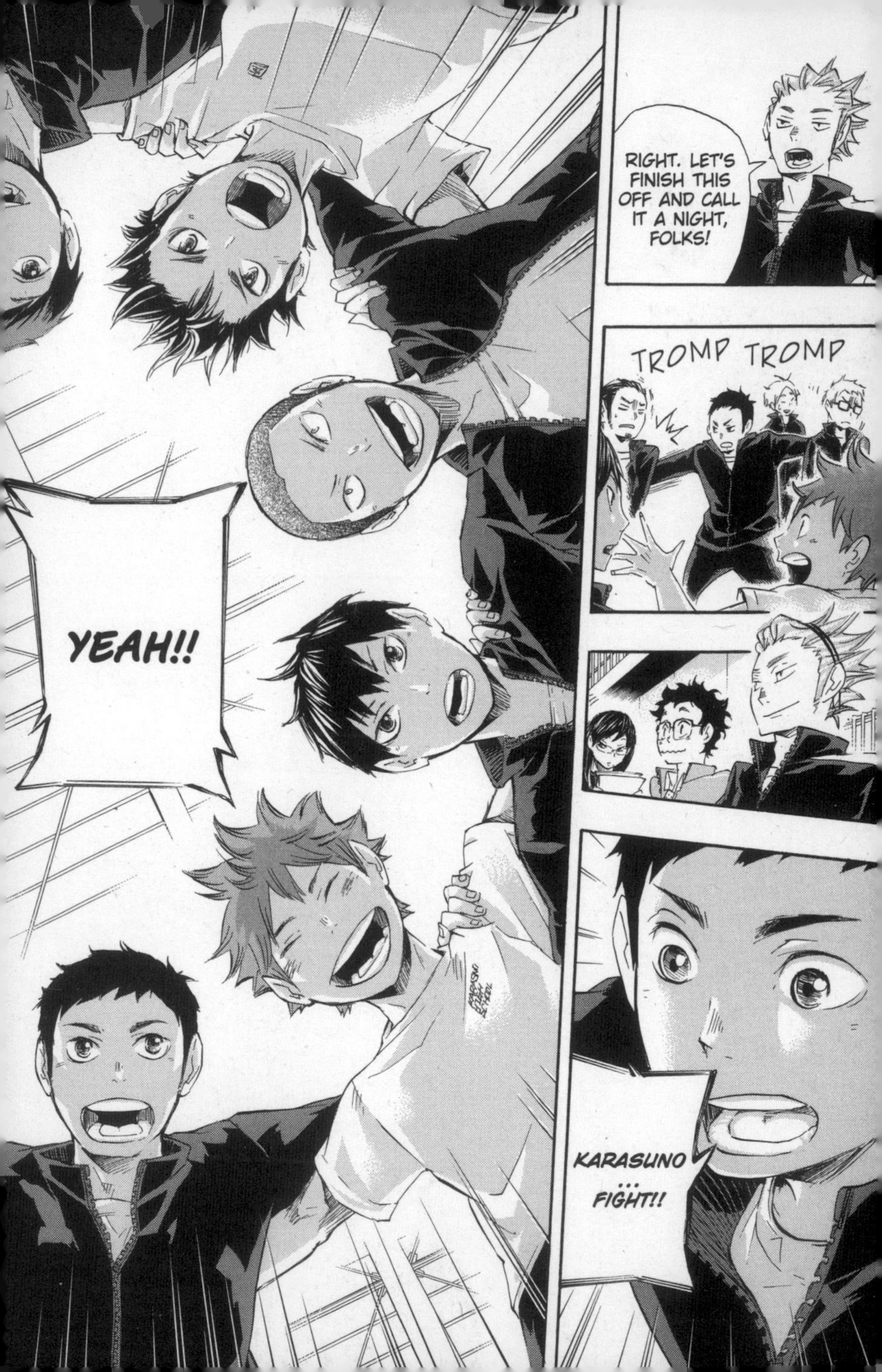
RIGHT. LET'S FINISH THIS OFF AND CALL IT A NIGHT, FOLKS!
TROMP TROMP
KARASUNO ... FIGHT!!
YEAH!!

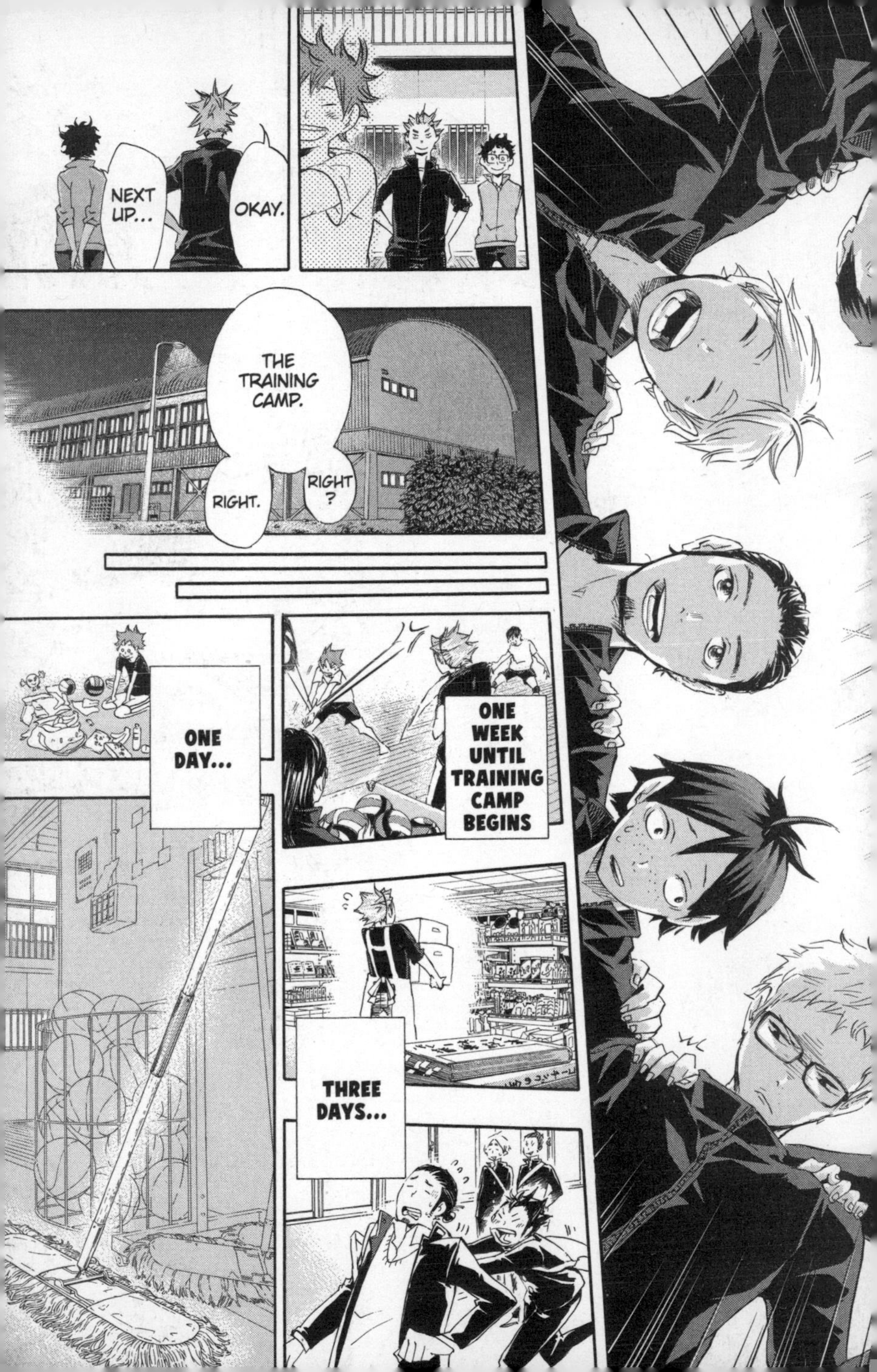
OKAY.
NEXT UP...
THE TRAINING CAMP.
RIGHT?
RIGHT.
ONE WEEK UNTIL TRAINING CAMP BEGINS
THREE DAYS...
ONE DAY...

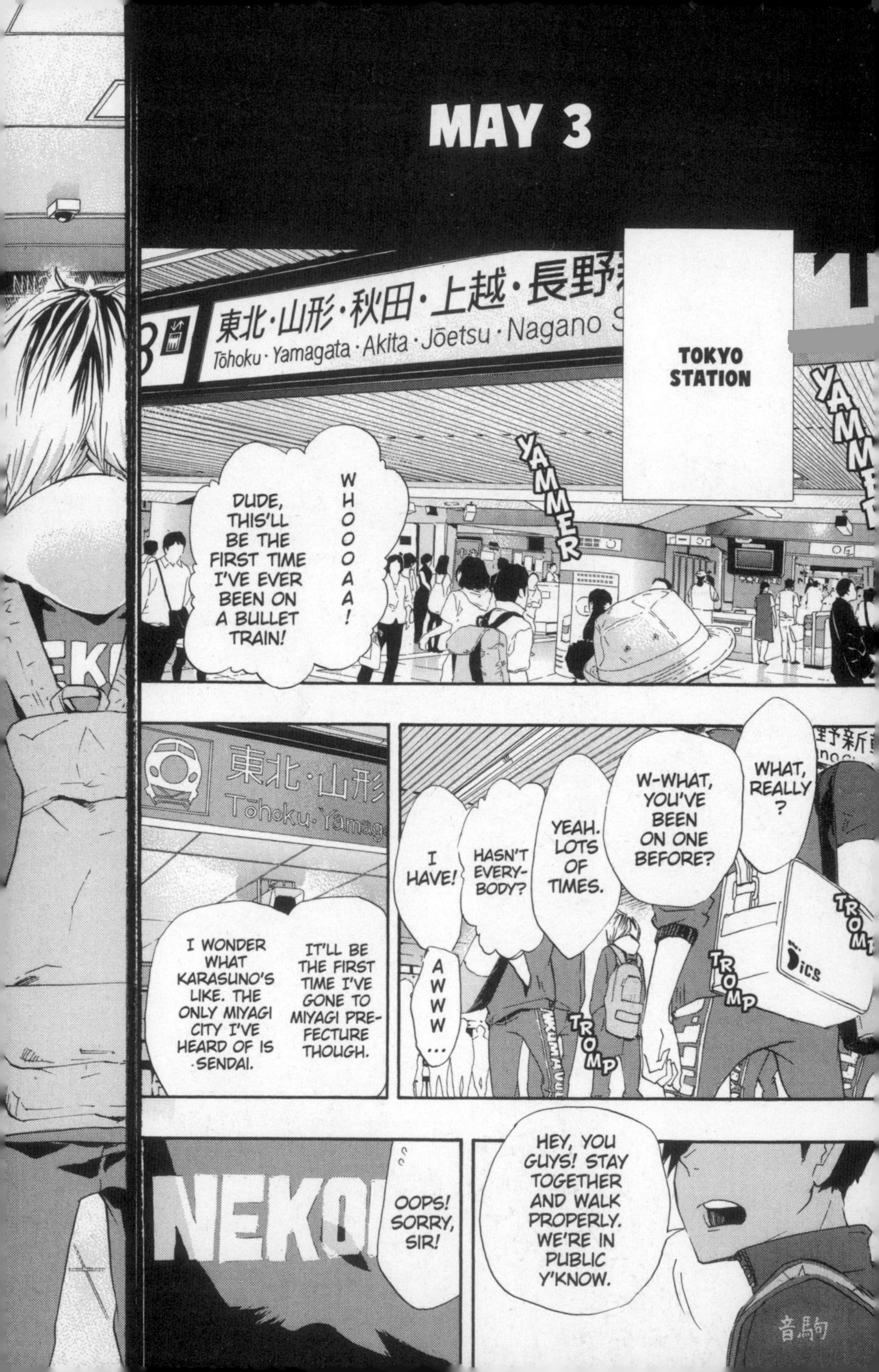
MAY 3
TOKYO STATION
YAMMER
東北・山形・秋田・上越・長野
Tōhoku · Yamagata · Akita · Jōetsu · Nagano
YAMMER
WHOOOOAAA!
DUDE, THIS'LL BE THE FIRST TIME I'VE EVER BEEN ON A BULLET TRAIN!
WHAT, REALLY?
W-WHAT, YOU'VE BEEN ON ONE BEFORE?
YEAH. LOTS OF TIMES.
HASN'T EVERYBODY?
I HAVE!
TROMP
TROMP
AWWW...
TROMP
東北・山形
IT'LL BE THE FIRST TIME I'VE GONE TO MIYAGI PREFECTURE THOUGH.
I WONDER WHAT KARASUNO'S LIKE. THE ONLY MIYAGI CITY I'VE HEARD OF IS SENDAI.
HEY, YOU GUYS! STAY TOGETHER AND WALK PROPERLY. WE'RE IN PUBLIC Y'KNOW.
音駒
OOPS! SORRY, SIR!

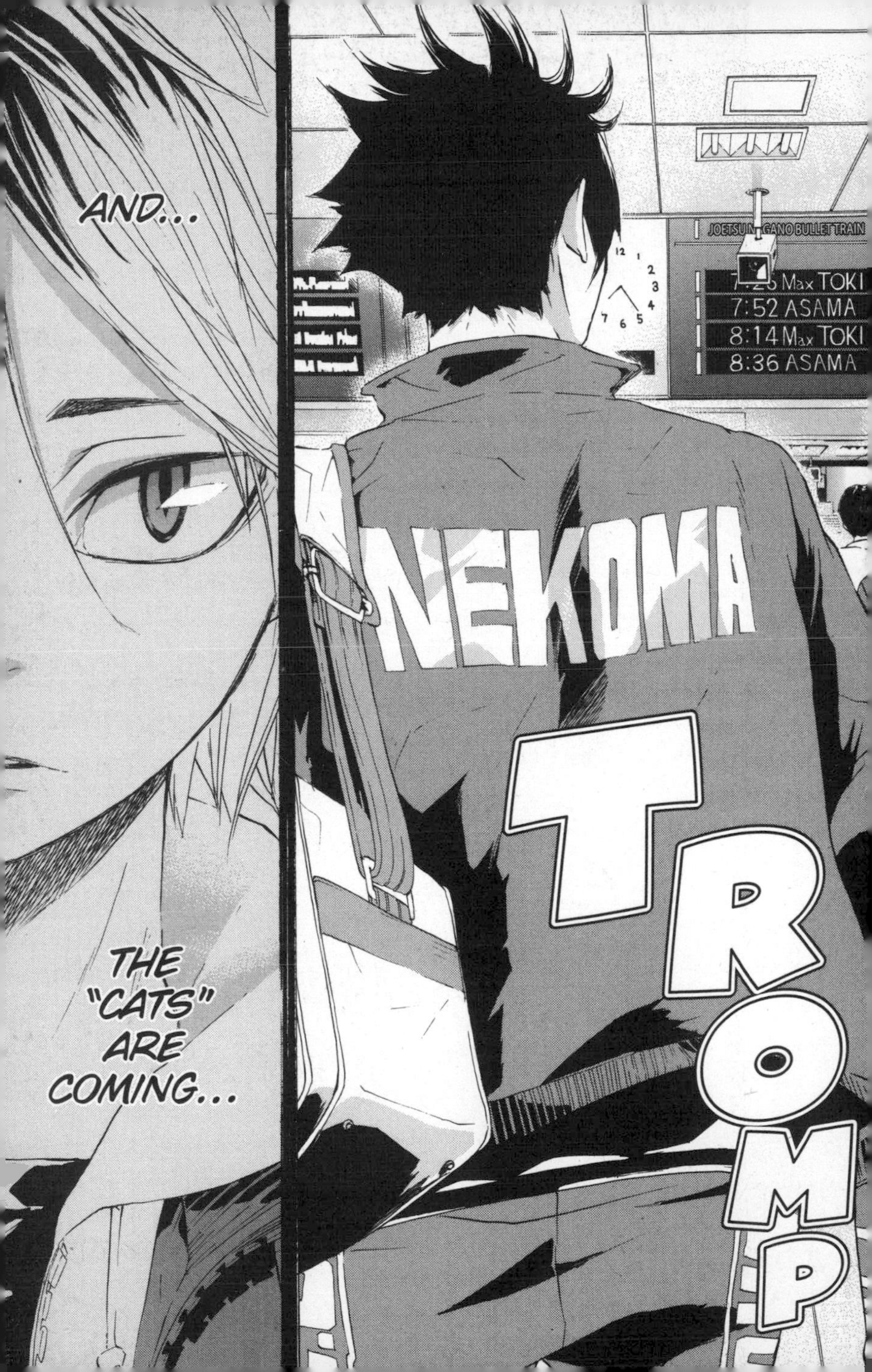
7:52 ASAMA
8:14 Max TOKI
8:36 ASAMA
NEKOMA
TROMP
AND...
THE "CATS" ARE COMING...

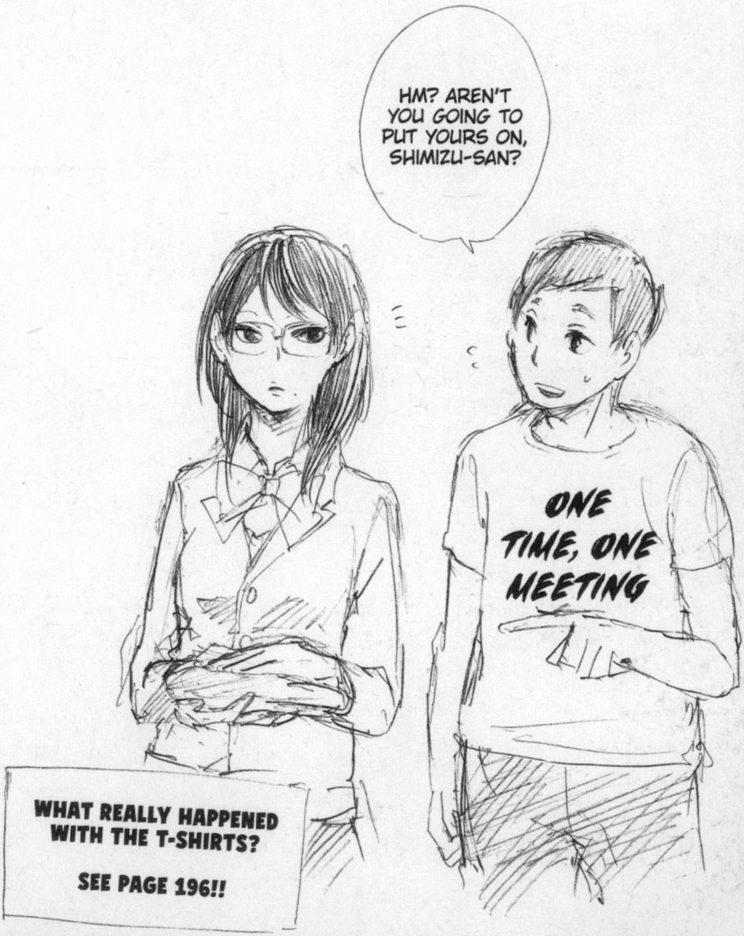
HM? AREN'T YOU GOING TO PUT YOURS ON, SHIMIZU-SAN?
ONE TIME, ONE MEETING
WHAT REALLY HAPPENED WITH THE T-SHIRTS?
SEE PAGE 196!!

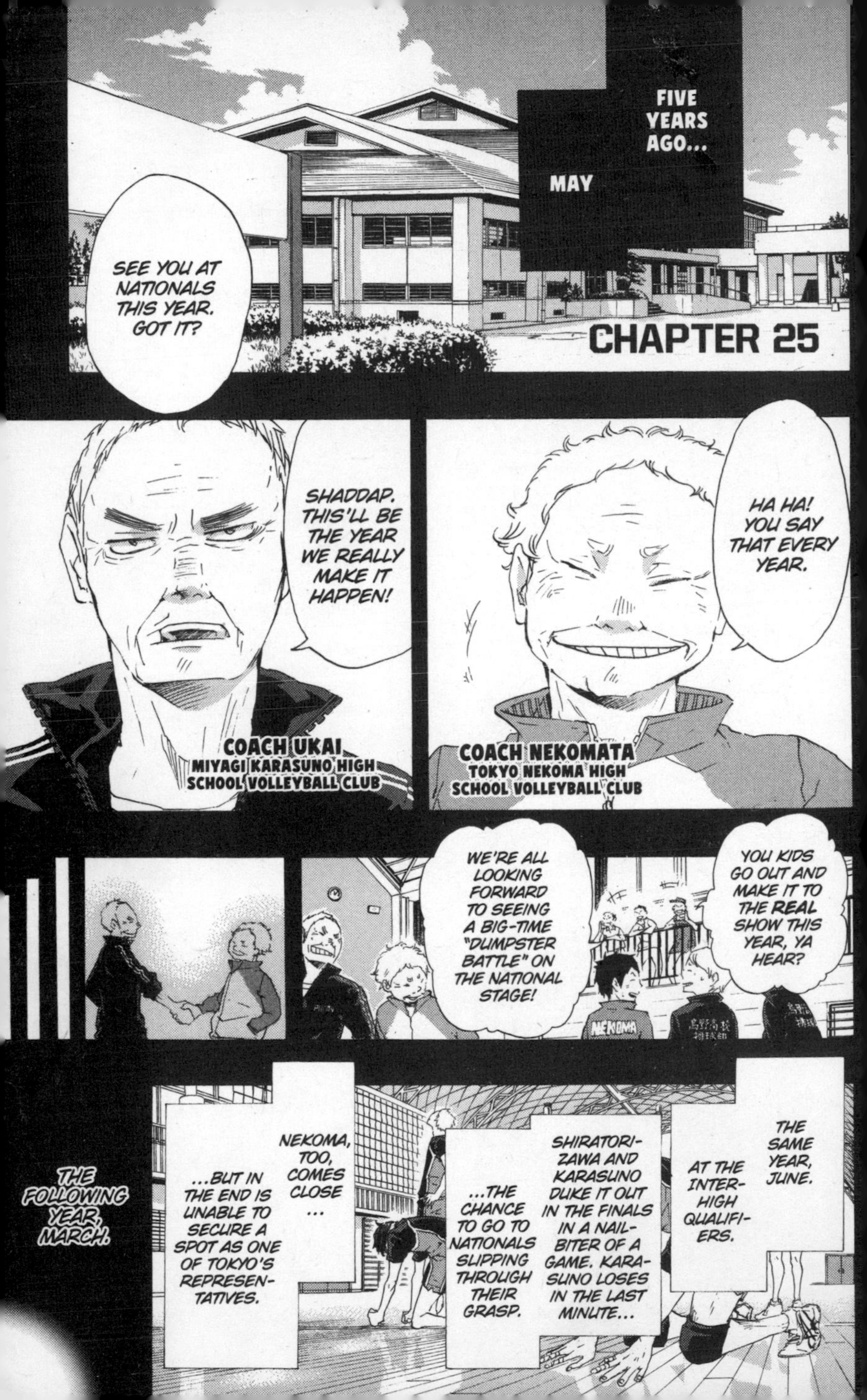

FIVE YEARS AGO...
MAY
CHAPTER 25
SEE YOU AT NATIONALS THIS YEAR. GOT IT?
HA HA! YOU SAY THAT EVERY YEAR.
COACH NEKOMATA
TOKYO NEKOMA HIGH SCHOOL VOLLEYBALL CLUB
SHADDAP. THIS'LL BE THE YEAR WE REALLY MAKE IT HAPPEN!
COACH UKAI
MIYAGI KARASUNO HIGH SCHOOL VOLLEYBALL CLUB
YOU KIDS GO OUT AND MAKE IT TO THE REAL SHOW THIS YEAR, YA HEAR?
WE'RE ALL LOOKING FORWARD TO SEEING A BIG-TIME "DUMPSTER BATTLE" ON THE NATIONAL STAGE!
NEKOMA
THE SAME YEAR, JUNE.
AT THE INTER-HIGH QUALIFIERS.
SHIRATORIZAWA AND KARASUNO DUKE IT OUT IN THE FINALS IN A NAIL-BITER OF A GAME. KARASUNO LOSES IN THE LAST MINUTE...
...THE CHANCE TO GO TO NATIONALS SLIPPING THROUGH THEIR GRASP.
NEKOMA, TOO, COMES CLOSE ...
...BUT IN THE END IS UNABLE TO SECURE A SPOT AS ONE OF TOKYO'S REPRESENTATIVES.
THE FOLLOWING YEAR, MARCH.

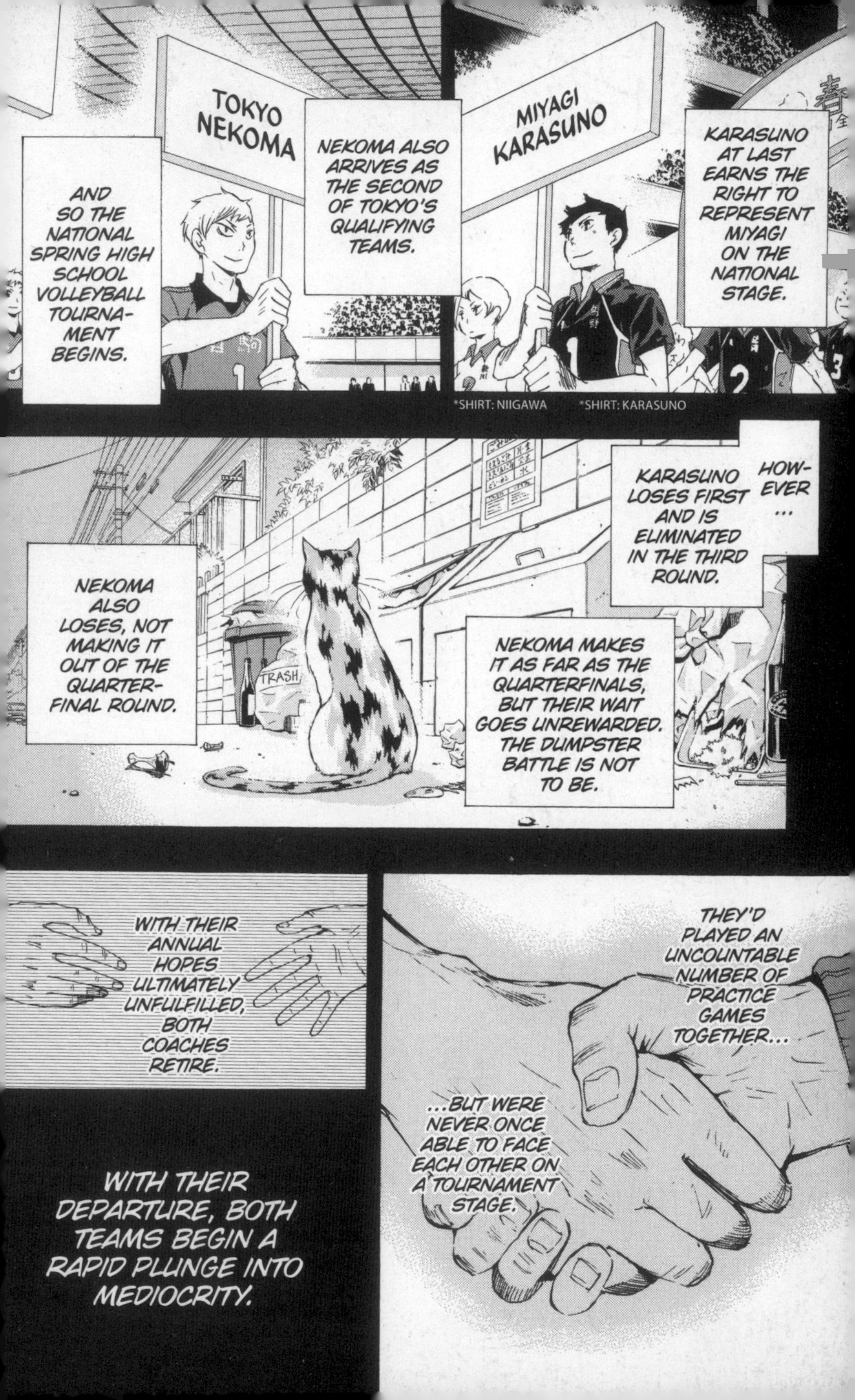
MIYAGI KARASUNO
KARASUNO AT LAST EARNS THE RIGHT TO REPRESENT MIYAGI ON THE NATIONAL STAGE.
*SHIRT: KARASUNO
TOKYO NEKOMA
NEKOMA ALSO ARRIVES AS THE SECOND OF TOKYO'S QUALIFYING TEAMS.
AND SO THE NATIONAL SPRING HIGH SCHOOL VOLLEYBALL TOURNAMENT BEGINS.
*SHIRT: NIIGAWA
HOWEVER...
KARASUNO LOSES FIRST AND IS ELIMINATED IN THE THIRD ROUND.
NEKOMA MAKES IT AS FAR AS THE QUARTERFINALS, BUT THEIR WAIT GOES UNREWARDED. THE DUMPSTER BATTLE IS NOT TO BE.
TRASH
NEKOMA ALSO LOSES, NOT MAKING IT OUT OF THE QUARTERFINAL ROUND.
THEY'D PLAYED AN UNCOUNTABLE NUMBER OF PRACTICE GAMES TOGETHER...
...BUT WERE NEVER ONCE ABLE TO FACE EACH OTHER ON A TOURNAMENT STAGE.
WITH THEIR ANNUAL HOPES ULTIMATELY UNFULFILLED, BOTH COACHES RETIRE.
WITH THEIR DEPARTURE, BOTH TEAMS BEGIN A RAPID PLUNGE INTO MEDIOCRITY.

CHAPTER 25: Random Encounter

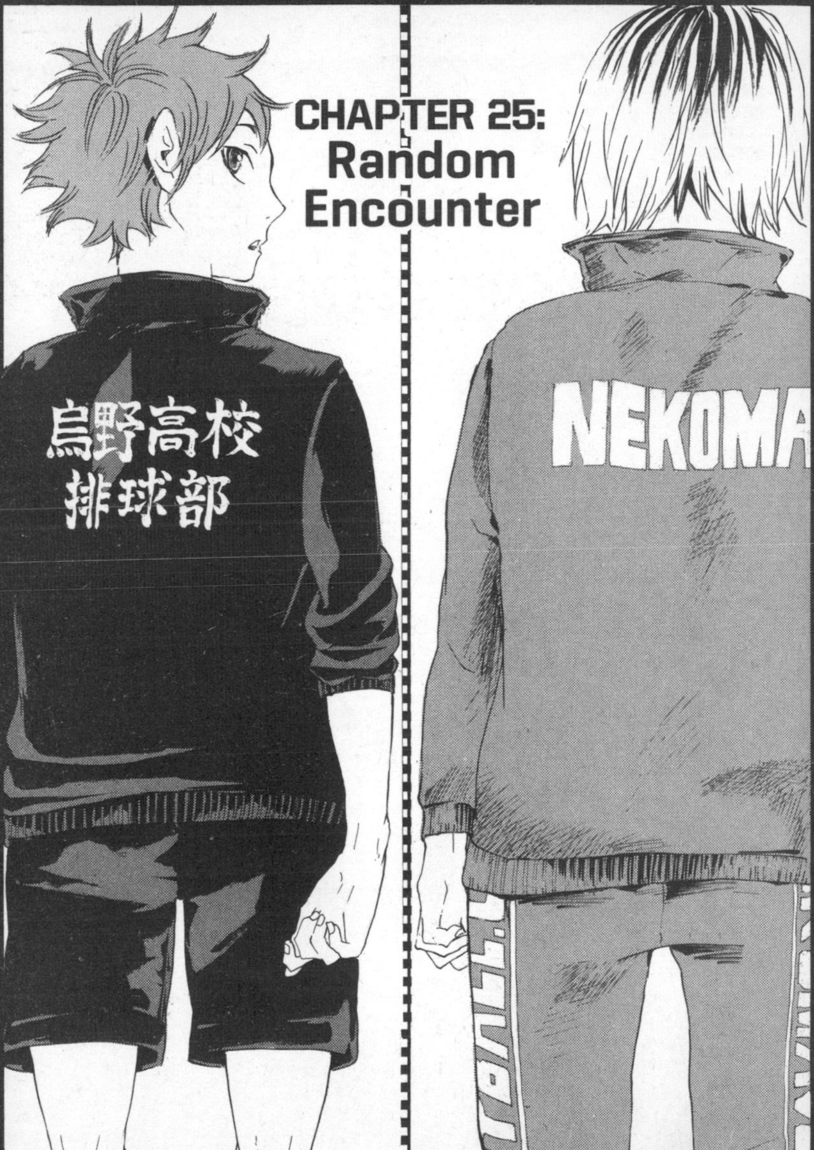
烏野高校
排球部
NEKOMA

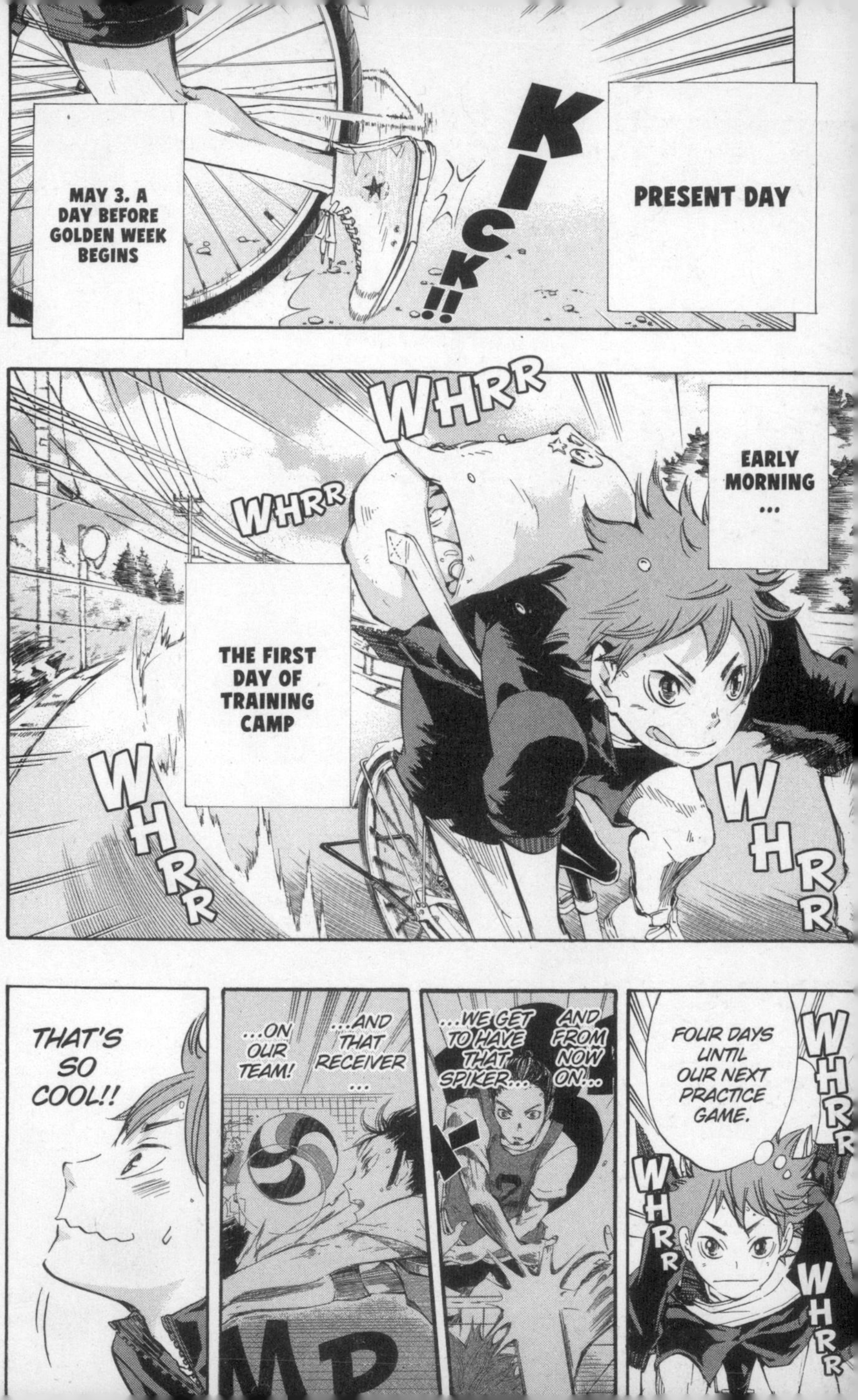
PRESENT DAY
KICK!!
MAY 3. A DAY BEFORE GOLDEN WEEK BEGINS
EARLY MORNING ...
WHRR
WHRR
THE FIRST DAY OF TRAINING CAMP
WHRR
WHRR
WHRR
FOUR DAYS UNTIL OUR NEXT PRACTICE GAME.
WHRR
WHRR
AND FROM NOW ON...
...WE GET TO HAVE THAT SPIKER...
...AND THAT RECEIVER ...
...ON OUR TEAM!
THAT'S SO COOL!!

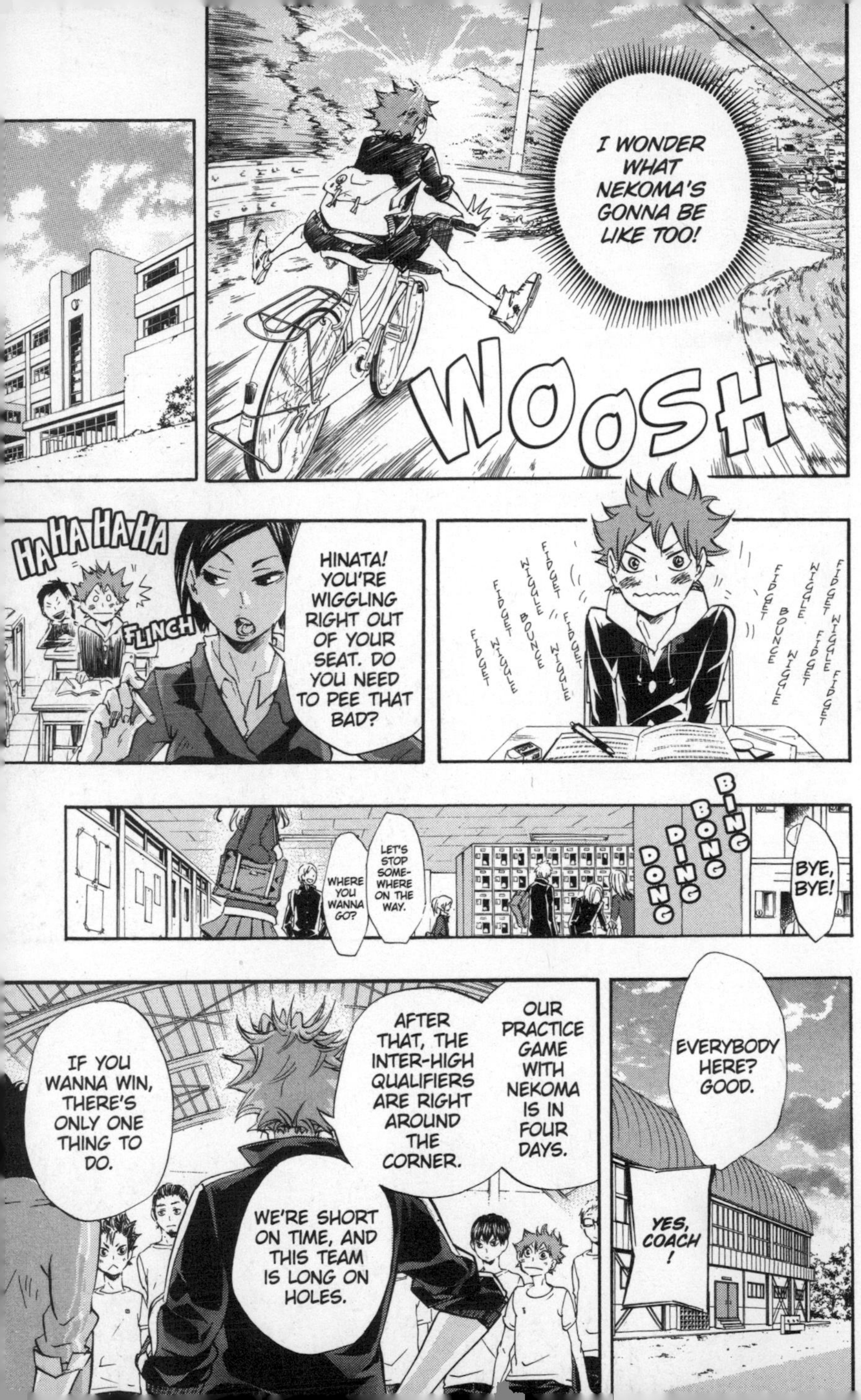
I WONDER WHAT NEKOMA'S GONNA BE LIKE TOO!
WOOSH
FIDGET WIGGLE FIDGET WIGGLE BOUNCE FIDGET FIDGET WIGGLE FIDGET
FIDGET WIGGLE FIDGET BOUNCE WIGGLE WIGGLE FIDGET FIDGET WIGGLE FIDGET
HINATA! YOU'RE WIGGLING RIGHT OUT OF YOUR SEAT. DO YOU NEED TO PEE THAT BAD?
HAHAHAHA
FLINCH
BING BONG DING DONG
BYE, BYE!
LET'S STOP SOME-WHERE ON THE WAY.
WHERE YOU WANNA GO?
EVERYBODY HERE? GOOD.
YES, COACH!
OUR PRACTICE GAME WITH NEKOMA IS IN FOUR DAYS.
AFTER THAT, THE INTER-HIGH QUALIFIERS ARE RIGHT AROUND THE CORNER.
IF YOU WANNA WIN, THERE'S ONLY ONE THING TO DO.
WE'RE SHORT ON TIME, AND THIS TEAM IS LONG ON HOLES.

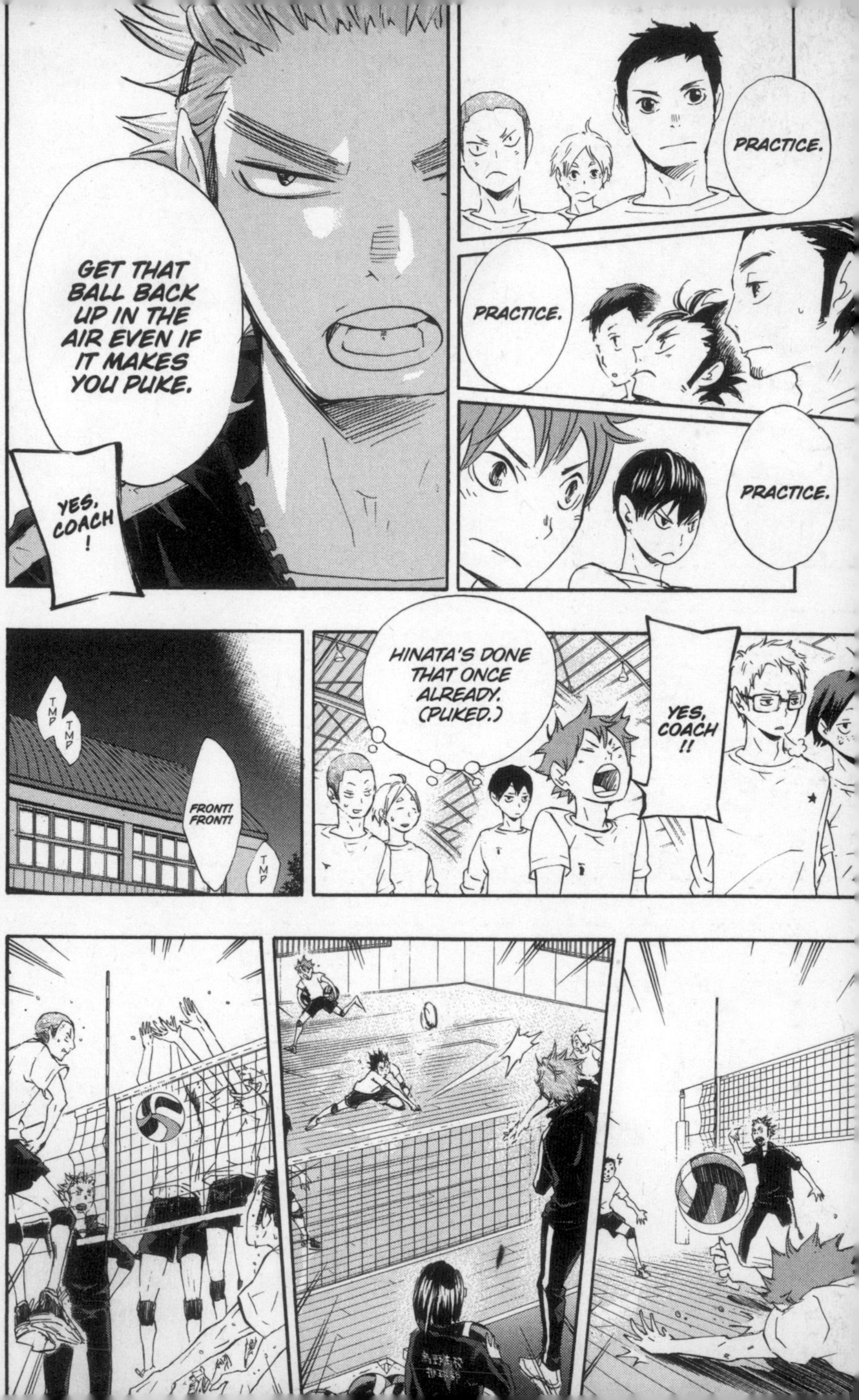
PRACTICE.
PRACTICE.
PRACTICE.
GET THAT BALL BACK UP IN THE AIR EVEN IF IT MAKES YOU PUKE.
YES, COACH!
YES, COACH!!
HINATA'S DONE THAT ONCE ALREADY. (PUKED.)
TMP TMP
FRONT! FRONT!
TMP

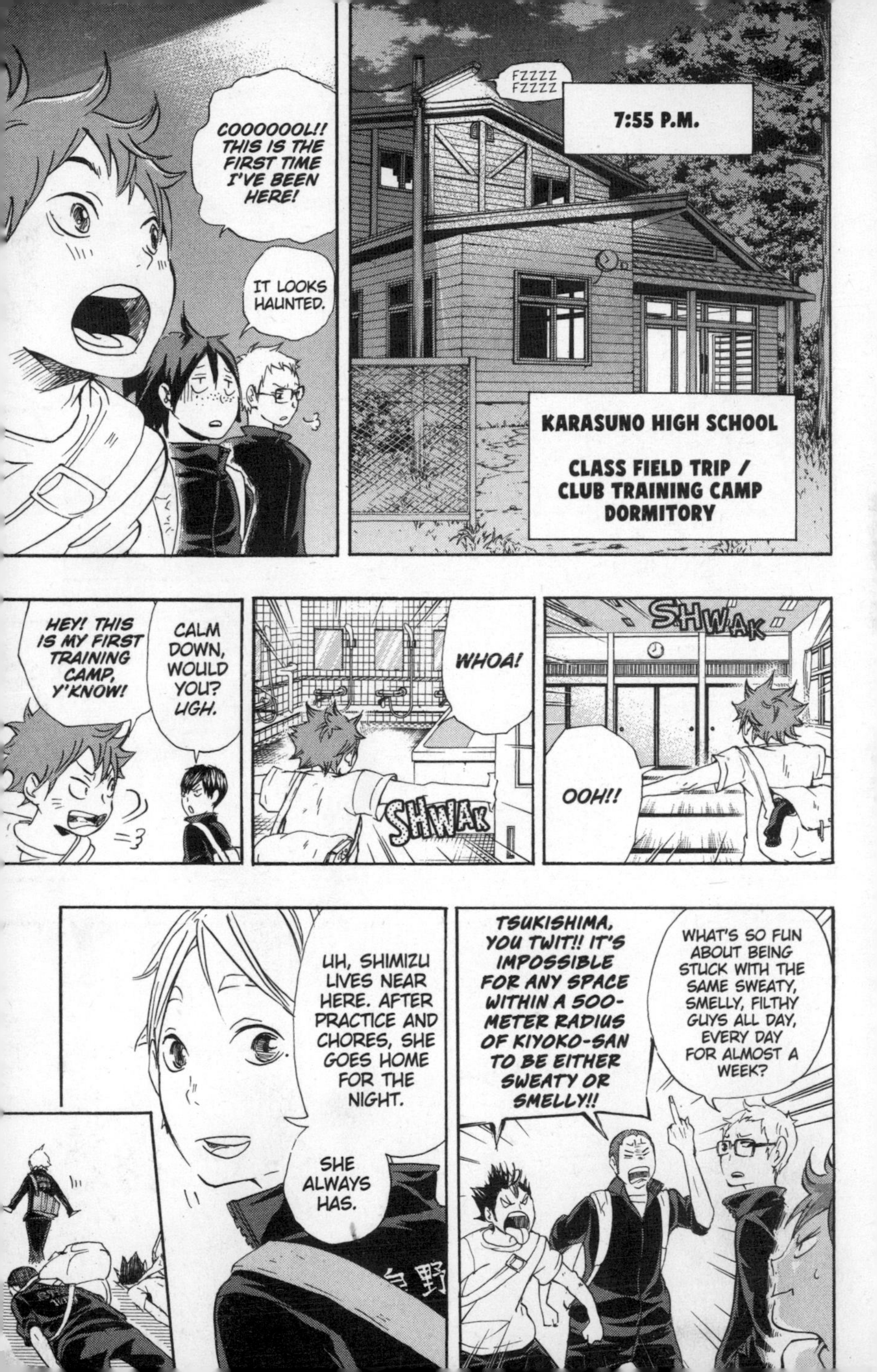
FZZZZ
FZZZZ
7:55 P.M.
KARASUNO HIGH SCHOOL
CLASS FIELD TRIP / CLUB TRAINING CAMP DORMITORY
COOOOOOL!! THIS IS THE FIRST TIME I'VE BEEN HERE!
IT LOOKS HAUNTED.
SHWAK
OOH!!
WHOA!
SHWAK
HEY! THIS IS MY FIRST TRAINING CAMP, Y'KNOW!
CALM DOWN, WOULD YOU? UGH.
WHAT'S SO FUN ABOUT BEING STUCK WITH THE SAME SWEATY, SMELLY, FILTHY GUYS ALL DAY, EVERY DAY FOR ALMOST A WEEK?
TSUKISHIMA, YOU TWIT!! IT'S IMPOSSIBLE FOR ANY SPACE WITHIN A 500-METER RADIUS OF KIYOKO-SAN TO BE EITHER SWEATY OR SMELLY!!
UH, SHIMIZU LIVES NEAR HERE. AFTER PRACTICE AND CHORES, SHE GOES HOME FOR THE NIGHT.
SHE ALWAYS HAS.

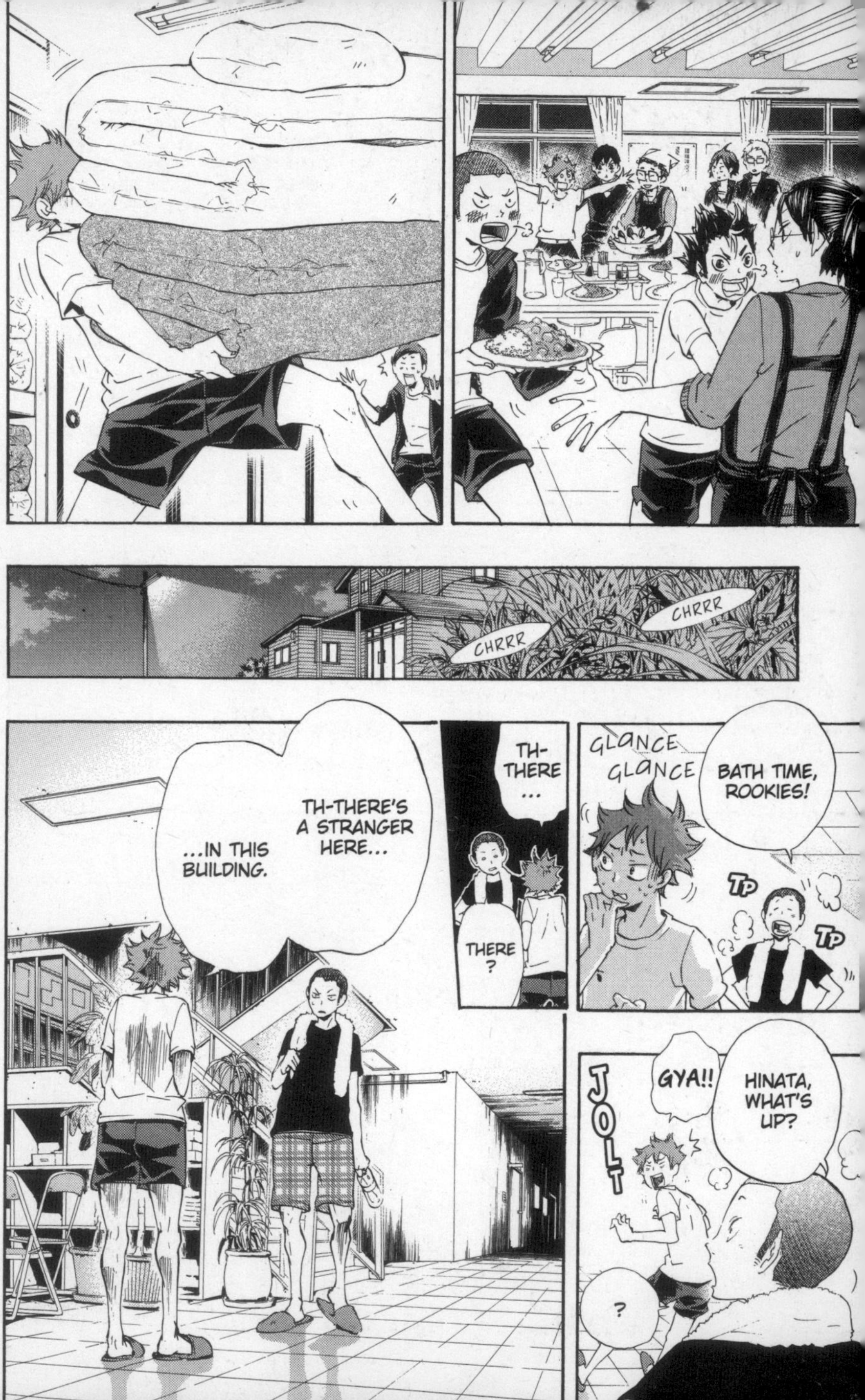
CHRRR
CHRRR
GLANCE GLANCE
BATH TIME, ROOKIES!
TP
TP
HINATA, WHAT'S UP?
GYA!!
JOLT
?
TH- THERE ...
THERE ?
TH-THERE'S A STRANGER HERE...
...IN THIS BUILDING.

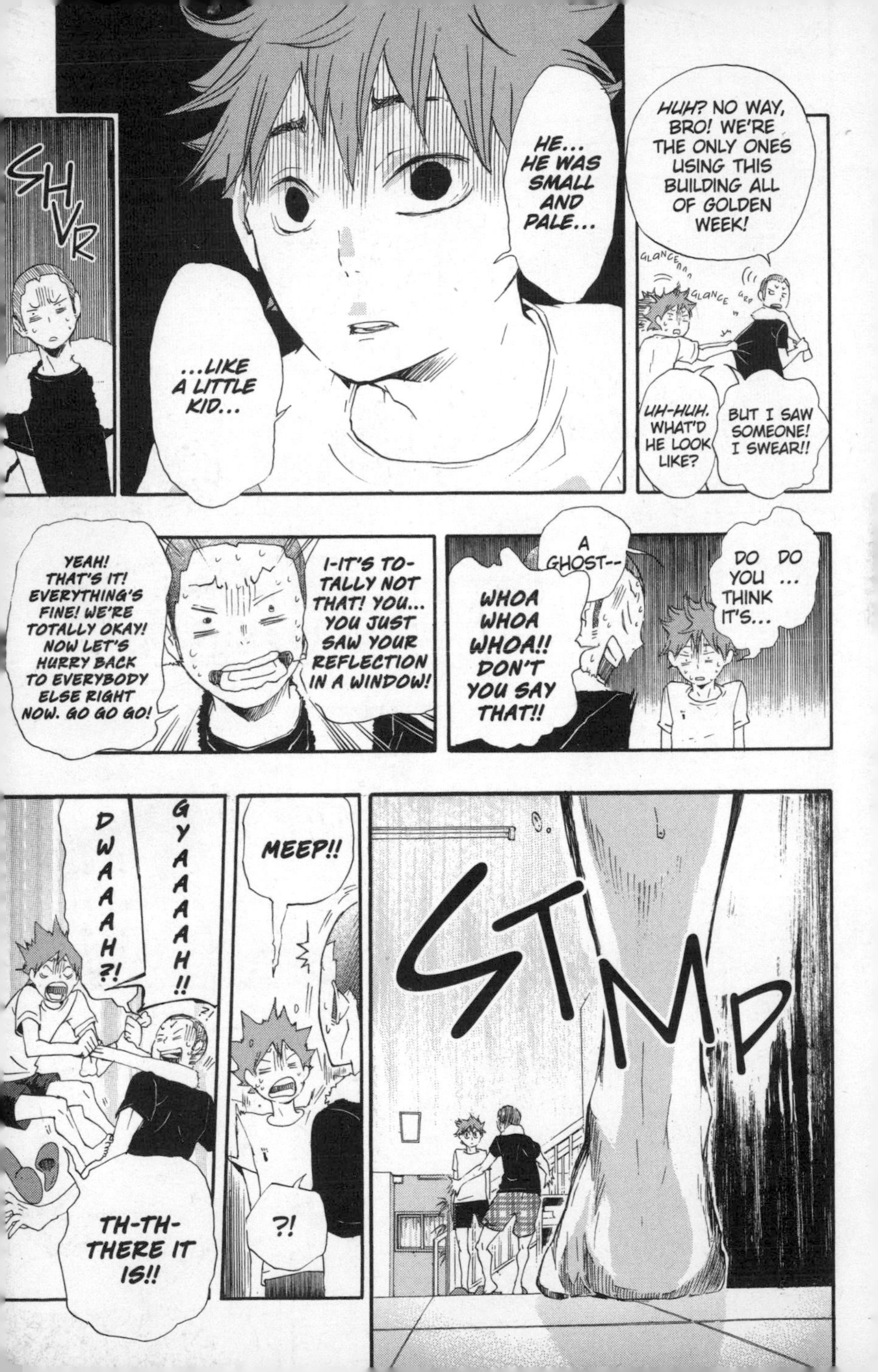
HUH? NO WAY, BRO! WE'RE THE ONLY ONES USING THIS BUILDING ALL OF GOLDEN WEEK!
GLANCE
GLANCE
BUT I SAW SOMEONE! I SWEAR!!
UH-HUH. WHAT'D HE LOOK LIKE?
HE... HE WAS SMALL AND PALE...
...LIKE A LITTLE KID...
SHVR
DO DO YOU ... THINK IT'S...
A GHOST--
WHOA WHOA WHOA!! DON'T YOU SAY THAT!!
I-IT'S TO-TALLY NOT THAT! YOU... YOU JUST SAW YOUR REFLECTION IN A WINDOW!
YEAH! THAT'S IT! EVERYTHING'S FINE! WE'RE TOTALLY OKAY! NOW LET'S HURRY BACK TO EVERYBODY ELSE RIGHT NOW. GO GO GO!
STMP
MEEP!!
?!
GYAAAAAAH!!
DWAAAAH?!
TH-TH-THERE IT IS!!

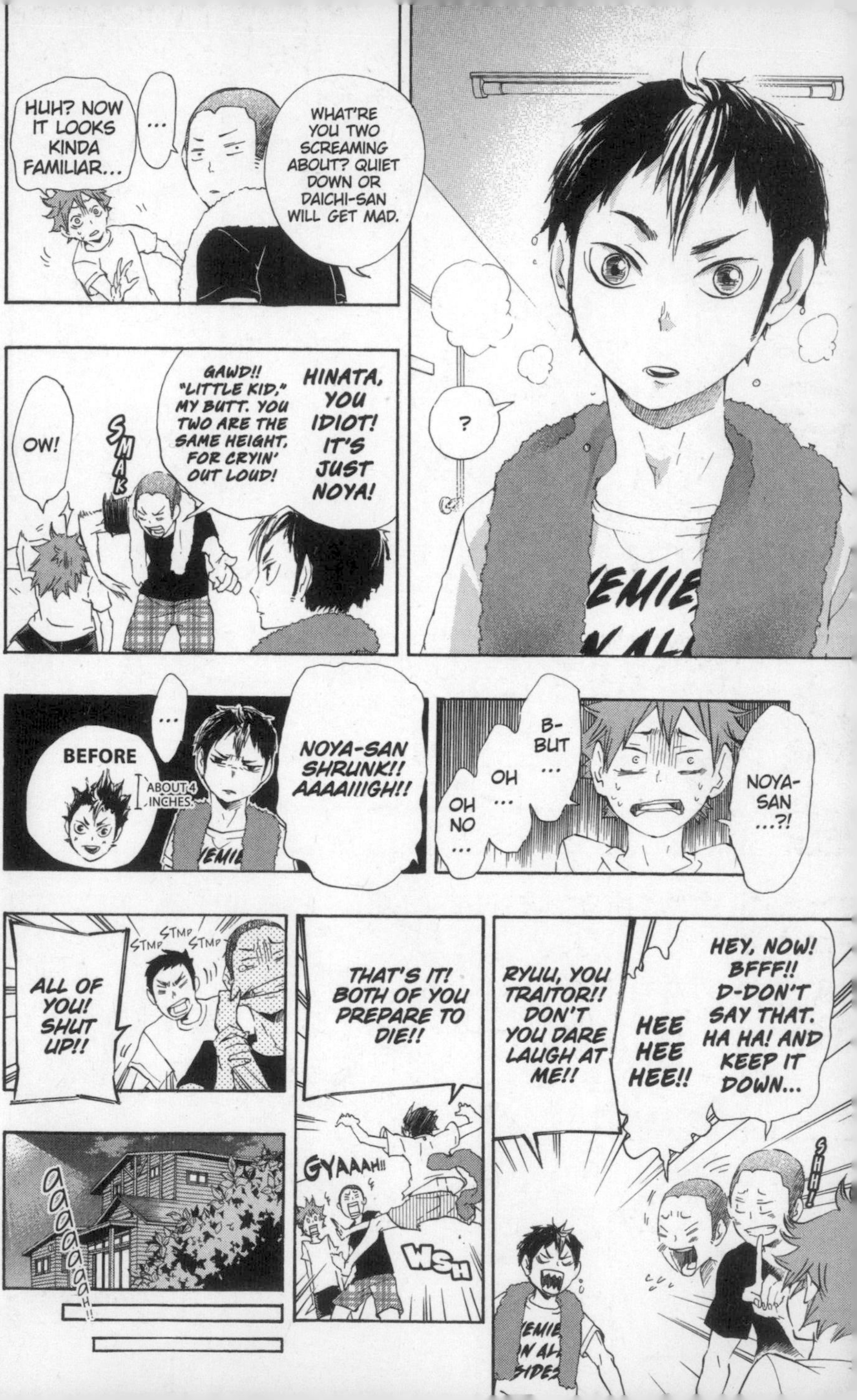
?
WHAT'RE YOU TWO SCREAMING ABOUT? QUIET DOWN OR DAICHI-SAN WILL GET MAD.
...
HUH? NOW IT LOOKS KINDA FAMILIAR...
HINATA, YOU IDIOT! IT'S JUST NOYA!
GAWD!! "LITTLE KID," MY BUTT. YOU TWO ARE THE SAME HEIGHT, FOR CRYIN' OUT LOUD!
SMAK
OW!
NOYA-SAN ...?!
B-BUT ...
OH ...
OH NO ...
NOYA-SAN SHRUNK!! AAAAIIIGH!!
...
BEFORE
ABOUT 4 INCHES.
HEY, NOW! BFFF!! D-DON'T SAY THAT. HA HA! AND KEEP IT DOWN...
HEE HEE HEE!!
RYUU, YOU TRAITOR!! DON'T YOU DARE LAUGH AT ME!!
SHH
THAT'S IT! BOTH OF YOU PREPARE TO DIE!!
GYAAAH!!
WSH
STMP STMP STMP
ALL OF YOU! SHUT UP!!

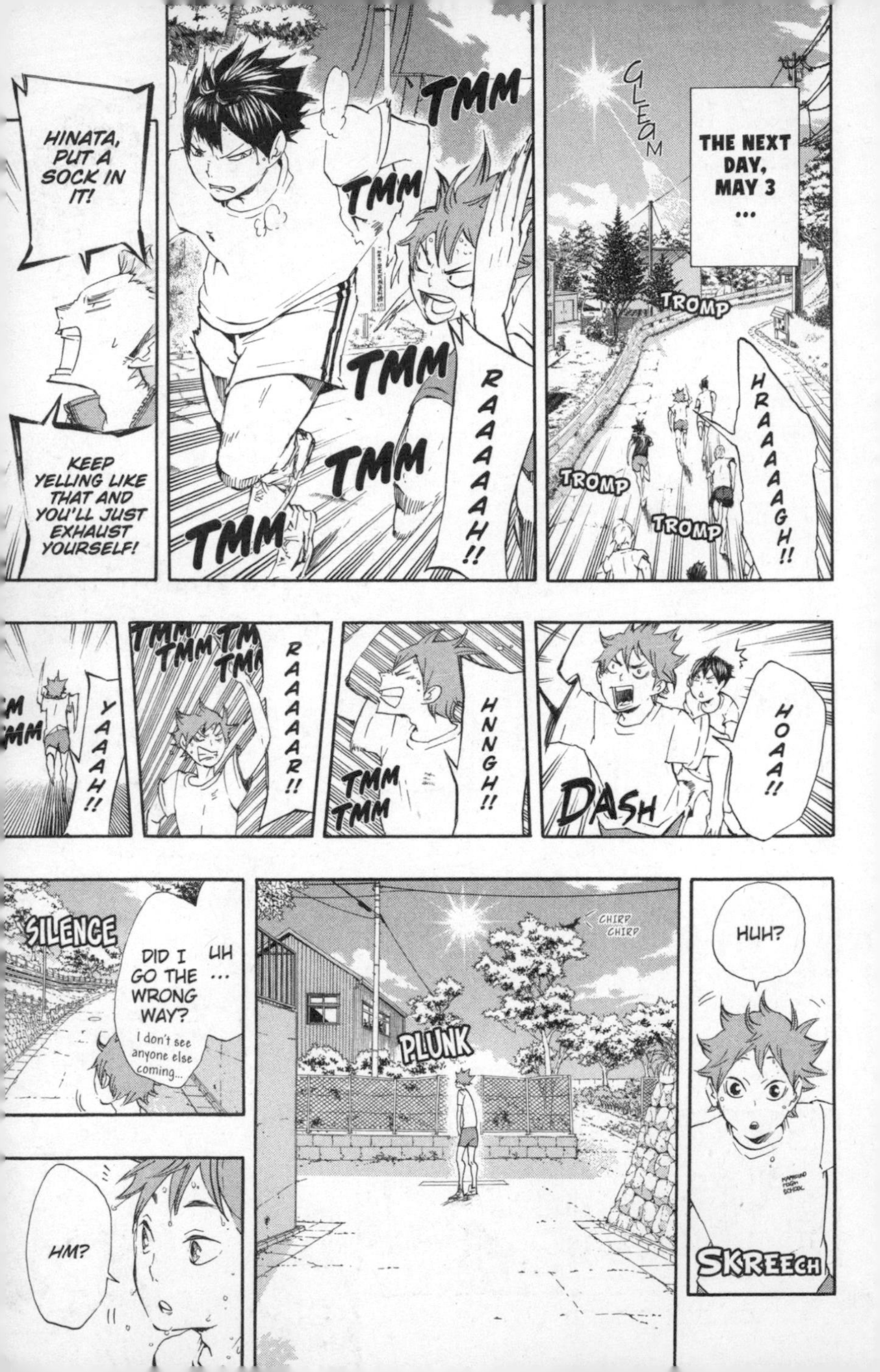
THE NEXT DAY, MAY 3 ...
GLEAM
TROMP
HRAAAAAAGH!!
TROMP
TROMP
TMM
TMM
TMM
TMM
TMM
RAAAAAAH!!
HINATA, PUT A SOCK IN IT!
KEEP YELLING LIKE THAT AND YOU'LL JUST EXHAUST YOURSELF!
HOAAA!!
DASH
HNNGH!!
TMM TMM
TMM TMM TM TM
RAAAAAAR!!
YAAAAH!!
HUH?
SKREECH
CHIRP CHIRP
PLUNK
SILENCE
UH ...
DID I GO THE WRONG WAY?
I don't see anyone else coming...
HM?

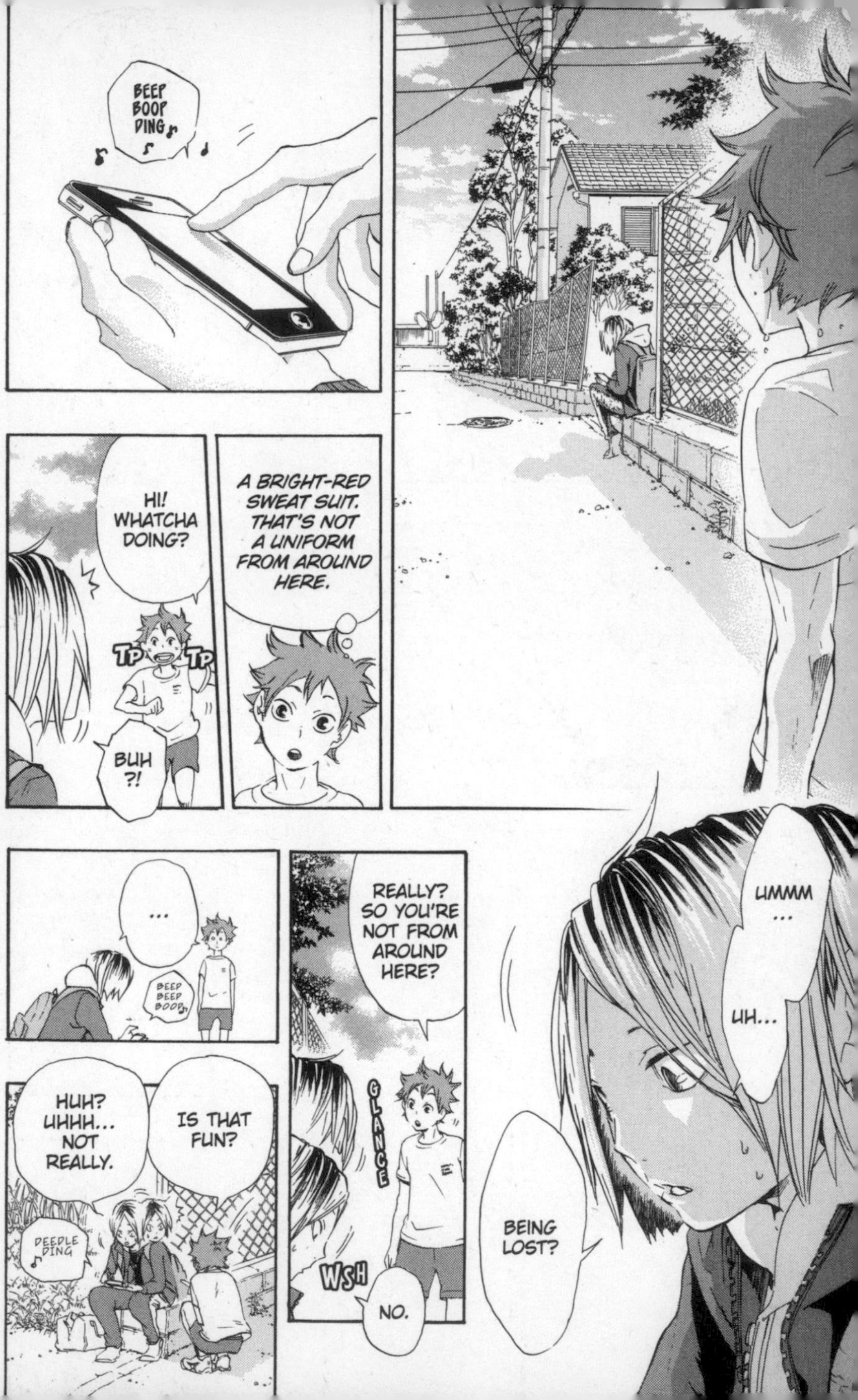
BEEP BOOP DING
A BRIGHT-RED SWEAT SUIT. THAT'S NOT A UNIFORM FROM AROUND HERE.
HI! WHATCHA DOING?
TP TP
BUH ?!
UMMM ...
UH...
BEING LOST?
REALLY? SO YOU'RE NOT FROM AROUND HERE?
GLANCE
WSH
NO.
...
BEEP BEEP BOOP
IS THAT FUN?
HUH? UHHH... NOT REALLY.
DEEDLE DING

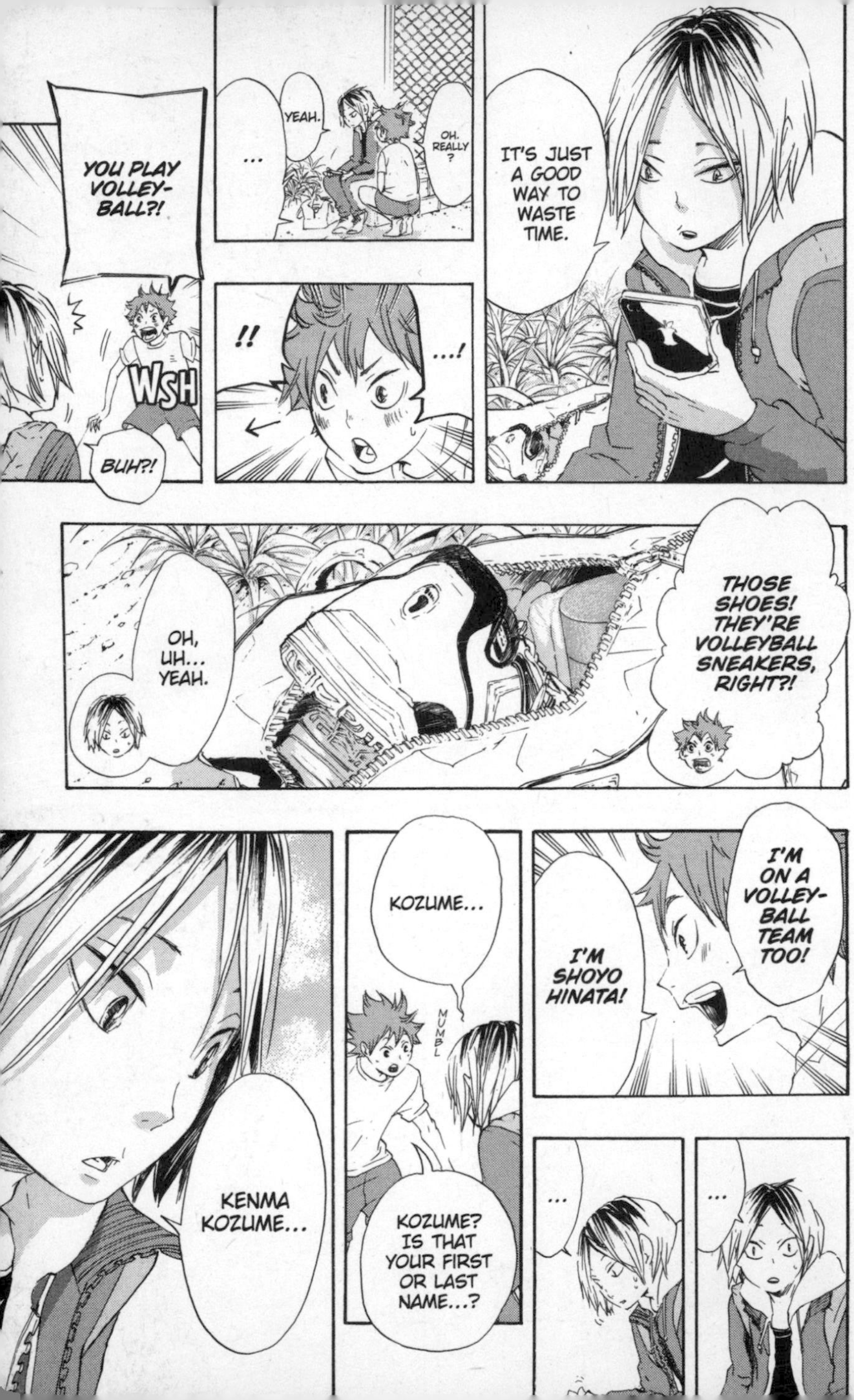
IT'S JUST A GOOD WAY TO WASTE TIME.
OH. REALLY?
YEAH.
...
...!
!!
YOU PLAY VOLLEY-BALL?!
WSH
BUH?!
THOSE SHOES! THEY'RE VOLLEYBALL SNEAKERS, RIGHT?!
OH, UH... YEAH.
I'M ON A VOLLEY-BALL TEAM TOO!
I'M SHOYO HINATA!
...
...
KOZUME...
MUMBL
KOZUME? IS THAT YOUR FIRST OR LAST NAME...?
KENMA KOZUME...

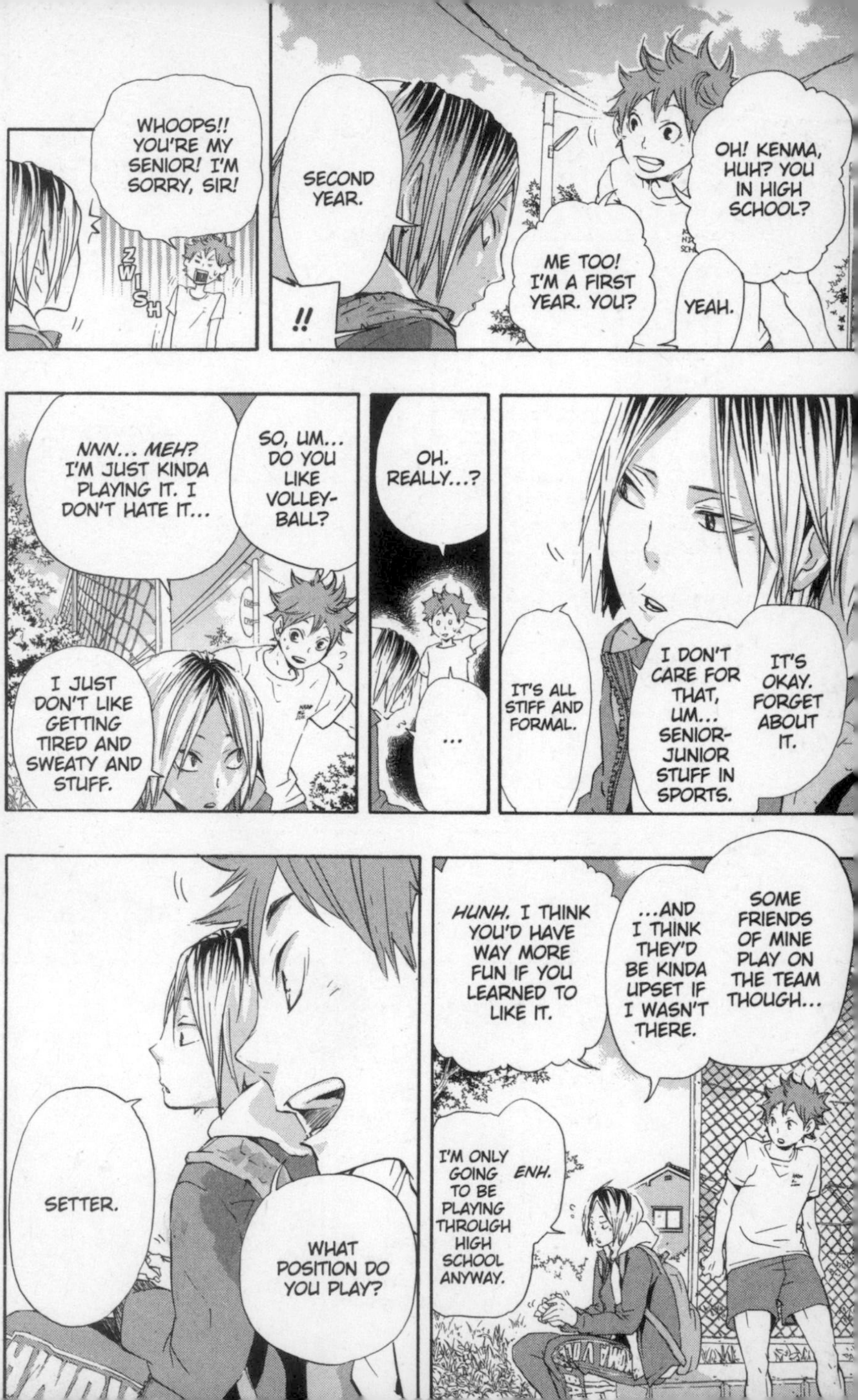
OH! KENMA, HUH? YOU IN HIGH SCHOOL?
YEAH.
ME TOO! I'M A FIRST YEAR. YOU?
SECOND YEAR.
!!
WHOOPS!! YOU'RE MY SENIOR! I'M SORRY, SIR!
ZWISH
IT'S OKAY. FORGET ABOUT IT.
I DON'T CARE FOR THAT, UM... SENIOR-JUNIOR STUFF IN SPORTS.
IT'S ALL STIFF AND FORMAL.
OH. REALLY...?
...
SO, UM... DO YOU LIKE VOLLEY-BALL?
NNN... MEH? I'M JUST KINDA PLAYING IT. I DON'T HATE IT...
I JUST DON'T LIKE GETTING TIRED AND SWEATY AND STUFF.
SOME FRIENDS OF MINE PLAY ON THE TEAM THOUGH...
...AND I THINK THEY'D BE KINDA UPSET IF I WASN'T THERE.
HUNH. I THINK YOU'D HAVE WAY MORE FUN IF YOU LEARNED TO LIKE IT.
ENH.
I'M ONLY GOING TO BE PLAYING THROUGH HIGH SCHOOL ANYWAY.
WHAT POSITION DO YOU PLAY?
SETTER.

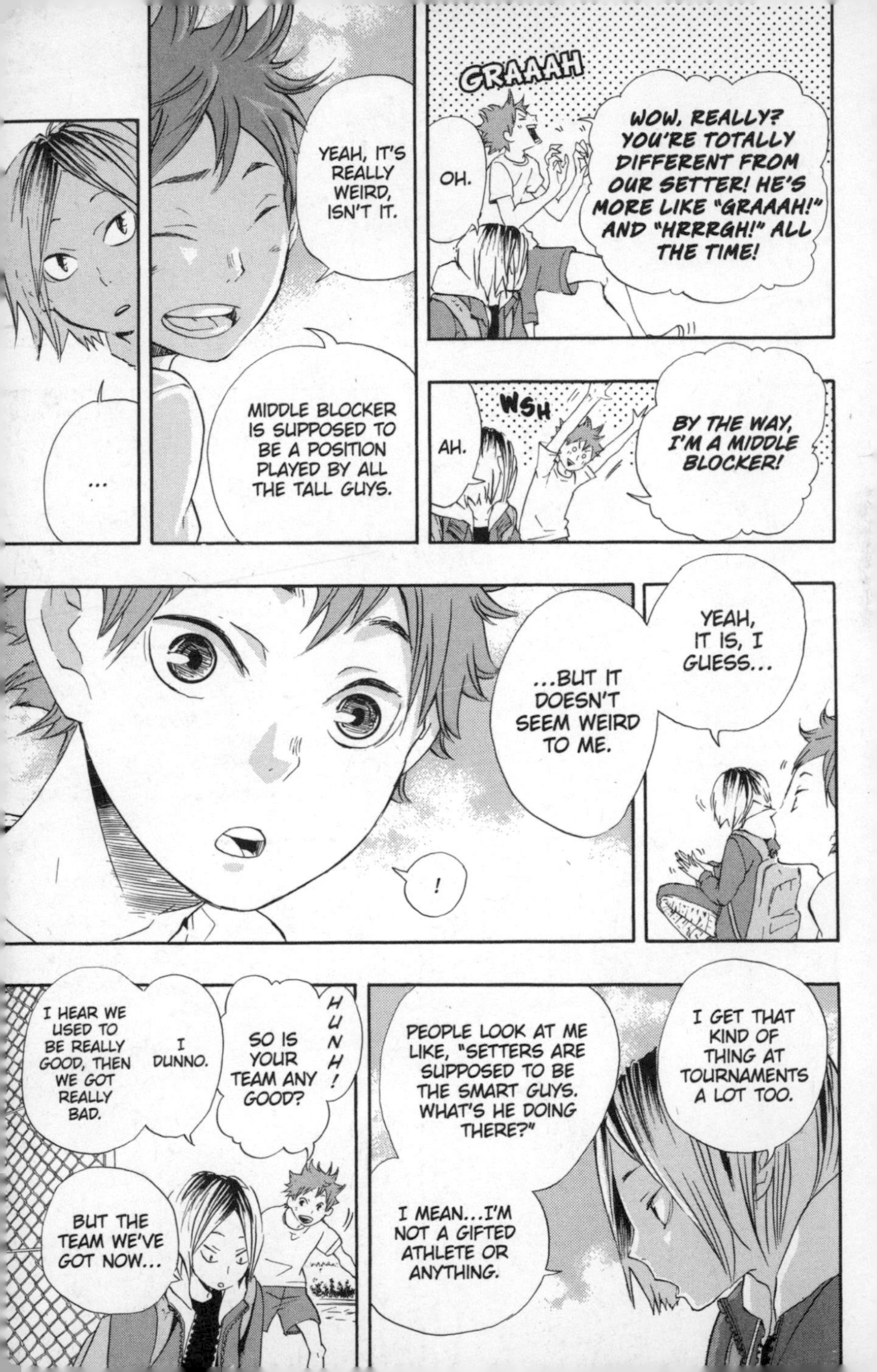
GRAAAH
WOW, REALLY? YOU'RE TOTALLY DIFFERENT FROM OUR SETTER! HE'S MORE LIKE "GRAAAH!" AND "HRRRGH!" ALL THE TIME!
OH.
WSH
BY THE WAY, I'M A MIDDLE BLOCKER!
AH.
YEAH, IT'S REALLY WEIRD, ISN'T IT.
MIDDLE BLOCKER IS SUPPOSED TO BE A POSITION PLAYED BY ALL THE TALL GUYS.
...
YEAH, IT IS, I GUESS...
...BUT IT DOESN'T SEEM WEIRD TO ME.
!
I GET THAT KIND OF THING AT TOURNAMENTS A LOT TOO.
PEOPLE LOOK AT ME LIKE, "SETTERS ARE SUPPOSED TO BE THE SMART GUYS. WHAT'S HE DOING THERE?"
I MEAN...I'M NOT A GIFTED ATHLETE OR ANYTHING.
HUNH!
SO IS YOUR TEAM ANY GOOD?
I DUNNO.
I HEAR WE USED TO BE REALLY GOOD, THEN WE GOT REALLY BAD.
BUT THE TEAM WE'VE GOT NOW...

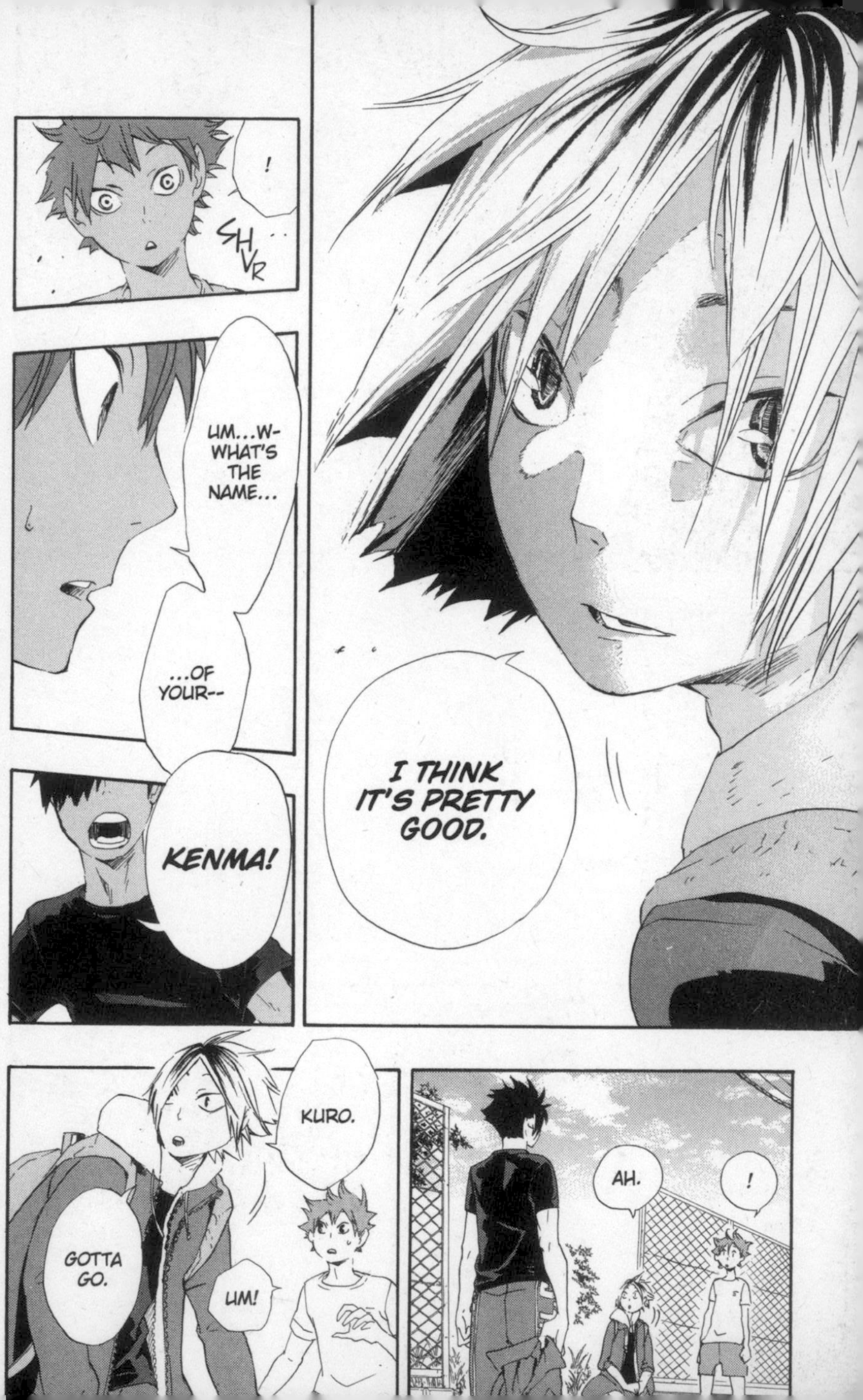
I THINK IT'S PRETTY GOOD.
!
SHVR
UM...W-WHAT'S THE NAME...
...OF YOUR--
KENMA!
!
AH.
KURO.
GOTTA GO.
UM!

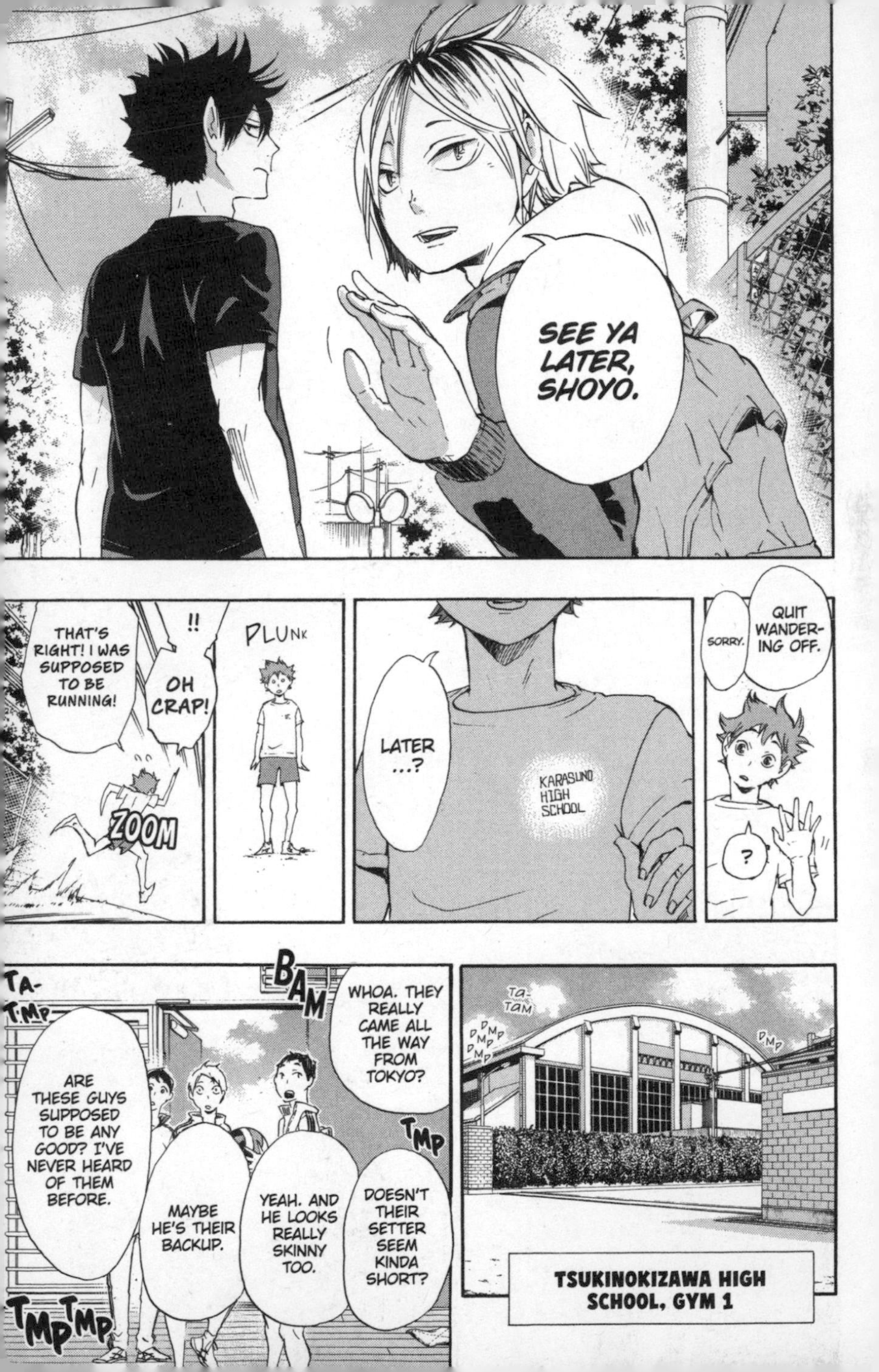
SEE YA LATER, SHOYO.
QUIT WANDERING OFF.
SORRY.
?
LATER ...?
KARASUNO HIGH SCHOOL
PLUNK
!!
OH CRAP!
THAT'S RIGHT! I WAS SUPPOSED TO BE RUNNING!
ZOOM
TA-TAM
DMP DMP DMP
DMP
TSUKINOKIZAWA HIGH SCHOOL, GYM 1
BAM
WHOA. THEY REALLY CAME ALL THE WAY FROM TOKYO?
TMP
DOESN'T THEIR SETTER SEEM KINDA SHORT?
YEAH. AND HE LOOKS REALLY SKINNY TOO.
MAYBE HE'S THEIR BACKUP.
ARE THESE GUYS SUPPOSED TO BE ANY GOOD? I'VE NEVER HEARD OF THEM BEFORE.
TA-TMP
TMP TMP

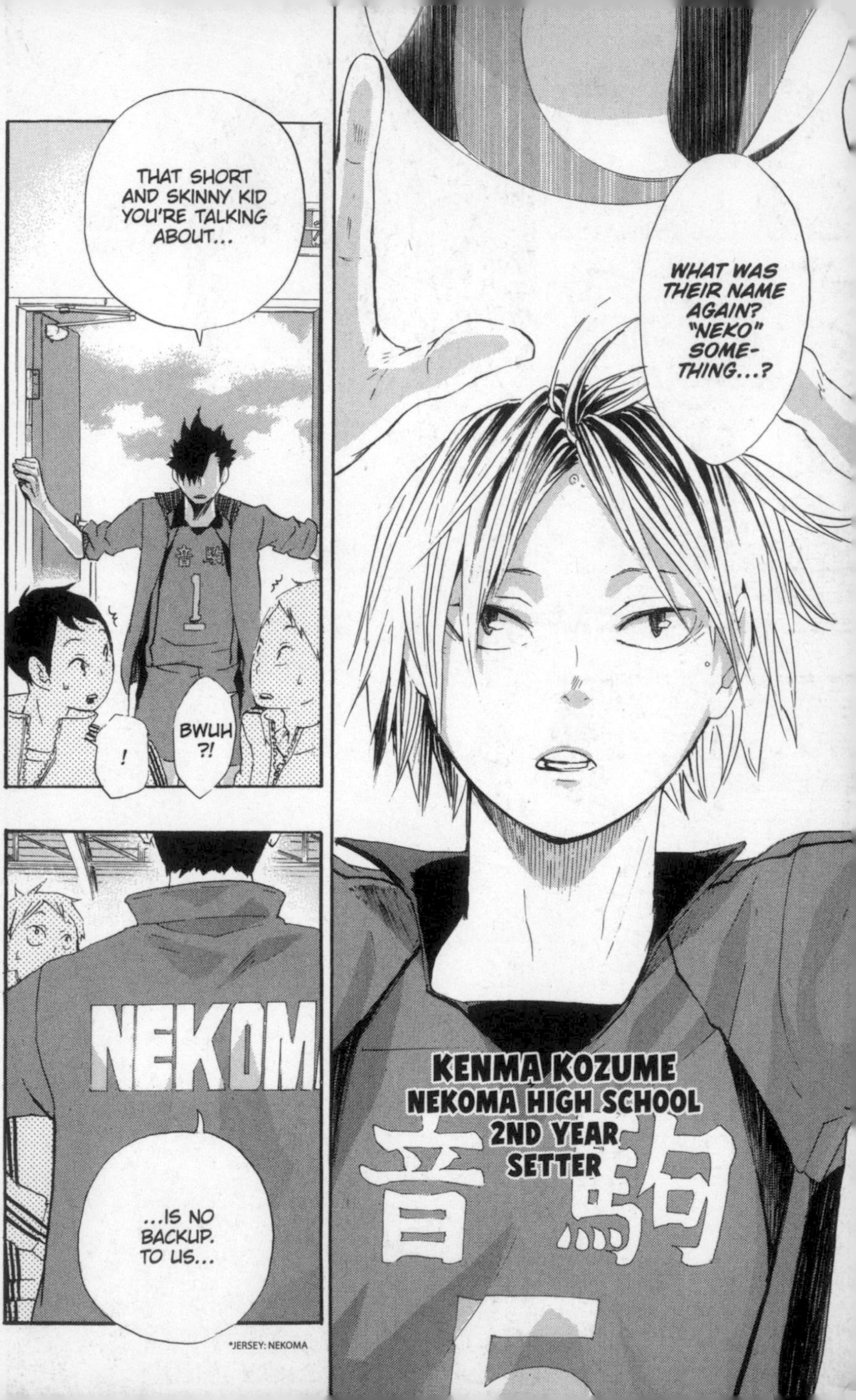
WHAT WAS THEIR NAME AGAIN? "NEKO" SOME-THING...?
KENMA KOZUME
NEKOMA HIGH SCHOOL
2ND YEAR
SETTER
音駒
THAT SHORT AND SKINNY KID YOU'RE TALKING ABOUT...
BWUH ?!
!
NEKOM
...IS NO BACKUP. TO US...

*JERSEY: NEKOMA

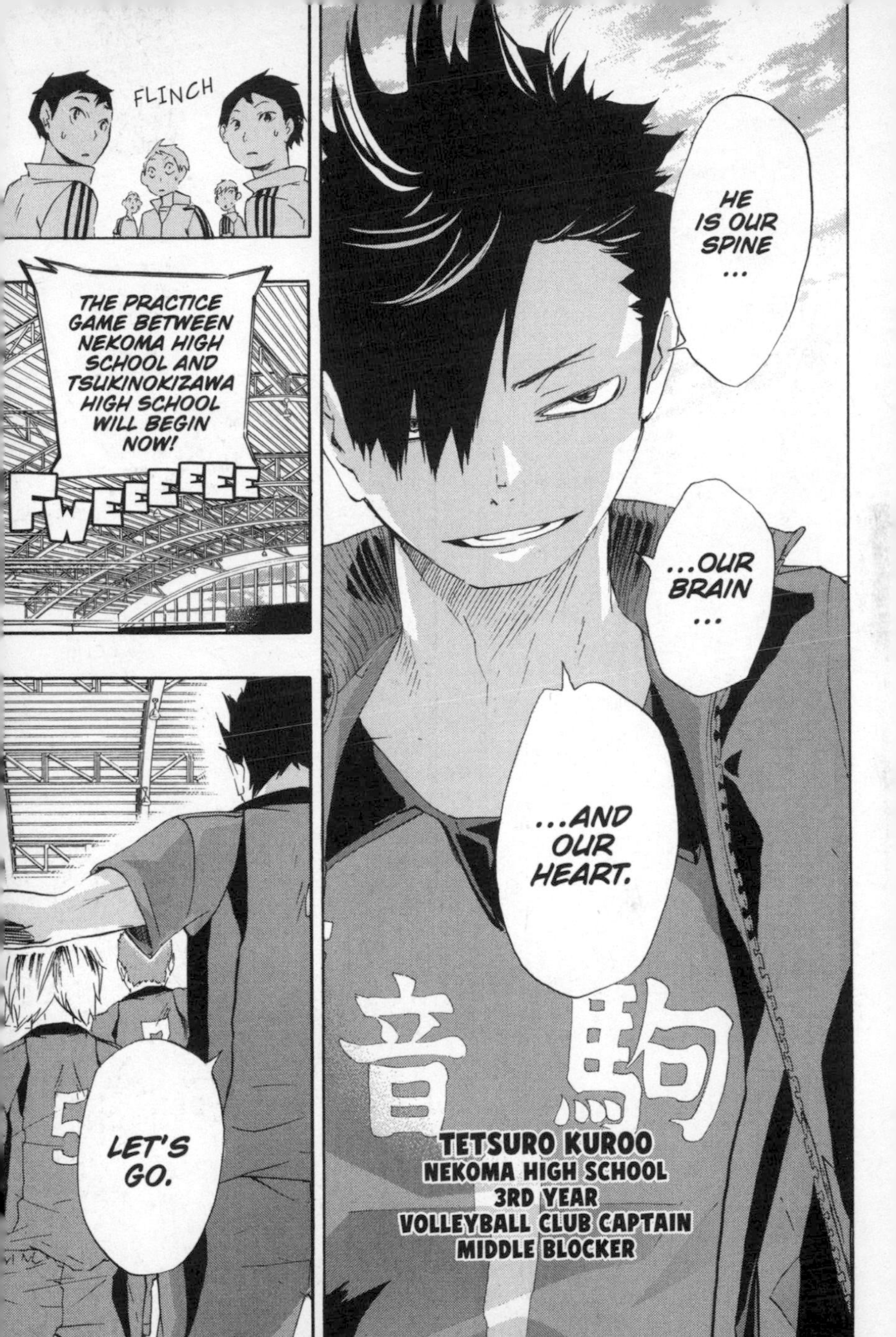
HE IS OUR SPINE ...
...OUR BRAIN ...
...AND OUR HEART.
音駒
TETSURO KUROO
NEKOMA HIGH SCHOOL
3RD YEAR
VOLLEYBALL CLUB CAPTAIN
MIDDLE BLOCKER
FLINCH
THE PRACTICE GAME BETWEEN NEKOMA HIGH SCHOOL AND TSUKINOKIZAWA HIGH SCHOOL WILL BEGIN NOW!
FWEEEEEE
LET'S GO.

HAIKYU!! VOL 3: GO, TEAM KARASUNO! (END)

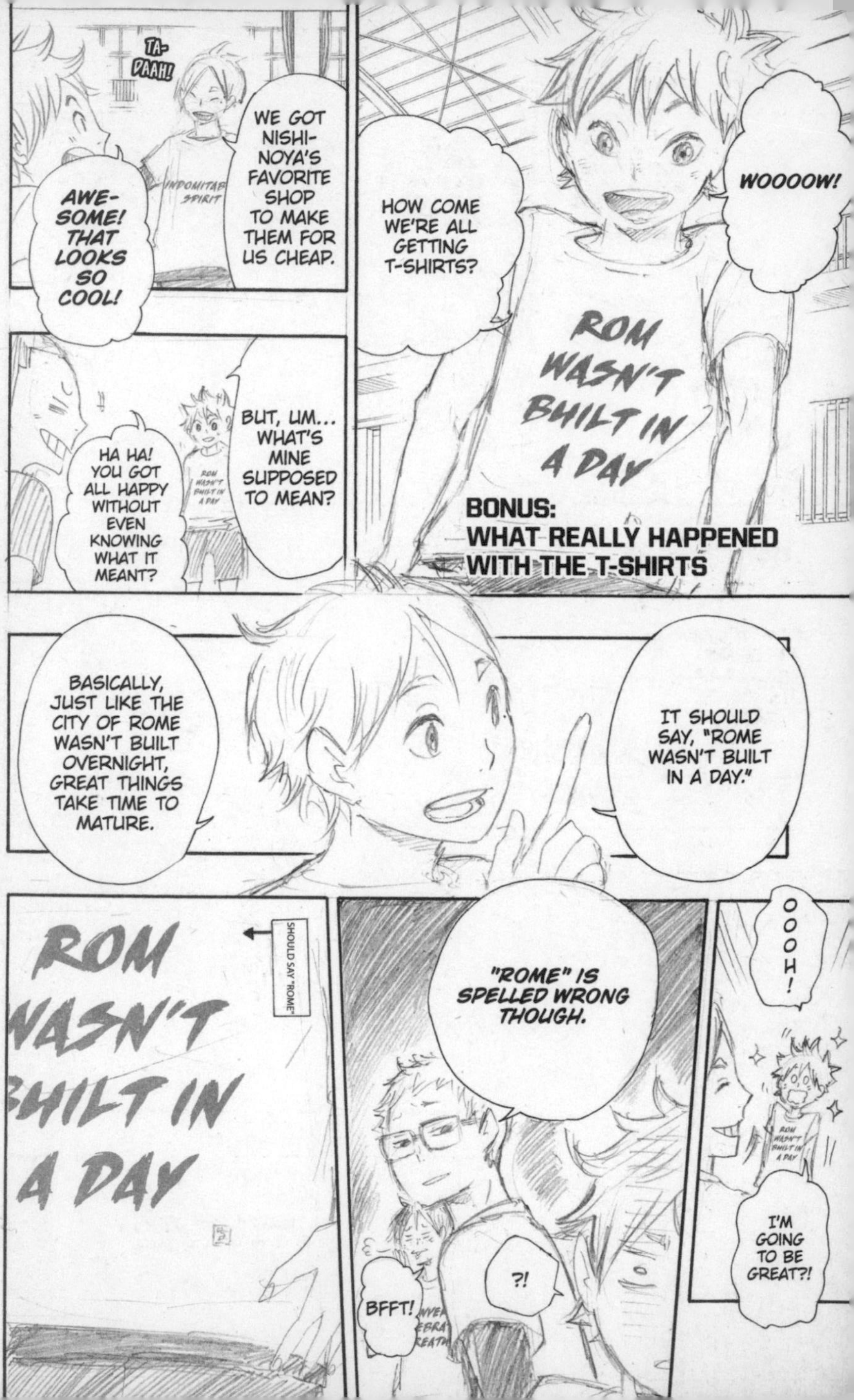
WOOOOW!
HOW COME WE'RE ALL GETTING T-SHIRTS?
ROM WASN'T BUILT IN A DAY
BONUS: WHAT REALLY HAPPENED WITH THE T-SHIRTS
TA-DAAH!
WE GOT NISHI-NOYA'S FAVORITE SHOP TO MAKE THEM FOR US CHEAP.
AWE-SOME! THAT LOOKS SO COOL!
BUT, UM... WHAT'S MINE SUPPOSED TO MEAN?
HA HA! YOU GOT ALL HAPPY WITHOUT EVEN KNOWING WHAT IT MEANT?
IT SHOULD SAY, "ROME WASN'T BUILT IN A DAY."
BASICALLY, JUST LIKE THE CITY OF ROME WASN'T BUILT OVERNIGHT, GREAT THINGS TAKE TIME TO MATURE.
OOOH!
I'M GOING TO BE GREAT?!
"ROME" IS SPELLED WRONG THOUGH.
?!
BFFT!
ROM WASN'T BUILT IN A DAY
SHOULD SAY "ROME"

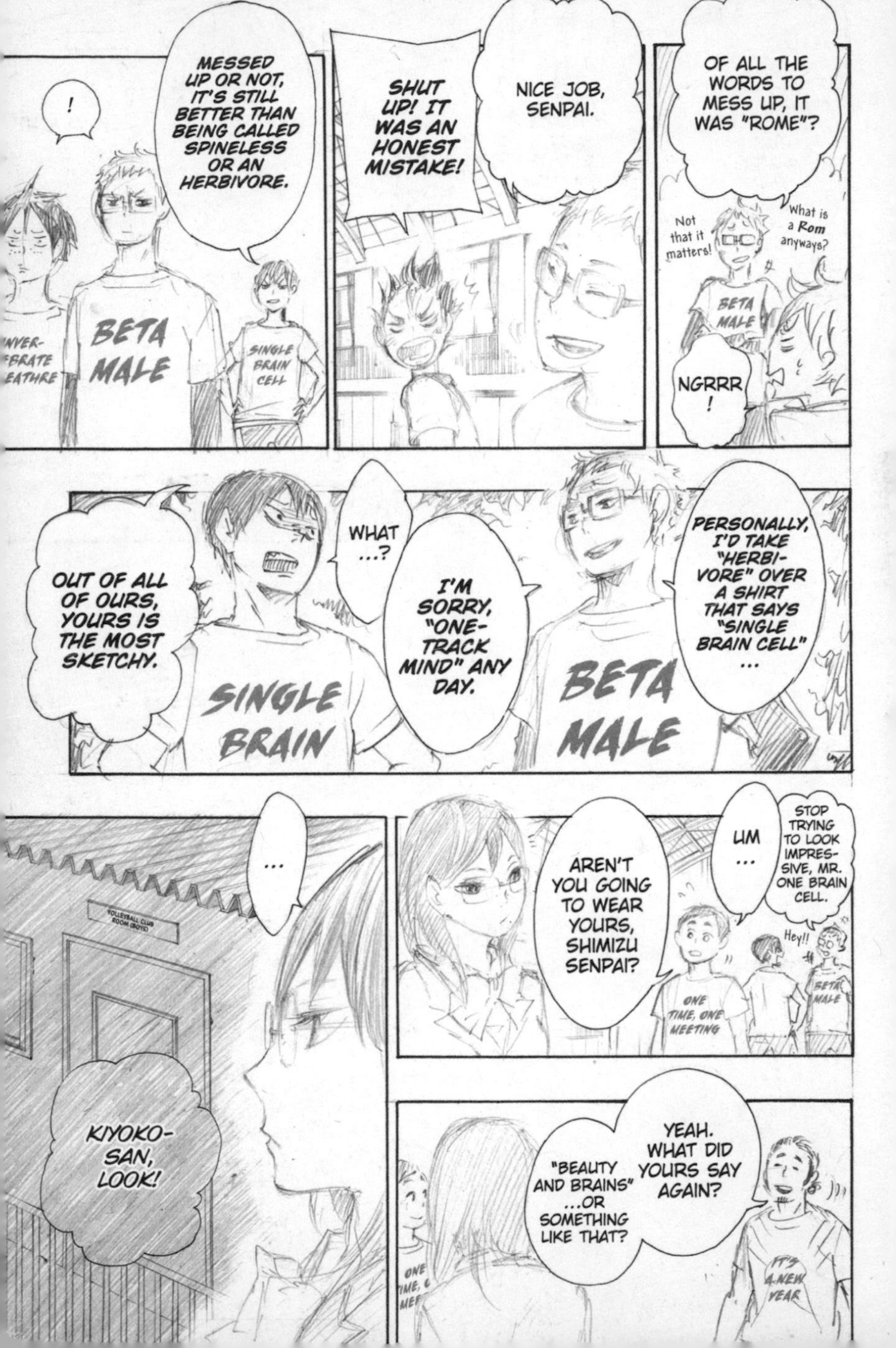
OF ALL THE WORDS TO MESS UP, IT WAS "ROME"?
What is a Rom anyways?
Not that it matters!
BETA MALE
NGRRR!
NICE JOB, SENPAI.
SHUT UP! IT WAS AN HONEST MISTAKE!
MESSED UP OR NOT, IT'S STILL BETTER THAN BEING CALLED SPINELESS OR AN HERBIVORE.
!
SINGLE BRAIN CELL
BETA MALE
PERSONALLY, I'D TAKE "HERBI-VORE" OVER A SHIRT THAT SAYS "SINGLE BRAIN CELL"...
BETA MALE
I'M SORRY, "ONE-TRACK MIND" ANY DAY.
WHAT...?
OUT OF ALL OF OURS, YOURS IS THE MOST SKETCHY.
SINGLE BRAIN
STOP TRYING TO LOOK IMPRES-SIVE, MR. ONE BRAIN CELL.
UM...
Hey!!
BETA MALE
ONE TIME, ONE MEETING
AREN'T YOU GOING TO WEAR YOURS, SHIMIZU SENPAI?
YEAH. WHAT DID YOURS SAY AGAIN?
IT'S A NEW YEAR
"BEAUTY AND BRAINS" ...OR SOMETHING LIKE THAT?
...
VOLLEYBALL CLUB ROOM (BOYS)
KIYOKO-SAN, LOOK!

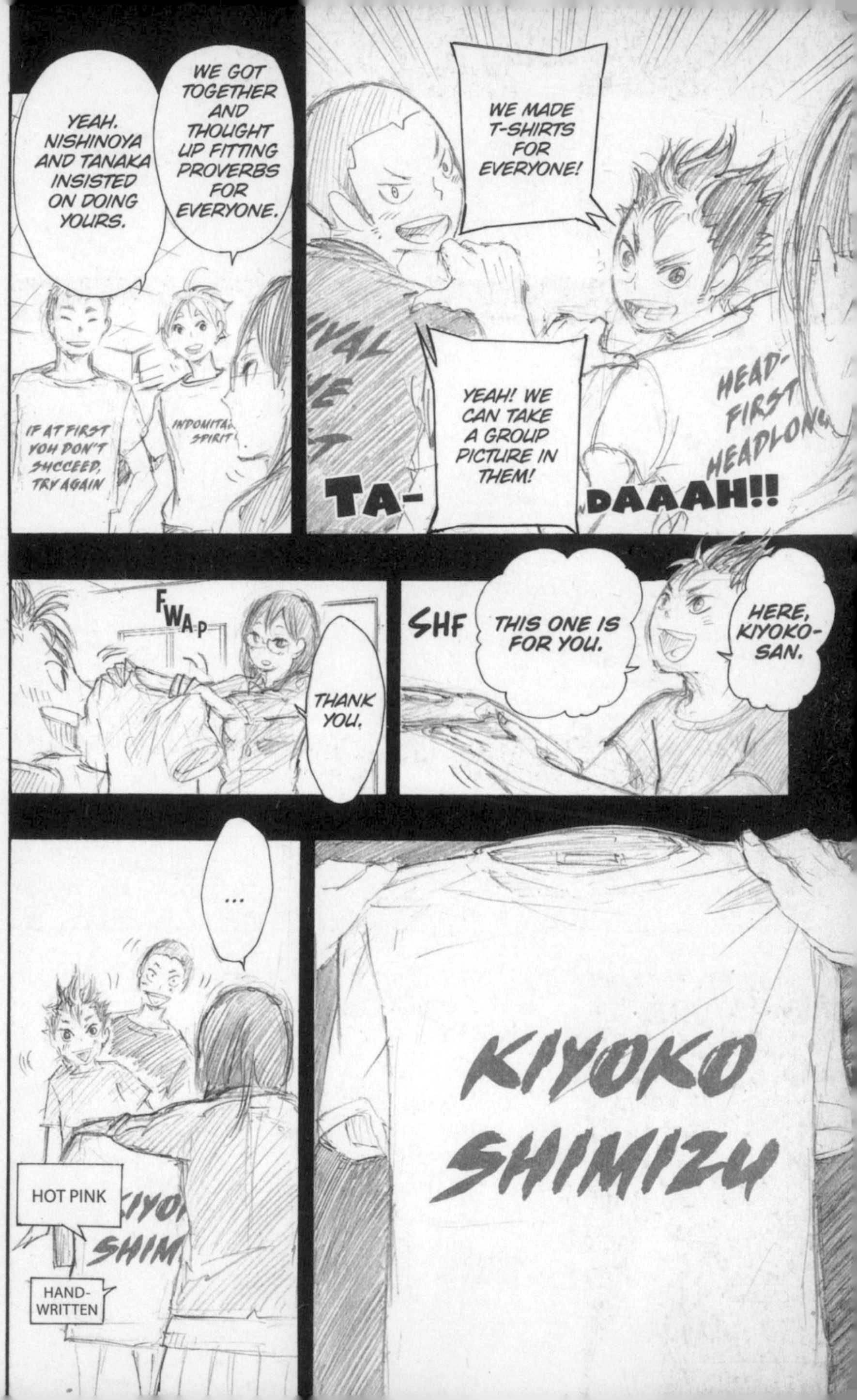
WE MADE T-SHIRTS FOR EVERYONE!
YEAH! WE CAN TAKE A GROUP PICTURE IN THEM!
TA-DAAAH!!
HEAD-FIRST
WE GOT TOGETHER AND THOUGHT UP FITTING PROVERBS FOR EVERYONE.
YEAH. NISHINOYA AND TANAKA INSISTED ON DOING YOURS.
IF AT FIRST YOU DON'T SUCCEED, TRY AGAIN
HERE, KIYOKO-SAN.
THIS ONE IS FOR YOU.
SHF
FWAP
THANK YOU.
KIYOKO SHIMIZU
...
HOT PINK
HAND-WRITTEN

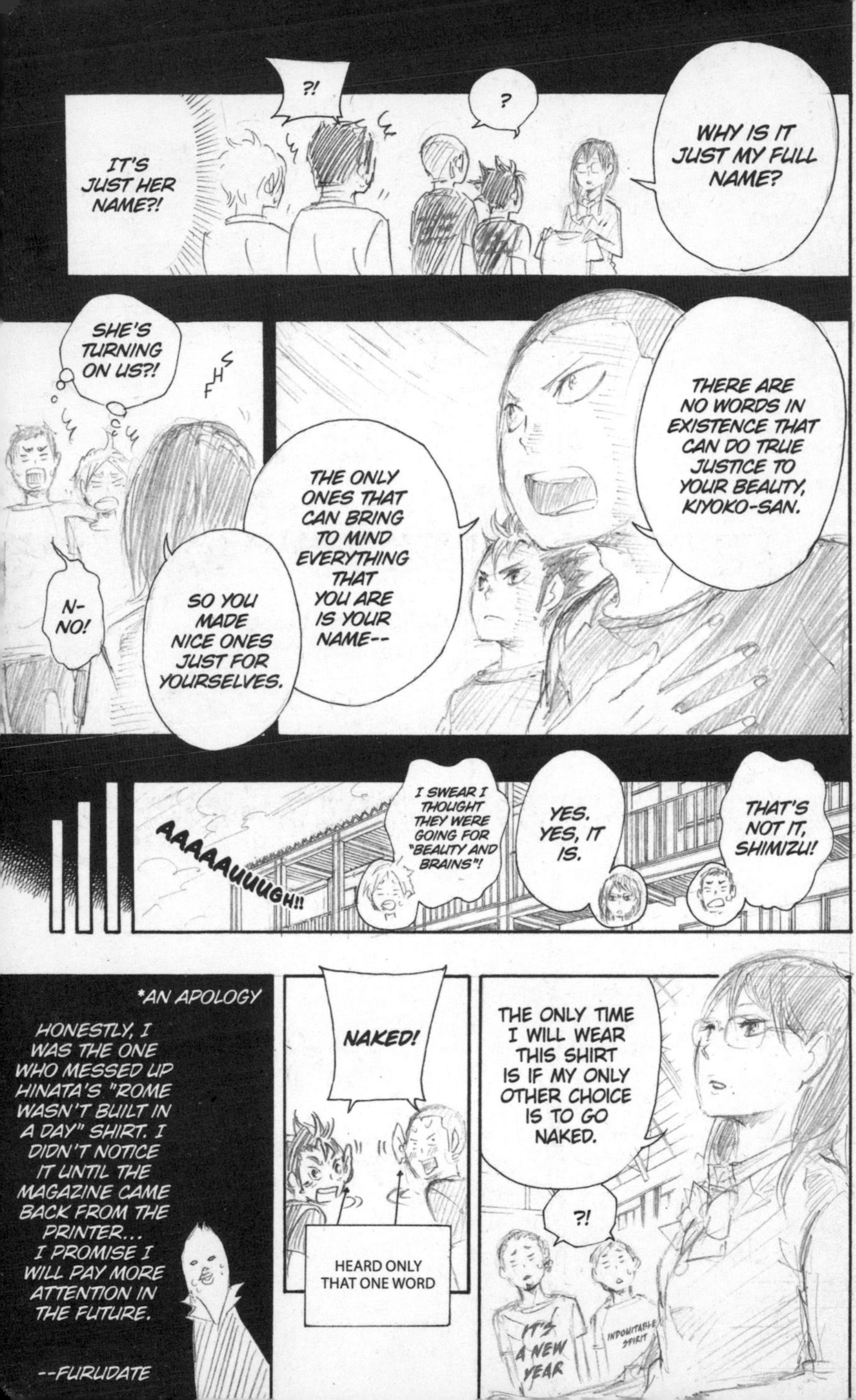
WHY IS IT JUST MY FULL NAME?
?
?!
IT'S JUST HER NAME?!
THERE ARE NO WORDS IN EXISTENCE THAT CAN DO TRUE JUSTICE TO YOUR BEAUTY, KIYOKO-SAN.
THE ONLY ONES THAT CAN BRING TO MIND EVERYTHING THAT YOU ARE IS YOUR NAME--
SHE'S TURNING ON US?!
SO YOU MADE NICE ONES JUST FOR YOURSELVES.
N-NO!
THAT'S NOT IT, SHIMIZU!
YES. YES, IT IS.
I SWEAR I THOUGHT THEY WERE GOING FOR "BEAUTY AND BRAINS"!
AAAAAUUUGH!!
THE ONLY TIME I WILL WEAR THIS SHIRT IS IF MY ONLY OTHER CHOICE IS TO GO NAKED.
?!
IT'S A NEW YEAR
INDOMITABLE SPIRIT
NAKED!
HEARD ONLY THAT ONE WORD
*AN APOLOGY
HONESTLY, I WAS THE ONE WHO MESSED UP HINATA'S "ROME WASN'T BUILT IN A DAY" SHIRT. I DIDN'T NOTICE IT UNTIL THE MAGAZINE CAME BACK FROM THE PRINTER... I PROMISE I WILL PAY MORE ATTENTION IN THE FUTURE.
--FURUDATE

EDITOR'S NOTES

The English edition of Haikyu!! maintains the honorifics used in the original Japanese version. For those of you who are new to these terms, here's a brief explanation to help with your reading experience!

When saying someone's name in Japanese, a suffix is often attached to indicate how familiar the speaker is with the person. Some are more polite and respectful, while others are endearing.

1 *-kun* is often used for young men or boys, usually someone you are familiar with.

2 *-chan* is used for young children and can be used as a term of endearment.

3 *-san* is used for someone you respect or are not close to, or to be polite.

4 *Senpai* is used for someone who is older than you or in a higher position or grade in school.

5 *Kohai* is used for someone who is younger than you or in a lower position or grade in school.

6 *Sensei* means teacher.

MY HERO ACADEMIA

IZUKU MIDORIYA WANTS TO BE A HERO MORE THAN ANYTHING, BUT HE HASN'T GOT AN OUNCE OF POWER IN HIM. WITH NO CHANCE OF GETTING INTO THE U.A. HIGH SCHOOL FOR HEROES, HIS LIFE IS LOOKING LIKE A DEAD END. THEN AN ENCOUNTER WITH ALL MIGHT, THE GREATEST HERO OF ALL, GIVES HIM A CHANCE TO CHANGE HIS DESTINY...

SHONEN JUMP

VIZ media
www.viz.com

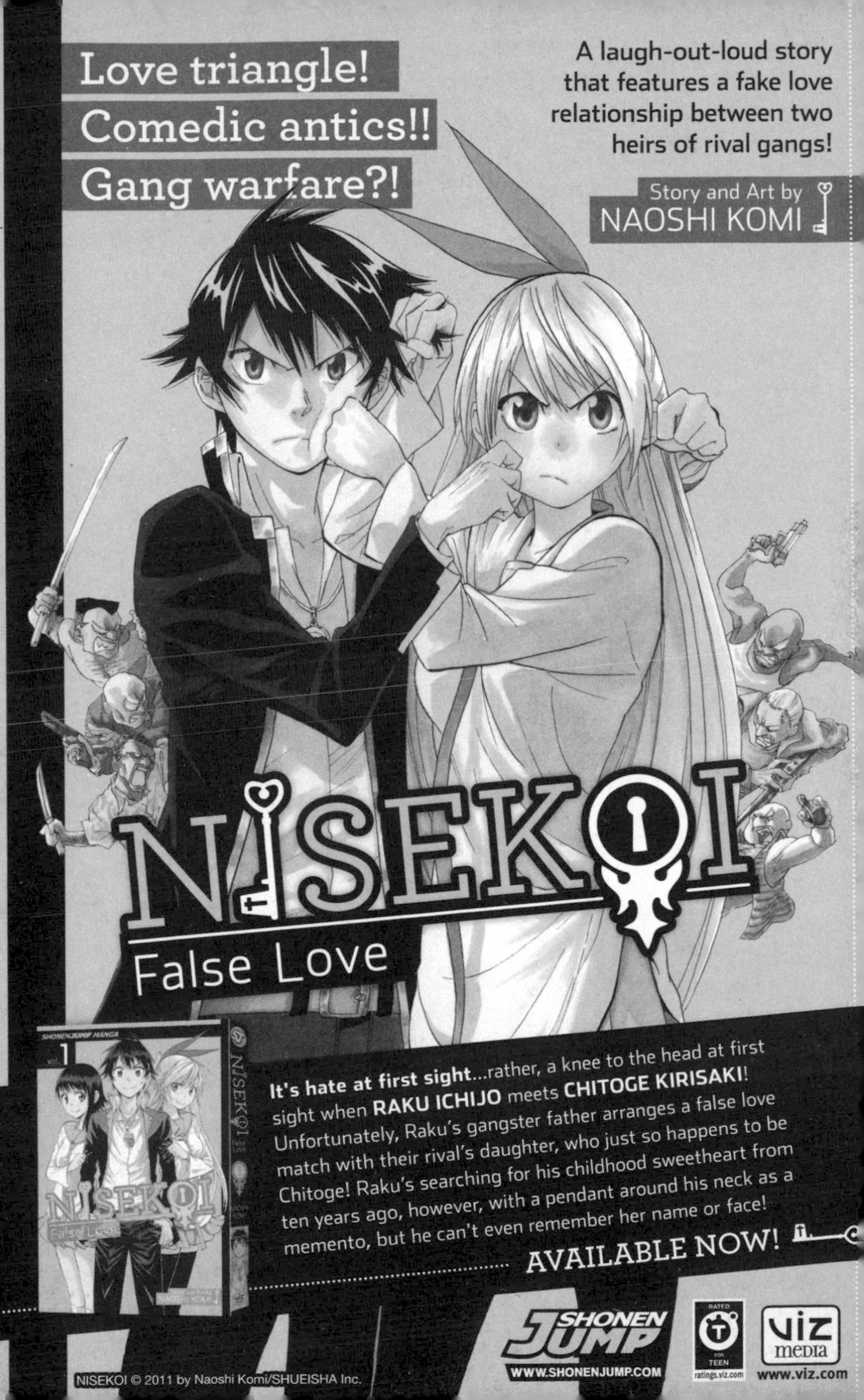
Love triangle!
Comedic antics!!
Gang warfare?!
A laugh-out-loud story that features a fake love relationship between two heirs of rival gangs!
Story and Art by NAOSHI KOMI
NISEKOI
False Love
SHONEN JUMP MANGA
vol. 1
NISEKOI
False Love
It's hate at first sight...rather, a knee to the head at first sight when RAKU ICHIJO meets CHITOGE KIRISAKI! Unfortunately, Raku's gangster father arranges a false love match with their rival's daughter, who just so happens to be Chitoge! Raku's searching for his childhood sweetheart from ten years ago, however, with a pendant around his neck as a memento, but he can't even remember her name or face!
AVAILABLE NOW!
SHONEN JUMP
WWW.SHONENJUMP.COM
RATED T FOR TEEN
ratings.viz.com
VIZ media
www.viz.com
NISEKOI © 2011 by Naoshi Komi/SHUEISHA Inc.

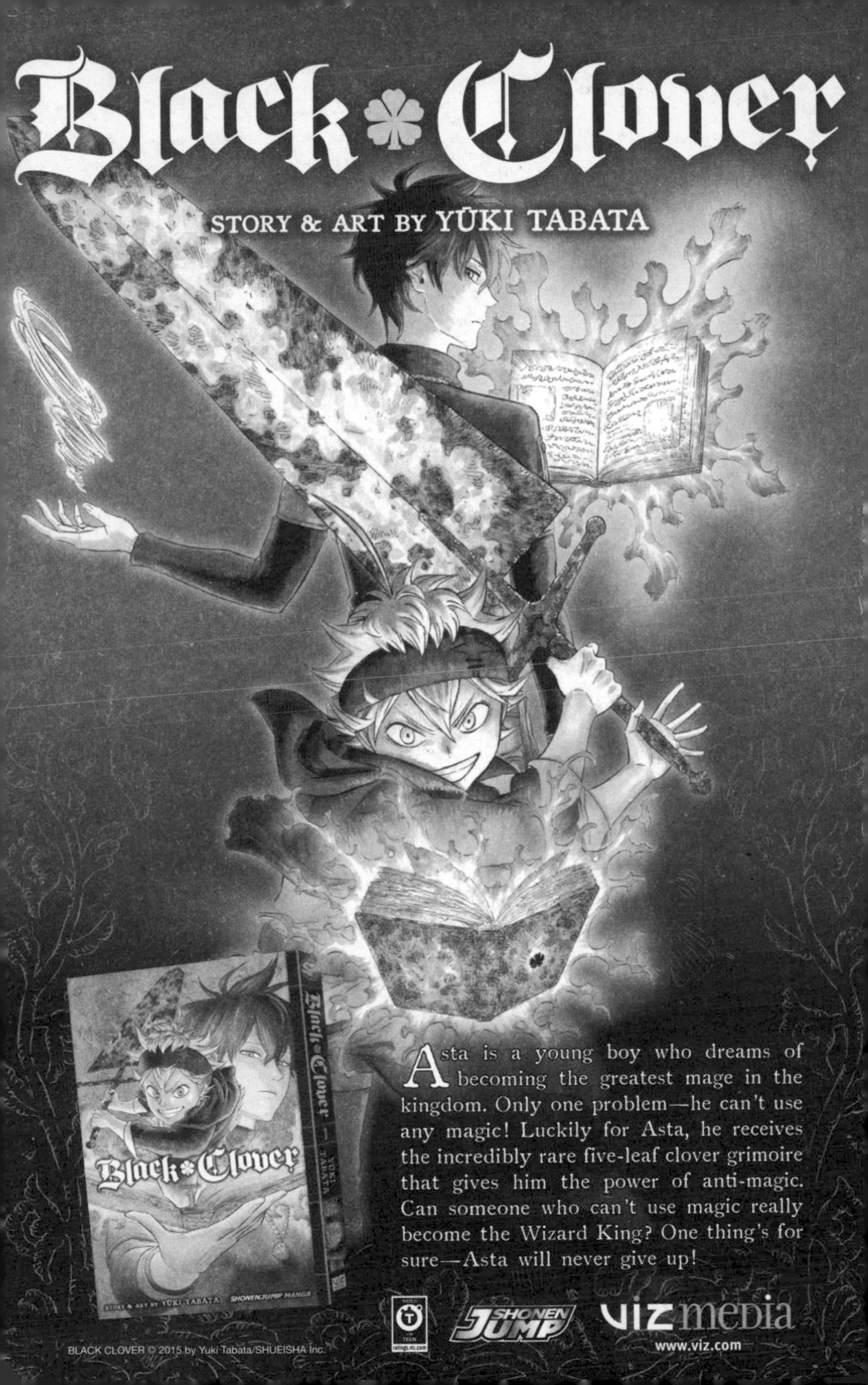

Black Clover
STORY & ART BY YŪKI TABATA
Asta is a young boy who dreams of becoming the greatest mage in the kingdom. Only one problem—he can't use any magic! Luckily for Asta, he receives the incredibly rare five-leaf clover grimoire that gives him the power of anti-magic. Can someone who can't use magic really become the Wizard King? One thing's for sure—Asta will never give up!
Black Clover
STORY & ART BY YUKI TABATA
SHONEN JUMP MANGA
SHONEN JUMP
VIZ media
www.viz.com
BLACK CLOVER © 2015 by Yuki Tabata/SHUEISHA Inc.

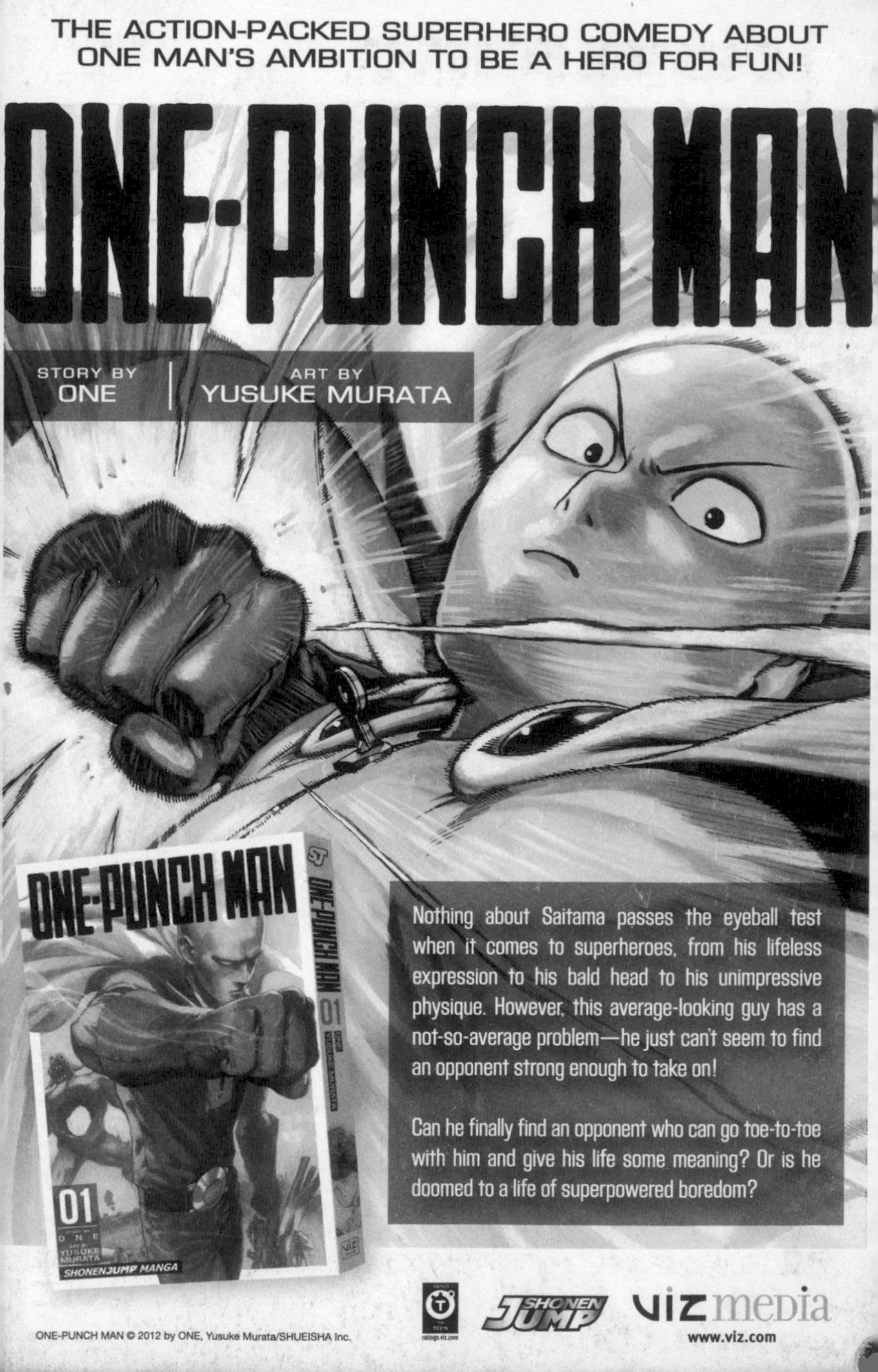
THE ACTION-PACKED SUPERHERO COMEDY ABOUT ONE MAN'S AMBITION TO BE A HERO FOR FUN!
ONE-PUNCH MAN
STORY BY ONE
ART BY YUSUKE MURATA
ONE-PUNCH MAN 01
Nothing about Saitama passes the eyeball test when it comes to superheroes, from his lifeless expression to his bald head to his unimpressive physique. However, this average-looking guy has a not-so-average problem—he just can't seem to find an opponent strong enough to take on!
Can he finally find an opponent who can go toe-to-toe with him and give his life some meaning? Or is he doomed to a life of superpowered boredom?
SHONEN JUMP MANGA
SHONEN JUMP
viz media
www.viz.com
ONE-PUNCH MAN © 2012 by ONE, Yusuke Murata/SHUEISHA Inc.

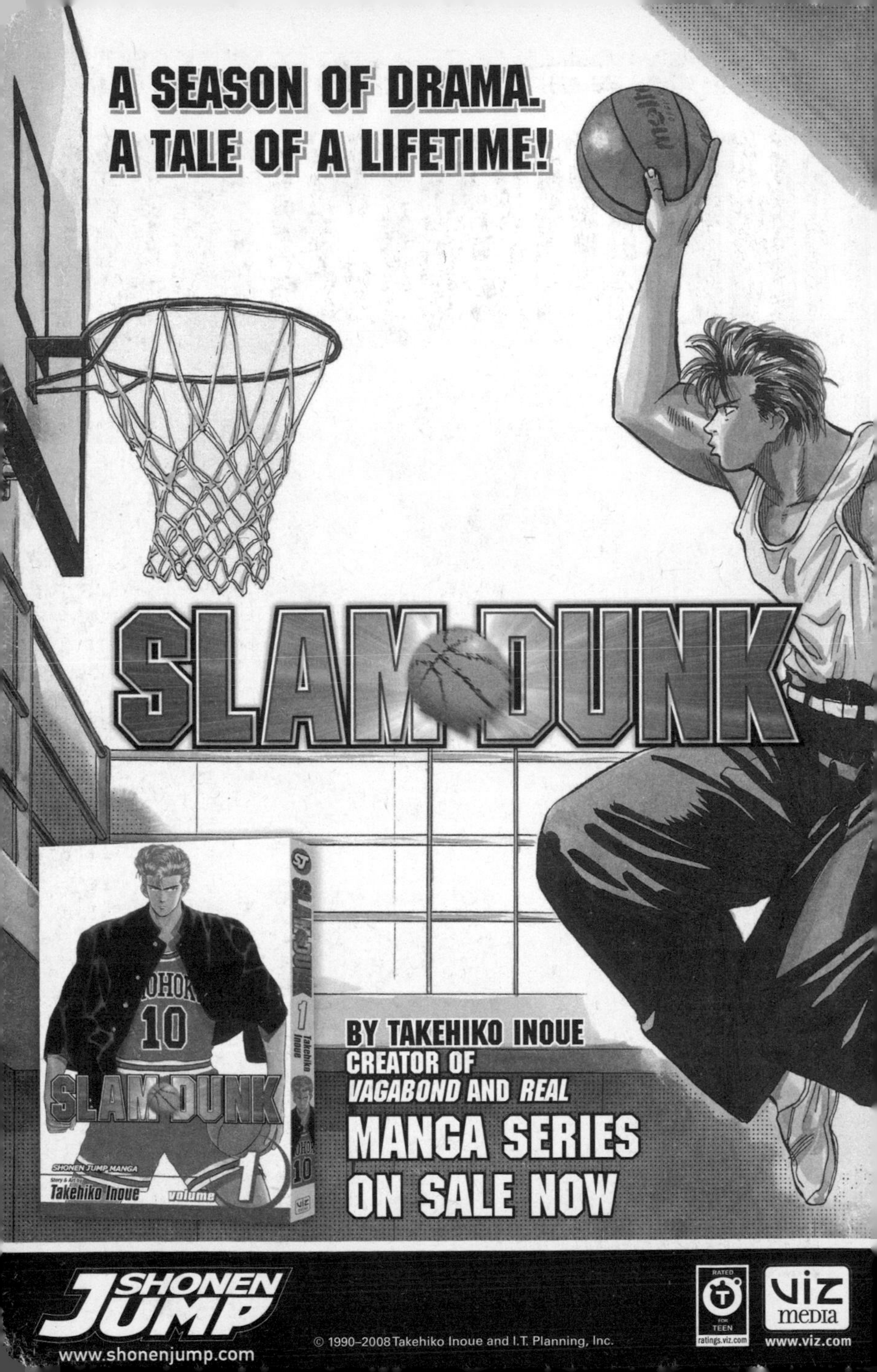
A SEASON OF DRAMA.
A TALE OF A LIFETIME!
SLAM DUNK
SHONEN JUMP MANGA
Story & Art by
Takehiko Inoue
volume 1
BY TAKEHIKO INOUE
CREATOR OF
VAGABOND AND REAL
MANGA SERIES
ON SALE NOW
SHONEN JUMP
www.shonenjump.com
© 1990–2008 Takehiko Inoue and I.T. Planning, Inc.
RATED T FOR TEEN
ratings.viz.com
VIZ media
www.viz.com

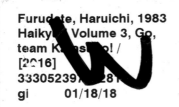

You're Reading the WRONG WAY!

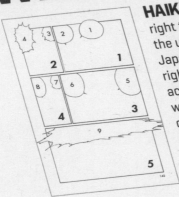

HAIKYU!! reads from right to left, starting in the upper-right corner. Japanese is read from right to left, meaning that action, sound effects and word-balloon order are completely reversed from English order.